We Are Already One

Thomas Merton's Message of Hope

Reflections in Honor of His Centenary (1915–2015)

Edited by Gray Henry and Jonathan Montaldo

Foreword by Paul M. Pearson

FONS VITAE

CENTER FOR INTERFAITH RELATIONS

First published in 2014 by
Fons Vitae
49 Mockingbird Valley Drive
Louisville, KY 40207
http://www.fonsvitae.com
Email: fonsvitaeky@aol.com

ISBN 978-1891785-719

Printed in Canada

Cover portrait by Terrell Dickey
Photographed by Annie Langan

Library of Congress Cataloging-in-Publication Data

We are already one : Thomas Merton's message of hope : reflections in honor of his centenary (1915/2015) / edited by Gray Henry and Jonathan Montaldo ; foreword by Paul M. Pearson.
    pages cm
  Includes bibliographical references and index.
  ISBN 978-1-891785-71-9
  1. Merton, Thomas, 1915-1968. I. Merton, Thomas, 1915-1968, honouree. II. Henry, Gray, editor. III. Montaldo, Jonathan, editor.
   BX4705.M542W4 2014
   271'.12502—dc23
                         2014033859

We Are Already One
is dedicated to the members of
The International Thomas Merton Society,
past, present and yet to come

This book is also dedicated to
the welfare of all life.
May it benefit countless beings.

Virginia Gray Henry
Owsley Brown III
December 10th, 2014

"Our glory and our hope—we are the Body of Christ.
Christ loves us and espouses us as His own flesh.
Isn't that enough for us? But we do not really believe it. No!
Be content. Be content. We are the Body of Christ.
We have found Him. He has found us. We are in Him. He is in us.
There is nothing further to look for except
the deepening of this life we already possess. Be content."

Thomas Merton
A Search for Solitude

With Gratitude for their Support

The Abbey of Gethsemani

Maydie and Nolan Allen
Mr. and Mrs. Eli H. Brown IV
Ben Eisner
Mary Lee and George Fisher
Susan Gatz, SCN
Gayle and George Hanratty
Barbara and James Hennessy
Deedee Baquie Jones
Doris Boland Jones
Rob Lehman
Mr. and Mrs. Eugene W. March
Avideh Shashaani and Ken McNeil

Rev. Dr. John Mulder
Tommie O'Callaghan
William O. Paulsell
Frank Peabody
Brother Paul Quenon, OCSO
Kitty and Dennis Riggs
Barbara N. Sandford
Glen Schilling
Douglas D. Stegner
Elizabeth and Gerald Terrell
Robert and Mary Ellen Toth

The Fetzer Foundation

*****

Center for Interfaith Relations'
Institute for Contemplative Practice

Owsley Brown III
Kathleen Lyons

Ambassador Thomas Graham
Sharon Potter

*****

The Fons Vitae Board of Directors

Nina Bonnie
Jill Cooper
Mary Nash Cox
Sara V. and James E. Haynes
Nana Lampton
Sally Meigs
Eleanor Bingham Miller
Anne Brewer Ogden
        and Judge Boyce F. Martin, Jr.

Tom Pike
Donovan Reynolds
Peter Schroeder
Shelly and Morgan Ward
Tom Williams
Terry Taylor
Jim and Libby Voyles

Contents

Contents, continued

Contents, *continued*

List of Illustrations

"I stand among you as one who offers a small message of hope that, first, there are always people who dare to seek on the margins of society, who are not dependent on social acceptance, nor dependent on social routine, and prefer a kind of free-floating existence under a stake of risk. And among these people, if they are faithful to their own calling, to their own vocation and to their own message from God, communication on the deepest level is possible.

"And the deepest level of communication is not communication, but communion. It is wordless. It is beyond words, and it is beyond speech, and it is beyond concept. Not that we discover a new unity. We discover an older unity. My dear brothers and sisters, we are already one. But we imagine that we are not. So what we have to recover is our original unity. What we have to be is what we are."

The Asian Journal of Thomas Merton

Foreword

Paul M. Pearson

A theme that occurs throughout the volume you are now holding and one that has struck millions of Thomas Merton's readers right from the publication of *The Seven Storey Mountain* in October, 1948 up until the present day as we celebrate the centenary of his birth, is the manner, indeed the gift, by which Merton speaks so intimately to his reader. The Episcopal bishop G. Porter Taylor wrote that Merton's autobiography was one of those rare books that "read me, as much as I read it," an experience of the phrase John Henry Newman would incorporate into his coat of arms upon becoming a cardinal, *cor ad cor loquitur*—heart speaks to heart. Parker Palmer sums this up succinctly writing Merton was "a kindred spirit who understood me better than anyone alive, better than I understood myself," a true soul friend.

As with countless readers before me, this was my own experience of discovering Merton or, just as accurately, of being discovered by Merton. Having been introduced to him as a teenager by a school chaplain, my own faith seemed to develop with him as a close companion on that journey, indeed, a soul friend. Let me expand on this a little.

I was introduced to Thomas Merton by a high school chaplain, Father Tony Cornish, who used to teach one religion class a term at the boys only grammar school that I attended in Plymouth, England run by the Irish Christian Brothers. He started off this particular lesson by telling us a little of Thomas Merton's story and about the book that contained that story—*Elected Silence*, as it was called in England, better known in the United States as *The Seven Storey Mountain*. (Many years later, in conversations unimaginable to that schoolboy and no doubt sparked by my British accent, Robert Giroux, the American editor of Merton's autobiography, would still express his horror at the nerve Evelyn Waugh had of not just thinking he could edit *The Seven Storey Mountain* better than Giroux, but then compounding his audacity by changing the very title of the book, a book that would become the unexpected bestseller of Giroux's long and distinguished career, thus adding insult to injury.)

I was very interested to learn more about Thomas Merton and to read the book the chaplain had spoken to us about. The impact of his short presentation about Merton was such that, all these years later, I can still close my eyes and picture the cover of the paperback edition that he held up for us that day. As I ponder that moment, a moment that would ultimately change the very direction of my life, I wonder how many of my classmates paid the slightest of attention to that talk? Was the chaplain aware of the impact his words would have? Indeed, are any of us ever aware?

However, *Elected Silence* was long out of print in England and, for some reason, I never thought of asking the chaplain to borrow his copy. Instead, in days far distant from the internet, Amazon and eBooks, I hunted in local libraries and bookshops searching for the book but without success. In fact, the only book by Merton that I could find in print and available at that time in England was *The Monastic Journey* which had just been published. There was quite a lengthy period in England when there was a real dearth of materials by and about Merton in print. This began to change with the publication of Monica Furlong's biography, *Merton: A Biography* in 1980 and the subsequent proliferation of books by and about Merton as the wheels of the "Merton industry" rolled into motion.

As it was the only book by Thomas Merton that I had managed to find, I gingerly invested a recently won school prize in purchasing *The Monastic Journey*. Not exactly the first book I would recommend to anyone asking where to begin reading Thomas Merton, especially not a teenager of fourteen or fifteen years old, which would have been my age at that time. Let me quote from the jacket blurb of the book to illustrate this:

> Thomas Merton wrote several books on monasticism including *The Waters of Siloe* and *The Silent Life* which became best sellers. But he also wrote many shorter essays and articles on the monastic life describing its beauties and demands and emphasizing its essentials: the basic values of silence, solitude, prayer and purity of heart . . . a selection, all written during the last decade of Merton's life, is published here in book form for the first time. It reflects his mature thought on both community monastic living and the solitary life . . ..
>
> The first three pieces describe something of the mystery of the monastic vocation and make a strong statement on the basic verities of the monastic way of life. The middle section discusses monastic themes in detail and the book ends with a deeply moving monograph in praise of the hermit life (*The Monastic Journey*, Sheldon Press, Jacket blurb).

"A deeply moving monograph in praise of the hermit life," not exactly the reading of most fourteen or fifteen year old boys, even in the days before satellite television, the worldwide web and Xbox 360! But I read *The Monastic Journey* and although, looking back on it, I probably did not understand much of it, yet it sowed a seed of desire for me in the same way that *The Seven Storey Mountain* had done for a whole generation in the years after the second world war.

I wanted to read more, and so my "love affair" with Merton began. It is hard to put a finger on exactly what the attraction was—what the attraction is. Initially there was something of a romantic view of monasticism—and it took a novitiate in a Benedictine monastery to partially break through that veneer.

However, as my own spirituality has grown and developed, Merton has frequently been one of the catalysts. I was brought up in a traditional Catholic family. Merton's early writings on spirituality, contemplation, the monastic life, and on the true and false self appealed to that background. But, as I continued to read him, his writings led me forward into a much broader, deeper, world-embracing spirituality. My interest in ecumenism and inter-faith dialogue developed hand-in-hand with my reading of Merton, as did my awareness and involvement in social issues.

I cannot, for certain, say those changes were a result of reading Merton; my actual life might have gone in that direction anyway, but Merton was certainly an intimate companion, a soul friend, through all these changes. This journey with Merton continues as new areas of Merton's life and thought appear on my horizon—his anti-poetry;

his interest in the Shakers; Merton's art, in particular his photography; his frequently overlooked writings on racism; his interest in Hinduism—a seemingly inexhaustible ability, so many years after his death, to continue to engage and challenge his readers.

In attempting to put a finger on the core of this attraction I would say that it is Merton's searching spirit that is central. St. Benedict in his *Rule* for monks makes it quite clear that the focus of the novitiate is to truly discover whether the novice is seeking God or not. Not a question of whether he is called to a particular kind of ministry, but simply whether the novice is seeking God. And it was this search, this deep, heartfelt desire that preoccupied Merton.

Merton's calling to seek God, his "love of learning and desire for God" (Dom Jean Leclercq, *The Love of Learning and the Desire for God: A Study of Monastic Culture*), led him to the contemplative and ultimately the solitary life. When he entered the monastery in 1941, he thought he was turning his back on the world. He soon discovered that this was not the case. If the search for God is really genuine, we find in that search not only God, but also our sisters and brothers and our true selves.

Merton's own search for God would continually stimulate his attraction to other earnest manifestations of God's spirit—the poetry of Blake and Hopkins, the Desert Mothers and Fathers, mystics of many traditions, the Celtic Hermits, and the Shakers. The Shakers belief in the manifestation of the Christ spirit was a realized eschatology, a witness to the living presence of Christ. It was this Christ Merton first caught sight of in Rome in the early nineteen thirties and whom he followed religiously, if you'll excuse the pun, for the rest of his life.

As I read the rich tapestry of personal experiences and insights into Thomas Merton that compose this volume, my own story and experience of Merton resonated time after time. I was reminded of a volume of love letters, but letters not just between two lovers, but representative of the countless lives that Merton has touched, changed and enriched. These "letters" are an incredible living testimony to Thomas Merton as he reaches his centenary and yet, as Merton's work itself continues to speak to readers, so in these letters Merton's witness and wisdom are distilled and read like letters back to each of us from him, sharing little beams from his multifaceted embrace of the divine, the human, indeed of all creation. As one side of a tapestry displays a multitude of threads and knots, hardly giving any inkling of the richness and beauty displayed on the other side, so these letters, these testimonies, come together witnessing to the working of the divine through this "brother of God" who learned "to know the Christ of the burnt men."

Merton had some insight into the power of the divine manifesting itself through our humanity when he was handed his first copy of his published autobiography and browsed the index, a "gathering of all the people I have known at a banquet to celebrate the publication of the Book" (*Entering the Silence*, 214). Then, as the years passed and Merton became an inveterate correspondent, so the index to his correspondence—from Popes, presidents and Nobel prizewinners, down to ordinary school children with whom he corresponded, provides yet another insight into the divine manifesting itself through our fragile human nature. As Merton's correspondence expanded through the fifties so did his insight into the power of this aspect of his writing. In a letter of November 10, 1958 to the recently elected Pope John XXIII, Merton writes a distillation of his thinking on his ministry as a correspondent. After noting that "this poor world has a right to a place in my solitude," Merton goes on to tell John XXIII that, in the light of this insight, an insight so clearly manifested for Merton earlier in March that same year on the corner of Fourth and Walnut in Louisville, that he perceives his apostolate as a cloistered monk going beyond "prayer and penance" to "a sympathy for the honest aspirations of so many intellectuals everywhere in the world and the terrible problems they have to face." Merton then goes on to tell Pope John of his experience of this apostolate through his contact with "artists, writers, publishers, poets, etc." who had become his friends through correspondence, writing "I have exercised an apostolate—small and limited though it be—within a circle of intellectuals from other parts of the world; and it has been quite simply an apostolate of friendship" (*The Hidden Ground of Love*, 482).

One of the most unique features of the circle of readers and friends of Thomas Merton, seen most especially in the International Thomas Merton Society and other such societies around the world, is the manner in which Merton's apostolate of friendship continues to powerfully express itself. That friendship was first extended to me through Tony Cornish and has continued over the years through countless friends, living and dead. That apostolate of friendship is profoundly witnessed to by each and every one of the diverse testimonies in this volume. In the midst of so much of the superficiality of our modern world, where the techno-babble of email, Facebook, Twitter, and numerous other insubstantial distractions draw us away from the great and mysterious breadth and depth of our uniqueness in the eyes of God, the value of such an apostolate takes on a renewed, urgent and immeasurable importance. From one who has experienced the profoundness of this apostolate of Thomas Merton's, my final thought is most simply expressed by Hector in the closing scene of *The History Boys*: "Pass the parcel. That's sometimes all you can do. Take it, feel it and pass it on. Not for me, not for you but for someone, somewhere, one day. Pass it on . . .."

Introduction:

Honoring Thomas Merton's Place In The Index Of Our Biographies

Jonathan Montaldo

All our salvation begins on the level of common and natural and ordinary things. And so it was with me. Books and ideas and poems and stories, pictures and music, buildings, cities, places, philosophies were to be the materials on which grace would work.

The coming war, and all the uncertainties and confusions and fears that followed necessarily from that, and all the rest of the violence and injustice that were in the world, had a very important part to play. All these things were bound together and fused and vitalized and prepared for the action of grace, both in my own soul and in the souls of at least one or two of my friends, merely by our friendship and association together. And it fermented in our sharing of our own ideas and miseries and headaches and perplexities and fears and difficulties and desires and hangovers and all the rest.

The Seven Storey Mountain

For those who love God all things work together for good.

Romans 8:28

Early in his life and until its ending, Thomas Merton ruminated upon the Holy Spirit's transforming relations with his inner self through the flow of events within his everyday life. He experienced the "Spirit of God's" providence for his good every day through the agency of his life's ordinary things, especially friendships that mentored him. In his autobiography, for example, describing his years at Columbia University in New York City, he focuses on "the real part Columbia seems to have been destined to play in my life in the providential designs of God." Columbia had given him his introduction to some of his life's best friends: "Strangely enough it was on this big factory of a campus that the Holy Ghost was waiting to show me the light, in His own light. And one of the chief means He used, and through which he operated, was human friendship." His friend, Robert Lax, was an important case in point. Although

Lax had his own share of confusions and perplexities, Merton asserted that it was by the agency of Lax's "voice" and personality that the "insistent Spirit of God was determined to teach me the way I had to travel" (*The Seven Storey Mountain*, 177, 237).

Merton's appreciation of a providential design for his life through the agency of his friendships is a recurring feature of his autobiographical writing and his lived theology. One guiding focus for meditation in his journals was excavation of a "hidden ground" that established a firm place for him and his friends to support one another in fulfilling their lives' profoundest destinies (*The Hidden Ground of Love*, 115). To describe this faith in divine providence for his life more simply, he matured to realize he was no self-made man and that no one gets born into his truest destiny alone. The school of his own experiences taught Merton that every person he ever knew had been a "word" for his instruction and guidance for his formation. Because his own life's destiny and those of his friends were interdependent, they co-created together the circumstances that fostered their vocations to become more deeply integrated human beings.

In a letter to the poet Czeslaw Milosz, Merton referred to a "church of his friends" as the incarnation of the "Spirit of God's" merciful presence in his life (*The Courage for Truth*, 85). This text and others even more significant aid our realizing that this monk never considered himself one of life's loners. He knew that the kindness of friends had enriched his person and propelled the trajectory of his life's vocations.

Merton's discovery of a "hidden ground of love" that guided his becoming a monk and writer did not originate after his having entered the Abbey of Gethsemani on December 10, 1941. Ten months before he would enter the monastery, while teaching at St. Bonaventure College in Olean, New York, he had written in his journals that the works of spiritual mercy on his behalf by various persons, some intimately known and others unknown, had prompted his decision to convert his life by taking up a practice of prayer. In writing about the providential influence of both friends and strangers on his life's true course, he excluded no one from the circle of his gratitude, neither Hindu nor Jew, not only the living but the dead. Even the prayer of "some child" affected the conversion of his life from a desperate restlessness toward a deeper stability in journeying toward loving God:

> How can anyone tell how much he owes to the goodness of those who love him? [. . .] I don't know what I have written that I could really call mine, or what I have prayed or done that was good that came from my own will. Whose prayer made me first pray again to God to give me grace to pray? I could have fought for years by myself to reduce my life to some order (for that was what I was always trying to do—even to ridiculous extremes and the most eccentric disciplines, all pseudo-scientific and pretty much hypochondriacal too; keeping records of what I drank, trying to cut out smoking by reducing the number of cigarettes each day, noting down the numbers in a book—weighing myself every few days, etc!) and yet I would have slowly eaten myself out, I think. But someone must have mentioned me in some prayer; perhaps the soul of some person I hardly remember—perhaps some stranger in a subway, or some child. Or maybe the fact that someone as good as Lilly Reilly happened to think I was a good guy served as a prayer. Or the fact that Nanny may have said my name in her prayers moved the Lord God to send me a little grace to pray again, or first to begin reading books that led me there again—and how much of it was brought on by the war? Or maybe Bramachari in some word to

the Lord in his strange language moved the Lord to let me pray again! These things are inscrutable and I begin to know them better when I can write them. How many men have become Christians through the prayers of Jews and Hindus who themselves find Christianity terribly hard (*Run to the Mountain*, 304-305)?

Merton's closest friends might have thought that he was abandoning them by entering a monastery, but nothing was further from reality in his religious imagination. He actually hoped for a more intimate union with his friends by becoming a monk, a hope he had detailed in his letter to Bob Lax dated December 6th, four days before he would arrive at the monastery's gate. This beautifully written "farewell" explains his motives as to why he chose to become a monk. The letter ends with his declaration that he was leaving no one behind. He would pass over through Gethemani's gate to his truest destiny with everyone he ever loved tucked in the pocket of his heart:

Finally has come the time to go to the Trappists and try to get in.

I cannot explain this except to say it in a lot of different ways: time to get out of the subway and go away to the clean woods, or time to get out of the party full of smoke and pray in a clean bedroom, like before sleeping and resting the way it is sweet. It is time to stop arguing with the seven guys who argue inside my head and be completely quiet in front of the face of Peace.

It is time for the midnight to get very quiet (through me giving to somebody else everything I am thought to be) so that my house may be at rest and the soul talk in peace and listen to Peace and learn from Peace. [. . .]

No, honestly: it is time to stop being sick, (better than before, of course) and really get well. It is time to be full of peace and silence. And if you have a free and real choice between a world that belongs in a book by John O'Hara and one that belongs in a book by St. Teresa of Avila, I guess you have to make a choice in order to be happy, and quit arguing as if the two books were even comparable.

Once I can be in the place where I belong entirely to God and not to anyone less than God, like belonging to some writer having my legal name, then I guess problems about writing and everything else will not be much problems any more. Harlem isn't for me. Nor is any college. Nor is New York.

Maybe St. Lucy's Day I start out for Kentucky, full of prayer. (Next Saturday.) And round His sunny tent like lambs rejoice. Also, there is absolutely no language to say the things that are to say about this except the language of love: but there He will teach me to use that language like a child and a saint. Until which I cannot talk about Him, Who is all I want to talk about.

And in Him, while I sing in the big church, will be also: Lax, Gibney, Seymour, Slate, Rice, Gerdy, Knight, Huttlinger, and Van Doren, and the Baroness, and Mary Jerdo, and my brother and my uncle and my aunt and my father and mother who died and Bramachari and the whole mystical body of Christ, everybody: Roger, Gil, all people, Jinny, Lilly. All people. The living and the dead. All days, all times, all ages, all worlds, all mysteries, all miracles. . . . (*The Road to Joy*. 163-164).

I love this letter not only for its beauty of expression, but because it reveals Merton's sustained engagement to stay in love with the world as a major feature of his spiritual and religious imagination until his death. The "Spirit of God's" will for his life would always manifest itself to him as a "word" spoken to him within the context of his object relations with everything he deeply loved. His letter to Lax makes clear that he consciously entered monastic life not to break his ties with everyone and everything in his past. On the contrary, his monk's life would be his means to conserve everything he had loved in his past in the archive of his heart. Becoming a monk would be his path on which to remain alive and awake to the seeds of contemplation his friends had scattered for his life's growth. His prayer and inner work as a cloistered monk would paradoxically make his ties to all his life's intimates, even extending to the living and the dead of all times, all the more actual and real.

When Merton's abbot, Frederic Dunne, first pressed into his hands a copy of his newly published autobiography, Merton wrote that he took most delight in his autobiography's Index:

> Robert Giroux had somebody do an index to *The Seven Storey Mountain*—the most peculiar collection of names you ever saw. Starts off with Abbot, Father, goes on to Adler, Alfred, Ellington, Duke, Fields, W. C., Smith, Pete is followed by Smith, Robert Paul, and there is Bob O'Brien the plumber at Olean House, and Pierrot the teamster at Saint Antonin, and the Privats at Murat, and Brother Fabian, who went to Georgia, and Mary Jerdo, and Helen Freedgood, and Burton, Jenny, and Flagg, Nancy and Wells, Peggy [. . .].
>
> I was fascinated. The index is beautiful. It is like the gathering of all the people I have known at a banquet to celebrate the publication of the book—and it is like a pledge that they will all belong to me somehow as trophies in heaven—or I will belong to some of them as a trophy. Blake, William; Francis of Assisi, Saint; Bonaventure, Saint; Aquinas, St. Thomas; Bernard, Saint. I think this index is a partial, optimistic preview of the General Judgment with the four Marx Brothers among the sheep.
>
> So God is very good. *Sanctus in omnibus operibus suis*—Holy in all His works (*The Sign of Jonas*, 106-107).

His autobiography's Index was a partial listing of those to whom Merton owed his formation, the index of those persons, known in the flesh or only in their books, who had intervened, consciously or not, to shape him into the person he had become at that moment on the cusp of his becoming a famous writer. His autobiography's Index was a foreshadowing of what he hoped would be an eternal "holy communion" with all those who were teachers in the school of his life, their voices having transmitted the "Voice" of the "insistent Spirit of God [who] was determined to teach me the way I had to travel."

When I present retreats, I often read these texts that memorialize the meaning of friendship for Merton's life, and then suggest a salutary exercise for us of using meditation time to create an index of all the names that would appear at the end of our own "autobiographies," those persons year by year who have formed us into the persons we are today by their love for us. This Index would reveal how wide and deep are the ranks of those who were and remain the messengers of hope and providence in the formation of our becoming the persons we are today.

I commend these Merton texts on the "mystical body" of his friends to your memory as you read this volume of reflections written to honor his centenary. Merton's voice embedded in his many texts has deeply impacted this book's authors by their friendship in reading him, first alone, and then in a community of readers wanting to hear his voice together. Even among this volume's contributors who knew him in the flesh, his published words, perhaps more than his actual presence, have formed them into the persons they are today. As I reviewed these reflections for publication, I was repeatedly taken aback by the good that Merton's writing has accomplished for and in so many. How many volumes of this size would it have taken to publish the reflections of those millions whom Merton has inspired since the appearance of his first book, *Thirty Poems*, in 1944?

The order of presentation of the reflections gathered in *We Are Already One* was intuitive on our parts. As each reflection is a unique personal statement, each standing on its own, we refused to segregate them from one another by imposing formal thematic sections. Gray Henry and I expressly requested that the reflections lean away from the academic and toward more personal statements. We asked that citations of texts be made parenthetically within the reflections, although we have provided a bibliography of citations from Merton's texts at the end of the volume.

Reading this volume in manuscript, contributor Thomas Del Prete wrote: "I was moved by what I read and by the totality of it. There seems a great deal of humble and authentic reflection in it, with Merton as guide and inspiration rather than simply as object of admiration. One gets the impression of all of us working hard trying to stay afloat in the same stream of awareness."

May this gathering of reflections to honor Merton's 100th birthday instigate new streams of awareness of his legacy of hope for us, that we can realize and act out of our essential kinship, of our being one humankind with one another. The reflections by so many young contributors to this volume sustains belief that Merton will continue to mentor succeeding generations in how to be alive and awake to their co-creating together a more peaceful and compassionate world.

A Friendship, A Love, A Rescue

Parker J. Palmer

> I stand among you as one who offers a small message of hope, that first there are always people who dare to seek on the margin of society, who are not dependent on social acceptance, not dependent on social routine, and prefer a kind of free-floating existence under a state of risk. And among these people, if they are faithful to their own calling, to their own vocation and to their own message from God, communication on the deepest level is possible. And the deepest level of communication is not communication, but communion. It is wordless. It is beyond words, and it is beyond speech and beyond concept.
>
> *The Asian Journal of Thomas Merton*

I met Thomas Merton a year after he died. I met him through his writing and through the communion that lies "beyond words," met him in the seamless way good friends meet again after a long time apart. Without Merton's friendship and the hope it has given me over the past forty-five years, I'm not sure I could have kept faith with my vocation, even as imperfectly as I have.

My vocational journey to what Merton calls "the margin of society"—at least, the margin of my known world—began in 1969 when I was completing my doctoral work at Berkeley. As the 1960s unfolded, the academic calling that brought me to graduate school had become less and less audible. Vietnam, a spate of assassinations, race riots and "the fire next time" in several major American cities—all of this had me hearing an insistent inner voice saying, "Your vocation is in the community, not the classroom." I turned down several opportunities to become a professor, and in July of 1969 moved with my wife and two children to Washington, D. C. to begin work as a community organizer. No one could understand what I was doing, beyond committing professional suicide. In truth, I could not explain it to myself, except to say that it was something I "couldn't not do"—despite the clear odds against success. I had no training or experience as a community organizer; much of the work had to be funded by grants I had no track record at raising; and I was an idealistic and thin-skinned young man temperamentally unsuited for the hard-nosed world of community organizing. Compared to accepting a salaried and secure faculty post, as such posts were back in the day, I was stepping off the edge into "a kind of free-floating existence under a state of risk." Companions would have been comforting, but few are to be found when you go over the cliff.

MEETING MERTON

After five months in D. C.—when the thrill of my free-fall had been replaced by the predictable bruises, cuts and broken bones—I walked into a used book store near Dupont Circle. A friend had recommended that I read *The Magic Mountain* by Thomas Mann. It was not on the shelf, but in the place where it would have been was another book I knew nothing about: *The Seven Storey Mountain* by Thomas Merton. I remember thinking, "It's about a mountain and the author's surname begins with M. Close enough . . . ." So I bought it.

That was early in December, 1969. Merton, I soon learned, had died almost exactly one year earlier. But he came alive as I read his autobiography, as he had for millions before me. I never felt that I had merely discovered a new author worth reading. Instead, I knew I had met a kindred spirit who understood me better than anyone alive, better than I understood myself, a fellow traveler who could accompany me on the strange path I had chosen—or had it chosen me?

Wanting to learn more about my new friend, I set out to read everything he wrote. As Merton devotees know, this turned into a lifetime project. The man published at least thirty books and that counts only those published while he was alive: I've lost count of how many more have been published since his death. Merton's posthumous literary output is, I believe, the first documented case of "perish and publish."

A few years after I began reading Merton, I learned about his correspondence with Louis Massignon, a French scholar who introduced Western readers to the life and work of al-Hallaj, a ninth century Muslim mystic. Massignon felt that his relation to al-Hallaj was not so much that of a scholar to his subject as it was "a friendship, a love, a rescue" (Herbert Mason, *The Death of al-Hallaj*, xix). He did not mean that he had rescued al-Hallaj from historical obscurity, but that the Muslim mystic had reached out across time to rescue him.

That's what Merton did for me as I read and re-read *The Seven Storey Mountain*. Forty years later, I'm still reading him, still finding friendship, love and rescue—essential elements in serving as a "messenger of hope." Imparting hope to others has nothing to do with exhorting or cheering them on. It has everything to do with relationships that honor the soul, encourage the heart, inspire the mind, quicken the step, and heal the wounds we suffer along the way.

Merton has companioned me on my journey and illumined my path, offering life-giving ways to look at where I've been, where I am right now and where I'm headed. I want to say a few words about four of those ways.

THE QUEST FOR TRUE SELF

First comes the pivotal distinction Merton makes between "true self" and "false self," which helped me understand why I walked away from the groves of academe toward *terra incognita*. No reasonable person would call my early vocational decision "a good career move." But looking at it through Merton's eyes, I came to see that it was a first step on a life-long effort to be responsive to the imperatives of true self, the source of that inner voice that kept saying "You can't not do this."

I grew up in the Methodist Church, and I value the gifts that tradition gave me. But at no point on my religious journey—which included religious studies at college, a year at

Union Theological Seminary, a Ph.D. in the sociology of religion, and active memberships in several mainline Protestant denominations—was I introduced to the contemplative stream of spirituality that Merton lived and wrote about. His notion of the quest for true self eventually led me to Quakerism, with its conviction that "there is that of God in every person." The quest for true self and the quest for God: it's a distinction without a difference, one that not only salvaged my spiritual life but took me deeper into it.

"Most of us," as Merton brilliantly observed, "live lives of self-impersonation (*The Inner Experience*, 4)." I cannot imagine a sadder way to die than with the sense that I never showed up here on earth as my God-given self. If Merton had offered me nothing else, the encouragement to live from true self would be more than enough to call his relation to me "a friendship, a love, a rescue."

THE PROMISE OF PARADOX

The notion of paradox was central to Merton's spiritual and intellectual life, not merely as a philosophical concept but as a lived reality. Given the many apparent contradictions of my life, nothing Merton wrote brought him closer to me in spirit than the epigraph to *The Sign of Jonas*: "I find myself traveling toward my destiny in the belly of a paradox." It is no accident that my first book featured a lead essay on Merton and was titled *The Promise of Paradox* (1980).

Merton taught me the importance of looking at life not merely in terms of either-or but also in terms of both-and. Paradoxical thinking of this sort is key to creativity, which comes from the capacity to entertain apparently contradictory ideas in a way that stretches the mind and opens the heart to something new. Paradox is also a way of being that's key to wholeness, which does not mean perfection: it means embracing brokenness as an integral part of life.

For me, the ability to hold life paradoxically became a life-saver. Among other things, it helped me integrate three devastating experiences of clinical depression, which were as dark for me as it must have been for Jonas inside the belly of that whale. "My God, my God, why have you forsaken me?" was the question that came time and again as my quest for light plunged me into darkness. In response, Merton's lived understanding of paradox came to my rescue. Eventually I was able to see that the closer I move to the source of light, the deeper my shadow becomes. To be whole I have to be able to say I am both shadow and light.

Paradoxical thinking can also save us from the crimped and cramped versions of faith that bedevil Christianity and are, at bottom, idolatries that elevate our theological *formulae* above the living God. Merton—who had a deep appreciation of Taoism, Zen Buddhism and Sufism—once put this in words so fierce that, if taken seriously, could generate enough energy to transform the Christian world:

> The Cross is the sign of contradiction—destroying the seriousness of the Law, of the Empire, of the armies . . . .. But the magicians keep turning the cross to their own purposes. Yes, it is for them too a sign of contradiction: the awful blasphemy of the religious magician who makes the cross contradict mercy! This is of course the ultimate temptation of Christianity! To say that Christ has locked all the doors, has given one answer, settled everything and departed, leaving all life enclosed in the frightful consistency of a system outside of which there is seriousness and damna-

tion, inside of which there is the intolerable flippancy of the saved—while nowhere is there any place left for the mystery of the freedom of divine mercy which alone is truly serious and worthy of being taken seriously ("To Each His Darkness" in *Raids on the Unspeakable*, 11-12).

THE CALL TO COMMUNITY

For several years after the 1948 publication of *The Seven Storey Mountain*, the Abbey of Gethsemani was flooded with young men who wanted to join Merton in the monastic life. Though I came to the party twenty years late, I too wanted in. But I had a few liabilities when it came to becoming a Trappist monk, including a wife, three children and Protestant tendencies. I needed to find another way into "life together" in a spiritual community.

So in 1974, I left my community organizing in Washington, D. C. and moved with my family to a Quaker living-learning community called Pendle Hill, located near Philadelphia. For the next eleven years, I shared a daily round of worship, study, work, social outreach, and communal meals with some seventy people in a spiritually grounded community that was as close as I could get to my image of the life Merton lived. That image was of a "community of solitudes," of "being alone together," of a way of life in which a group of people could live more fully into Rilke's definition of love "that two (or more) solitudes border, protect and salute one another" (*Letters to a Young Poet*, 50).

This is not the place to write about the many ways a decade-plus at Pendle Hill deepened and strengthened my sense of vocation, a topic I have explored elsewhere (*Let Your Life Speak*, 2000, and in *The Sun Magazine*, Nov. 2012, Issue 443). Suffice it to say that in the Quaker tradition I found a way to join the inner journey with social concerns, and eventually founded a national non-profit, the Center for Courage and Renewal, whose mission is to help people "rejoin soul and role" (www.CourageRenewal.org). My experience at Pendle Hill also gave me the impetus to take one more step toward "the margin of society." For the past quarter century, I have worked independently as a writer, teacher and activist, unsheltered by any institution.

When my courage to work at the margins wavers, I take heart in what Merton said in his final talk, given to a conference of monks in Bangkok a few hours before he died. Quoting a Tibetan lama who was forced to flee his monastery and his homeland, Merton advised the monks, "From now on, Brother, everybody stands on his own feet." In words that ring true for me at a time in history when our major social institutions—religious, economic and political institutions—are profoundly dysfunctional, Merton goes on to say:

> We can no longer rely on being supported by structures that may be destroyed at any moment by a political power or a political force. You cannot rely on structures. They are good and they should help us, and we should do the best we can with them. But they may be taken away, and if everything is taken away, what do you do next (*The Asian Journal of Thomas Merton*, 229)?

HIDDEN WHOLENESS IN A BROKEN WORLD

As the Nigerian novelist Chinua Achebe famously reminded us, "things fall apart"

(*Things Fall Apart*, 1994). But in "Hagia Sophia," one of Merton's most lyrical pieces, he writes about the "hidden wholeness" the spiritual eye can discern beneath the broken surface of things—whether it's a broken political system, a broken relationship or a broken heart:

> There is in all visible things an invisible fecundity, a dimmed light, a meek name-lessness, a hidden wholeness. This mysterious Unity and Integrity is Wisdom, the Mother of all, *Natura naturans* (*A Thomas Merton Reader*, 506).

These words, too, have served as a source of hope for me. Once one has eyes to see it, wholeness can always be discovered, hidden beneath the broken surface of things. This is more than a soothing notion. It's an insight that can shape what the Buddhists call "right action," if we have eyes to see. Here's an instance of what I mean.

In the early 1970s—as I was reading Merton and learning about organizing for racial justice in a rapidly changing neighborhood—I began to understand that my job was not to try to compel people to do things they did not want to do, such as protesting against unscrupulous real estate practices like blockbusting and redlining. Instead, I needed to give them excuses and permissions to do things they really wanted to do—things related to the justice agenda—but were too shy or fearful to do under their own steam.

For example, the people in the neighborhood where I lived and worked had already run from "the other" once, driven by the fear that animates white flight. But in their heart of hearts, they had come to understand that there is no place left to run, no place to escape the diversity of the human community, and that embracing it might bring them peace *and* enrich their lives.

I knew that step one in stopping real estate practices that manipulate fear for profit was simple: give the old-timers and the newcomers frequent chances to meet face-to-face so they could learn that "the other" came bearing blessings, not threats. But instead of asking folks to do the impossible—e.g., "Just knock on a stranger's door and get to know whoever answers"—my colleagues and I began creating "excuses and permissions" for natural interactions: door-to-door surveys, block parties, ethnic food fairs, and living room conversations about shared interests, to name a few.

Amid the racial tensions of our era, we helped people act on their deep-down desire to live in the "hidden wholeness" that lies beneath the broken surface of our lives. And it worked. Over time, because of our efforts and those of many others, a community that might have ended up shattered became diverse and whole (*The Company of Strangers: Christians and the Renewal of Public Life*, 1983).

Things do not always work out so well, of course. History is full of tragically failed visions of possibility, and the more profound the vision, the more likely we are to fall short of achieving it. But even here, Merton has a word of hope for us, a paradoxical word, of course:

> Do not depend on the hope of results. . . . You may have to face the fact that your work will be apparently worthless and even achieve no result at all, if not perhaps results opposite to what you expect. As you get used to this idea, you start more and more to concentrate not on the results, but on the value, the rightness, the truth of the work itself (*The Hidden Ground of Love*, 294).

As long as we are wedded to "effectiveness" we will take on smaller and smaller tasks, for they are the only ones with which we can get results. If we want to witness to important but impossible values like love, truth and justice, there must be a standard that trumps effectiveness. The name of that standard is "faithfulness." At the end of the road, I will not be asking about outcomes. I'll be asking if I was faithful to my gifts, to the needs I saw around me, to the ways in which my gifts might meet those needs, to "the truth of the work itself."

For helping me understand this—and for imbuing me with the faith that, despite my many flaws, I might be able to live this way—I owe a debt of deep gratitude to Thomas Merton, friend, fellow traveler and messenger of hope.*

---

* I have saved my favorite Merton line for the end of this piece, relegating it to the status of a footnote to keep myself from prattling on about it: "I had a pious thought, but I am not going to write it down" (*The Sign of Jonas*, p. 37).

Thomas Merton As A Messenger Of Hope

James Forest

On pilgrimage in Asia in 1968, Thomas Merton was both far from home and at the same time very much at home. His at-homeness on the far side of the planet shines through the remarks he made while in Calcutta, ten time zones east of his monastic community in Kentucky: "My dear brothers and sisters, we are already one, but we imagine that we are not. So what we have to recover is our original unity. What we have to be is what we are."

Merton's insight is not a poet's wishful thinking. The human race is indeed one family—not only the Book of Genesis but our DNA confirms it. We are one and every one of us lives at the same address: the third planet out from a single star we call the sun. We are at home on this planet no matter where on the globe we happen to be. We are and always have been one. The only problem, as Merton points out, is that we imagine our differences are more important than what we have in common. Those differences become the fuel of wars. Our challenge is indeed to recover our original unity. Countless lives, and the health of our souls, depend on it. It's quite a challenge.

From an early age, one of Merton's major concerns was war, the cruelest expression of our failure to live in unity. World War I is the main reference point in the opening sentences of his autobiography, *The Seven Storey Mountain*:

> On the last day of January 1915, under the sign of the Water Bearer, in a year of a great war, and down in the shadow of some French mountains on the borders of Spain, I came into the world. Free by nature, in the image of God, I was nevertheless the prisoner of my own violence and selfishness, in the image of the world into which I was born. That world was the picture of Hell, full of men like myself, loving God and yet hating Him; born to love Him, living instead in fear and hopeless self-contradictory hungers. Not many hundreds of miles away from the house where I was born, they were picking up the men who rotted in rainy ditches among the dead horses . . . in a forest without branches along the river Marne.

In the population of Europe and North America, Merton was one of the rare men of his generation to refuse to take part in war. Instead, after a great deal of thought, conversation and prayer, he decided to seek recognition as a conscientious objector. In the end he became a monk instead—thus part of a fragment of the U. S. population automatically exempt from conscription.

What stood behind his conscientious objection? For Merton the question of overwhelming importance was not political or ideological but simply what would Christ do—what weapons would he carry, what flag would he march behind, who would he kill, by whose authority would he be commissioned to kill? In *The Seven Storey Moun-*

tain, Merton expanded on his decision in a text that must have startled many readers, appearing as it did just after World War II and in the early days of the Cold War:

> [God] was not asking me to judge all the nations of the world, or to elucidate all the moral and political motives behind their actions. He was not demanding that I pass some critical decision defining the innocence and guilt of all those concerned in the war. He was asking me to make a choice that amounted to an act of love for His truth, His goodness, His charity, His Gospel . . .. He was asking me to do, to the best of my knowledge, what I thought Christ would do . . .. After all, Christ did say, "Whatsoever you have done to the least of these my brethren, you did it to me (*The Seven Storey Mountain*, 311-312).

Not many Christians, still fewer Catholic Christians, were struggling with such questions or making similar decisions. Nor were many Christians making significant contact with people of other religions. In *The Seven Storey Mountain*, parts of which seem parochial by today's standards, Merton makes a point of drawing attention to non-Catholics who played key roles in his spiritual and intellectual formation.

One of the influential people was a Hindu monk, Bramachari, who had been sent from his ashram in India to take part in a Congress of Religions in Chicago. In fact he had arrived too late for that event but stayed on in America anyway, living from the hospitality of friends. Merton had been part of a small welcoming committee when Bramachari arrived in Manhattan in 1938. In the weeks that followed the two of them spent a great deal of time together. Merton was deeply impressed by Bramachari's deep kindness. "He was never sarcastic, never ironical or unkind in his criticisms: in fact he did not make many judgments at all, especially adverse ones. He would simply make statements of fact, and then burst out laughing—his laughter was quiet and ingenuous, and it expressed his complete amazement at the very possibility that people should live the way he saw them living all around him."

Bramachari gave Merton life-changing guidance: "He did not generally put his words in the form of advice, but the one counsel he did give me is something that I will not easily forget. 'There are many beautiful mystical books written by the Christians. You should read Saint Augustine's *Confessions* and *The Imitation of Christ* . . .. Yes, you must read those books'" (*SSM*, 198). Reading *The Imitation of Christ* in his apartment on 114th Street, Merton started praying again "more or less regularly" (*SSM*, 201).

It's not altogether surprising that, thirty years after their encounter in New York, Merton, now in Bramachari's homeland for the first time in his life, should be speaking about the bonds that unite us even as wars are being fought. The theme of peace and human unity is one of the golden threads running through Merton's writing throughout his adult life.

Through letters and very occasional visits at the monastery, Merton built relationships with various people outside the monastery who were involved in efforts to end wars and to prevent a nuclear holocaust. I was among the beneficiaries of his affection and care. During the last seven years of his life we exchanged letters on a more or less monthly basis.

The greater part of his correspondence to me has been published in *The Hidden Ground of Love*, 254-308. Of these, the letter that has been most widely circulated and has had the most impact on others was without doubt one he sent me dated February 21, 1966. The text has often been published with the headline "Letter to a Young

Activist" (294-297). I would like to quote from that letter and briefly comment on these extracts.

By way of background, let me explain that the letter to which Merton was responding expressed the exhaustion, bordering on despair, I was then experiencing in my work. I was at the time secretary of the Catholic Peace Fellowship, which several friends and I had founded the previous year. Merton was a member of our advisory board. Much of the Fellowship's work was focused on ending the Vietnam War and promoting conscientious objection. While in many ways our efforts were going well, the Vietnam War was getting worse by the day. It was to continue nearly another decade, not ending until 1975.

Merton's letter began:

Do not depend on the hope of results. When you are doing the sort of work you have taken on, essentially an apostolic work, you may have to face the fact that your work will be apparently worthless and even achieve no result at all, if not perhaps results opposite to what you expect.

It wasn't until I received Merton's letter that it had occurred to me that peace work is of its nature apostolic work—quite a dignity and also quite a responsibility. It was not an altogether comforting linkage. The apostles, few of whom died of old age, experienced a great deal of failure and ridicule.

As you get used to this idea, you start more and more to concentrate not on the results but on the value, the rightness, the truth of the work itself.

The shift from focusing not on the satisfaction of measurable results but rather on the value, rightness and truth of the work we were doing required a major shift of perception. We had to think of counseling prospective conscientious objectors in terms not merely of assisting them in their refusal to participate in a manifestly unjust war but, far more significantly, of assisting in the shaping of vocations in which the works of mercy were the main event.

And there too a great deal has to be gone through, as gradually you struggle less and less for an idea and more and more for specific people. The range tends to narrow down, but it gets much more real. In the end, it is the reality of personal relationships that saves everything.

That last sentence has been for me one of the most important insights that I ever received from Merton. It sums up incarnational theology. Words and slogans and theories are not nearly as important as how we see and relate to each other. In the context of peace work, it suggests getting to know, as best we can, the people and culture being targeted by our weapons. (Along these lines, in 1967 the Catholic Peace Fellowship began to develop "meals of reconciliation" during which Vietnamese food was eaten by participants and Vietnamese poetry read aloud.)

You are fed up with words, and I don't blame you. I am nauseated by them sometimes. I am also, to tell the truth, nauseated by ideals and with causes. This sounds like heresy, but I think you will understand what I mean. It is so easy to get engrossed with ideas and slogans and myths that in the end one is left holding the bag, empty, with no trace of meaning left in it. And then the temptation is to yell louder than ever in order to make the meaning be there again by magic. Going through this kind of reaction helps you to guard against this. Your system is complaining of too much verbalizing, and it is right.

Movements require words and use slogans to sum up goals. These have their place but it's secondary. In a talk to his novices, Merton once said, "He who follows words is destroyed." One of Merton's main contributions to many people who were involved in peace efforts was the witness given by his contemplative monastic life in which prayer and meditation were integral elements of every activity, with each day having a liturgical and sacramental foundation.

> *The big results are not in your hands or mine, but they suddenly happen, and we can share in them; but there is no point in building our lives on this personal satisfaction, which may be denied us and which after all is not that important.*

For me the last few words—"after all [satisfaction] is not that important"—were especially helpful. It's not that important that we personally get to see the results of our efforts, however worthy our goals may be. Here Merton suggests what I think of as a cathedral builder's attitude, a metaphor that easily comes to mind as I live just a minute's walk from a cathedral whose construction began in 1470 and which wasn't completed until 50 years later. As cathedral construction goes, half-a-century was relatively fast. Those who laid a cathedral's foundations knew they wouldn't live to see their building roofed; perhaps their grandchildren would have that satisfaction.

> *The next step in the process is for you to see that your own thinking about what you are doing is crucially important. You are probably striving to build yourself an identity in your work, out of your work and your witness. You are using it, so to speak, to protect yourself against nothingness, annihilation. That is not the right use of your work. All the good that you will do will come not from you but from the fact that you have allowed yourself, in the obedience of faith, to be used by God's love. Think of this more, and gradually you will be free from the need to prove yourself, and you can be more open to the power that will work through you without your knowing it.*

Building an identity in one's work is so basic an element for all of us living in a career-driven, results-oriented society that it's hard to imagine another way of identifying ourselves. Asked who we are, we tend to respond with information about what we do. It's not easy to think in other terms and indeed any more basic answer (what would that be?) might be embarrassing. But if what you do is rooted in attempting to follow Christ, in trying to live a life in which hospitality and love of neighbor is a major element, a life nourished by the Eucharist, that foundation may not only keep you going in dark times but actually, ironically, make your work more effective.

> *The great thing after all is to live, not to pour out your life in the service of a myth: and we turn the best things into myths.*

In my own case the problem was less making myself the servant of a myth than the servant of an ideology, both pacifism and even Christianity. Our myths so often are packaged as ideologies—closed systems of ideas and concepts.

> *If you can get free from the domination of causes and just serve Christ's truth, you will be able to do more and will be less crushed by the inevitable disappointments. Because I see nothing whatever in sight but much disappointment, frustration and confusion . . ..*

It is after all Christ's truth that matters, a truth we experience from time to time but which can never be adequately expressed in words or be obtained by movements and causes. Trying to live within Christ's truth certainly doesn't mean we will live an undented life, a life free of disappointments, but it may help prevent disappointment from becoming despair.

> *The real hope, then, is not in something we think we can do but in God who is making something good out of it in some way we cannot see. If we can do His will, we will be helping in this process. But we will not necessarily know all about it beforehand.*

The end of the letter circles back to its beginning: not to live a results-driven life but to have confidence that God will somehow make use of our efforts even though we ourselves will probably not live long enough to see them bear fruit. Referring back to the book Bramachari successfully urged Merton to read years before he found his vocation as a Trappist monk, it all has to do with the imitation of Christ.

Of Transformation And Marginality

Bonnie Thurston

There is not much evidence that Thomas Merton was particularly attracted to the demon consistency, that "hobgoblin of little minds." In fact he remarked in the December 10, 1949 entry in *The Sign of Jonas* "I am the impression that will change." And change he did. Although the conversion was never complete, the European became an American. The big man on campus and playboy became a Cistercian monk. The traditional Roman Catholic convert became a progressive who influenced the thinking of Vatican II. From a young monk upset with Anglicans, he became a mentor to Protestant seminarians, a friend to Jews, Muslims and Buddhists, and an important voice in inter-religious dialogue.

Perhaps it is kindest to say Merton was multifaceted. Some are troubled by this late 20th century chameleon. For some readers Merton's changeability was a sign of an unstable personality. For others he was maddeningly intellectually inconsistent. A creative person Merton was. A systematician he was not. Merton the man and Merton the writer and thinker changed, and thereby gave us permission to change, and not only to change, but to be transformed. His was an evolutionary life, one able to adapt as circumstances altered, as they did massively between the First World War and the 1960s. The perhaps astonishing thing is that he did so within the relatively rigid context of Cistercian life and while keeping its cardinal vow of obedience. His last Abbot, Dom Flavian Burns, once remarked to me that Dom James Fox (with whom Merton often seemed at loggerheads) said he had no more obedient monk than Merton.

Thomas Merton taught me a lesson I have observed in the lives of other monastics and religious: it is possible to evolve, transform and deepen in the precise circumstances in which one finds herself. We can change geographic locations, but we take ourselves with us. Merton demonstrates the wisdom of the intention of the vow of stability. He is an exemplar of how very fruitful that vow can be in a life in which it is faithfully kept. In his life of geographic stability and remarkable personal change, Merton's Christian and monastic convictions were the primary "still points" of his turning world (as I suggested in "The Christian Center of Thomas Merton's Thought" in the Winter, 2002 *Merton Seasonal*).

The second lesson he taught had to do with his conscious choice of marginality. In the late 1930s Merton appeared destined for a literary life in the American center of that industry, New York. But he became a monk in rural Kentucky with a monastic stability that involved marginality at many levels. I don't have in mind the image from his own self parody which opens his essay "Is the World a Problem?" published in *Contemplation in a World of Action*: ". . . due to a book I wrote thirty years ago, I have myself become a sort of stereotype of the world-denying contemplative—the man who spurned New York . . . heading for the woods with Thoreau in one pocket, John of the Cross in another, and holding the Bible open at the Apocalypse." The marginality of which I speak is choosing to remain on the sidelines when he was challenged to enter the game. That challenge forms the core of the correspondence between Merton and Rosemary Radford Ruether (*At Home in the World*, 1995).

Merton eloquently describes this marginality in the introduction to his collection of sayings of the desert Christians, *The Wisdom of the Desert* (its introduction may be my favorite of his essays). In that extraordinary piece he notes that those who "believed that to let oneself drift along, passively accepting the tenets and values of what they knew as society, was purely and simply a disaster" [*WD*, 3]. The desert Christians were people "who did not believe in letting themselves be passively guided and ruled by a decadent state, and who believed that there was a way of getting along without slavish dependence on accepted, conventional values" [*WD*, 5]. They went out into the desert in part because "the opinions of others had ceased . . . to be matters of importance" [*WD*, 10], not because they hated society and people, but precisely because they loved both. "They knew that they were helpless to do any good for others as long as they floundered about in the wreckage. But once they got a foothold on solid ground . . . they had not only the power but even the obligation to pull the whole world to safety after them" [*WD*, 23]. Merton's French contemporary Madeleine Delbrel makes the same point in the closing essay of the collection of her writing *We, the Ordinary People of the Streets* (Eerdmans Press, 2000). She writes "The solitude into which we are driven by God brings us into conscious solidarity with every living human being that comes into the world."

Merton's 1958 "Fourth and Walnut" experience recorded in his journal on March 19, 1958 (see *A Search for Solitude*) and reprinted in *Conjectures of a Guilty Bystander* provides clear evidence of his profound sense of relatedness to others, his involvement with the human condition. Further evidence is found in Merton's participation in civil rights, the anti-Viet Nam war movement and writings against nuclear war (See, for example, *Seeds of Destruction* and *Faith and Violence*). In loving a society on whose margins he chose to live, he refused to be co-opted by the corruptions of the "American dream" (about which he wrote so eloquently in the long poem "Cables to the Ace"), but also by the machinery of the church or the monastery. He indicates that we can love an institution without becoming embroiled in its functioning; in fact, that every institution needs a loyal, loving opposition.

There are advantages to marginality, to being "outside the camp" whether the camp is the intellectual and literary establishment of New York or the cenobitic life of a Cistercian house. One can see the game more clearly from the sidelines than when embroiled in playing it. Every country and society, every church and university needs the people who choose to live at its edges, not because they don't love it, but because they do. Societies and institutions may neither appreciate nor understand these people, but they need them.

By nature a non-joiner and solitary, I suffered in childhood from being considered "backward." Merton helped me understand these personal quirks as part of the mystery of my identity and vocation. Perhaps no Christian spiritual writer in the late 20th century wrote more articulately about God-given identity, the "True Self," than Thomas Merton. Many current, popular books on the "self" are re-workings of Merton. It was Merton who drew the connections between identity (who we are and were made to be) and vocation (what we are called to do). A non-joiner may both *be* that and be *called to* it for God's purposes, precisely for the perspective and detachment that "location" affords. It helps her articulate failings and perhaps facilitates change.

A mere century is not nearly enough time to evaluate the importance or influence of a person (or a movement for that matter). It is soon enough for gratitude for the life and example of one who challenges us to change when change is called for and to maintain enough distance and detachment from our own social location, institutions and received opinions to see them clearly and critically. Merton might be gratified to know that his work and example could be part of a foundation and formation from which one moves on when it is outgrown or no longer serviceable. Merton was novice master at Gethsemani from 1955-1965. His job was to form mature monks and launch them into monastic life, not to keep them in a perpetual novitiate. Many learned from Merton and moved on, some into the monastery, some back into "the world," most with gratitude for a master who could teach and then let them go.

Like the desert Christians at the collapse of the Roman Empire, Merton thought those living in the latter half of the twentieth century were living in a time of collapse and disintegration. Like them, Merton found that in "leaving" the world for the monastery, he was, in fact, returned to it. A. M. Allchin (of blessed memory) wrote of this paradox in a 1976 essay published in *Cistercian Studies* (vol. 11, no. 2), "'The Cloud of Witnesses': A Common Theme in Henry Vaughn and Thomas Merton." I give him the last word.

> They [Merton and those 4th century monastics] were called to preserve human values, as well as to bear their uncompromising witness to the absolute nature of the demands of God. To find God, they tell us that we must leave all things. . . . But having found God, we find that in him all things are given back to us. The world, which in one sense represents human society closed to God's action, in another sense is seen as his creation, full of hints and glimpses of his glory.

Thomas Merton, Citizen Of The World, Or Why Merton Matters Now

Susan McCaslin

Will it come like this, the moment of my death? Will You open a door upon the great forest and set my feet upon a ladder under the moon, and take me out among the stars?

The Sign of Jonas

A Book Flies Off a Shelf

In 1968, when I was an undergraduate majoring in English at the University of Washington in Seattle, a hardcover copy of *The Seven Storey Mountain* practically spun off the shelf of a used bookstore into my hands. That well-worn, heavily annotated volume of his best-selling spiritual autobiography nestles in my bookshelf as one of my most treasured possessions. Around the same time, photos I saw of Merton suggested a roguish, middle-aged monk roughly of my parents' generation. Now that I'm going on 67, the 53-year-old monk who died in Thailand seems young. Yet he remains for me a master of the spiritual path. The journey I began with Merton at the age of twenty-one has become a lifelong passion.

What was compelling about *The Seven Storey Mountain* was that it told in evocative, poetic language the story of a young man's quest for meaning and purpose. It extolled renunciation of the world (not the world of nature, but the world of outer success and material progress). It embodied a flight, a mystical quest and a grounding. As a young woman brought up Presbyterian, I had temporarily abandoned my childhood religion (but not my faith) to become a hippyish, Vietnam War protestor, but was also beginning to publish poetry in university literary magazines.

From childhood I had been drawn to the path of both the poet and the mystic. Accounts of visions, transformations and direct experiences of the divine drew me in. I had begun to read the European mystics in university, beginning with John of the Cross and Teresa of Avila. Then William Blake became the subject of my studies in graduate school, and I came to see myself as "a Blakean Christian." To my delight, I learned that Merton had done his Master's thesis on William Blake. Merton's gift to me was to validate and contemporize these older mystical streams.

Merton led me not only to mysticism, but to its central practice, meditation, or what he called contemplative prayer. You might say that as a poet and a scholar I've been in a mind-heart clench with Merton ever since. I've dreamed about him and even had a vision of him in the afterlife as a fully realized unitive teacher. Merton for me isn't just an academic pursuit, but a spiritual mentor.

His books on contemplative prayer have helped inspire recognition in the west of the need for a grounded spiritual practice embedded in daily life. He continues to encourage people within and without traditional religions to plumb the inner depths and engage with the world.

As an English instructor at a Canadian college, I went on to write poems and scholarly papers on Merton, some of which explore his love of William Blake, his attraction to Rainer Maria Rilke and his brief friendship with the poet Denise Levertov at the end of his life. Whenever I think I'm ready to move on and turn to other subjects, he sneaks up on me again. My delving into his mystic-poetic affinities led to a depth study of Merton's long poem *Hagia Sophia*, a meditation on the feminine figure of Holy Wisdom from early Christian and Eastern Orthodox sources. Merton also opened me to the wisdom of the east, its Zen sages and wisdom teachers, both ancient and modern.

A Hermit-Monk Lays his Finger on the Pulse of the World

It was important to me that Merton wasn't merely a systematic theologian or philosopher, a person of fixed ideologies, but a spiritual pragmatist, an imperfect pilgrim "on the path" to integral being. Increasingly, both contemplation and action became his yin and yang—inseparable and complementary. He upheld the tension of the contraries, the vital dynamic between interior development and social justice. Though cloistered for most of his life, through his lively correspondence, his Cold War letters where he spoke out against the Vietnam War, and his positions on racism and nuclear weapons in his essays and poems, he became increasingly a man of his times. The mystic and the political activist were for him non-dual aspects of a single consciousness. More recently, Merton's example inspired me to engage in a successful initiative to save an endangered rainforest near my home.

Merton lived with apparent contradictions. He wrote that he was "travelling toward destiny in the belly of a paradox" (*The Sign of Jonas*, 11). He's a loquacious apophatic (one aware of the limits of language), a logo-centric poet whose words spring from and return to silence. Yet balancing the writer with the monk or solitary who speaks from the margins is characteristic of his mystic predecessors who likewise aspired to the heights and depths of mystical unity. One has only to think of John of the Cross and Teresa of Avila who were simultaneously mystics and socially engaged, prolific writers. The host of mystics Merton studied throughout his life modeled how to live at the pivot between silence and speech, a font of peace and place of roiling energy.

A Young Woman Named Proverb Clasps Merton in the Marketplace

In a journal entry of 1958, Merton relates a dream-vision in which Holy Wisdom in the form of a young, dark-haired Jewish girl passionately accosts him in the street: "I am embraced with determined and virginal passion by a young Jewish girl. She clings to me and will not let go . . . . I ask her name and she says her name is Proverb" (*A Search for Solitude*, 176). This mystical experience has to be understood in the context of Merton's later Fourth and Walnut revelation described in *Conjectures of a Guilty Bystander*, where he records an epiphany about the shining light emanating from ordinary humans (mostly women, in the context of his journals) on a street corner in Louisville. It is also informed by his Sophianic studies at the time. Proverb (Sophia, Wisdom) is not merely God in a skirt, or God's feminine assistant, but an essential coherency (consubstantiality) within the Godhead. Wisdom isn't just playing at the foot of the throne as a consort, but is the *ousia* or dark ground of being and becoming. The recovery of the sacred feminine is an essential but underestimated strand in Merton's spiritual legacy. For me, his embrace of the sacred feminine in himself, the world and in each person is one of his central contributions.

The full story of Merton and Proverb includes the psycho-spiritual drama of his own healing, the restoration of the feminine in himself. Despite being wounded by the loss of his mother at the age of six, his profligate youth (impregnating a woman while at Cambridge) and his seeking refuge in a patriarchal community, the divine feminine kept breaking through in dreams and writings. Sophia was implicitly present in his early veneration of Mary, as evidenced by his tribute to Our Lady of Cobre written about his visit to Cuba as a young man, but she presents herself ever more insistently and intimately as he matures. My own sense is that it was precisely because he lost his mother at the age of six that he unconsciously set forth on a lifelong quest for the feminine.

Poetry seems to me Merton's primary means of healing and transformation. He may be more remembered as a writer of prose, but his prose itself is highly charged, layered and resonant as poetry. "Found poems" are embedded throughout his journals. Though Merton's poems are not as widely read as his contemplative writings, I believe they will last as long and be rediscovered in ever new contexts.

Hagia Sophia, a long poem centered on the feminine divine, is Merton's masterwork. It enacts his steady recovery of the tender, peace-making feminine through his Proverb-Sophia dreams and Sophianic explorations. Jonathan Montaldo has recovered many of Merton's sketches of the faces of the feminine in his glorious *Dialogues with Silence: Prayers & Drawings* (2001). Merton's *Hagia Sophia* presents the poet at his most vulnerable, rising from sleep at the call of Wisdom's soft voice to make his way on the earth. It's no accident that for Merton the recovery of wisdom and reconnection to the earth go hand in hand, as she is the power of embodiment, of incarnation. Furthermore, *Hagia Sophia* links the recovery of the feminine to the very salvation of the world. Here his peace work and the divine feminine are tightly interlaced. One of the books that nourished this poem is Russian mystic Paul Evdokimov's *Woman and the Salvation of the World* (1945), a daring challenge to Christianity's androcentrism, which the later Merton took to heart.

It's significant that Merton's embrace of the feminine wasn't wholly a matter of his readings and dreams. There is additionally the matter of the young nurse with whom he fell in love. Despite not being able to commit himself to quotidian life with M (for complex reasons we might never untangle), I see his relationship with her not as a lapse, but as an emotional and spiritual breakthrough. It was the first time Merton was able to imagine being with a living woman as co-equal, loving and being fully loved.

Shortly after, Merton's lively eighteen-month correspondence (1966-1968) with budding feminist theologian Rosemary Radford Ruether adds another real-life dimension to his dialogue with the feminine. Ruether was a feisty young woman who didn't agree with Merton on the value of monasticism and took him to task for being a recluse. Yet perhaps Ruether's cheeky feminism was just the palliative he needed. Though some of her analyses seem simplistic, I read with delight her ability to approach the revered man as an equal: "I'm just as fleshy as you, baby, and I am also just as much of a 'thinking animal' as you" (*At Home in the World*, 49). I'm equally impressed with Merton's humility and willingness to open himself to her critiques.

The point is that Merton moved beyond merely writing and studying the great Sophianic traditions, but engaged authentically with a strong-minded woman who was anything but the soft and sweet feminine stereotype. This correspondence, coming after his emotional and sensual relationship with M. and before his journey to the east, reveals that Merton opened himself to both the nurturing and the intellectually rigorous feminine. It would have been easy for him to pull rank on Ruether, taking a "you don't really know who I am" stance, but he makes himself vulnerable. Though Ruether's challenges to Merton can seem superficial at times, she penetrates to the heart of his existential dilemma. At one point he asks her to be his "confessor" and admits that there are times when he'd like to abandon monasticism.

Integral to Merton's embrace of the feminine is his lifelong embrace of nature. Not only was he becoming more inclusive spiritually, but he had an early and lifelong sensitivity to ecology. He read Rachel Carson's *The Silent Spring* not long after her seminal environmental work first appeared. His love of nature and Thoreau-like observations punctuate his journals. When reading Merton, we are never far from the natural world as the feminine matrix that births and sustains us and on which we are entirely dependent.

A Man from the West Stands Barefoot before the Buddhas

Merton's stillness and absorption before the giant statues of the Buddhas at Polonnaruwa recorded in his *The Asian Journal of Thomas Merton* sum up for me the cumulative power of his witness: full integration. His life and works point to not only an integration of the self (male and female, matter and spirit), but the meeting place of the mystical traditions both east and west. Merton's universality at the end of his life is not a facile syncretism, but a hard-won unity that respects every step of his sojourn through monasticism and the Christian mystical traditions. At the gate from which heaven and earth spring, he is a citizen of the world. The most startling and significant aspect of Merton's life is his ever increasing inclusivity, his steady evolution out of a parochial religion into a universal "interspirituality," or what his friend, the Vietnamese monk *Thích Nhất Hạnh*, calls "Interbeing."

Why Merton Matters Now

How do we reconcile the contradictions posed by the many faces of Thomas Merton? It is time to look not just at Merton's outer personality, the masks and personas (memoirist, poet, theologian, contemplative, activist, calligrapher, photographer, naturalist, journal-keeper, etc.), but at the *geist* of his longing, its broad sweep and long trajectory.

It's remarkable that throughout his relatively short lifespan, he kept expanding, maturing, going beyond himself. One hundred years after his birth, he shines forth not merely as a progressive, contemplative monk and prolific religious writer, but as a universal spiritual teacher. The whole of his journey is a dramatic action-parable of a movement toward integration with the nameless mystery some call God and others call Unitive Being or the One. However named, it is that place of mystery where language bows.

Like each of us, Merton was flawed, but he kept moving beyond dualities and false either/ors. One doesn't have to choose a favorite work, the poetry over the prose, his later over his early works. What matters is the constant evolution of both his life and his work—the always surging, expanding presence. The way he makes a gift of his own fragility gives us hope that each of us, with our own finitudes, flaws and failures, may also touch holy ground. He's not removed from us, but a brother. The core of our being, like his, intersects with the luminous core, *point vierge* or point of nothingness that is a "pure diamond" (*Conjectures of a Guilty Bystander*, 158). When we read him, we are invited to linger at this juncture, this *no place* where we don't know exactly who we are, where we're going or our final destination—only that we are always here, always now, always interconnected.

Reverdurance In The Wind

Gray Matthews

Thomas Merton, to me, was a poet of silence who taught us how to listen to the deep silence that pervades a culture of noise and how to contemplate the Life of our lives so often lost in commotion. He teaches us, in essence, how to reverdure in this world. I write with gratefulness for this opportunity to say something very simple about how Merton has helped me learn to reverdure with evergreen hope.

Silence penetrates reality in endless ways of creative expression. I have always heard silence and I have always sensed a natural calm in it, a calm that dispels any anxiety to explain the silence, any anxiety to replace silence with words. I have always sensed, too, that this silence seems to breathe by its nature, as if reality itself breathes and you can hear the breathing, as if you can feel everything breathing quietly. I have never been concerned about its source as much as I've been struck by the unrelenting necessity to simply pay attention. The silence bends you. It bends you like a string. You walk as if strummed, vibrating in contemplation.

Unfortunately, the rhythm of silence in and through everything around me, as well as in and through me, often seems rudely interrupted. Since early childhood, I have not wanted to disrupt the silence and have always worn soft-soled shoes. It was unnecessary if not impossible, when I was a child, to talk about this sensibility. In a way, you almost have to keep it to yourself, or so it seems; but that never works very well, actually it does not work at all.

Later, I began to wrestle with the social ramifications of this matter: How can I find a way to say something in or with the silence without destroying it? Like trying to walk without making noise, I wanted to speak as to affirm the silence instead of shatter it. This was less about being quiet, shy, introverted, or any other standard explanation for such a sensibility, and more about a deep longing to walk in the wilderness of reality without stepping on twigs. In seeking ways to walk in the silence, I soon realized I was looking for some kind of discipline for honoring the task by undertaking it with respect.

It was not until I was in my early 20s that I found someone who could communicate about it, someone from whom I could learn the needed discipline I was lacking. Somehow I knew such communication would have to be quiet, probably written instead of spoken. I needed to read something, I felt. There is something quiet about the way words work on paper; rare authors are those who write as if they heard the words first voiced by trees and then translated their speech into books. Such writers write by listening to the silent life. When I discovered the writings of Thomas Merton, I found such a listener. Here begins a simple story of how my life became turned inside out by trying to hear what Merton heard.

As I read Merton's writings, I felt someone was speaking deep within me, admitting, declaring, sharing, probing, witnessing, showing me my own life. I identified with Merton immediately when he declared "my life is a listening" (*Thoughts in Solitude*, 74). I felt, though, that I was always a few steps behind him, as if there was a slight delay between reading and hearing. I would understand what he said and then wait for the echo, a moment in which I heard—understood—my own life reflected in Merton's words. Slowly, over years, I learned so many things and absorbed so much of his thought that it has become extremely difficult now to tease out his influence from my own accounts and experiences of living contemplatively.

The first Merton book that invited me into this communal conversation with silence was *No Man is an Island*. It first attracted me, in part as I recall, because I felt I understood the title. Later, when I realized that this book was published in 1955, the year I was born, I developed a peculiar identification with it as if I was reading the story of my origin. Merton writes in the final chapter about silence, of which he declares that silence is the "mother of hope" and the "strength of our interior life" (*No Man is an Island*, 258-259). Buoyed by my first reading, I began reading other books by Merton, one after another, and then, like most Merton readers, when I had finished them all, I began rereading them. Next, I began reading everything I could get my hands on that Merton read or referred to. I began following leads to other trails as the discipline of listening to silence expanded in new and unexpected directions. If Merton mentioned anything that suggested another good vantage point, I went there to see for myself. I wanted to see what that poet, the artist, the Sufi, the Buddhist, the philosopher, the mystic saw. Hearing became synonymous with seeing as my senses dovetailed in contemplative, receptive action. Everything began opening. Contemplation became unbounded. I was learning to contemplate deeper and deeper and wider and wider and higher and higher and longer and longer. All of life continuously opened to reveal glimpses of a hidden wholeness in wonder. Scientists tell us that the whole cosmos is expanding. Well, you can see it happening! You can hear it in the silent breathing of Life within ever-expanding life.

And yet, the most essential lesson I continue to study, because I constantly struggle with it, regards how to contemplate the silence at the heart of communication with others in the midst of the world of human culture. Similar to Hölderlin and Heidegger's wonderment about the role of a poet in destitute times, I agonize over the challenge of saying something, anything, into a seeming cultural void of noise. Although Merton teaches me that it is not our speaking that breaks the silence, but rather it is the anxiety to be heard that fragments the wholeness of relational experience and distorts the unexplainable intimacy of communion with all of life, there are times when one must speak. One can speak into silent spaces and be heard by the other, but it is absurd to speak into the cluttered zones of noise and expect a hearing, a response, an understanding, or real relations. Why is this so important? To me, my entire sense of life is bound up with that silence from which my being is expressed. To focus only upon what I say, think and do in this world—as if that defined or completed my *life*—is tantamount to existential treason. To avoid such treason, I had to learn discipline.

There is a discipline of hope in being attuned to the silence in genuine communication that deepens into communion—and it is for this deep encouragement that I am grateful for Merton's testimony of the struggle to express one's soul:

Everything healthy, everything certain, everything holy: If we can find such things, they all need to be emphasized and articulated. For this is it is necessary that there be a genuine and deep communication between the hearts and minds of men, communication and not the noise of slogans or the repetition of clichés. Genuine communication is becoming more and more difficult, and when speech is in danger of perishing or being perverted in the amplified noise of beasts, perhaps it becomes obligatory for a monk to try to speak (*Seeds of Destruction*, 243).

Yet, as my life seemed to lead to graduate school in communication studies and on to the profession of teaching communication in higher education, I found my self lost and feeling a bit stranded as if my self had become an island. I was in the middle of a liquid cultural world and the relationship between silence and communication became less and less stable to me. Too few seemed to agree with Merton, hence with me, that we are already one and were in a frenzy, instead, to force communication into a process of making constant contact and connections over and over and over again.

While I remained steadily committed to a contemplative way of living, my career seemed to reward only activity if not hyperactivity. I was a contemplative in an analytical world. I wanted to talk about silence but was obliged to talk about language, texts, symbols, media, messages, discourse. I wanted to talk about solitude and stillness, but was quickly being asked to conform to the latest crazes in social media. I felt I was cheating my students as well as myself when I felt there was so much more to communication than making connections, interpreting messages, keeping up with the world of chatter. I felt as if I was now being called to live in two different worlds, two different realities. One promised a lifestyle, the other life itself. I was being torn in two and had to find a way to reconcile multiple tensions of contemplation in a world that I began to describe as: "The Commotion." Over time, I learned with Merton's help to reconcile many of the tensions between contemplation and action, at least enough to develop a contemplative approach to teaching communication and honor a deeper calling, but the Commotion of the world refused to pause and let me pass.

I use the term "the Commotion" as a metaphor for our hyper-modern world and in reference to the externalization of the agitation of the soul, the racket of systemic evasion, an accelerated state of hurried disregard, and diversion of the Life of our lives. The Commotion is the exploitation of vanity and a grand impatience with the realities of life such that action is displaced by activity and contemplation is supplanted by data analysis. Today, we tend to live in commotion while in fear of communion.

A hyper-modern world is not easy to abandon for its reach is overwhelming, but the injustice and suffering that results from it demands our compassionate response. It is terribly sad and frightening to witness the deterioration of the world, the continued destruction of the earth and the atrophy of human civilization in the throes of a pragmatic nihilism so clear that it is almost invisible. The paradox that you have to leave the world to find it is the real journey that Merton described as "interior" because you must venture through the interior of reality itself. You have to go *through* your culture, *through* your religion, *through* your media, *through* your pretensions, *through* your self, piercing and penetrating everything until all is behind you. As Merton puts it, "this is the test of those who wish to cross the frontier" (*No Man Is An Island*, 255). When you cross that frontier, in silence, you are transformed to respond to the world that no longer envelops and dominates you.

This way of interior passage, to me, is a calling to *reverdure*, a challenge, as well as discipline, of healing. Reverdure is a French word for restoring the life of a natural area, to become green with growth again, to recover, to heal. Wendell Berry has written a beautiful poem entitled "Reverdure" in which he says "the slope whose scars I mended/turns green now/Healing becomes health/Reverdure is my calling" (Wendell Berry, *Clearing*, 48-52). Merton teaches us that reverdurance is our calling, too: As the practice of cultivating care in careless times, as a way of going through one's life in order to come to life, and as a necessity to persevere in the midst of deadening forces. In short, reverdurance means *enduring with reverence*.

Each day I wake up, I am challenged to affirm the Life of a world that obscures it, a world that seems to deny its own life. My actions feel so small, like desperately opening windows or doors to let the breeze be felt by others who prefer artificial air; it is such a fleeting, small act, hardly heroism, but it seems like it is the most one can do sometimes. The temptation, of course, is to give up in futility, to let the Commotion sweep you off your two feet, but we must resist that temptation. We must reverdure. Merton has convinced me of the hope of healing, of the necessity to reverdure.

Reform is just a ticket for another ride at the amusement park; revolution merely changes the park's theme. What we need is a *Resumption*: Enough reverdurance to resume our living lives, to rediscover the life of the world that has gone out of it, to replant our roots in the healing silence.

To me, Merton's writings have fulfilled T. S. Eliot's call to "clear the air, clean the sky and wash the wind" ("Murder in the Cathedral," *The Complete Poems and Plays: 1909-1950*, 231). In conclusion, I wish to share a poem of my own as a way to convey my gratefulness to Thomas Merton for all that I have learned from him about the hope and discipline of contemplating silence like trees swaying in the air as they purify it and mystics swinging like chimes in the Wind that blows where it pleases.

Reverdure in the Wind

When the wind dawns on you
follow it, keep your face,
keep facing and follow
wherever it leads you.
Note the feathers, maybe,
fluttering around you,
as they drift, curl and pitch
without rhythm or song;
hollow-boned and light weight,
human institutions
flip unreasonably
in the breeze of wisdom's
passage through trivia.
Your first following step:
desire discipline,
care for wisdom enough
to leave all the feathers
in flight—the pillow fight—
to push on through the night,
endure with reverence,

loving and observing
the incorruptible
laws of the aisling wind,
the wind of Sophia
wherever she pleases.
Keep the vigil for her.
Keep the vigil for her!
Reverdure in the wind.

"I Know And Have Seen
What I Was Obscurely Looking For"

Fiona Gardner

These words are part of the description given by Thomas Merton when he stood in front of the large Buddhist statues in Polonnaruwa. I first read the account of this epiphany in *The Other Side of the Mountain* (1998), the last volume of his *Journals*, and found it electrifying. As the Quaker George Fox might have said, 'it really spoke to my condition.'

At that point I was spiritually in a limbo space. I had been a Quaker, a member of The Society of Friends for about twenty years, but for much of that time had felt that something was missing. At the same time I had experimented with different Buddhist groups: Tibetan Buddhism, then the Order of Western Buddhists, and finally a Zen group, and I was seriously involved in yoga and had studied *Patanjali's Yoga Sutras*, *The Upanishads* and *The Bhagavad Gita*. I had travelled to India in search of 'enlightenment'— but returned ill. At that point I stopped attending Quaker meeting and let go of the searching. It didn't seem possible to find whatever it was I was obscurely looking for.

In the early 1990s, as part of that obscure looking, I had read a second hand copy of *The Seven Storey Mountain* and had felt absorbed by the narrative, identifying in many ways with Merton's early life; but the fervor of his conversion and subsequent arrival at Gethsemani had felt like only something I could imagine. However, in 1999 I fell over, literally, *The Other Side of the Mountain*. Some copies had been stacked on the floor of the local bookshop, rather symbolically I later thought, between the religion and psychology sections, and as I picked myself up I also picked up one which I then bought. The cover helped—it seemed as if Merton was smiling and encouraging me to have a look. He also looked fun. Here was someone, a person I already knew a bit about, now writing about a journey to India, so perhaps he could help.

After reading volume seven I was hooked and so read one by one, working randomly in no particular order through each of the earlier *Journals,* and loved them. However this was not just a literary venture; it became transformational. I now realize that this reading was a form of preparation for my own conversion and that in some way my mind was becoming open to welcome Jesus Christ. Everything changed. In 2001 I began to attend Bath Abbey, a large building and congregation where I could be inconspicuous, and eventually joined a confirmation class. I was the only adult and this meant I enjoyed one to one time with a warm and encouraging woman vicar, and generally elicited amazement from friends who said that usually people left Anglicanism to become a Quaker.

Late in 2001 I went to a day retreat about Thomas Merton and then joined The

Thomas Merton Society of Great Britain and Ireland. I found the first residential conference I attended inspirational. It was terribly exciting. In addition to all the intellectual insights, I gained a welcome sense of a community of like-minded people. In part, as a way of expressing my gratitude for the transformation that was effected in my life through reading Merton, I have been involved in promoting his work and spiritual experiences ever since.

So what was it about Merton that spoke to my condition? William Shannon wrote of Merton as a theologian of experience. I would now add to this that he is also a theologian of feeling. It was the very human and real way in which Merton spoke about his emotions and his inner life that attracted and continues to attract me. I liked how he included both the positive and negative and seemed able to express and communicate in such a human way universal difficulties in the spiritual life. He felt like a friend. As many others have found, it sometimes seemed that he was writing especially for me. I could really connect to the experiences I was reading. In the Celtic tradition there is a term *anam cara* where in Gaelic *anam* means soul and *cara* friend, and in the Celtic understanding there need be no earthly limitations to this friendship. From the time that I seriously began to read Merton he has become such a soul friend.

His ideas on the false illusory self and the hidden true self resonated both personally and professionally as I had trained and worked for many years as a psychoanalytic psychotherapist and more recently as a spiritual director. In both analytic thought and in Merton's work there is emphasis on recognizing and discarding the false self and through this process uncovering and recovering the true self. While the context of psychotherapy and spirituality are different, there is also much to connect the work of Merton with both the analytical psychologist Carl Jung and the psychoanalyst Donald Winnicott. The ideas of both Jung and Winnicott have been central to my personal and professional understanding of the inner world, and Merton's writings add a further dimension that have enlarged and enlightened me spiritually. The relationship between therapy and spirituality has continued to fascinate and puzzle me and has been the subject of a number of books and articles I've written and talks and workshops that I've given. Merton has been a key figure in all of these.

Merton's writings on contemplation have helped me in a way that the Buddhist groups and teachings and years as a Quaker were unable to. This is because of Merton's writings on the personal relationship with God. This is clarified for me in one of my favorite pieces by Merton which is his last lecture to the novices before he becomes a full-time hermit. In the recording of this you can hear the full range of his emotion, intellect, insight and humor—he is in fact very funny. The written version is "A Life Free from Care" found in *Thomas Merton, Essential Writings*, (2000). Merton reminds the novices of the purpose of the solitary life which is to put away all care, and he draws on the work of Jean Pierre de Caussade on the need for surrender and self-abandonment to God, where God "offers to take upon Himself the care of our affairs." This is what love is. Towards the end of the talk Merton says our vocation is the same as the vocation of Mary Magdalene and the disciples at Emmaus which is to see the Lord.

My experience of reading Merton, writing about him and speaking about him has been that he acts as a liberator. Quite recently I discovered that Donald Allchin, the late President of the Thomas Merton Society of Great Britain and Ireland, wrote this about Merton many years ago, that Merton "set out at the beginning to liberate us from the illusions of the world" and I would emphasize from the illusion of our self and our false self. Merton knew that salvation lies within the psyche and that there is a need for the opening of a door unlocked from the inside. By helping me to unlock the door Merton did and indeed *is* still helping me to find what I was and am obscurely looking for.

Scholarship, Community And Communion:
A Jewish Perspective

Edward K. Kaplan

Thomas Merton's reflections on "messengers of hope" have helped me to clarify the meaning of my lifelong commitment to Merton scholarship and teaching—all of which nourish my personal quest for faith, for God and my efforts (not always consistent) to be a good Jew. Professionally, my involvement in religious studies is subordinate to the field of French literature in which I earned my Ph.D. (1970, Columbia University); French poetry is the academic specialty on which tenure and intellectual validation depended.

Merton became a mediator. Assuming the risk to work in fields usually considered antithetical (e.g. French is a notoriously secular culture), it was a special opportunity for me to teach Merton's life and works for over forty years, parallel to my teaching and writing on the life and works of Abraham Joshua Heschel (1907-1972), Jewish theologian and activist. They knew and admired each other, and both the rabbi/professor and the monk/priest were writers. Heschel was, and remains, my Jewish role model. Merton inspires me as a brother.

My trajectory as a religious studies scholar began during the beginning of my graduate program in French at Columbia University, in 1965, when I first met Heschel, professor at the nearby Jewish Theological Seminary (JTS). The short version is that my father, Kivie Kaplan, a businessman and civil rights activist, had arranged for me to be introduced to Heschel who was known as "a mystic." (His official title at JTS was Professor of Jewish Ethics and Mysticism.) At that time in life I was bored with the prosaic rationalism of the American Reform Judaism in which I was brought up, and fascinated with Hindu philosophy and Eastern spirituality which promised intense experiences. At the same time, I was enthralled by Heschel's book, *Man Is Not Alone*, which was the first Jewish book I ever read which convincingly evoked God's presence. After forming a mentor-like relationship with Heschel, I made a personal decision to seek answers to my perplexities through Judaism. While completing my doctoral dissertation on the French Romantic historian Jules Michelet (1798-1874), I found that the witness of Heschel and Merton provided standards of spiritual and ethical meaning in the modern world.

To the budding academic that I was, Merton and Heschel were indeed "messengers of hope" during a period of social and political turmoil. Competing with my peaceful literary studies were the civil rights movement, opposition to the American intervention in Vietnam, the June 1967 war in the Middle East, student rebellions at Columbia University and then in Paris, and of course Vatican II—you get the picture. Heschel and

Merton integrated contemplation, study and social conscience; they lived both within and at the margins of institutions, sharing—and not always in silence—intuitions of "original unity," human and divine. (Jules Michelet, in his secularized Christian, anti-clerical idiom, exemplified a similarly prophetic view of the writer's mission.)

As an advanced graduate student, I taught courses on French language and literature at Barnard College, while delaying my dissertation during the rebellion at Columbia University. Learning more than I wanted to about academic politics, I began to write essays as a sort of ethical journalism: an article in the *Jewish Times* of Boston about the Columbia events and mimeographed newsletters about demonstrations in Washington D. C. of clergy and laity against the Vietnam war—national gatherings in which I participated with Heschel. I was flattered that he invited me to take long walks with him on Shabbat afternoons, as he obsessively bemoaned the horrors of the Vietnam war about which he read daily in the *New York Times*. Naïvely, I was annoyed that he would speak rarely about intellectual and spiritual issues that bothered me. Only after his death did I realize that the agony he expressed over the victims of war (American and Vietnamese) was his theology. On such walks down Broadway or Riverside Drive, Heschel did tell me that he had received letters from Thomas Merton, but I did not follow up this glimpse of spiritual affinity until years later. During this same period, I also started writing about Heschel's poetic style. Heschel felt keenly that his works were badly understood, and he agreed with me that a literary approach would be helpful.

A year after completing the Ph.D., I became an assistant professor of French at Amherst College. When interviewed for the job, the Dean of Faculty, Bruce Morgan, asked about my writings on Heschel. Soon I was invited to offer a course from the Religion Department that I called "Mysticism and the Moral Life," connecting inner spirituality of the most radical kind—unmediated encounter with God—and ethical (even political) judgments leading to action, visible public acts or writings—as well as private, intimate, prayerful intuitions. The authors we consistently studied were Abraham Heschel, Howard Thurman and Thomas Merton. My students came from the "five college consortium" (Mount Holyoke, Smith, Hampshire Colleges, the University of Massachusetts, and Amherst) and were earnest seekers like their teacher. Perhaps too earnest.

These were the most passionate courses I ever taught. I did not hide my enthusiasm in the classroom nor in my academic publications and conference papers. But I was denied tenure. Despite recognition in distinguished journals in two fields (French literature and religious studies), I was deemed "too personally involved." The new Dean of Faculty (Bruce Morgan had since left) candidly wrote to inform me that the College tenure committee found my publications "devoid of critical distance" and that I was more interested in "religious mysticism" than French literature (even though my first book, *Michelet's Poetic Vision* (UMass Press, 1977) was in page proofs), as if there were an intrinsic opposition. My colleagues at Brandeis University, where I arrived in 1978, have judged otherwise.

CONTEMPLATIVE SCHOLARSHIP

I do not believe there is a quantum leap between the college classroom and the world outside (usually called, for some crazy reason, "the real world"). Those of us who publish as well as teach may depend on professional organizations for academic or personal self-validation, contact with new information or ideas, as well as a shared reading list of classics in the field, books in common. This is academic "community." Colleagues share their love (or disdain) for certain texts, certain ideas. In a word, we are usually motivated by more or less obvious ideological convictions. To put it another way, academic methods such as careful analysis and peer reviewing can help protect us from being blinded by our unwitting advocacy. Or we can "advocate" more objectively. Isn't this "critical distance" more likely "critical sympathy"?

We usually choose research and teaching topics close to our heart, to our values. The methods of scholarship must be as objective as possible; the decision to choose a sedentary, solitary life among books is a subjective, even a spiritual choice. How can we communicate and share our intimate commitments? When do colleagues become friends? To recall Merton, how do we pass from communication to communion?

My point is that for Merton and Heschel there is no neutrality. Nor is there neutrality among scholars of Merton and Heschel.

Here is how I found a "religious" community in the ITMS (International Thomas Merton Society). (I also belong to literature associations such as the MLA and Nineteenth-Century French Studies as well as the Association for Jewish Studies.) While I was still at Amherst College, the August 1974 issue of *St. Anthony Messenger* featured an article on the resurgence of Merton studies in North America; included was my course, "Mysticism and the Moral Life." I was quoted as "a Jewish professor" who proclaimed that Merton's vision of Catholicism will "save the Church." (What chutzpah for a non-Christian! and yet, unwittingly, Merton's spiritual openness had already become part of my identity as a Jew. Somehow, Merton, Dorothy Day, and the *Catholic Worker* to which I subscribed, and my restless students, had ushered me into the *Zeitgeist* of Vatican II.) About three years later Donald Grayston and Michael Higgins invited me to present a paper on Heschel and Merton at the 1978 Merton Conference at Vancouver, British Columbia. There I experienced a combination of estrangement and sympathetic fascination, as the only Jew at the meeting.

The 1978 Vancouver conference was, for me, the prototype of what became the ITMS. Put another way, I am a committed Jew teaching and writing about an exemplary Catholic writer, thinker and spiritual master. Where was my place at the Christian feast?

The ITMS is a community of serious (and humorous) Christians (not solely Roman Catholics) devoted to God and intellectual independence, and practicing, in the words of Abraham Heschel, "spiritual audacity." Merton's vision of the future has indeed become general knowledge: On one end of the arch there is immense nostalgia for the good Pope John XXIII and, on the other, immeasurable hope to revive the values of Vatican II with the papacy of Pope Francis.

The ITMS is an academic community at its very best. A vast, international and diverse readership is nourished by Merton's literary legacy. Everything has deliberately been made available, published or preserved in the archives at Bellarmine University in Louisville, Kentucky. Merton's books, poems and worldwide correspondence, and even his private diaries, are expertly edited and published without censorship. We can learn about practically anything we want to from these materials. His diary, for example, reveals the deepest secrets of his thoughts, dreams, even his body, including the "Love Journals" which explore his infatuation with a student nurse. No one has more access than others to the development of the writer's consciousness. That openness, I believe, and love for an imperfect man (Thomas Merton), save us from nasty sibling rivalries that often afflict the heritage of famous writers.

As a worship community, the ITMS is open to people of all religions or none, although the majority of its membership remains Roman Catholic. Merton himself started as a convert to the triumphal Church before opening himself to diversity beyond the cloister. At its biennial meetings, to integrate "academics" and worship, the ITMS provides Mass to which all are invited. I meditate prayerfully but do not kneel, nor do I take Communion. That dimension of community is limited for me.

However, communion can go two ways. The ITMS also provides weekend retreats at the Abbey of Gethsemani, alternating with its academic conference. There, I have shared my family's Friday evening Shabbat home service with the community. The monastery provides the Jewish challah bread, candles and the sweet Manichevitz wine, while Brother Paul Quenon, in his Trappist robes, holds the ceremonial hand washing bowl for me, as if I were at the altar. We recite the blessings over candles, wine (*kiddish*), and bread (*motzi*), and wish each other "Shabbat shalom." On one such occasion, Sister Jose Hobday, a Franciscan nun and native American, thanked me by saying, "This is the first time I prayed in the language in which Jesus prayed." What validation for a Jew with my fragile faith!

For me, the interfaith dimension of the Merton community is the heartbeat of our community, of our communion. Together we have made tremendous progress. In 2001 I was invited to organize a conference on Merton and Judaism; the papers, previous publications on the topic and Merton's correspondence with Jewish thinkers have been edited by Beatrice Bruteau and published by Fons Vitae with ecumenical passion and professional expertise (the ITMS standard). Spirituality has been advanced by Merton. A devout Catholic theologian, Christopher Pramuk, has combined sophisticated analysis and love in his book, *Sophia. Thomas Merton's Hidden Christ.* He applies the Jewish theology of Abraham Heschel to translate the Incarnation into universal, as well as Christian, terms. A new, interfaith chapter of the ITMS has begun to blossom in Delaware. Those of us who study and teach Thomas Merton have good reasons, perhaps holy reasons, to hope.

What We Have To Be Is What We Are: Merton's Unfinished Agenda

Joan Chittister, OSB

Merton's continuing insistence that there is no real spiritual development until we plumb the depths of the self to determine who we are—without the masks, without the labels—is a call to honesty and to self-criticism. The difficulty lies in the fact that both qualities are long lost in the Madison Avenue approach to life. In this world, life becomes a matter of creating images of who I aspire to be rather than setting out to understand who I really am. What really drives me, what I really think and want and care about are the raw materials of me. It is out of these things that the self emerges, shapes and forms itself, and finally, finally, finally comes to fullness.

What Merton calls us to do as part of this slow but fulfilling process depends on the raw and ruthless debunking of the self to the self that is the ground of humility. He challenges us all to cling to the reality that is ourselves rather than enshroud ourselves in the cosmetic world around us, mere specters of who we are each meant to become. He calls us to the most daring truth of all, the truth of who we really are. In the center of the self. In the heart of us. Behind the veils.

But it is not a simple process. To discover the real self implies the peeling away of the layers of persona we have so carefully cultivated for the sake of fitting into a plastic world full of other plastic images. It requires, as they say in publishing, the courage to refuse to believe our own press. Until that happens we risk the danger daily of falling down the rabbit hole of the self. We begin to see ourselves as above, beyond, different from, superior to all the other mere mortals around us. In political language we call it "exceptionalism." In spiritual dialects we call it "holiness." We find ourselves outside the pale of basic spiritual disciplines, above the appetites that score the rest of the human race, psychological robots made out of the stuff of a papier-mâché world.

It is the task of a lifetime to work with the basic instincts and urgings, soul shifts and values, desires and hopes within us to become the fullness of the raw material of the self. But unless we do, we doom ourselves to buy into the empty images every new world creates to define itself: successful man, tough urban cowboy, wealthy woman, clerical dandy, wonder woman, obedient disciple, leader, stereotype of whatever becomes the fashion of the time.

The spiritual excavation of the real person is the central adventure of life. Merton is right about that. But it is not simply the discovery of the possibilities of the self that constitute its wholeness. It is as well the awareness of what defines us from outside ourselves that is necessary to bring us to spiritual wholeness.

Or to put it another way, we must learn at the same time to be what we are not.

And what we "aren't"—essentially—is American or Indian, Polish or Chinese, Italian or Turkish, Brazilian or Australian, English or African. In fact, we aren't any of them. Rather, we must come to realize that we are all of them. Regardless of whoever it is who tells us we are not.

The problem is that everything in the world, including religion too often, wars against the discovery of the essential self for the sake of the public self. The most dangerous of wars have a religious component, from the Crusades to Kosovo, from Hitler's search for the super race to fanatic Islam and its worldwide terror. We kill one another because the gods we make for ourselves tell us to do so, we declare, for the sake of the soul of the planet. And few religious figures stand up together—rabbis and imams and Christian clergy and Hindu swamis and monastics of all ilk—and witness together to the absurdity of such pseudo-theology.

Neither nationalism nor religion prepares us to simply be ourselves, to be humans together. Neither religion nor society prepares us to simply be ourselves, men and women together, as equal participants in both the life of grace and the affairs of humanity everywhere and anywhere.

And so we all live separated by the very institutions we have a right to expect will bind us together. We go on seeking oneness behind the walls we have built against one another. And we talk about the discovery of our "real" selves, the religion we live inside ourselves, while our societal selves cling to the masks we continue to live behind in public.

It is a kind of spiritual schizophrenia that we are negotiating now in a world highly pluralistic but attempting to live in both isolation and unity at the same time. While the national boundaries of the world seep everywhere and the religions teach oneness but practice separation, we need to realize that unless we unmask our public selves as well as our inner selves, our "real" self—the self we were born to become—we will never be either fully alive or spiritually whole.

Indeed, what we have to be is what we are, individuals on the way to universal oneness where uniformity is no substitute for unity. As Philipp Melanchthon puts it: "In essentials, unity; in differences, liberty; in all things, charity," is only possible when the inner self is so real that the public self is itself changed by it.

Seeing The World As It Really Is:
The Prophetic Legacy Of Thomas Merton

Daniel P. Horan, OFM

Although Thomas Merton never lived to see his one-hundredth birthday—the milestone we now celebrate—his influence, insight, wisdom, challenge, and humanity continue to be present in the prophetic voice he left behind. There are times that I read the sage words and reflections of this twentieth-century monk and feel as though his voice is responding to the immediate and urgent needs of our time. His insight into prayer and spirituality, criticism of violence and discrimination, and genuine interest in interreligious dialogue and interfaith experiences still touch the hearts and lives of women and men of our age. And, surely, the relevance and appeal of his thought and writings will continue to inspire generations to come. I believe, above all else, that the reason he continues to live on in this way, long after his bodily death, is because Thomas Merton was a prophet.

By prophet I do not mean, as Merton himself once dismissed, one who has certain magical abilities as in "the sense of sudden illuminations as to what is going to happen at some future moment." Instead, I recognize in Merton the prophetic life and voice that he called others to adopt, "in the sense that we are so one with the Holy Spirit that we are already going in the direction the Spirit is going" (*The Springs of Contemplation* 49). A prophet, as Merton attests, is not some kind of fortuneteller or a predictor of what is to come, but someone whose life is so open to God's Spirit that she or he cannot help but begin to see the world in a new way. What distinguishes prophets from other people, even other people of faith, is that they can begin to see the world as God sees it or, to put it another way, prophets see the world as it really is.

To understand what that means and the implications that arise from such a way of living in the world, we need to look a little closer at the meaning of prophecy and the prophetic vocation. In doing so, it is my hope that we might not only come to a deeper appreciation for the prophetic legacy that Merton leaves us in his writings, but that we might especially come to see how we can follow Merton's own example and become the much-needed prophets of our own time.

THE PROPHETIC VOCATION

Unlike the more colloquial use of vocation, whether in the secular world to discuss a trade and career path, or in the religious context to refer to a state of life (e.g., marriage, religious life, single life, etc.), Merton's notion of vocation is much more inclusive. He recognized that each person was individually created into existence with a particular identity known to God fully and known to us partially as the "True Self." In this sense, everybody has a calling (a "*vocare*," meaning "to call," which is the Latin root word for vocation) from God to be the person each was created to be, which is an entirely unique, unrepeatable and wholly loved identity. Yet, Merton also wrote about a more universal sense of a vocation. This sense of the term referred to what was shared among the baptized, what each Christian was called to do and be in light of our communal commitment to following the Gospel. To talk about a prophetic vocation is to talk in this more general way, as a characteristic of our collective Christian identity. Its manifestation will necessarily appear differently in the lives of various people by virtue of the differences in lifestyle, social location, familial commitments, religious profession, and so on. But a general call for all Christians to be prophets in the world is universal.

Not everybody, however, lives up to this call, just as not everybody lives up to each aspect of baptized life. Nevertheless, when someone does respond, usually unwittingly or unconsciously, they are immediately recognized as "different from the pack."

We see this differentiation going back to the prophets of the Hebrew Scriptures. Those called by the Lord to speak the truth in society and within the faith community are remembered because of their stance within the community and the message they proclaimed. What is both comforting and discomforting at the same time is that none of these historic prophets wanted to accept the call they had received. Jeremiah is one of my favorite examples, in large part because his main excuse is that he is too young. We read at the beginning of the Book of the Prophet Jeremiah the call that echoes each of the prophets of Israel:

> Now the word of the Lord came to me saying, "Before I formed you in the womb I knew you, and before you were born I consecrated you; I appointed you a prophet to the nations." Then I said, "Ah, Lord God! Truly I do not know how to speak, for I am only a boy." But the Lord said to me, "Do not say, 'I am only a boy'; for you shall go to all to whom I send you, and you shall speak whatever I command you. Do not be afraid of them, for I am with you to deliver you, says the Lord (Jeremiah 1:4-8, NRSV).

As someone who entered the Franciscan Order at the relatively young age of twenty-one, right after graduating from college, I can appreciate Jeremiah's hesitancy and insecurity with regard to what is being asked of him. To commit one's self to religious life today, something that Merton describes time and again as a prophetic stance in the world, is an intimidating venture and one that, like Merton's own experience in his time, is filled with both euphoric highs and surprising lows. It makes perfect sense to me that Jeremiah, while still in his youth, would instinctively dismiss the call of the Lord.

Merton, coincidentally, was also struck by Jeremiah's story of call and resistance. In the retreat he gave at the Abbey of Gethsemani for religious sisters in the late 1960s, the text of which was later published as *The Springs of Contemplation*, Merton writes:

> Read the prophets in the Old Testament. Their biggest problem was that they were prophets. Jeremiah didn't want to be a prophet. In some sense, we're in the same boat. God lays on us the burden of feeling the contradictions in our world and Church and exposing them, insofar as we are honestly able to do that (*Springs*, 157-158).

Merton sees in Jeremiah an example for all of us. We, too, are called to be prophets in our time, but most reject that possibility outright. This is not necessarily done consciously or with malice but, in order to live a prophetic vocation, one's story must be God's story, the narrative of faith and not one of the many other competing narratives of the world.

One of the medieval figures that deeply influenced Merton's thought and theological worldview early on was Bonaventure, the thirteenth-century Franciscan friar, saint and doctor of the church. Bonaventure had a lot to say about prophecy, particularly in terms of how St. Francis of Assisi exemplified the prophetic vocation in both word and deed. Merton's understanding of prophecy was very likely shaped, if in implicit ways, by Bonaventure's theology. Merton even mentions St. Francis, as Bonaventure did, in *The Springs of Contemplation*, in which he writes: "For him, too, there is a radical break with the world into a prophetic and free life" (133).

In his presentation of St. Francis as prophet Bonaventure compares the medieval Italian saint to John the Baptist, the great herald of Christ, who is generally hailed within Christianity as one of the greatest prophets of history. John's particular greatness stems from his proximity to Jesus, both chronologically and spiritually, as he is the most immediate forerunner of the Lord and, according to the New Testament canon, the first to recognize the Lord for who he really is. The way Bonaventure highlights the meaning of prophecy is rooted in the tradition of the great prophets of the Hebrew Scriptures. It is not, as Merton rejects earlier, the notion of one's ability to foretell the future, but instead to see reality as it truly is. In this sense, the meaning of prophecy is more in line with the Greek word *propheteia*, which bears the connotation "to speak forth" more than it signifies "foretelling" or something magical. The ability "to speak forth" was unique, among the charisms that St. Paul names in his epistolary, not because of the content so much as the grounding for what was being proclaimed. The grounding of one's prophetic pronouncements came from the appropriation of the scriptural narrative that is another way to talk about embracing "God's Story." Bonaventure insists that a prophet is one who focuses his or her life on scripture and, over time and by way of divine inspiration, comes to arrive at its spiritual and fuller sense. In sum, we become prophets when we become people of scripture imbued with God's revelation in a way that shades and shapes our perception. It is only then that a prophet can begin to see with "God's eyes."

This is what we might say is the formative process for becoming a Christian prophet, something that Merton described in his comments to the sisters published in *The Springs of Contemplation*. Time and again he returns to the importance of scripture and the role of the Holy Spirit in shaping the outlook of women and men who follow their call to live out the Christian prophetic vocation. But this is not the end of the story. Prophets, as one might recall about any of the famous (or even not-so-famous) prophets in the tradition, do not keep silent and do not keep their way of seeing the world to themselves. As if unable to contain the pain of seeing the incongruity recognized in the way people live in the world contrasted with the way God intends the human family to live in this life, the prophet speaks out against the increasingly more recognizable instances of injustice, pain, suffering, abuse, and other troubles in the world. The true prophet, like all his or her prophetic predecessors, necessarily becomes a marginal person because this way of seeing reality inevitably pushes one to the margins of the socially acceptable and of the *status quo*. It should come as no surprise that prophets are often viewed as outsiders; in truth they could live no other way. They enter the realm of what some postcolonial theorists have recently taken to calling the "location of the surplus," or that marginal space from which a different perspective is gained because that marginal space does not align with nor is it subsumed into the predominant power system or structure of a given society, institution or place.

Prophets become a nuisance to those who have vested interests in the maintenance of power or control because they point out the disconnect between the way those in power or those with authority act and the way God intends the human family to relate to one another and the rest of creation. Merton made this point well when we said: "The prophetic struggle with the world is the struggle of the Cross against worldly power" (*Springs*, 81). This struggle with the world and against worldly power will inevitably result in friction and suspicion on the part of those whose identity and interests are threatened by the prophet's public acknowledgement of the incongruity of lived reality versus the reality God intends. Merton sees this as inherently painful for those who follow the call of the Holy Spirit to become prophets in their time:

> To live prophetically, you've got to be questioning and looking at factors behind the facts. You've got to be aware that there are contradictions. In a certain sense, our prophetic vocation consists in hurting from the contradictions in society. This is a real cross in our lives today. For we ourselves are partly responsible (*Springs*, 157).

This is not simply a societal issue for Merton, but something that affects the prophet personally and ecclesiastically, for the more one starts to see the world as it really is and observes the ways in which we consistently fall short of God's loving desire, the more we see the inherent contradictions in our own lives and in the church.

THOMAS MERTON'S PROPHETIC LEGACY

This was the sort of prophet that Thomas Merton was and continues to be long past his earthly death. He was able, with time, to see more and more of what God's vision for the world was and how the way in which humanity exercised its collective freedom in myriad ways was far afield from that divine intention. It didn't happen overnight and, I would argue, Merton was not at the beginning of his religious pilgrimage the prophet he would eventually become and remain. The prophetic legacy he leaves us and from which we continue to glean inspiration arose out of a life of conversion, a life committed—in imperfect, finite ways—to following the call of the Holy Spirit.

I am certainly not the first to highlight Merton's prophetic legacy as one of the central gifts the twentieth-century monk has left us. From Gerald Twomey's tellingly titled 1978 collection of essays, *Thomas Merton: Prophet in the Belly of a Paradox*, to the more recent volumes including Paul Dekar's *Thomas Merton: Twentieth-Century Wisdom for Twenty-First-Century Living* (2011) and Mario Aguilar's *Thomas Merton: Contemplation and Political Action* (2011), scholars and enthusiasts of Merton's life and work have identified the threads of prophetic intuition and proclamation that continue to speak to the pressing concerns and unsettling times of our own day. Along with these authors, I am continually struck by the insight that emerges from the writing of a man whose social location (a member of a cloistered monastic community in Kentucky) and personal identity (a white, highly educated, celibate, Roman-Catholic cleric) would appear far-too removed from the experiences of those whose struggles with justice, violence and power today are most pressing. Yet, his ability to cut to the heart of the matter is reflective of the true prophetic heritage from which it arises.

Many people might be quick to assume that, because Merton was a cloistered monk remotely situated in relationship to the urgent concerns about the economy, justice, race, and violence of his day, he was less able to respond to the "signs of the time" (*Gaudium et Spes*). However, in light of what we know about true prophets in the Christian tradition, it was precisely this lifestyle and location that provided the very condition for the possibility of fostering his prophetic vocation.

There is much to be said for his lived example of a life devoted, at least in principle, to prayer, study (especially of scripture) and reflection that ultimately cultivated an environment capable of imbuing God's narrative in his heart and mind. In a sense it is a real spiritual luxury to live in a milieu so singularly dedicated to living the Gospel. In truth, each monk in the monastery—just as each person in any walk of life—must willingly respond in freedom to the Holy Spirit's call, and simply being a member of a religious order is not enough without the commitment of the individual to *live* the life. Nevertheless, the conditions of religious life are intentionally designed to enable a person to let God's story become more and more that person's story, to let scripture become the pacemaker, and to allow prayer to guide the thoughts and actions of each member of that community.

In the case of Merton this spiritual landscape within which he was located, a terrain shaped by daily recitation of the psalms, hearing the scripture and celebrating the church's liturgies was an ideal locale for the formation of a prophet. Removed, in part, from the more common distractions of life in his time, Merton could—if he so chose—focus more dedicatedly to becoming a person of scripture, a man whose own story began to look at lot more like God's story, a monk whose eyes could glimpse the world with some of God's vision of reality.

In the beginning this was not the case. Merton's most popular books and essays early on do not reflect the thought of someone who we could call a prophet. He was more like a "prophet-in-training" (something to which we should all aspire in our own ways). His focus was on the life of prayer and scripture, and his writing reflected it. Texts like *Seeds of Contemplation* and *The Sign of Jonas* reveal a Christian grappling with the meaning of evangelical life in the modern world. But it was these periods of intense gazing and spiritual struggle that enabled the later Merton—the author of *Conjectures of a Guilty Bystander* and *The Cold War Letters*—to become who he was. By the time his eyes were opened to the condition of the world in which he recognized himself as a fellow citizen with the rest of humanity, Merton was already at the margin of society living an ancient monastic life in a complex modern time. His location was, without his knowing it, a place of theological and social "surplus," a place at once removed from the systems of *status quo* and the ordinary.

With years of living a life of scripture, having become saturated daily with the inspired word of God, Merton looked out of his monastery at the world around him and saw the disconnection between what God intended and the way his sisters and brothers were living. The disjunction appeared in stark relief because of the injustices and abuses of his time made manifest in racial inequality, international threats of violence and war, economic disparity, and so many other iterations of systemic sin. With this vision of what God intended for the human family placed in contrast alongside his vision of reality, Merton could not help but cry out and call attention to the problems.

He did this the best way he knew how: through writing.

Merton's writing is the medium by which his prophetic legacy is passed on from one generation to the next. The entire written corpus provides us with a holistic vision of his lifelong conversion from idealistic young monk to prophet. At times subtle, the shift in emphasis that is generally expressed as a move from solitude and contemplation toward social justice and interreligious dialogue is not as fragmented or demarcated as some would have us think. In embracing the prophetic vocation one doesn't move away from a life of prayer and scripture, but is instead sustained in their authentic Christian call precisely through that faithful living of modern discipleship. This is important to remember. Merton could not be a prophet without a continued personal and, on some level, communal commitment to a life of prayer and scripture. Sure, he could have been a so-called "secular" radical, perhaps even committed to many of the same concerns. But, as we know and Merton affirmed, to be a prophet requires one's life to be transformed by the Holy Spirit and to allow one's story to align with God's story in scripture. Merton's prophetic legacy transcends the sectarian or ideological strictures that generally limit other well-meaning peoples' concerns; God's concerns are not limited to partisan interests, but touch on the wellbeing of all people and the entirety of creation.

THE NEED FOR PROPHETS IN OUR OWN DAY

In what would be one of the last few addresses of his life, Thomas Merton gave an informal and unscripted talk on monasticism at the Temple of Understanding in Calcutta, India in October 1968. Throughout the short reflection the often-eloquent monk struggled to find the words and the images he needs to express the feelings he wished to convey. He was moved by the fundamental unity that connected all human persons together beyond the superficial distinctions, cultural variation, perceived differences, and other things that separate people from one another. He concludes that address with the affirmation that, "We are already one. But we imagine that we are not. What we have to recover is our original unity. What we have to be is what we are" (*The Asian Journal of Thomas Merton*, 308). This realization that there is an intrinsic feature of our existence that binds us together in an inseparable way is in part an articulation of the scriptural vision of humanity that reflects reality as it really is. This is, in the truest sense, a prophetic expression of who we are as human beings. All the exterior differences and struggles to divide people are iterations of worldly narratives that do not align with God's vision of reality.

In the same talk, Merton makes it abundantly clear that he recognizes the prophetic dimension of what he is saying, while at the same time he reaches beyond his own experience to call his audience—to call us—to follow that divine impulse toward being prophets in our day. Merton explains what this entails:

> And so I stand among you as one who offers a small message of hope, that first, there are always people who dare to seek on the margin of society, who are not dependent on social acceptance, not dependent on social routine, and prefer a kind of free-floating existence under a state of risk. And among these people, if they are faithful to their own calling, to their own vocation, and to their own message from God, communication on the deepest level is possible.

As discussed above, Merton was very aware of the marginal lifestyle that being a true prophet necessarily entailed. In one sense he warns his hearers of what to expect, while in another sense he encourages them, nevertheless, to be "faithful to their own calling, to their own vocation." This is a message for you and me as much as it was for his audience in Calcutta more than four decades ago. We need prophets in our own day who are willing, in whatever state of life such people find themselves, to follow the example of Merton and become people committed to prayer and scripture in ways that enable transformation from a worldview shaped by the narratives of our cultures and societies to a vision of reality as it really is from the vantage point of God.

Do we "dare to seek on the margin of society" in an effort to cry out for justice in our world? Are we willing to follow the direction of the Holy Spirit in our actions and words? Can we become people of prayer and scripture in our various states of life, from the married and committed partnerships to those in communal religious orders? This is our task today, to follow in the footprints of Thomas Merton in discovering who we are in discovering what God has in store for all of us. There are, as Merton says above, inherent risks that come with this embrace of our call: the risks of marginalization, the risks of upsetting the *status quo*, the risks of doing what is right and just.

Thomas Merton's prophetic legacy can only continue in the lives, words and actions of you and me. What better way to celebrate his one-hundredth birthday than to commit ourselves to following more closely the prophetic call that all Christians have received on the day of our baptism? Just as Merton ultimately gained that spiritual clarity through prayer and scripture that opened his eyes to God's vision, may we too continually strive to see the world as it really is and become the much needed prophets in our own day.

Communion Through Dialogue

Judith Simmer-Brown

Raised a Methodist minister's daughter in a Nebraska small town full of Polish immigrants, I knew nothing about Thomas Merton until college. Provincial Protestantism had taught me suspicion of Catholics ever since my first-grade classmate Betty had jumped off the other end of the teeter-totter screaming that I was going to hell for not being a Catholic. My parents encouraged me to wear orange on St. Paddy's Day, and I was always pinched by my many Catholic schoolmates. It was supposed to be a banner of pride.

As a Religious Studies major in a good liberal arts college, everything changed. My natural childhood curiosity about world religions blossomed into an enduring passion for India, and I went on a study abroad program to a Gandhian ashram college in the mid-60s. There I learned interreligious toleration, and began a self-styled meditation practice. Thomas Merton entered the periphery of my mind when I read of his death in Bangkok in 1968, the year I graduated from college and began graduate school.

It was not until much later, after I had become a committed Tibetan Buddhist practitioner, that I came to know Merton's work. In 1978, I had come to teach Religious Studies at the original Buddhist-based college in the west, Naropa Institute (now University). Chogyam Trungpa, its founder and my root teacher, had asked me to work with him organizing a conference on Buddhist-Christian meditation, the first of an annual series that extended through the 1980s. He began these conferences in honor of his relationship with Thomas Merton, whom he had met in India in 1968, and with whom he had an instant rapport. Their conversations began a respectful, collegial interreligious connection that sustained Rinpoche in his early years as a western dharma teacher, and he dedicated this series of conferences to Merton's memory.

As a result of Rinpoche's appreciation for Merton, I began a study of Merton's interreligious writings, curious about his impact on my teacher. Delving into this relationship and into Merton's interreligious vision has deeply impacted my own Buddhist journey, and I'm honored to contribute to this volume. It is largely through the influence of these two great contemplative visionaries that I have committed to a lifetime of contemplative interreligious dialogue. They both recognized that, when we delve deeply in our own spiritual journeys, we are no longer limited by the doctrines, scriptures or rituals of our respective faith traditions. We meet each other, with all our delicious spiritual specificities, in an intimate communication that that honors difference and relishes resonance.

Living as a Buddhist in a Judeo-Christian or secular world, interreligious dialogue has enriched my life immeasurably. I find pilgrims from many traditions whose treasures and challenges inspire me, and I appreciate the generosity of their sharing.

Buddhists from other lineages, cultures or countries become my companions in an environment of personal sharing. Spiritual seekers who are not comfortable in any institutional setting open me to the openness of practicing without tradition, and I find myself converted again and again. In short, I have found a *sangha* in many unexpected corners of my life.

The greatest blessing in my teaching is the opportunity to introduce students to the dialogue of contemplative practice. Through my years of teaching dialogue at Naropa University, I have been gratified by the growth in openness, curiosity and empathy that these dialogues have brought to my students and their dialogue partners. Of course, there have been glitches. Occasionally dialogue relationships have become defensive early on and closed down, but these occurrences have been rare. For the most part, the dialogues have generated accelerated progress in appreciating differences and developing curiosity, mutual respect and new ways of listening and speaking with religious others.

I know that Merton spoke of "communion," and that the title of this book suggests "we are already one." That sounds beautiful—but that is not my experience. Communion can mean unity or oneness—or it can mean intimacy that honors difference. I do not want to be one with everyone, I am not one with everyone, and neither are you. I do not want difference to be annihilated, and it seems forced to ask that it be. The pressing issue of our time is the challenge of living beautifully in a world of difference. Raimundo Panikkar wrote "What to do with the barbarian" is the central question in the age of pluralism. We all have some notion of barbarian in our minds or lives. Our life is learning to befriend or connect with the other, whoever that person may be.

It seems to me that for Merton "communion" could be understood as "dialogue." Dialogue is the art of thinking together, or of "talking through—dia-logue." When we encounter each other this way, we can respect the other and ourselves, and do not pressure the other person to be like us, nor pressure ourselves to conform with the other. We can develop harmony, a kind of dance with someone who is not us. This is the skill we need individually and communally for peace work in our time.

When Merton spoke of communion, he manifested dialogue. He respected difference and was stimulated by it. He was nurtured spiritually by difference. He learned depth from Asian religious traditions without trying to make them just like his own. In one of his last talks, Merton affirmed:

> I think that we have now reached a stage of religious maturity at which it may be possible for someone to remain perfectly faithful to a Christian and Western monastic commitment and yet learn, in depth, from a Hindu or Buddhist discipline or experience. Some of us need to do this in order to improve the quality of our own monastic life (*The Asian Journal of Thomas Merton*, 313).

This is a life of dialogue, not communion.

Thomas Merton and the Dalai Lama, fabric quilt by Penny Sisto, 2013. To commemorate the auspicious meeting of these two authentic spiritual leaders in Dharmsala, India in 1968. The quilt is inspired by a famous photograph taken by Harold Talbott. The two young men stand squinting into the sun, close as brothers. The quilt shows their bodies almost splintering into the surrounding trees and sky. There is a golden light around their heads, perhaps divine inspiration.

Confluence Of Merton And The Sixties Counter Culture Movement

Richard Sisto

I was fortunate in this life to be part of a counter culture movement that embraced the spiritual path as the primary motivation for living. We came to this realization as a result of peak experiences, which were both aesthetic and supernatural and which changed our lives forever in the most significant way. This happened in the 1960s and flourished in the 1970s and included mostly younger people as well all ages and social and economic profiles. We were lumped together in a group known by various names such as hippies, freaks, flower children, counter culture revolutionaries, and back to the land dropouts.

In reality the movement included all of these categories, but there were serious differences between them. For my part, as I have already stated, the prime directive was the spiritual search and the location where this quest took place was the college and university campus. In my junior year at Northwestern University I took a philosophy course which whetted my appetite for reading mystical spirituality both east and west. The course included works by Merton. I was in search of a transcendent experience rather than merely the intellectual knowledge. The reading included many of the classics of the time, with a special interest in Zen Buddhism. I had begun meditation practice with a Japanese Roshi in a very small house, which he called The Zen Temple of Chicago located near Lincoln Park Zoo. Learning to sit in the strict *zazen* meditation posture was a discipline that produced mostly pain and the exaggeration of time moving very slowly.

Around this same period many of us in schools around the country had begun experimenting with a new hallucinogenic drug called LSD or Lysergic Acid Diethylamide. A graduate friend and I were able to buy LSD, which at that time was legal, directly from the Sandoz Pharmaceutical Company, the sole manufacturer of the drug. We were following the guidelines of three Harvard professors, Leary, Alpert and Metzner who had begun their extensive research a few years earlier. Our manual for the LSD sessions was *The Psychedelic Experience* by Timothy Leary. Each session, in which we consumed varying amounts of LSD, was preceded by two or three days of preparation which included fasting, meditation, reading, and arranging for a proper environment and guide to help us reach a profound ego loss state of awareness. We were also receiving college credit, for an independent study in the psychology department, of the results of our psychedelic "trips." The approach we took and the serious nature of our LSD experiments was a far cry from the thrill seeking, hedonistic orgies of "hippies" of the Haight Ashbury Era. One of the defining events of that time was to "drop" a large dose of street LSD and experience the effects while listening and dancing to the music of The Grateful Dead in a large auditorium with a huge crowd. For me this approach was absolute madness and very dangerous for many reasons. My hippie friends were never able to convince me to attend one of these "concerts."

My introduction to the writings of Thomas Merton was a result of my Catholic upbringing and my experience in a preparatory seminary in Chicago. I spent the first two years of high school at Quigley Preparatory Seminary on Rush Street, which was also, strangely, a popular night life center of that time. I remember walking past various nightclubs on the way to school where jazz was played and where there were many establishments of a more dubious nature. Although I was able, with downcast eyes, to avoid the lure of the strip joints, jazz had already gotten into my blood. I began to learn to play jazz vibraphone in the 8th grade and was continuing that process along with my seminary study. By the time I reached my junior year my jazz interest won the battle and I transferred to a Catholic high school that had a prominent jazz program run by a swinging Holy Cross priest.

All of this was a great preparation for my time at Northwestern. I was engrossed in reading a wide range of spiritual writings, including the later works of Merton that were beginning to be published, especially those dealing with Zen. Ingesting LSD as a sacrament, sitting *zazen* with Sensei, practicing and listening to the "contemplative" music of Bill Evans and Miles Davis, both of whom I was fortunate to hear live at the numerous jazz clubs, took up the rest of my time.

I remember that, even before I met Merton at Gethsemani, his wisdom had helped me through the "problem" of my Catholic orientation. Although during this period I was not a "practicing" Catholic I still felt a great attachment to my roots and to the teachings of Jesus Christ. Merton, perhaps in part because he was a convert but more as a result of the deep awareness he had of the connection of everything, helped me realize I could retain my identity as a disciple of Christ and a student of Catholic mystics and at the same time practice Zen Buddhism and the shamanistic use of sacramental hallucinogens.

I moved from Chicago to Louisville, Kentucky and was playing jazz in the clubs, including a place called 118 Washington St. One night after the gig was over the club owner informed me that the monk was in again listening to the music. I knew who he meant. Shortly after that a good friend by the name of Fr. Vernon Robertson, who was in close communication with Merton, took me to the Abbey to meet him. The first meeting was simply in a room in the guest house and, like so many others, I felt a great warmth and presence from Merton. He seemed very interested in what I had to say, which was mostly about Zen meditation and the weekly practice evening I was hosting in my apartment on St. James Court in Louisville. I invited him to join us if possible which he didn't dismiss, although it never happened. We exchanged a few letters during that time in which we remained focused on the inner dimension of meditation and some discussion of LSD and of course jazz.

The most significant meeting was a picnic on a Gethsemani lake with a small group of folks, including Merton's close friend from the "old days," the poet and hermit Bob Lax. It was Lax who took a photo of myself and Merton drinking Schlitz beer and engrossed in conversation. Lax appeared more than a decade later at the first "Merton convocation" at Bellarmine College and unceremoniously and silently walked up to me and handed me the photo. I have always been grateful for that generous gift from Bob

Lax. He was living at the time in Greece. The photo has a prominent place inside the cover of my CD and in the Merton Documentary, both entitled *Soul Searching,* and was the only photo of any kind I had saved from that era. I remember that our picnic occurred on the

day of Brother Paul Quenon's Solemn Vows. In fact, Paul and his family passed our party on their way and we were introduced. We have been spiritual friends ever since that day. It was soon after this that Fr. Louis (Merton) was scheduled to leave for his Asian journey.

The untimely death of Thomas Merton in Bangkok, Thailand was a shock to all who knew him or had been influenced by his writings. For me, it became a time to

Richard Sisto and Thomas Merton, photograph by Bob Lax.

move on, having realized how much the relationship and proximity to him meant. I had friends in northern California who were joining various communes in the Sierra Nevada Mountains and the spirit of change and new beginnings was infectious. I packed the old VW Bus with a few things including a healthy collection of Merton's books which inspired and filled me with a sense of spiritual anticipation for my new life in the mountains. Before I left Louisville, I was asked to play a jazz dedication piece at the public funeral. It took place in the cathedral to a packed audience and the celebrant was the Gethsemani Abbot, Dom Flavian Burns. I performed a solo vibe rendition of "Nardis" by Miles Davis and Bill Evans. Tom would have liked it.

My first year in California I lived at Ananda Meditation Retreat on a vegetarian diet, practicing hatha yoga, spiritual scripture study and meditation. My reading companions were Merton's early journals on life in the monastery. What he spoke about had great relevance for the path of communal sharing and spiritual discipline. Like the monks, we were required to give up all intoxicants, shed our city clothes for simple yoga garb and work together to grow our food, build our shelters and practice our spirituality. Our goal was inner peace and illumination. The writings of Merton that spoke to me on the deepest level were the same ones that he pointed to as the essence of his search. The experience and knowledge beyond concept and idea had become his obsession, especially after he began living in the hermitage. The life he was leading there was the same model that we had embraced. The prayer and meditation he practiced was our practice. In his last writings on Monastic Experience and East-West Dialogue he ended with a beautiful description of the kind of person who is called to a spiritual destiny. He was that kind of person and so were we. His words ring true into eternity:

And so I stand among you as one who offers a small measure of hope, that first, there are always people who dare to seek on the margin of society, who are not dependent on social acceptance, not dependent on social routine, and prefer a kind of free-floating existence under a state of risk. And among these people if they are faithful to their own calling, to their own vocation, and to their own message from God, communication on the deepest level is possible.

And the deepest level of communication is not communication, but communion. It is wordless. It is beyond words, and it is beyond speech, and it is beyond concept. Not that we discover a new unity. We discover an older unity. My dear, brothers and sisters, we are already one. But we imagine that we are not. And what we have to recover is our original unity. What we have to be is what we are" (*The Asian Journal of Thomas Merton*).

Thomas Merton in a Lush Field, fabric quilt by Penny Sisto, 2000. Thomas Merton stands in a lush field. A line of hooded Trappist monks march pass a pond. The Cross and Wagon Wheel is a landmark that they are approaching Merton's hermitage which is seen through the trees. Merton looks out of the quilt, staring past the viewer into his own distance.

The Writer

Ross Labrie

In the 1950s, having been relatively secluded in a Jesuit high school and then a Jesuit college for a number of years, I found myself in 1957 in a graduate school at a secular university, where religion was something that serious academics didn't discuss. While browsing through one of the many bookstores near the university, I was drawn to the paperback cover of Merton's *Seven Storey Mountain*. Since the book was essentially about a man who had turned away from a university career, I wasn't sure where my interest lay, but I recall that Merton caused me to think about academia in relation to religion in a way that I was to find helpful. This was in part because of Merton's gratitude for the wisdom of some of his professors at Columbia, particularly Mark Van Doren and Dan Walsh. Furthermore, in spite of his decision not to become an academic or a writer, Merton's sacrifice was more complex than it initially appeared, a truth that was later verified by his return to writing, and especially to poetry, in the late 1950s. In addition, what struck me about *The Seven Storey Mountain* was its ambivalence about art, especially literary art, and religion. Art and religion, for example, seemed reconciled, Merton observed, in William Blake, whose integrity in this respect Merton praised. The same could be said of his view of Gerard Manley Hopkins.

The other thing about Merton that would register with me during the 1950s, both in *The Seven Storey Mountain* and in *The Sign of Jonas*, was that both were exceptionally fresh and convincing. Indeed, he managed to make his life at his monastery in Kentucky seem so different from the culture around him that it seemed to me almost exotic. In spite of the apparent narrowness of Merton's circumstances in his Kentucky monastery he enabled readers to somehow see the relevance of his monastic setting to their own inner journey. He did this by writing not about the tenets of his religion but rather by dramatizing the experience of the soul in its search for direction. The inclusivity of Merton's vision would develop throughout the 1950s and 1960s so that even the atheism of someone like Albert Camus came to be part of a spiritual journey that he saw as beckoning within the human soul. It was this paradoxical universality arising from the ostensibly narrow vantage point of a Trappist monastery that caught my attention. Moreover, to someone like myself who had been schooled in the dogmatic strictures of the Council of Trent, Merton threw open a window through which I could begin to relate my sheltered, religious upbringing to the secular culture in which I found myself in graduate school.

In this connection somehow, in spite of Merton's monastic isolation, he conveyed an underlying freedom that I found attractive. An example was his reaction to James Joyce's *Portrait of the Artist As a Young Man*, a book that, for much of the twentieth century, was on the Catholic church's list of prohibited books. I became interested in Merton's reaction to the "Mission" sermon on hell in Joyce's novel at a time, when while living in New York, he was drawn towards Catholicism. Instead of being repelled by the sermon, which Joyce had clearly meant to satirize Catholicism, Merton was impressed by its clarity and substance. These Catholics, he confided, at least knew what they believed.

Merton's valuing of a text that Catholics were told to avoid suggested an openness to the contraries of experience that attracted many like myself. I was reminded of this later on, when in his journal in June of 1959 he declared that he had to "live in the fresh air." Paradoxically perhaps, in the passage in which he says that he needed to live in the fresh air, he qualified this by saying that, with regard to his recurring, restless desire to move to where he would be able to live a hermitage life, he would try to discern what God appeared to want of him. Nevertheless, his freedom expressed itself eloquently in the 1960s when he challenged the viewpoints of many Catholics, including some in his own Order, with taking an un-Christian attitude in acquiescing not only to the Vietnam War but to the acceptance of the inevitability of war in an age dominated by weapons of mass destruction. In spite of Merton's dark consciousness during the Cold War of the world being on the edge of disaster, his writings were essentially hopeful. This stemmed from the fact that he was a humanist, a Christian humanist as he thought of himself.

If *The Seven Storey Mountain* had contained strong elements of Augustinian guilt in a world tainted by evil, the later writings affirmed the inextinguishable presence of human goodness in both individuals and in the variegated cultures that spanned and enriched the planet. For those of us reading Merton in the 1950s this represented a sea change in the atmosphere surrounding religion, and Roman Catholicism in particular. Shortly before his death Merton was considering writing a book in which the concepts and terminology used by contemplatives in different religious traditions would be compared, a comparison that he felt would yield fresh insights into as yet unnoticed similarities. For Merton all religions, even those generally regarded as primitive, had a significance from which all could benefit. One of the reasons why Merton was able to recognize the value of cultures that did not figure in his own background was that he had already bridged in his own life a number of antitheses, Europe and America, being an example, classicism and modernism being another. One of these sets of antitheses was that between religion and art which, as already noted, brought Merton as a writer to a pause in the late 1940s and early 1950s. Moreover, Merton's consciousness of a tension between religion and art sprang from his reading of Catholic poetry in the 1930s and 1940s. He became wary of religious, especially of Catholic, poetry that was heavily didactic and in which the religious content of the work, the beliefs upheld in the poem, were seen as a sufficient basis on which to value the work. The subordination of art to the role of embellishing doctrine annoyed Merton. One of the famous Catholic poems that raised his ire was Francis Thompson's "Hound of Heaven," a poem that I can recall having to wade through in my early schooling. What had brought this situation about was the culture of the Council of Trent, which, in reacting to the Reformation, had placed a high value on the formulation of doctrine and a relatively low value on art, which was felt to have no significant cognitive function.

Gradually, however, Merton recognized that both religion and art were united in that they are both forms of contemplative experience. Apart from anything else religious and artistic contemplation tended to heighten, Merton felt, they assisted one's grateful consciousness of being alive, of being a part of creation. The following passage, taken from his journal in December, 1950, will illustrate the point:

> Yesterday there was snow again and wind froze ribs on top of the drifts along the hillsides; sun shone through the copper grass that grew above the snow on St. Joseph's hill, and it looked as if the snow were all on fire. And there were jewels all over the junk the brothers dumped out there where the old horse barn used to be. A bunch of window screens were lying about and they shone in the sun like crystal (*Entering the Silence*, 446).

These prosaic objects, seen in the winter light as shining jewels, give one a sense of the back-lit beauty which Merton perceived as present in creation. Moreover, the resplendence of the moment, captured through the writer's analogical vision, illustrates his ontological perception that we are fellow creatures with nature, struck from the same, divine, creative source.

If the artist in being a contemplative had much in common with the religious contemplative, so too did the religious contemplative with the artist. This was the gist of Merton growing conviction in the 1960s that the artist had increasingly taken on a role that had traditionally been that of monks. That role was to illuminate the self, which for Merton was another term for the soul. He saw the self as having been hijacked by a consumerist society on the one hand and a tendency to politicize everything else on the other. Capitalism and Marxism, Merton argued, had both ignored and thereby alienated the self within, whose life had been designed by the creator to recognize its hidden orientation towards both solitude and thereby towards ultimate reality. Where Merton caught my attention was in his consciousness that Marx's view of humanity was entirely collective. Missing in such a world, Merton insisted, was a sense of the importance of the individual, whose life, Christianity had argued, was central. In the 1960s especially he focused not only on the plight of the hidden self with its imprinted orientation towards God and towards ultimate reality, but he showed how the self was made invisible by public discourse. Throughout the 1960s, in works like *Cables to the Ace*, for example, he emphasized that modern society with its blankets of advertising and its imposition of its own specious versions of the self, excluded human beings from themselves.

Increasingly in the 1960s Merton's attention shifted to literature where he recognized the prophetic and therefore the cognitive role of the writer, arguing that literature often overtook the work going on in theology. Frequently, he characterized the artist, especially the literary artist, as prophetic, by which he meant that artists were *sapiential* rather than religious in a formal sense. By *sapiential* Merton understood the deepest and ultimate truths of human experience. Indeed, in the reflections by Merton on James Joyce cited above, he made the point that, although he had been at odds with Catholicism, Joyce had successfully recreated the Catholic Dublin of his youth. In this way Joyce had held true to the primary task of the artist, separated from any extrinsic commitments which a particular artist might have to a particular set of religious beliefs. Indeed, writing in his journal in June of 1959, he echoed the observation by the Protestant theologian, Paul Tillich, that there was more ultimate reality in an apple painted by Cezanne than in a portrait of Jesus by the pious German painter, Heinrich Hofmann.

I found especially meaningful Merton's showing how modern writers like Camus and Faulkner gave rise in their works to truths of human experience that compared with the great biblical stories. In Faulkner's novel, *The Wild Palms,* and in the short story collection, *Go Down, Moses,* Merton traced a continuum between Faulkner's writings, which were ostensibly secular, and the great religious myths of the flood and of the fall. Moreover, Merton regarded the Bible as essentially in form a work of poetry, certainly in the case of the stories of the Old Testament and the Book of Revelation. Both religion and art constructed myths. As an example both characteristically drew together pieces of time that had no chronological relationship to one another into a creative vortex in which the similarities and analogies of discrete historical events suddenly became apparent and instructive. For Merton myth and symbol imaginatively imbued human experience with universal meaning that a child might understand and that an adult might later cling to.

Moreover, in the midst of a tendency in literary criticism in the 1960s to sever literature from knowledge, Merton insisted, and I greatly valued his constancy in this, on the ontological significance of symbolism in both religion and art. The recognition of meaning in symbols depended on the reader's or spectator's experience with the beings or things that were used as symbols. In this way, without the need of a mediating explanation or argument, the symbol communicated directly to the reader or spectator. Merton emphasized that symbolism, either in religion or art, reminds us of the wholeness of creatures as well as their relationship to all of being. In art we see creatures in the round as it were, often including their conflicting qualities as Merton observed in the case of Blake's famous tiger, a troubling symbol because of its pre-Darwinian shadowing for readers like myself. Creatures like Blake's tiger spoke of something in themselves but also of something in all of creation and in the mind of God, as it were, even when this pointed to something that is quite mysterious. This kind of mysteriousness with its accompanying reticence is certainly something that Merton believed was shared by art and religion.

This restraint in both the religious and artistic contemplative, Merton saw as an aspect of a vocational asceticism shared by each. Renderings of ultimate reality by both religion and art would be limited from the start and in that, Merton concluded approvingly, lay their wisdom, modesty and their enduring power. In Merton's estimation both religion and art enhance our understanding of the self and its inherent dignity in a culture that cares little for this sort of thing. The reticence of both religion and art stemmed in Merton's view from the enormity of creation and of the creator. Faced with this enormity, the true prophet either in religion or art would hold back, aware of the distances to be covered. This sort of reality-probing awareness was somewhat akin to what Merton thought of as apophatic contemplation, and appropriately he saw both the religious and artistic contemplative as committed to a vocational asceticism. For Merton myth was a suitable form, limited but suggestive, for the contemplative believer or artist who, while projecting a light into the darkness, never forgot the extent of that darkness.

As an academic I have been grateful to Merton for his affirmation of the cultural, psychological and especially spiritual values of religion and art, which he characteristically saw as intertwined. Apart from this gift to the world he wrote some very fine literary criticism as can be seen in the publication of his essays in respected journals like the *Hudson Review* and the *Sewanee Review.* He wrote in a period when the connection between art and meaning was increasingly treated as an irrelevancy, and he challenged this view of art by elucidating the spiritual significance of artists even when they had no explicit connection to religion. Flanked by a culture steeped in technology, Merton in his hilly, Kentucky retreat seems an odd fish indeed. As it turned out, his vantage point, that of someone on the outside looking in, was exactly what Western culture in the 1950s and 1960s needed if it hoped to survive. Through celebrating the dignity and richness of the self and the sacredness of what he called the ground of being, Merton breathed into his art and criticism a vitality that came from the timeless wisdom of monasticism. At the same time he showed us the contemporaneity of the ancient and the traditionalism of the modern. How wonderful to have heard from him, even within his limited lifespan, since it now seems, more than ever, that he was like no other.

Thomas Merton's Conjectures
For A Twenty-First Century English Professor

Lynn R. Szabo

> We are in search of *meaning* and the search is consistently frustrated, not
> only by the fact that traditional symbols seem to have lost their efficacy,
> but the fact that artists, poets and so on have suddenly become hostile and
> uncommunicative, frustrating the desire for meaning by declaring that there
> are no meanings left and that one has to get along without them. . . . Mean-
> while, of course, what is indecipherable by squares remains significant to the
> artist and his friends; it is either meaningful or a substitute for meaning, a
> significant enigma.
>
> *Conjectures of a Guilty Bystander*

In the postmodern contexts of the late twentieth century, a host of literary critics
came to accept, as almost *de rigeur,* hermeneutics for reading literature which are best
engaged by strategies of irony and infinite deferrals of meaning. The powerful influences of deconstructionist philosophers of language such as Derrida, Foucault and
Saussure have been embraced in English studies with an enthusiasm that has nearly
totalized the discipline and in many respects, the entire Western culture. The instabili-
ties of fragmentation and subjectivity have been seized as the conditions of language,
producing a critical discourse that has fundamentally departed from the previous priv-
ileging and authorizing of texts as autonomous literary artifacts. One of the prepon-
derant outcomes of this shift has been the replacement of literary studies with cultural
studies in university English departments; therein, literature becomes a site for social
and philosophical inquiry, often enmeshing literary scholars in the eruption of "culture wars" as they attempt to relocate their discipline amidst the clashes of competing
Marxist, feminist, post-structuralist, and psychoanalytic hegemonies.

Just as for Christian scholars in other disciplines, such tensions have been com-
pounded by the simultaneous marginalization of Christianity in the secular academy
and by cultural influences which have seemingly deposed the relevance of any form
of institutionalized religion. In such a context, Christian scholarship in literature is
intensely interrogated by deconstructionist suspicions about language and meaning,
about any willingness to assign authority to literary texts, sacred or otherwise. In this
frame of reference, the approaches of earlier criticisms are perceived as naïve, provoking amusement, if not castigation. Texts are now designated as constructs around and

through which readers are forever destined to negotiate interpretations which resist closure and cohering meanings. Surrounded by this uncertain climate, some scholars have clung to their old paradigms, hoping the storms of postmodernism would abate, leaving in their wake known and calmer seas. Others, not wanting to be left behind, have leapt aboard the ships setting sail on uncharted and sometimes futile journeys into the ingenious extremes of theories not yet ready to be tested for seaworthiness and integrity.

For my own scholarly pursuits, the writings of Thomas Merton, monk and renowned American writer, have provided a fertile category of engagement which offers ballast to both of these extremes. At its foundations is his profound and prophetic capacity to embrace and espouse the fundamental unity in all things while refusing panacean responses to the apparent dissolution of that unity. One can imagine that, were he alive today, his prophetic insights would continue to provoke conjectures which lend themselves to the rediscovery of unifying principles in the cosmos. Merton's ontology is his apprehension of the "hidden Wholeness . . . [the] mysterious Unity and Integrity . . . *Natura naturans*" of all things, embedded in the acknowledgment that it is in the identity and power of God that all things are imagined and incarnated; that it is God's desire for humanity to recover its lost and paradisial Wisdom; that language and literature, indeed *Logos*, is its Ground of Being.

Another significant and reaffirming aspect of Merton's writings for those of us who devote ourselves to the act of creating and reading literature is the centrality of literary and religious texts as influences on his conversion. Following from his studies of Étienne Gilson's *The Spirit of Medieval Philosophy*, Augustine, Thomas à Kempis, and, in particular, William Blake, and G. M. Hopkins, Merton acts with astonishing directness in pursuing his conversion to Christianity. He continuously endorses belief in the incarnational powers of language and literature and their transcendent possibilities, both in his personal experience and in his legacy of lifelong engagement with the *literati* of his times.

Merton's embrace of mystery, silence and solitude is a fecund hermeneutical space from which I have come to re-envision my own approaches to literature and spirituality. In this cosmology, language and narrative arise from silent places which hold the secrets of the *imago dei*—the indestructible presence of God in the world—and unleash His creativity and incarnational powers in all Being. This mystery arouses in me a compassion for the often-silenced beauty and brokenness of the human story and an enduring hope for reconciliation and redemption for the world it portrays; it is at the core of my scholarly pursuits.

As a Christian scholar mentored by Merton's literary writings on spirituality, in particular his poetry, I have been given opportunities to engage in meaningful and satisfying dialogue with others whose interests go far beyond the academy. I have discovered that Merton creates space for profound dialogue in a pluralized culture where authentic inquiry often intersects with literary and religious writings in prophecy and power; where Charles Taylor and Salmon Rushdie find their voices welcomed both at once, the acknowledgement of one voice permitting the recognition of another. In such moments, the honor of participating in inter-religious and interdisciplinary dialogue with respected scholars from traditions other than my own enriches and pleasures my studies immeasurably.

Promisingly for professors of literature as a whole, more recent shifts in literary criticism are turning towards an ethics of reading and scholarship that seeks to encourage alliances among critics who can find mutually fertile grounds for engagement of texts and theories, just as Merton might have hoped. Such an agenda currently seems to be spawning new collectives of scholars, programs and disciplines related to literature. It has the markings of interdisciplinarity not before seen in its crossing of boundaries—cultural, religious, spiritual, and historical. It is also giving rise to new genres of literature in which previously narrowed fields of interpretation and production are amalgamating: for example, nonfiction life writing, such as the compelling and literate journals of Merton, is now one of the most prolific and ascendant literatures, providing creative cultural and spiritual engagement for readers, writers and theorists in their attempts to re-imagine and identify authentic human experience. Into these new wineskins, I enduringly find the new wine of Merton's hopes for language and humanity ready to be poured, imbibed and savored by his readers in their thirst for meaning and wisdom.

As always, the most respected of Christian literary scholars will need to demonstrate an agility of mind and heart that allows them to acknowledge and own the failures of Christianity that are so elaborately depicted in contemporary narratives of all kinds. With humility and tenacity, such scholars will be required to address the study of new cultural theories whose agenda clearly marginalizes Christian scholarship and refuses Christianity's historical and religious value, culturally and politically. Such scholars will be neither reactionary nor revolutionary in their response, realizing that integrity in scholarship and demeanor transcends apologetics and polemics.

In sum, the Christian literary scholar today faces organic and dynamic challenges that may seem overwhelming in their complexities and influences. To serve literature and its reading, to demonstrate courage and indefatigable creativity, and to commit oneself to openness of mind and heart, calls for a life of faith and scholarship that is fed by one's embrace of and by Christ, the Incarnated God who is all and is in all. For me, it is to be grounded in the "Hidden Wholeness" who is Sophia "dancing in the waters of life," portrayed by Thomas Merton in his radiant and life-giving literary art, the heart of my scholarship as a Protestant Christian literature professor, gratefully mentored by a Catholic cloistered monk.

Beat Of The Heart:
A Personal Reflection On Thomas Merton

Angus Stuart

Back when I was about twenty or twenty-one years old my brother gave me a copy of *Contemplative Prayer* by Thomas Merton. I suspect it was an attempt to broaden my theological horizons which at that stage in my life were relatively narrow. My brother, John, who is fourteen years older than I am and had studied theology at Oxford, explained to me that Merton, who was one of his main spiritual guides and influences, was something of a paradox: a silent monk who had written dozens of books. My brother read Merton in his teenage years, but I in my early twenties was not ready for him yet. I attempted to read *Contemplative Prayer* but I found it hard-going, and it made little sense to me. I put it aside, and there it remained for the next few years with a bookmark in it, moving from house to house, awaiting the time when I would return to it. But the name "Thomas Merton" kept cropping up—in the writings of Henri Nouwen and others who were popular with post-evangelicals searching for a deeper spirituality, and I remember listening to an interview with Canadian singer-songwriter Bruce Cockburn who cited Thomas Merton as a major influence on him. All the while I was accumulating mental notes that I needed to check out Thomas Merton.

Then, in my late-twenties, I went to theological college to study theology myself and to begin training for ministry in the Anglican Church. All new ordinands were given a book voucher by S. P. C. K. (Society for the Promotion of Christian Knowledge) to be spent in one of their bookshops. So, in common with many of my fellow students, I purchased C. K. Barrett's commentary on the Greek text of John's Gospel and *A New Eusebius*, a compendium of early Christian texts. This left me with a little left over, so I thought to myself that perhaps I could find something "for my own spiritual benefit," to nurture my own soul, as it were—in contrast to these more academic tomes! There was a display in the shop of a new paperback edition of *The Seven Storey Mountain* which had just been republished by S. P. C. K., and it cost almost exactly the right amount to use up the remaining credit on my voucher. So, given my predisposition for reading biographies, and the whole stack of mental notes that I needed to get to know Thomas Merton, this seemed perfect serendipity. I bought the book.

That's where my reading of Thomas Merton began, in common with many others: *The Seven Storey Mountain.* I loved it. I loved the story, I loved the writing; I bristled a bit at some of the side-swipes at Anglicans and others, but even then I knew there was more to Thomas Merton than the character who wrote *The Seven Storey Mountain.* This was the beginning of a journey, and *The Seven Storey Mountain* was the pre-amble, setting the scene, the initial trail to the base of the mountain, if you will. I have returned to it many times since, re-reading the whole book or reading parts of it; for example, the chapters covering his years in France when I was on vacation there and visited many of the places mentioned in the book, or the New York chapters when I participated in a pilgrimage there organized by the Thomas Merton Society of Canada. As my reading continued on, *The Seven Storey Mountain* was swiftly followed by *The Sign of Jonas*, which has become one of my all time favorites—comfort reading for readers of Thomas Merton. From there I began to read everything I could lay my hands on either by or about Thomas Merton, for I was eager to understand how Merton was seen through the lenses of others.

In my final year at theological college we were all required to write a dissertation on some aspect of ministry, and I determined to use this as an opportunity to read and study as much as I could about Thomas Merton. The title of my dissertation was, "Busy Being Born: Towards a Spirituality for Ministry," and was really about developing a more contemplative outlook in the practice of parish ministry which, to my eyes, often appeared to be overly activist, with priests leaping in and out of cars, running here, there and everywhere with their daybooks at the ready. I drew on the work of existentialist writers as I also felt an affinity with their outlook, and on Henri Nouwen, whom I'd been reading for some time (*the* Catholic writer hip for post-evangelicals), and on Thomas Merton of course, the study of whom was really the ultimate purpose for which this dissertation provided the pretext. "Busy being born" is a quote from a Bob Dylan song, "It's Alright Ma, I'm Only Bleeding," where he sings, "he not busy being born is busy dying." I discerned in these words the irony of priestly busyness leading to their own spiritual demise and the need to work consciously towards spiritual rebirth and continual renewal. It was in the course of working on this dissertation that I came at last to engage with Merton's *Contemplative Prayer* and begin to appreciate its call to "*metanoia*, that deep change of heart in which we die on a certain level of our being in order to find ourselves alive and free on another, more spiritual level" (*Contemplative Prayer*, London, 1973, 89).

I was struck how many echoes (and indeed direct quotes) there were in this book of the writings of the so-called "existentialist" writers that I had also been reading in connection with that dissertation, especially Heidegger, Buber, Marcel, and Jaspers. Merton seemed to me to be "an existentialist monk" concerned very much with the authenticity of spirituality, and with identifying what is false in the "false self" and cultivating the truth and reality of the "true self." It is probably for this reason that I have always found his more autobiographical writings to be particularly accessible, his letters and his journals. That is not to say I have not appreciated the treasures contained in *New Seeds of Contemplation* or *Raids on the Unspeakable*, for example, but in his journals and letters I appreciate how much of what he is saying comes out of his own lived experience. His words and his conversations were rooted in the world as he was living it, and for this reason found connection with me as I consciously or unconsciously compared and related it to my own experience of life.

That same year I first read *The Seven Storey Mountain* I also read Jack Kerouac's *On the Road* for the first time. Here I found another author to whom I was immediately drawn and who wrote primarily out of his own experience of life, though apparently a very different experience from Merton's. I found myself reading both Merton and Kerouac at about the same time, exploring the writings of each of them, and finding in both that something was being ignited by them in my own soul. So it was, as if he was expressing my own thoughts when Robert Inchausti described Merton as "Jack Kerouac's monastic elder brother" in his *Thomas Merton's American Prophecy*. This began my ongoing exploration of Thomas Merton and the Beats (the writers of the so-called Beat Generation), primary among them Jack Kerouac. The parallels and links between the two seemed to multiply the more I looked into them: their near contemporaneous experience of Columbia University in New York, including Mark Van Doran's course on Shakespeare; their mutual friendship with Robert Lax; the involvement of Robert Giroux in their early publications; their experience of the Catholic Church; their interest in Buddhism and the traditions of the East; the francophone influence on each; their early experiences of death and bereavement, and so on. But more than this, they provide two different but complementary views into the world, and especially America, at that turbulent time of change in the years following World War II. In many ways this was a time of questioning and challenge to American society as it was emerging by mid-twentieth century, and both Merton and Kerouac (and the other Beat writers), in their different ways, turned away from the stultifying conventionality of that society in pursuit of a more radical authenticity. In a sense, Merton was something of a "Beat monk" who like Kerouac and other Beats was one of those "who dare seek on the margins of society, who are not dependent on social acceptance, nor dependent on social routine, and prefer a kind of free-floating existence under a state of risk" (*The Asian Journal*). Reading these informal remarks Merton made at the Temple of Understanding in Calcutta in 1968 makes me realize again just how Merton was just as much a "father" of the 1960s counterculture as Alan Watts, Ginsberg, Kerouac, and the writers of the Beat Generation.

As the years have passed, I have come to value more and more Merton's breadth of conversation with other traditions. His writings on and especially his letters with those involved in Sufism, Buddhism and Daoism, in particular, have struck chords in me that have set me off in new directions of study and exploration. Merton is not the last word when it comes to interfaith dialogue and exploring other traditions but, for me, he has often been the first word. I am struck too how all his seemingly disparate interests actually all relate together. For example, I can see how the famous "Fourth and Walnut Epiphany" in 1958 came out of his studies of Zen Buddhism and his correspondence with D. T. Suzuki in the preceding years. Yet at the heart of all this I discern a deep appreciation for the mystery of the incarnation as expressed in the Christian tradition, which brings me to what is probably my favorite quote of Thomas Merton. Of course, there are so many golden passages from which to choose: the "Fourth and Walnut Epiphany," already mentioned, is an obvious one; another might be his famous prayer from *Thoughts in Solitude* that begins "My Lord God, I have no idea where I am going" (I have actually seen the original manuscript of this at the collection in the library at Columbia University)—so many of us can identify with that; and another delicious passage for me is the last couple of pages of *New Seeds of Contemplation* where he talks about the General Dance, I love that whole piece, imbued as it is with both Sufism and Vedanta and the imagery of Japanese art. But if I had to choose just one passage, I think it would be this:

> If I allow the Holy Spirit to work in me, if I allow Christ to use my heart in order to love my brother [or sister] with it, I will soon find that Christ loving in me and through me has brought to light Christ in my brother [or sister]. And I will find that

the love of Christ in my brother [or sister], loving me in return, has drawn forth the image and the reality of Christ in my own soul. This, then, is the mystery of Christ manifesting Himself in the love which no longer regards my brother [or sister] as an object or as a thing, which no longer treats him [or her] merely as a friend or an associate, but sees in him the same Lord who is the life of my own soul (*Disputed Questions*, London, 1961, 126).

I came across these words very early on in my reading of Thomas Merton, and quoted them in that dissertation in my final year at theological college, and I have continued to return to them many times since, and have shared them with others on many occasions. For me they contain a profound truth about the mystery of our true identity, our underlying identity with Christ which I take to be a code word for the manifestation of the human face of God, who is the "hidden ground of love." These words are also a reminder to me that "God" is not a static, sterile, exterior conception, but is brought forth in the very act of love and living. Love is brought forth in loving; life is brought forth in living. In these words I hear a call, a vocation, a gracious invitation for each of us to become, like Merton, a messenger of hope.

An Ever-Widening Circle, A Not So Small Hope

Christine M. Bochen

When I try to visualize Thomas Merton's legacy, the first image that comes to mind is that of an ever-widening circle—a circle that began with the people whom Merton counted among his friends and collaborators and expands to include all who find themselves inspired and challenged by Merton's example and vision. Paradoxically, the monk who sought silence and solitude in a Trappist abbey in rural Kentucky had a penchant and, indeed, a remarkable capacity for friendship. Some years ago when William Shannon and I were teaching an Elderhostel, one of our students, who was also a student at Columbia, recalled that whenever she saw him he was always surrounded by friends. It is not surprising then that throughout Merton's monastic life, his hunger for solitude existed alongside a desire for companionship and communion. In "Day of A Stranger," Merton wrote of the "reassuring companionship" of poets and sages; hermits, mystics, and church fathers; philosophers and prophets. Merton's friends—living and dead—had come to inhabit his solitude in ways he could not have foreseen in 1958 when Merton wrote to Pope John XXIII that it seemed to him that he need not "lock" himself "into solitude and lose all contact with the rest of the world; rather this poor world has a right to a place in my solitude." Merton was intent on engaging what he termed "an apostolate of friendship" (*The Hidden Ground of Love*, 482).

In his letters, we see just how Merton was able to make room for others in his solitude. The publication of five volumes of Merton's letters under the general editorship of William Shannon, and the continuing publication of Merton's exchanges of letters with friends and publishers, enables us to see the breadth and the depth of his contacts with people all over the world. Merton's circle of friends and companions on life's journey included his Columbia University friends and his family members of course, but also so many others. There were writers and poets with whom he felt a special kinship and solidarity in the common quest for truth; activists and peacemakers with whom he shared a commitment to eradicate war, violence and injustice; and social and political leaders to whom Merton reached out to offer encouragement and from whom he sought support. There were also men and women religious with whom he shared faith and struggles, leaders and followers of the world's religious traditions, people of no religion with whom he felt a unity that transcended difference, and ordinary folks—young and old—who sought his advice and were blessed with his wisdom and often with his humor. Merton's ability to initiate and sustain friendships, largely through correspondence, is both remarkable and exemplary. He could talk people's language—entering into their lives and inviting them into his. He translated what it meant to be a monk into a new idiom; mapped the terrain of inner experience for us; and reminded us, as he did his fellow monks, that "we are living in a world that is absolutely transparent, and God is shining through it all the time" (*Thomas Merton: Essential Writings*, 70). He was able to bridge the distance that separates people whatever the causes and so offers us the hope that we can do the same. Reading Merton's letters, I can almost hear him saying: "Meet my friends, listen to our conversations and join in the work for peace and justice."

I am grateful for that challenging invitation and most especially thankful that my experience of studying and teaching Merton has drawn me into Merton's ever-growing circle. While I recognize that I belong to a worldwide community of Merton readers whom I will never come to know personally, I am especially thankful for the bonds of community and friendship that I enjoy because of Merton.

My own work on Merton began at the "invitation" of William H. Shannon who shortly before his retirement had begun offering a course on Thomas Merton and who, when he retired from Nazareth College, suggested that I start teaching the course. I did so gladly but not knowing then what I do now, that Thomas Merton would become such an important part of my professional and personal life. Nor did I foresee that the teaching would lead to collaborating with Bill in editing several books and, together with Patrick O'Connell, writing *The Thomas Merton Encyclopedia*.

Teaching a course on Merton and introducing students to him in other courses has been and continues to be a privilege. In ways that continue to astound me, he easily bridges the decades between his time and ours. My students are intrigued by Merton: the young convert of *The Seven Storey Mountain* whose spiritual journey eventually leads him to the Catholic Church and then a Trappist Abbey where he is willing to give up his calling to be a writer to become a monk (fortunately for him and for us, he would discover that he could be both monk and writer), the spiritual guide who speaks to them about their own selves and of God in ways that are eye-opening and real, a Catholic grounded in his faith in a way that opens him to the wisdom of the world's religions. Merton demystifies the language of faith, breaking open terms and concepts such as tradition, prayer, holiness, solitude, silence, grace, and church. His honesty, humility and humor touch my students deeply. Reflecting together on his work, we come to see ourselves and each other differently.

It has been my experience that Merton creates community in the classroom. Of course, this happens in the courses focused on Merton's life and work which I have taught at the graduate and undergraduate levels. But the seeds of community begin to take root whenever I present even a bit of Merton's work. Then, inspired by Merton's candidness and honesty, students begin to identify and speak about issues of spiritual and social concern. Merton has the uncanny ability to touch students living in the 21st century. "He could have written that yesterday," they insist. Some identify most easily with Merton the seeker whose spiritual journey took him by a somewhat circuitous route to find his place and purpose in life. Others resonate with his prophetic critique of violence, war and injustice. Others find themselves drawn by his invitation to silence and solitude, if only occasionally and in small doses. All of them find themselves drawn to this man of wisdom and paradox.

In 1987, Bill invited me to attend the founding meeting of the International Thomas Merton Society, the brainchild of Brother Patrick Hart; Robert Daggy, the director of the Merton Center; and Bill Shannon. By the end of the meeting, I had been elected corresponding secretary, a job that would give me first-hand knowledge of the early days of the Society. We had declared 1988 the year to "celebrate Merton" and resolved to hold the first General Meeting of the Society at Bellarmine University in 1989. In 2015, Merton's centenary year, we will return to Bellarmine for the Fourteenth General Meeting. During the intervening years, the ITMS—its chapters and its affiliates around the world—have created local communities that bring together scholars and life-long readers of Merton, along with some quite new to Merton, for lectures, discussions and retreats. And so the circle expands. Most note-worthy is the intentionality with which the ITMS reached out to young adults through the Daggy Scholarship Program which brings young people from North America and beyond to ITMS General Meetings. Some have become presenters at future programs and taken on leadership positions in the Society. How exciting it is for young people who have also read and studied Merton to meet other young people who share their interest. And how moving it is to witness and participate in inter-generational conversations of Merton scholars and readers. The International Thomas Merton Society and its chapters and affiliates are certainly about the work of expanding the ever-widening circle of Merton readers.

As I think back, I see clearly that the ever widening circle of friendships that Merton developed during his lifetime continues after his death and this ever-widening circle is an integral dimension of his legacy and, for me, a source of hope. I am grateful to have had the opportunity to meet people who knew Merton and people who are Merton readers, students and scholars. Our experience mirrors the ever-widening circle of relationships and friendships that Merton developed during his lifetime—a circle that continues to grow even as we prepare to celebrate the centenary of his birth. Just as during his lifetime Merton became part of an ever widening circle of friendship and collaboration, so too he has left us a legacy of friendship and collaboration.

In retrospect, it is apparent that Merton's message at Calcutta—in his words "a small message of hope"—were altogether too modest. Merton was and continues to be one of those people who witness to the possibility of communion among people and the reality of unity among us. His message of hope is not "small" at all and his witness has been and continues to be inspiring and life giving to generations of readers. An important aspect of Merton's message is that community and communion are possible despite our many differences. What unites us is ever stronger than what divides us. The ever-widening circle that Merton inspires is a reminder that we are called to be part of a greater circle—the human family. In Merton's words: "We are already one . . . . What we have to be is what we are."

Playing Bongos With Merton

Rob Peach

> We claim the present as the pre-sent, as the hereafter.
> We are unraveling our navels so that we may ingest the sun.
> We are not afraid of the darkness, we trust that the moon shall guide us.
> We are determining the future at this very moment.
> We now know that the heart is the philosopher's stone.
> Our music is our alchemy.
>
> Saul Williams, "Coded Language," from *Amethyst Rockstar (2001)*

Though he has remained an ever vigilant presence in my life since I was first gifted *The Seven Storey Mountain* by a close friend and mentor in the fall of 2001, my first semester of college at Philadelphia's La Salle University, it's been a long time since I've thought seriously about Merton—a man I consider, like so many other of his readers, to be a spiritual father.

This is ironic, in a way, because he led me through my undergraduate years as a student of religious studies, and continued to accompany me both personally and professionally through two masters programs—in English Literature at Arcadia University in Philadelphia and Systematic Theology at the Jesuit School of Theology at Santa Clara University (JST-SCU)—and a slew of Merton Society meetings. Indeed, I first came to Berkeley, California, my current place of residence, almost four years ago with the intent of making him the focus of a Ph.D. at the Graduate Theological Union (GTU), where I am currently engaged in doctoral work that has very little to do, at least ostensibly, with Merton.

Upon acceptance into the GTU's common M.A. program in the spring of 2010, however, Merton was front and center. Taking up work I had already started at Arcadia, I wanted to engage Merton as a mouthpiece for the politics of mysticism and its role in facilitating societal transformation. I had it in mind to further what scholars such as Lynn Szabo and Ross Labrie accomplished with their own detailed exploration of Merton's mystical poetics and to examine the ways in which Merton's poetry has implications for a shift in social consciousness necessary to creating a more just society. Undergirding this claim is the still strong belief I have in the power of literature to influence human rights discourse and, as American political philosopher Martha Nussbaum posits in *Cultivating Humanity: A Classical Defense of Reform in Liberal Education* (1997), nurture "powers of imagination that are essential to citizenship" (85).

For sure this is a tenet that Merton himself would hold true. Hence his prophetic "Message to Poets" and "Answers on Art and Freedom" that close his prose-poetic *magnum opus, Raids on the Unspeakable* (1966), which became the centerpiece of my GTU master's thesis. In it I interpret the text as a political theology using work by Christopher Pramuk and Johann Baptist Metz to sharpen my hermeneutical lens. In returning to *Raids*, I find Merton there embodying perhaps more fully than any of his previous works the *parrhesia* (Greek for "free speech") that he does so well to unpack in theoretical terms in *The New Man* (1961) and which Jonathan Montaldo treats deftly in his manuscript "To Uncage His Voice: Thomas Merton & Parrhesia [Free Speech]." Merton likens the concept—which refers traditionally to the "rights and privileges of a citizen in a Greek city state" to "speaking one's own mind fully and frankly in the civil assemblies by which the state is governed"—to human intimacy with God "in work as well as in contemplation" (*NM*, 72). Merton meanwhile culls from the writings of the church Fathers and his own allegorical reading of the Judeo-Christian creation myth to interpret *parrhesia* as the "symbolic expression" of the human person's self-actualization in love (*NM*, 74). This happens by way of laboring with "some consciousness of the value of human society" that puts us "in dialogue with reality" (*NM*, 80)—a figurative "conversation with God" which Merton understands as the "free spiritual communion of being with Being" (*NM*, 76) that duly manifests not only in the fact of being human, but in the intimacy of being-for-other (read: human relationship).

As an expression of *parrhesia, Raids* provided Merton the space to come most fully into himself as activist, artist, global citizen, monk, poet, and theologian who tears the fabric of social orthodoxies through the power of "free speech" in order to do his part, as Martin Luther King, Jr. said of his own work, in ridding the world of social evil and thereby come into deeper intimacy with God. This is no small task to say the least. And it is one that Merton challenges his readership to take up in *Raids* when he urges us to dispel the magic of political propaganda through love (*caritas*)—giving witness through his own "free speech" to an underlying eschatological faith-hope in the possibility of "the word" to usher in a new dawn of fidelity to life in "the Spirit" rather than to artificial systems; to human solidarity rather than to the mere collectivity of the herd (as illustrated by Eugene Ionesco's metaphor of "rhinoceritis" which Merton expounds in "Rain and the Rhinoceros"; see also *RU*, 156-57).

That being said, I closed *Raids* with the completion of my master's thesis and the prospects of doctoral work at the GTU looming on the horizon in the spring of 2012, wondering: *Where do I go from here? What more, if anything at all, do I want to write about Merton? What do I do with the work he has left me to take up?*

Feeling as though I had exhausted my stint with Merton, I have to admit that, by the time I submitted a second thesis on him, I was itching to explore new terrain; to bid happy farewell to the figurative parent who reared me intellectually in the mystery of *parrhesia* and find my own voice as the would-be poet to whom Merton addressed his penultimate essay of *Raids*. This led me to ask the further question about what most enlivens me, about what makes me feel most fully myself (and therefore a poet as Merton would have it), particularly in terms of continuing the academic route on which I was set.

Thomas Merton Playing Bongos,
photograph by Ralph Eugene Meatyard.

Like Fr. Louie playing bongos inside of his Gethsemani hermitage, photographed in the iconic black and white picture taken by Ralph Eugene Meatyard in 1968, I found myself drawn to the sound of the drums, specifically as elicited in the work of my favorite rap artists. Along with Merton, it was hip-hop that kept me in step to the rhythms of life through my formative years. When finally it came time for me to solidify a set of research questions that would take me through yet another degree, I turned my attention away from Merton's poetry and toward the poetics and politics of rap music.

Indeed, before Merton even entered my world, hip-hop that taught me what it means to really "dance in the water of life" as when I was nine years old and first heard the jazzy interplay of sampled vibraphones, bass and drum on A Tribe Called Quest's "Award Tour" bumping out of my stereo, tuned to the frequency of Baltimore's rap radio station 92 Q. It was then that I first learned, at least unconsciously at that point, what *parrhesia* is all about.

Yet it is with the image of Merton on the bongos in mind that I presently engage what I call, riffing on American jazz drummer Max Roach, the "politics in the drums" which lies at the heart of a now global cultural phenomenon that post-colonial theorist George Lipsitz, appropriating the terminology of humanist intellectual Antonio Gramsci, coins a counter-hegemonic "war of position" (see Lipsitz, "Diasporic Noise: History, Hip Hop, and the Post-Colonial Politics of Sound" in *Dangerous Crossroads: Popular Music, Postmodernism and the Poetics of Place*, 27, 38). Deeply informed by Merton's self-identification as poet on the margins—clapping stretched canvas in happy protest of the "hegemonies that be" or listening to jazz and blues records as they spun on the turntable situated in the cosmopolitan space of his hermitage—I have found in rap music a medium of and variation on *parrhesia* that has allowed society's most disenfranchised to take ownership over their own lives, as well as the means of production, through the power of the word—what in West African parlance is called *Nommo*.

In this, Merton has provided the inspiration, the necessary push, for me to enter the dance of *parrhesia* as it takes place in hip-hop culture as well as my work as a student of the rap academy, rife with street-level philosophers whose gift of "free speech" signifies the "combined functions of hermit, pilgrim, prophet, priest, shaman, sorcerer, soothsayer, alchemist, and bonz" (*RU*, 173). By entering into conversation with these figurative high priests of rap-inflected *parrhesia* as (ra)*parrhesia*—including the likes of Nas, Jay-Z, 2Pac, Kanye West, Kendrick Lamar, Killer Mike, Shabazz Palaces, Ab-Soul, Erykah Badu, Lauryn Hill, Talib Kweli, Mos Def, Project Blowed, among many others—I enter into deeper intimacy with God, embodying my own capacity for "free speech" in the process of interpreting for and with others the insights gleaned from what a former GTU professor of mine calls "message music." Insights that reveal a deeply invested commitment, riffing on Merton, to the pursuit of political solutions to problems "that endanger the freedom of man [sic]" (*RU*, 171)—not least of which is institutionalized racism as it operates in a global capitalist economy that, in the post-industrial predicament of American cities, has blighted once prosperous North American urbanscapes populated mostly by racial/ethnic minorities.

Inasmuch as my current academic pursuit entails an examination of the ways in which black cultural production in the form and content of rap music (read: *[ra]parrhesia*) fosters new ways of being in and for the world that are deconstructive of the white supremacist status quo, I am being challenged to keep in check the egoism of the "false self" by which I have been conditioned in a socio-economic milieu that privileges both my whiteness and my maleness. Positioned in many ways as the well-meaning "white liberal" to whom Merton addresses his searing essay on American race-relations in *Seeds of Destruction* (1964), my work implicates me in a practice of hermeneutic self-reflexivity that is an act of intersubjective *parrhesia* in its own right.

It invites me, echoing James Baldwin in *The Fire Next Time* (1963), to "fruitful communion with the depths of my own being" that serves to decenter my subjectivity (and the assumptions that inform it) in encounter with the so-called "other" (130 ff) and there root out what Merton calls in *Seeds of Destruction* the "cancer of injustice and hate which is eating white society and is only partly manifested in racial segregation with all its consequences" (*SD*, 45-46). Such an act of "free speech" is grounded in the purpose of fulfilling the democratic promise upon which the American project is founded, a mission Merton himself worked to accomplish during his own lifetime as a prophet of *parrhesia*.

Rap music, as a cultural platform for minority youth in particular and young people in general to embody the freedom of self-expression, is in its own way empowering me to answer Merton's injunction in Seeds of Destruction to "think black" (60)—to reorient my understanding of the world by adopting an epistemology informed by the plight of those who suffer the injustices of systemic racism. In this performative dialogic, this dance of "free speech," between me and the racialized other, I am called to further engage the "crisis in which we find ourselves" (*SD*, 60) as a society still deeply entrenched in what black feminist bell hooks calls the "imperialism of patriarchy" (see bell hooks, *Ain't I a Woman: Black Women and Feminism*, 1999).

Furthermore, it is cluing me into the "streets" and the "ghettoes" where, as Merton notes in *Learning to Love* (1967), "much of the real germinating action in the world, the real leavening" lies (231). In this, I am being summoned (along with rap's actual practitioners and other like-minded "hip-hop heads"—be they black, brown, white, red, or yellow) to plumb the depths of my own unique possibilities for civic engagement and thereby conduct a Mertonian "raid on the Unspeakable," implicating rap music, and my love for it, in what black cultural critic Huey Copeland calls, à la the intellectual contributions of black literary theorist Saidiya Hartman, a "rhetoric of redress" aimed at reparative justice (See Huey Copeland, "Fred Wilson and the Rhetoric of Redress" in *Bound to Appear: Art, Slavery, and the Site of Blackness in Multicultural America*, 2013).

So it is to the imagined boom-bap of Merton's playful bongo beats that I march into the matrix of cultural production that black public figures from Afrika Bambaataa, Queen Latifah, Grandmaster Flash, and the Furious Five to Tupac Shakur and his figurative protégé, Kendrick Lamar, have helped shape, remapping the global landscape into a social sphere more livable through electronically-based, rhymed storytelling that functions to develop the essential moral capacities, recalling Nussbaum's insight into narrative, necessary for a kind of *(ra)parousia* to occur—understood in the context of American race relations as the realization of the Ellisonian dream of democracy that the Harlem Renaissance-era author espouses in his seminal *The Invisible Man*.

Signifying on traditional conceptions of what constitutes literacy so as to create an entirely new lexicon that is at once textual, verbal and non-verbal, rap music acts as kind of "Talking Book," to borrow a trope from black literary theorist Henry Louis Gates, Jr. (*The Signifying Monkey: A Theory of African-American Literary Criticism*, 1988), which provides its practitioners, particularly those in ghettoized or under-represented communities where the "real leavening" takes place, a means of enunciating a specific stance, location and visibility within a broader cultural framework that has historically reduced them to the status of the invisible or, in Frantz Fanon's terms, "the wretched."

In the same way learning to read and write allowed slaves a means to contest their oppression and use the master's tools of literacy to speak themselves into subjecthood, rap music's *Nommo*, as an African-derived variation on *parrhesia*, empowers its practitioners (and its audience) to disarticulate, or dissemble, the oppressive historical circumstances in which they find themselves, and rearticulate their discursive terrain in a speech act of forthright self-assertion. As such, rap music offers the necessary resources for a subtextual analysis of history, on the part of artist and audience, which discloses unpopular political truths pertaining to systemic evils such as racism and, as black critical theorist Houston Baker Jr. argues in terms of the blues, serves to reorient historical discourse from the perspective of the oppressed (see Houston Baker, Jr., *Blues, Ideology and Afro American Literature: A Vernacular Theory*, 1984).

Rap is in this way an exercise in an expansive kind of literacy which challenges us, as did Merton's mystical poetics, to re-conceptualize language as more than the mere manipulation of words. Put another way, it pushes us to take language, and the way we use it, more seriously. As with Merton's "Message to Poets," rap's underlying ethos invites us to see language as an embodied act of self-fashioning that takes on many forms, styles and articulations, and has everything to do with keeping in step to the soul's beat—that embodied metronome of rhythm and rhyme which empowers its speakers to "claim the present as the pre-sent" and, in an eschatological turn, determine the future "at this very moment." In this same way it gestures toward the love and hope that undergirds a sturdy "politics of conversion"—what in *Race Matters* (1994) black cultural critic Cornel West deems the antidote to the problem of "spiritual impoverishment" in America.

That said, I'm grateful to Merton for awakening me to the narrative play that is inherent in the gift of "free speech," as intimate conversation with God, and the many ways it manifests through different forms of poetry—be it the anti-poetics of the Trappist monk's later prose poems that constitute *Raids;* the politically polemic poetics of such Golden Era rap classics as Public Enemy's *It Takes a Nation of Millions to Hold us Back* (1988); or, with Sophia's blessing, my own work as an aspiring hip-hop scholar. And I'm also grateful for the opportunity and space this essay has given me to enter into a figurative "cipher" with someone whom I consider a dear father, brother and friend in Sophia. [A "cipher" is a situation in which two or more rappers form a circle and play off of each other in an informal performance of freestyle, or improvisational rapping/talking.]

Hers is a wisdom that Merton would find resonant in rap's vernacular *Nommo*, resplendent with a message of hope for our time in its function as a kind of "free speech," a *(ra)parrhesia*, imbued with potential for bringing us into deeper intimacy with God, as if in cipher, through deeper intimacy with each other and ourselves. An intimacy which, thinking of Merton in (ra)parlay with Baldwin, takes us beyond words and into a kind of "wordless communion."

I have no doubt that were Merton still alive at the time of hip-hop's burgeoning, and even still today as the genre continually evolves into new forms and patterns of "free speech," he would be tuned in to the sonic frequency which is rap, "routed" in the Afrodiasporic politics of the break beat—what spoken word poet and rapper Saul Williams allegorizes in his invective, "Coded Language," quoted in the epigraph, as the "missing link connecting the diasporic community to its drum woven past." Indeed, I can hear Merton right now, in the spirit of *(ra)parrhesia*, chanting with fellow anti-poet Williams: "Motherfuckers better realize!/Now is the time to self-actualize!"

Thomas Moore On Thomas Merton

Thomas Moore

People I've met who knew Thomas Merton tell me you can't write about him if you didn't know him. All right, then I'm going to write about my "inner Merton." As with any influential, bigger than life personality, you encounter both the person and the hero. By hero I mean someone who has so fulfilled his destiny as to shine like a star and become a figure of fantasy for others. Maybe in this case it's the difference between Father Louis and Thomas Merton, the latter the hero of the imagination.

Merton was a real factor in my life when I was in my early twenties and living in the Servite Order, a small mendicant society founded in Italy in 1233. We were not at all like the strict Cistercians that Merton joined, but we lived a monastic style of life, and Merton's reflections on monks and the Church and mysticism guided me in those heady days when formal religion was widely popular.

As part of my training for the priesthood I went to Northern Ireland to study philosophy. Most of the classes used the medieval approach of Thomas Aquinas—appeal to the Bible, the early Church theologians and tradition, all taught in the relatively simple Latin of Aquinas. But one or two contemporary philosophers, trained at Louvain, found their way onto the faculty, and I began to wake up in my thinking through the influence of phenomenology and existentialism.

I was interested, then, to read of Merton's life in New York, an earnest search for an intellectual home and a sustainable path toward a meaningful life. The intensity of that search, told so feverishly in *The Seven Storey Mountain*, served as a mythic mirror for my own calmer but no less urgent quest.

I felt I could trust Merton because he straddled two sides of a road that I was walking in my own way. He was the secular intellectual flirting with radical ideas, and at the same time he knew that the meaning he longed for had to be religious in some way. His ending up with the Catholic Church and the Cistercians must be a shock to anyone who reads his early autobiography with a similar urgent draw toward a radical solution to the hunt for meaning.

He not only became a monk but used his high-flying and probing intellect to study monasticism in its many forms and to write book after book on mysticism, letters that offer biting comments on the issues of the times, and journals that show best, perhaps, the style of his thinking. In this way he continues to inspire me and others to make significant ties between history and contemporary issues, the rarified concerns of meditation and contemplation on one side and matters of daily living on the other, and a model for fusing the spiritual and the mundane. Since we as a culture are still miles away from achieving these reconciliations, we still have much to learn from Merton.

The Merton within—I use the phrase somewhat tongue in cheek—is a strong presence saying: "Be worldly and otherworldly. See the holy in improbable places. Don't succumb to secularism or religionism. Don't hesitate to travel far into the ethers of a serious and adventurous spiritual life. If I can be a Cistercian monk and write about current cultural issues, you can be in the thick of culture and go far into experiments in the mystical life." Merton had a broad, embracing mind along with a courageous heart.

I've seen criticisms of Merton for not being a model pious monk. But I join him in appreciating an alternative to the monk who is blankly obedient and silly in his piety. Merton took life seriously and refused to hide out in a saccharine approach to religion, which is only an escape from reality. He was his own person, neurotic like all of us, driven by needs and passions. He didn't let his monk's habit cover up those passions but tried to be a good monk and himself at the same time. This is my ideal, as well, and so I am inspired not by some plaster statue version of the monk Merton but by his example of being the imperfect monk. Hearing his voice within, I can more effectively be my imperfect self while also pursuing a certain kind of perfection.

He wrote about perfection with considerable depth and subtlety. He understood perfection as restoring the original beauty and nature of the person. He did not picture an ideal, flawless image of a self. He said, "A weird life it is to be living always in somebody else's imagination, as if that were the only place in which one could become real."

This point is crucial in the spiritual life. You have to live out your own imagination of who you are at the deepest level, not someone else's ideal that is either gracefully given to you or forced upon you. In his last talk in Thailand, he said now we are on our own. We can't rely on the institutions as we have in the past. This statement was one impetus among others that inspired me to write my book *A Religion of One's Own*. Merton is a good model of someone who lived his religious life in his own way, even though he was a member of a strict monastic order. He made the life his own, which I assume is what a monastic person should do, what we all should do. The time of surrendering entirely to someone else's imagination of what you should be is over. Now is the time to be faithful to the deep source of our vitality and identity, a source I call the soul, following ancient traditions and language, as Merton often did.

It's interesting for me to look at the arc of my spiritual life over years of profound changes, knowing that at each stage Merton was there as one of my chief models. Because of his loyalty to his own destiny, I was able more easily to follow mine. He was not an example of what I should become but of how I could be both traditional and radically individual at the same time. He was a person in motion, always thinking his way to the next step, re-inventing himself within the limits of his chosen monastic lifestyle, stretching the limits when he had to.

In his appreciation for all spiritual traditions he was ahead of his time, and it seems mysteriously appropriate that he should die in Asia, one of his spiritual homes that for many years he had imagined from a distance. If he could be a Christian monk not limited by the culture of his chosen religion, then I could be anything without limiting myself unnecessarily. I strongly advocate developing a religion of one's own, drawing on the world's spiritual traditions in a serious way. I understand the danger of being superficial in taking elements of this or that tradition, but I also know from my own experience that you can be affected deeply through excursions into other religions. Again, I have the model of Merton, who was in no way superficial as he drew insights from many traditions that he had studied thoroughly.

There is an important clue. Merton studied intensely. You only have to read one of his books on the spiritual life to see immediately how deeply he delved into his subject. Like every good monk, he understood that study is a spiritual practice. It's what a monk is called to do in life. I urge ordinary people today to learn from monks how to be spiritual, and one way is really to study whatever subject is relevant to your spirituality. I don't see workshops being given on study as a spiritual practice, and yet monks have always collected books and manuscripts, translated and interpreted them, and spread the ideas around. I am like Merton, and think of him as I work, forever opening a book in Latin or Greek, studying the language carefully, relying more on classical texts than modern writing.

I am also inspired by Merton's practice of photography. Notice that I connect his art with his spiritual life, as he did in his writing. It makes complete sense that he would have discovered an art that smoothly connected his contemplative life with the world around him in a form analogous to his writing. There is no doubt that he saw himself as a writer, which is different from spelling out your ideas. Obviously he wrote his books and his casual writing, if you can call it that, as an artist, careful with his style, even though he was such a master at it that it seems easy and natural. Most artists move from a primary art to a secondary or complementary one, and Merton's turn to photography was a major movement in his life.

Merton's photographs inspire me to connect the arts to the spiritual life as integrally and as tightly as possible. When I encourage people to engage an art as a spiritual practice, I often remind them how in history and around the world religion and the arts have been linked so closely that it's difficult to imagine one without the other. But Merton refines that idea. He invites us to zoom in on it and notice that our meditations are complete when we can use the lens of a camera to see the interiority or the art forms of the world around us. The camera frames our world so that we can transform it into an image that speaks to the soul and spirit and is an object of contemplation. Each of us could follow Merton's example and give new dimension to our spirituality through our own active experience of an art.

Drawing all these thoughts together, we can see that Thomas Merton sequestered himself in a strict and limited lifestyle with the result, if not the purpose, of being more engaged with all aspects of cultural life. He wrote about politics, historical events, public personalities, and the arts. In his scope he was global, cultural, spiritual, and artistic. A complete man.

I am a born and experienced introvert. I love to hide out and do my work at home. But Merton inspires me to be part of a greater world and to employ a variety of portals for my art of writing. I, too, have a complementary art—music—but for the most part I keep that work private. My wife is a serious painter, and I am engaged in visual arts largely through her expertise and connections. All my life I've had as an ideal my own kind of religious humanism, a love of arts and letters fully compatible with an active religious and spiritual life.

Spirit is unfulfilled without matter, is incomplete without a rich life of the senses, and is far too limited without full enjoyment of secular living. The sacred and the secular are two sides of a coin, inseparable and mutually enriching. I see how Merton accomplished this union, and I learn how to do it in my own life. I know that he was not a saint in the sense of being perfect, but he lived the kind of life I admire and want to emulate in my own way.

The Spirit Of Thomas Merton At Santa Sabina Center

Susannah K. Malarkey and
Harriet Hope Berman

Let there always be quiet, dark places in which people can take refuge. Places where they can kneel in silence. Houses of God, filled with God's silent presence. There, even when we do not know how to pray, at least we can be still and breathe easily . . .. Let there be a place somewhere in which you can breathe naturally, quietly . . . a place where your mind can be idle, and forget its concerns, descend into silence, and worship God in secret. There can be no contemplation where there is no secret.

New Seeds of Contemplation

It was a defining moment when we two, Susannah and Harriet, identified the spirit that had drawn us together in a rare collaboration of retreat ministry, the spirit that would define and guide the Santa Sabina Center in San Rafael, California for the next twenty five years: Contemplative Ways of Being.

Susannah had been raised Catholic in Oregon by an enlightened convert mother who, when she entered the Dominican community of San Rafael at Santa Sabina in 1949, gave her the just published *The Seven Storey Mountain* by Thomas Merton, to bring along with her. In the summer of 1982 she had come full circle, back to the contemplative place of her beginnings, the former Dominican novitiate that she had loved, returning to become the director of the Santa Sabina Retreat Center that had been established the decade before in that beautiful monastic setting. In the intervening years as a teacher and administrator she had continued to be nourished by Merton's writings, particularly *Thoughts in Solitude*, *New Seeds of Contemplation* and *Conjectures of a Guilty Bystander*.

Harriet had been raised in a Jewish family in New Jersey, and lived in Southern California while raising two boys and pursuing a Master's and Doctor's degree in Humanistic Psychology. Meditation and yoga practice had led her in 1982 to Bombay, India for the ITPS Conference, and from there to Delhi and Nepal, before returning to California. Harriet's eldest son's early interest in Christianity, along with the impact of Mother Theresa in Bombay, led her to embrace the spiritual/human depth of the Christian gospel. In the fall of 1983 Harriet was staying at a retreat center in the Napa Valley, where she found Jim Finley's book, *Merton's Palace of Nowhere*. With Finley's book in hand, Harriet arrived at Santa Sabina in October of 1983, to pursue the notice of a weekend on Thomas Merton to be given at Santa Sabina Center presented by, in a remarkable coincidence, James Finley!

The rest, as one might say, is history. Harriet never left Santa Sabina for long; she was soon baptized into the Catholic faith by Fr. Joe Watt, Santa Sabina's good friend and a former novice of Thomas Merton. She became the Program Director of Santa Sabina, traveled to Louisville for Merton Conferences, was elected as International Secretary of the Thomas Merton Society, and became good friends with many Friends of Merton who eventually found their way to Santa Sabina to give a series of profoundly affecting retreats that spoke directly to Santa Sabina's identity and vision as a Center for *Contemplative Ways of Being*: Flavian Burns, William Shannon, Robert Daggy, Jim Forest, Mary Luke Tobin and Jane Marie Richardson, Jim Conner, Michael Higgins, Basil Pennington, Bonnie Thurston, Larry Cunningham, Jim Finley, Daniel Berrigan, Myriam Dardenne, John Eudes Bamberger, Denise Levertov, and Jonathan Montaldo.

All of these Santa Sabina retreats were silent, of a deeply contemplative nature, with a morning and evening prayer in the quiet, steepled, monastic chapel, a simple Eucharist in the candle-lit circle of the warmly oak-paneled Prayer Room, morning and late afternoon talks by the presenter with long stretches of silent time in between (including meal times) for rest, for quiet walks in the gardens and surrounding hills, for sitting in the peace of the cloistered garden, or in the straw-bale Hermitage on the hillside, for silent exploration of the resources of Harriet's basement Art/Meditation space, for just being. And then in the quiet, dim light of the evening chapel, the Night Prayer of Compline: the "completion," or "folding together" of the day. We were, and remain, deeply nourished by the wisdom of Thomas Merton unfolding within us during these retreats.

Some time in our 4th or 5th year together at Santa Sabina, we began what became the core of our own deepening encounter and sharing of Merton's richly human/spiritual/contemplative way of being. In a twenty year series of monthly "Thomas Merton Reflection Evenings," we read, first separately on our own, and then together in the evenings with a group of 12 to 15, all of Merton's essential works, beginning with *The Seven Storey Mountain*, his Letters, two Biographies: (Jim Forest's *Living with Wisdom* and Lawrence Cunningham's *Thomas Merton: Spiritual Master*), and then concluding with the books of Merton's personal Journals, ending with *The Asian Journal* and finally the beautifully edited work by Patrick Hart and Jonathan Montaldo, *The Intimate Merton*.

The format of these Merton Reflection Evenings was exceptional in itself: the Gathering in silence in the Pillow/Fireplace Room in a candle lit circle; 20 minutes of Listening to selected excerpts from the month's Merton readings (chosen and read aloud by both of us, alternating); Silent Sitting meditation; Personal Time for continued meditation/reading/chapel time; finally Gathering back in our circle for shared Reflection through the ritual of passing the "speaking stone": one chance to silently pass the stone, or to speak to what "echoed in your soul." Through these evenings, the spirit of Thomas Merton seeped deeply into our souls, and echoed there: his wisdom, his humanity, his humor, his searching soul, his contemplative depth, his marvelous observations of the natural world in all its times and seasons.

During the course of our twenty years of deepening our connection with Thomas Merton through readings and retreats, we were also able to give Presentations on Merton's Life, Thought and Prayer at various conferences, both at meetings of the International Thomas Merton Society in its various bi-annual locations: Louisville, Kansas,

North Carolina, Alabama, Vancouver, San Diego, Ontario/Canada; and also at several places locally, here in Northern California, at different retreat centers, churches, or other places where we were invited. We used slides, without commentary, accompanied by Gregorian chant music and readings from Merton's own works to address such integral Merton topics as Merton's Way of Prayer (which we presented several times), Springs of Compassion, Merton's Transforming Vision, The Monastic Tradition, and Thomas Merton's Prophetic Challenge. Each half hour presentation would begin and end with Silence, the sound of the singing bowl, and again, Silence. The sound of the singing bowl, from the Zen Buddhist tradition, had become our way of introducing and closing all of our Merton retreats, evenings of reflections and presentations. It had a powerful effect of suspending talk and drawing us inward to a place of attention and deep listening.

We, Harriet and Susannah, no longer live at Santa Sabina; after twenty five years we have moved on, but not without Thomas Merton, whose spirit lives in us. And his library and all those Merton readings live on, as well, in Harriet's basement office and Reading Room at Santa Sabina, where she comes and goes weekly, preserving the blessing of our twenty five years together of contemplative being. Each week those who find their way down the basement stairs, beyond the cloister garden, into this quiet space are blessed to reach up and bring down from the shelves all the riches of Merton's living thought that dwell there.

We remain deeply grateful for our several times spent in personal retreat at Gethsemani, most recently in the spring of 2010, in the lovely Hermitage by the lake arranged for us by Jonathan Montaldo at Bethany Spring, in the warm welcome received at the Monastery by Jim Conner, in the visit to Merton's own Hermitage on the high hill behind the monastery, accompanied by Patrick Hart in his trusty truck. Merton's spirit breathes there most specially; the white dogwood blooming there beside the hermitage forms a curve of grace that draws us in and back to the places where we, and so many others over these years of Merton's life, have been so deeply nourished.

The Long Look From Grace's House—
Cuttings From A Weekend Journal

Rusty C. Moe

FRIDAY

Sixty-five years, eight months, and ten days of being born have brought me to the skin of this moment: up early, I'm sitting alone on the porch of a house called "Grace's House," looking out onto gentle Kentucky landforms settled in 1848 by a band of French Trappists from a monastery in Brittany, that had been established in the twelfth century by rebel monks from a monastery in Citeaux, which itself had been formed during the previous century to live more devotedly to the *Rule* written by Saint Benedict for the monks at Monte Cassino, the Italian monastery he established in the early part of the sixth century—a *Rule* that was infused by the lives and insights of the desert mothers and fathers, but most especially by Anthony of Egypt, who, in the last decades of the third century, took two of Jesus' first-century ideas (*Go, sell what you have and give to the poor, and do not be anxious about tomorrow . . ..*) to the desert alone and was there for twenty years, seeking after what is unknowable but still worth seeking.

Thomas Merton prayed me here (my surrendered reading of his journals and poems—or the collective spirit and effect of them over almost half-a-century—move in me as ceaseless prayer)—

> No blade of grass is not blessed
> On this archetypal, cosmic hill,
> This womb of mysteries.
>
> I must not omit to mention a rabbit
> And two birds, bathing in the stream
> Which is no road, because
> Alas, there is no road to Grace's house!

"Grace's House" in The Collected Poems of Thomas Merton, 331

Tim can't be here for these few days, and already I'm realizing that he is more present to me than when we're sitting in the same room, talking together. Absence has distilled his essence; he is more discernible. Perhaps that's one of the reasons people become more *entire* to us after they have died: their utter absence compresses and clarifies them in ways their personalities defined and eclipsed them.

SATURDAY

Brother Conrad Fleishman, who handed over the key to Grace's House to me, told me it was designed as a solar house by Jasper Ward, a Louisville architect, and built on these out-lying acres in 1975, by monks and locals. Twenty-some years later, it was remodeled for a Canadian hermitess, who lived here until 2006, "or thereabouts," and Father Damien Thompson spent most of a year in solitude here after retiring from his term as the ninth abbot of Gethsemani. Fences of woven and barbed wire keep horseback riders out and the monks in, "and vice versa," Brother Conrad said.

The furnishings here are either hand-me-downs or have been bought for cheap, though the pillow-top mattresses are firm, and the bedclothes are of an impressive thread count. Tables wobble, upholstery is stained by God-knows-what or rubbed thin where elbows rest, the window blinds in the kitchen are on the garish edge of teal while the ones in the other rooms are dust-coated and bone-white. Walls, ceilings, ceiling beams, stair rails, doors, are white, too. Glassware, cookware, tableware—most are delightfully dented or chipped, or in the case of the silverware (with not much pressure), bendable. I know Grace's House like I know any place I happen at any moment to be, even my own home—as a guest.

Here at Grace's House, there are no rules or bounden duties; there isn't the embarrassment of having a face, or a need to operate within the narrowness of a name. There's no need to listen *to* anyone *for* anything. Reality can be anything I want it to be—or not to be. Here, the clutch of history dissolves, and the future (an irrelevant fantasy) never arrives. Life proceeds out of my own innocence and my body's natural desires and their satisfactions. May the premium the civilized world places on sanity be gradually dismantled by the shadows of cloud drifts and the creekwater giggling between its banks outside the bedroom windows.

A forenoon of great fluidity. Shadows jivver and plummet, the angle of the sun mutes certain surfaces to a silvery green. I wonder: is heaven (or awakening or *satori* or simple maturity) the realization that everything depends on everything else around it for its own definition but doesn't surrender its essence? The fact of my own impermanence presses itself upon me. Information, perceptions, conclusions shift in their own time, their roars diminish to murmurs; nomad-mind rambles, rests, is spurred on once again by the promise of yet another championship notion. No wonder I feel tossed about most of the time: as long as awareness is spiraling and consciousness is evolving, nothing I experience is durable. Is there an anchorhold in this everlasting revelation? Perhaps. Perhaps it is in learning to be a witness to, a watcher of, my cerebral somersaults. If I relate *to* my mind's perpetual risings and fallings, rather than *from within* them, I'm steadier, more fit to live with; my breath doesn't stick to my lungs.

I walked the path that sides the barn where Brother Paul Quenon has slept for decades, down beyond a small pond where a tractor and several monks were at some work I didn't care to make sense of, past an abstract heap of stone chunks, rusted fencing, and plastic and metal pipes, and bore left onto another path that led me a quarter-mile deeper into the woods to a garden shed that had been dragged there in the 1950s for Thomas Merton to use as his first hermitage. He named it St. Anne's, which was the name of the church in Soho, London, where his parents, Owen and Ruth, were married in 1914. I wonder: was that church in his mind when he named the shed?

It's a raunchy, windowless wreck nowadays. Inside, on either side of the doorframe, are lopsided bookshelves littered with rat droppings and yards of spider silk, and the gritty, sand-strewn floor is springy with rot and criss-crossed with snail trails. Within these walls, Father Merton wrote—

> It seems to me that St. Anne's is what I have been waiting for and looking for all my life, and now I have stumbled into it quite by accident. Now, for the first time, I am aware of what happens to a man who has really found his place in the scheme of things . . .. Everything that was ever real in me has come back to life in this doorway wide open to the sky! I no longer have to trample myself down, cut myself in half, throw part of me out the window, and keep pushing the rest of myself away. In the silence of St. Anne's, everything has come together in unity, and the unity is not my unity but yours, O Father of Peace (*A Search for Solitude*, 182).

And on a day in March of 1958, from the doorway, while a red-shouldered hawk swam tender circles in its airy ocean, Father Merton made an entry in his journal that would, in time, blossom into his most beloved piece of prose:

> Yesterday, in Louisville, at the corner of 4th and Walnut, I suddenly realized that I loved all the people and that none of them were, or could be, totally alien to me. As if waking from a dream—the dream of separateness, of the "special" vocation to be different. My vocation does not really make me different from the rest of men or put me is a special category except artificially, juridically. I am still a member of the human race—and what more glorious destiny is there for man, since the Word was made flesh and became, too, a member of the Human Race!
>
> Thank God! Thank God! I am only another member of the human race, like all the rest of them. I have the immense joy of being a man! As if the sorrows of our condition could really matter, once we begin to realize who and what we are—as if we could ever begin to realize it on earth.
>
> It is not a question of proving to myself that I either dislike or like the women one sees on the street. The fact of having a vow of chastity does not oblige one to argument on this point—no special question arises. I am keenly conscious, not of their beauty (I hardly think I saw anyone really beautiful by special standards) but of their humanity, their woman-ness. But what incomprehensible beauty is there, what secret beauty that would perhaps be inaccessible to me if I were not dedicated to a different way of life. It [is] as though by chastity I had come to be married to what is most pure in all the women of the world and to taste and sense the secret beauty of their girls' hearts as they walked in the sunlight—each one secret and good and lovely in the sight of God—never touched by anyone, nor by me, nor by anyone, as good as and even more beautiful than the light itself. For the woman-ness that is in each of them is a once original and inexhaustibly fruitful bringing the image of God into the world. In this, each one is Wisdom and Sophia and Our Lady—(my delights are to be with the children of men!) (*The Intimate Merton*, 124).

I returned by the same way, past the barn, past the monastery, but cut across the secular cemetery. Such a lively sleeping-place: whenever I'm there, someone, two others, or small groups are meandering among the headstones and markers. I looked over toward the Trappist cemetery. What a fine thing that men who give themselves to the Abbey of Gethsemani and try to live, in their unique ways, *into* the ideas and spirit that inspired it, are folded back into its soil when they die.

As common an event as death is, the reality of it can still bare-knuckle me. How is it that someone who moves and speaks and sees (someone who is an active verb) is, after a final breath, instantly and forevermore not? Is un-sensed, ex-souled? Father Merton is now a noun not far beneath my feet, an emptied body as silent as the tattered sod over his grave. Where beings go when they die, I have no earthly idea nor am I much concerned, but *that* they—we—die, are de-verbed—how is that? The punctuation—the period—of the grave: the dead are complete sentences. "In my ending is my meaning," Father Merton wrote.

Back at Grace's House, while a TV dinner (Salisbury steak) cooked, I pulled out my wrangled-up copy of Lynn Szabo's exquisite selection of Father Merton's poetry, *In The Dark Before The Dawn*. I read "The Trappist Cemetery—Gethsemani" (pp. 32-34) out loud, the poem that begins—

> Brothers, the curving grasses and their daughters
> Will never print your praises:
> The trees our sisters, in their summer dresses,
> Guard your fame in these green cradles:
> The simple crosses are content to hide your characters.

and ends—

> Then will creation rise again like gold
> Clean, from the furnace of your litanies:
> The beasts and trees shall share your resurrection,
> And a new world be born from these green tombs.

How good it was to read this poem into the air (that has no ears), at the trees (whose only language is silence, rot and rebirth), to other creatures (for whom my creaturehood is worthless), a poem that signals my irrelevance while reminding me that I am here, in this random and particular form, in this random and particular time, because Creation knows more than I and has called me forth!

I blow the candle out on this day. Tree crickets have begun. Layers of cloud-bellies drag across the duskening sky like lowered peacocks' trains. A catbird quits its long song, mid-melody. That moist smell coming in from the window behind me—is it mint or pine? (It's both.) Thoughts married to the urgency of sunlight begin to gutter. My part in this Mystery Play has something to do with being grateful for the cunning, common senses I have that allow me to receive it.

SUNDAY

The world is an overwhelming extravagance to anyone with senses and common sense: why, then, does my species, this creature that declares its dominion over everything not itself, insist on scarring it, shaping current events into forms of fear, basking in the security that having an enemy provides? There are times when I'm exhausted from hoping that my hope is relevant, and I toil to remember that creation never perishes—out of extinctions, she re-fertilizes herself; out of catastrophes, she grows new forms of herself; out of ignorances, she re-seeds herself.

There is no path—and we are always on it. Thomas Merton, pray for me.

Thomas Merton Found Me By Chance, Six Years After His Death

Robert Grip

It happened as I was taking the first elective of my double major at Boston College. One of the required textbooks in my Zen Buddhism class was *Zen and the Birds of Appetite* by two authors previously unknown to me, D. T. Suzuki and Thomas Merton. Merton's ability to connect with me touched me in a way that J. D. Salinger did with *The Catcher in the Rye*. Unlike the other prominent Catholics about whom I had read to that point, Merton's life had not been sanitized by hagiographers. He was not perfect. As we later learned in his letters and private journals, he did not intend to hide his faults. He had been determined to live authentically and not "as a role model for children in Catholic schools."

Unlike other textbooks that I either sold or gave away, *Zen* was a paperback that remained on my bookshelf unopened for years until I spotted a copy of Monica Furlong's biography of Merton. It was for sale amid hundreds of other books in a traveling Catholic book show set up in the lobby of the public school where our parish in Virginia Beach, Virginia, was meeting. Reading Furlong's book prompted me to read *Zen* again. With the patience of a good friend, Merton was waiting to renew our acquaintance, albeit this time at a deeper level.

In case I needed another tap on the shoulder, Paul Wilkes' documentary on Merton aired on the local PBS television station (*Merton: A Film Biography*, 1984). I finally had a face and a voice to put with the author who seemed to be writing just to me.

As I was moving from Virginia back to Alabama, I felt compelled to make a pilgrimage through Kentucky to visit the Abbey of Gethsemani and Merton's grave, but—new to this—I didn't know if I would be allowed there. After learning where Wilkes lived, I am now embarrassed to say that I, a complete stranger, called him at home on a Sunday to ask his advice. Wilkes was most gracious and told me to ask for Brother Patrick Hart; I did so when I arrived at the Abbey outside Bardstown. Brother Patrick, one of the guardians of Merton's legacy said, "Any friend of Paul's is a friend of ours," and thus began our relationship, under, if not exactly false, then certainly at least shaky pretenses.

Coincidences kept piling up. A woman sitting next to me on an airplane told me that Sister Thérèse Lentfoehr had been her teacher and that Sister Thérèse had been disconsolate at Merton's death and had spent the days after his death sitting outside his hermitage, fed by the kindness of the monastic community who brought her sandwiches and beer.

A former actress who had a small role in the movie "From Here to Eternity" approached me in Mobile, after hearing me serve as a lector during the 12:10 daily Mass at our Cathedral, to tell me she knew Merton as a little boy. The story stunned me for a second, but she later explained how, as a young woman, she had worked at Grosset and Dunlap for Merton's grandfather, and how "little Tom" would come to work occasionally and sit in the corner to read dime store novels.

A man in Mobile introduced himself and explained he had been at Gethsemani with Merton and helped him staple copies of *Monks Pond*. He gave me a copy of a 1927 Baptist hymnal that Merton had given him. Inside, in pencil, was written the name of Merton's great-grandmother, Mary Jenkins.

Throughout the years, while on vacation, my wife and daughters endured side trips which involved visits to either Cistercian ruins or abbeys, from Caldey Island off the coast of Wales, to Mount Melleray in Ireland, to Spencer or Conyers in the United States, to a school named after Merton in Toronto, Canada.

Merton helped to introduce me to members of God's family with whom I would have never become acquainted, such as Msgr. William Shannon of Nazareth College and the late director of the Thomas Merton Studies Center, Robert Daggy, who encouraged me to use my training as a journalist to search through U. S. government records to see if Washington was watching the monk; it was. A series of requests through the Freedom of Information Act revealed that the FBI did indeed have a file on Merton, complete with anonymous tips and reports on his letter of recommendation to a young man requesting conscientious objector status from the military draft. The CIA sent a copy of an envelope and the letter it held from Merton to Russian author Boris Pasternak, an intercept that was illegal at the time.

All whom I have met through my encounter with Merton have helped enrich my life, encouraging me to "pray as I breathe" and help others find and share the gift of Merton's life and communion with others . . . much like Merton's epiphany at Fourth and Walnut, but at my own intersection, and in my own time.

Thomas And Me

Michael W. Higgins

My interest in Thomas Merton is quite multi-layered: personal, spiritual, intellectual, and professional. And it began decades ago.

I suppose I was a mite uncommon as an adolescent as I spent more hours mining the riches of our local Toronto library than I did consorting with my peers, evading parental censure, tweaking authority, or wrestling with hormonal upheaval. Of course, I did all those things as well, but the light, the sanctuary, offered by the library was too compelling to resist.

And I *know* that I was singularly unconventional in that the stacks that lured me were those given over to ecclesiastical history, theology and spiritual autobiography. They were not peopled with those of my chronology.

Still, I didn't mind. The other browsers may have looked suspiciously at me but I was indifferent, I was safe, I was alone with my books.

One day in the 1960s, a couple of years prior to my entering a missionary order seminary, my eye caught a cover that especially intrigued me with a title that seduced me to probe what lay between its covers. Sounds lurid but it was not.

More Than Sentinels by Naomi Burton (later Naomi Burton Stone) fascinated me and introduced to me a character whose presence in the book was determinative. That character was Thomas Merton. I came to Merton indirectly and by means of a literary genre that would have abiding interest for me: the memoir/conversion story/spiritual autobiography.

It was a short hop from there to Merton's other writings contained in the library, principal of which were the devotional and contemplative works. I devoured *Life and Holiness* but the lack of narrative and autobiographical details disappointed me. After all what normal teenager, or even moderately eccentric one, is enthralled with an *enchiridion*.

My next TM encounter would come shortly: just before I began my studies in the seminary I read *The Seven Storey Mountain*. It seemed the required thing to do; it seemed the appropriate rite of passage for all those aspiring to the religious or clerical life; it seemed more important than the Scriptures. And so, dutifully, devoutly and deter-minedly I read it and the overwhelming feeling it induced was not awe, nor gratitude, but annoyance. I couldn't quite see the fuss.

Just before I parted company with the seminary—in the penultimate year of my undergraduate studies—I read the special *Continuum* issue dedicated to Merton's memory and I was hooked. *Continuum* did what *The Seven Storey Mountain* had failed to do for me: it made Merton compellingly interesting, the various submissions in the issue crafting a portrait of TM as a Catholic thinker, essayist and poet of non-sectarian appeal. I thought at the time I would come back to Merton, read him more closely, explore more deeply a personality that now struck me as endlessly fascinating. But how and when I had no idea. I was about to begin my graduate studies in English literature on a fellowship at Canada's most secular academy, York University in Toronto, and Merton would surely have no role to play in this undertaking. How wrong I was.

In a class on the poetry, drama and prose of T. S. Eliot with Professor D. E. S. Maxwell (one of the pre-eminent Eliot scholars in the world at the time) we were invited to use the last class of the year—it was a rigorous full-year undertaking—to speak about a modern poet whose work attracted us and about whom few in the class may have yet heard. I thought instantly of Merton, scrambled to recover a copy of *Selected Poems*, the one with the introduction by Mark van Doren, chose five poems, and made my presentation. Not one in the class had heard of Merton, but Professor Maxwell was impressed by the quality of his craft and suggested that there was a dissertation here yearning to be born. I stored his suggestion away but only temporarily as I was to retrieve it the following year when taking a course by the poet/critic Eli Mandel on the visionary poetics of Christopher Smart, William Blake and W. B. Yeats.

Blake was to be my hermeneutical key to understanding Merton.

And what I have come to appreciate over the years of research and writing as I continue to investigate the depths, prescience and abiding relevance of many aspects of his thinking—a truly visionary thinking—is Merton's essentially universalist sensibility, his capacity to transcend narrow and constrictive modes of thinking, his openness to the risks of disruptive insights, his embrace of the wondrous and luminous in all traditions of faith, his very temerity of mind and spirit. I think these are genuinely Blakean qualities and Merton was his astute, critical and discerning disciple.

Not surprisingly in a keenly secular academic environment a healthy skepticism defined the approach to any figure or body of study, but perhaps most especially a religious one. Theology was considered quaint, monasticism of historical significance only, ecclesiastical matters seen as parochial, and therefore of no interest to probing academics. That was the environment in which I studied and competed. And Merton appealed to them—professors and fellow students—on the basis of the quality of his mind, his skill as a poet, the integrity of his life.

From the outset of my studies Merton was always secular property, if you like, and when I consulted, wrote and narrated various radio and television programs for the Canadian Broadcasting Corporation (*Thomas Merton: Extraordinary Man; Out of Silence—a Voice; Monk on the Run; Heretic Blood: A Spiritual Audiobiography*) I had to do so in a way that was more catholic than Catholic, more interdisciplinary than discipline-specific, intelligible to a highly educated audience that did not limit itself to any form of theological boundary.

Merton introduced me to a genuine ecumenicity of mind, an unfettered Catholic way of being in the world, an intellectual vulnerability that eschewed certitude in favor of exploration—humble, tentative and fearless.

Merton was a public Catholic intellectual distinguished by a rigorous self-scrutiny, possessed of a literary voice of singular virtuosity and bold eclecticism. He was a contemplative, restless, chronically unsure, poised at many a liminal point—spiritual and emotional—ever aching into holiness.

Hope—"A Tune That Never Stops"

Monica Weis, SSJ

Emily Dickinson captures it well: "Hope is the thing with feathers/That perches in the soul/And sings the tune without the words/And never stops—at all." How often we have seen this quotation on greeting cards or posters and had a "feel good" moment, a kind of warm, fuzzy experience—but then we just go on about our daily lives. Have we ever really pondered these words? Accepted their challenge?

What strikes me this year as we commemorate the 100th anniversary of Thomas Merton's birth is the phrase "sings the tune without the words." Surely, Merton, a self-declared bystander on the margins of society, sang the tune—often with words his contemporaries could not comprehend. His critique of the Vietnam war, and war itself, his caution about the dangers of technology, his defense of the rights of indigenous people, his censure of racial injustice, his challenge to America to develop an ecological conscience—all were prophetic words whose deep meaning we are just discovering—words that we now know to be true on multiple levels.

Every one of us is called to sing a tune in our world and, in our own unique way, to witness to the outrageous love of a God who every moment is creating the entire cosmos and holding it—us—me—in being, in loving embrace. Granted, we do this with limited voice, often without the "proper" words, but how aware are we of the significance of what we are doing? Yes, we often sing from the margins, in a place of fragile uncertainty, yet we sing. Yes, we sing to celebrate the splendor of this world and the glorious in-breaking of the Reign of God and, occasionally, we catch a glimpse of what that glory is. In special moments of grace, human imagination surges ahead of the mundane and quotidian to recognize some new, often dazzling, whole—an experience of singing the tune without the words, an experience of hope.

Two characteristics of such experience seem related—awareness and persistence—and both Dickinson and Merton apparently understood this. How many times Merton calls us to be alert to the spiritual reality around and in us—to re-discover the older unity of our oneness with each other and with all creatures on planet Earth. How often and how urgently Merton challenges us to go one step more, to be more, to move from an old reality to a fresh one—to sing a tune with or without all the proper words.

Indeed, awareness and persistence remind me of other examples of hope, both literary and contemporary. Thoreau's repeated wake-up call to his Concord neighbors in *Walden* concludes: "only that day dawns to which we are awake"; moreover, "the sun is just the morning star." In other words, there is always more to human experience. These two characteristics remind me, too, of Pope Francis' symbolic Holy Thursday ceremony at the Casal del Marmo in which he encouraged the young detainees whose feet he had washed to "not let yourselves be robbed of hope."

Thomas Merton's Message of Hope

Awareness and persistence reveal themselves in many guises. Last year, my local church of Rochester, New York commemorated the 50th anniversary of Vatican II with complementary lectures by our Bishop Emeritus Matthew H. Clark and Howard J. Hubbard, Bishop of Albany—lectures later published by St. Bernard's School of Theology and Ministry as *Messages of Hope*. Clark's reflection focused on what he continues to experience as key insights and fruits of the Council, as well as specific initiatives of the Council he hopes will reach fulfillment: genuine subsidiary in the Church; pastoral authority that listens and learns; appropriate structures to honor contributions of women; wider pastoral embrace of gays and lesbians; celebration of the gifts of lay ecclesial ministers; and greater attentiveness to those who struggle to remain in the Church. Our diocese has been blessed for the last thirty-three years with this compassionate and forward-thinking Shepherd who knows how to sing the tune and, in his retirement, will continue to be a voice of hope.

On the global scene, there are many initiatives of hope to praise. I celebrate the recent news about a series of computers stationed outside in the poorest sections of India. There, young kids, yielding to their natural curiosity and playfulness, are discovering—without teachers—how to access the Internet and stretch themselves in a world of knowledge. And I revel in the new studies of cosmology that broaden our perspective to see how we are part of the more than 13 billion-year unfolding of God's love. Each of these examples of breakthrough moments—of singing a new tune—gives me hope for humankind and for our planet.

In my professional circles, I experience many of what Elaine Prevalet, SL has called "pockets of hope." I interact with college students who are committed to service as part of their lives, giving up vacation time to paint houses in Appalachia or participate in an Urban Plunge—a week-long sampling of ministries sponsored by the Sisters of St. Joseph of Rochester. I meet with adult students in our graduate liberal studies program who never want to stop learning and others who come by medi-van to campus, entering the classroom with the aid of a walker and intent on doing all the work for the course, even though they are just auditing it. And I witness our vets warmly welcomed to our campus, becoming an integral part of a receiving and giving academic community.

What do I see as my role? To be aware of each of these graced moments, to give thanks, and to encourage the enriching and enriched life they represent. Their enthusiasm challenges me to new levels of awareness and persistence. As professor, I need to be about "professing"—to share my knowledge, certainly, but to foster, to mentor, to nurture, to share my love of life. And while, from one perspective, I am at the center of campus life, I am also paradoxically, like Merton, on the margins, resisting the common herd mentality, raising difficult questions about the drift of society, looking with different eyes at our consumer world, urging colleagues and students to question the status quo, while at the same time contributing to a more intense and authentic community. Each of these "pockets of hope" challenges me to continue to sing my tune—and never stop at all.

So, thank you Emily Dickinson for offering a metaphor that suggests a way of accomplishing Thomas Merton's challenge to the human community: to continually strive for the deeper communion that reflects our older unity—the one beyond concepts, beyond words. Let's keep singing the tune—with or without the words—and never stop at all.

Abbey of Gethsemani, watercolor by Jim Cantrell, 1994.

Merton Changed My Life

Jeannette Cantrell

"Merton changed my life." I cannot begin to tell you how many times I have heard that phrase over the years. I'll never forget the first time I heard a customer speak those words. It was such a transforming moment in his life that he recalled "It was on page 58 in *New Seeds of Contemplation*." Another would say someone gave them a Merton book, or others picked up a Merton book in a bookstore not knowing why, but these books were read and their lives were changed.

I suspect in many ways Merton changed my life as well. It all began in 1980 when a call came from one of the monks at the Abbey of Gethsemani (12 miles from us) asking if I would be interested in adding Merton books to our Bardstown Art Gallery. He proceeded to tell me they didn't have a gift shop anymore and said they were looking for a place that had the right atmosphere, but also wanted me to know they couldn't finance me should I accept the idea. After hearing such a nice compliment, I was indeed interested. Of course, I had no idea what was in store for us. My initial thinking was (not knowing a thing about the book business)—Thomas Merton—he probably wrote a few books; one author, one publisher. How hard could it be? Besides, I felt people who read would also have an appreciation for the arts, and we could meet some interesting people. Indeed we have. Many over the years have shared their life stories with me, and we keep up with one another when they make their annual visits to the monastery, or telephone with an order, send a letter or email.

Little did I dream I would also meet and become friends with some of the authors and scholars of Merton's writings! The first such surprise came when Fr. Bill Shannon came into the gallery. I think I had only one title of his at the time, *Thomas Merton's Dark Path: The Inner Experience of a Contemplative*. He was so gracious and kind. My husband Jim's paintings hit a responsive chord with him. He began making an annual stop to visit and eventually commissioned Jim to paint a small portrait of Merton. He was starting a Merton Reading Room in the library at Nazareth College in Rochester, New York. He sent several of his favorite images of Merton. When Jim had completed one oil painting, he couldn't decide whether he had captured Merton's personality. So he did another, then another, and after the fifth one, we asked some of the monks to come to the gallery to view them. Each monk seemed to select a different one. I laughed and surmised we must have been playing "Will the Real Thomas Merton Please Stand Up?!" Jim had obviously captured different aspects of Merton's personality. We sent three to Shannon so he could select which one he wanted. He liked all three. He decided to use two to alternate in the library and wanted to keep the one of Merton in his wool cap for himself. Bob Daggy decided the Merton Center should have one. Jim had wanted me to destroy the fifth one. Fortunately, I didn't, and it was sold to a fine collector/Merton scholar/dear friend a couple of years ago. Shannon also requested permission to use the one of Merton in his cowl on the cover of *The Silent Lamp*, Shannon's biography of Merton.

After that commission, Jim decided he wanted to do a larger portrait of Merton but he didn't want to use someone else's photograph. The opportunity arose when Brother Joshua Brands invited us to see the monastery's archives. What an afternoon! Seeing rare and priceless objects, collections of ledgers and invoices from the inception of the Abbey back in the 1800s, and then the plethora of Merton objects, photographs etc., was quite a heady experience. Jim spotted a small snapshot of Merton. He liked his expression and asked to borrow it for reference. I asked Brother Patrick Hart if we could borrow a cowl so I could photograph Jim in it to insure he could get the lighting and shadows in the folds, etc. It turned out to be Merton's cowl that Brother Pat let us use!! Again, as the painting progressed, we asked some of our monk friends to come and make an assessment as to whether Jim was capturing Merton—since neither of us had ever met him in person. Their suggestions were taken and changes made. Finally we asked Father Matthew Kelty, one of Merton's spiritual directors, to come see it. When he came in and tears came to his eyes, I knew Jim had captured the right essence of Merton, the mature spiritual master. We eventually designed a poster for the Thomas Merton Books business and used that image.

Prior to the addition of Thomas Merton Books at Bardstown Art Gallery, I had the opportunity to purchase a letterpress printer and was learning to print and getting frustrated. So I decided to take a hand press printing workshop from Gay Reading (nephew of Carolyn Hammer and wife of Victor Hammer who published a number of limited edition Merton books) at King Library Press. Among the participants was a rare book dealer who learned I dealt in Merton books. He suggested if I worked at it, I could become known as THE source for Merton material. I ignored him thinking he was a bit audacious. A couple of years later a woman from New York came in and couldn't get over my "extensive" selection of books. When questioned she said, "Yes, everything is available in New York, but not in one spot." So my competitive nature kicked in, and I decided to listen and learn from willing mentors (and later great friends) like rare book dealer Marshall White, Merton Center Director Bob Daggy and Merton's secretary Brother Patrick Hart.

When I was out of stock of any of the books, many times I would be asked to mail it to the person when it was restocked. Jim suggested I utilize my press and print up a list and price of the books along with an order form. It eventually grew too much for me and I finally just had it printed. I would have a new catalogue printed every two years. Although I can no longer print and mail a catalogue, I have kept my mailing list of now over 3500 Merton readers (hard to believe!). The list consists of people who have either come into the gallery to purchase a book or ordered from my catalogue or by phone. I now have a website, www.thomasmertonbooks.com, and a growing email list as my only means to notify those interested in learning about new Merton related books, CDs, etc.

As my skills improved I set out to handset the type, print and hand bind a book all on handmade paper. Brother Patrick Hart had given me a short piece he had written about the first and last time he saw Merton. We decided to call it *First & Last Memories* and print an edition of 250 copies. Sweet memories come to mind when I think about our "binding parties" where I, Jim, Brother Patrick, and Brother Benedict would get together to work on the binding process. The book sold out, and Patrick encouraged me to do an offset edition of 500. I hand printed the wrapper and had the text printed by a local printing company. I was amazed when it, too, sold out.

Oh my, the memories! One day a group of women came to the gallery. They had been on retreat at the Sisters of Loretto. We began discussing the possibility of my printing a book on Merton written by a woman. One of the women asked if she could go around the other side of the gallery and meditate while the rest of us dealt with this issue. No problem. Soon thereafter a few tourists came into the gallery and were browsing. They didn't stay long. The woman who had been meditating came to us with a big grin on her face when they left. It seems the tourists had come around the section of the gallery where she was on the floor in a seated yoga position. They looked at her and commented that she looked like a piece of sculpture. Then one lady walked up to her, touched her cheek and said, "It looks like sculpture, but I don't think it is." The woman then opened her eyes and said, "I'm real. See all these books in here? They're about contemplation. So it's okay to meditate here." I've often wondered since if, when those friends get together, they reminisce about that time in the Bardstown Art Gallery and encountered what one of them thought was a sculpture!

Our first "Merton experience" outside the gallery came when Sr. Elena Malits invited us to bring books to sell during a winter weekend lecture series she had organized at St. Mary's College in Notre Dame, Indiana. Even though we were faced with blizzard conditions, we excitedly drove and arrived about 4:00 A.M. the morning of the first session—astounded to see so many young college students out and about! We were staying in an alumni house with the speakers: Larry Cunningham, Michael Mott, who had just been contracted to write the official biography of Merton, and Paul Dinter. Wow, great conversations among those men were mesmerizing. I had much to learn and discern.

A year or so later Fr. Shannon invited Jim and me to bring books to sell during a small gathering he had organized at Nazareth College. I believe it was his initial effort to begin organizing the ITMS. All the presentations were held in the same room with my tables of books in the back. The attendees were so enthused about all the books available they had a hard time settling down to listen to the next speaker. As hard as I tried, it was impossible to keep the bags from rattling and people asking questions when someone was purchasing. It became obvious I needed to be in a separate area if there was to be another such gathering.

I feel blessed to have been involved in the world of Thomas Merton before and since the 1987 inception of the International Thomas Merton Society and their biennial meetings. I have been the book vendor for every conference they've had in the U. S. and the first meeting held in Canada. I tell people it is very much like a family reunion as many of the same people attend. Jim calls himself my roadie as he helps load, unpack and set up for these events. He noticed I was spending so much time reuniting with so many of my now regular customers/friends that I wasn't getting the books out and organized when others were anxious and ready to look and purchase. So he made wooden boxes I could fill as if they were bookshelves. All we had to do was unload the van, set the "shelves" on the table and most of the initial work would be done. He could take care of customers while I continued socializing for a bit.

It was during of the ITMS conferences when I met Paul Pearson who was attending from England. He would purchase nearly every title I had as many of the books were not easily available in the UK. He eventually started the Thomas Merton Society of Great

Britain and Ireland. One year I suggested he invite us to set up books in England for their next conference. He did, and my Merton world really expanded. Most of their meetings are held in Oakham where Merton went to boarding school. I began getting orders from all over the world. When I seemed to get fairly regular orders from Turkey for awhile, the Post Office here would tease me about "yet another letter from my boyfriend."

In between the major conferences, I have been fortunate to be able to participate in smaller gatherings. One in 1988 that took place in Berea, Kentucky comes to mind. The limited edition, fine press book, *The Alaskan Journal*, from the Turkey Press in California was fresh off the press. I called and asked if they could overnight a couple of copies to the Boone Tavern Hotel so I could have them available for an interested audience. I believe the edition of 140 copies were priced at $250.00 each. We arrived and got set up. I went to the Hotel to collect my delivery. They found nothing addressed to me. I checked later in the day. Still nothing. I was frantic by now. The seminar ended and we went back to Bardstown quite disappointed. I called the press. It had indeed been shipped. They had no idea what could have happened. A couple of days later, Boone Tavern Hotel called. They had found the box. It had been put in the restaurant freezer! It seems the press had used a recycled food box in which to pack the books. The box from Turkey Press indicated it should be refrigerated upon arrival. Whoever got the delivery assumed it was pressed turkey. Thus it lay in cold storage until someone finally realized it wasn't addressed to the restaurant but to me and that it probably wasn't food! The folks in California sent a "we're so sorry" note and signed it "From a Depressed Turkey."

When Bob Daggy died, Jonathan Montaldo was named Director of the Merton Center. He began to recruit Paul Pearson, working in the United Kingdom, to succeed him as director. I can't say enough about the help and friendship of these three people. I couldn't do what I have done without their counsel. Paul has kept me in the loop by bringing Merton Elderhostel groups to the gallery on their way to the Abbey and by inviting me to set up books for the various lecture series the Center sponsors at Bellarmine University. It has been a lifeline what with the advent of Amazon and now the monastery's reopening of their gift shop in their new Visitor's Center. It is heartening to still have many of my old customers stop by or call and place an order.

Just this past summer a group from Mississippi stopped by on their way for an annual retreat at the Abbey. Their visits go back maybe more than 15 years. Anyway, I had just been diagnosed with breast cancer. They said they would keep me in their prayers. They did and one day a package arrived in the mail. The wives of the men belonged to a group that made prayer shawls and one had been made for me. It provided much comfort as a physical reminder that many were praying for my healing. The leader of the group, Rev. John Staggs, and his wife made a trip to Ireland and even had a Mass said for me while they were in Iona, Scotland. Another regular, Deacon David Nolan, found out about my cancer and sent a lovely wood container he had turned on his lathe along with a note about the healing power of wood and these directions: 1. Open box, 2. Insert anxieties, worries, fears, etc., 3. Close box tightly, 4. Worries, etc. GONE! All the Merton family kept me in their prayers and hearts. I truly believe I am now cancer free.

I'm proud and humbled when I think about the "Merton tapestry" that has evolved and entwined itself around our lives. It certainly isn't anything I planned, but it definitely is the work of the Holy Spirit speaking to me through so many people. I give thanks to God for showering me with the grace to be open to His guidance and pray to be worthy of His abundant blessings.

Thomas Merton II, oil on canvas by Jim Cantrell, 1986.
In the collection of Rev. William Shannon and the Nazareth College Library,
Rochester, New York.

God Alone, watercolor by Jim Cantrell, 2000.
Abbey of Gethsemani

Thomas Merton/Spiritual Master, oil on canvas by Jim Cantrell, 1995.

Thomas Merton's Call To Discover Our Older Unity

Matthew Fox

First, I commend the organizers of this book and subsequent events for working to keep the spirit and life and teachings of Father Thomas Merton alive as distinct from becoming frozen in some kind of hagiographic fog or pious nostaglia that he himself would have found utterly distasteful. For a number of years I have known Michael Toms of New Directions Radio and he has always called himself "a Thomas Merton Catholic." I think that is a happy phrase (I know others who call themselves a "Dorothy Day" Catholic for example) and it is not the same thing as calling oneself a "Mertonian" (or a "Jungian" or a "Thomist," since Jung said he thanked God he was not a Jungian, and the real Aquinas I am sure has often been misused by Thomists, just as Jesus has sadly often been misrepresented by "Christians").

So I too celebrate the centennial of Thomas Merton, this great soul, generous monk, passionate citizen, and gracious writer to whom we all owe so much. My own debt is quite personal, not only because of his many books that influenced and inspired me from his *The Seven Story Mountain* that I read as a teenager to his notes in his last Journal that "Eckhart is my lifeboat," but also because he is the one who advised me to go to the *Institut Catholique de Paris* for my doctoral studies in spirituality—thus I owe him for all the trouble I have gotten into since. For it was there that I met my mentor, Pere M. D. Chenu, OP, who named the creation spirituality tradition for me along with many other teachers who set me on my somewhat controversial theological/spiritual way.

I love the citations that have been chosen from Merton's many pregnant words for our common reflection. I like his reminding us that there are deeper levels of relating than "communication" and that is "communion" which is wordless and beyond words, beyond speech and beyond concepts. (It is also beyond "laws" including canon laws.) Here I hear echoes of Meister Eckhart who says God is "superessential darkness that has no name and will never be given a name" and that we all ought to "quit flapping our gums about God and speak from an inner wealth of silence" and that we, like he, "pray God to rid us of God." Merton too celebrates the God of silence as he writes that "all things are on fire" and "all their silence is on fire." All this talk from Merton and Eckhart is, of course, talk of the *apophatic Divinity* and, if I were a betting man, I would bet on the next era of God-talk being an epoch that celebrates the apophatic Divinity of the *Via Negativa*.

Why would this be so? For several reasons.

First, because we have heard too much cheap talk of God lately. The righteous surety with which fundamentalists pronounce on how they know with rigid certainty exactly who God is and what God demands is both scary and tends to the idolatrous, this whether we are talking of Protestant fundamentalism or the Vatican kind, whether

Islamist fundamentalist or the Hindu or Jewish kind. In America we have God's name stamped on every coin and dollar bill, and probably on MX missiles as well. The apophatic approach is essentially more humble and less arrogant and sure of itself and I think such a breath of fresh air is sorely needed in religion and society today.

Second, the apophatic Divinity encourages listening more than pronouncing, being-with rather than proselytizing, and we are in a time when we all ought to be listening more deeply for one another's wisdom and not just shouting about our own. Deep Ecumenism requires deep listening; deep listening is what meditation and contemplation provide. We need to speak from hearing and listening, not from tired scripts and yellow-paged theological position papers. And part of what we need to listen to is the news, the good news and the hurtful news, the suffering of the world as well as the beauty of creation which is in such jeopardy today. We need to listen to the oceans and the fishes, the forests and the soil, the four-legged ones and the feathered ones, not just to fellow humans. But of course we need to listen to each others' rich and generous spiritual traditions as well and ask what they each have to teach us as individuals and as communities of faith and as citizens on a rapidly deteriorating planet.

The apophatic Divinity also invites us into depth and darkness ("The ground of the soul is dark," says Meister Eckhart). It teaches us not to be afraid of the dark but how to be more at home with and more at ease in the darkness and the depths of not knowing and the darkness of waiting and the darkness of mutuality and the darkness of shared pain and suffering. If the ground of the soul is dark, surely the ground of compassion also comes from a dark place. Of course not only is the soul dark in its depths but so too is the earth, the sea and the cosmos. Many of the astronauts and cosmonauts who returned to earth as mystics were converted, as some have told me, by the deep silence they experienced in space and the deep darkness of the depths of the cosmos against which our shiny blue planet glistened like a rare gem.

I was struck this past year to learn that Thomas Merton's conversion actually happened at a shrine of the Black Madonna of Cobre, Cuba while he was recuperating from an illness there in 1940. As an explicit acknowledgment of this encounter, Merton dedicated his first Mass as a priest to Her in 1949. Clearly he had a special devotion to and owed a debt to the Black Madonna and she is an integral part of the apophatic Divinity that is asserting itself in our times in so many ways. She herself is appearing to many in dreams and messaging in our time and for good reason. Among other dimensions to her archetype is the emerging voice of the vast majority of our species who are people of color. She is rising; they are rising and with many gifts to offer. The Divine Feminine is also dark.

Our species is involved today in a collective Dark Night. I call it the "dark night of our species." Our knowledge has so outpaced our wisdom, our ability to spend our intelligence on nonsense, like more and more effective weapons, on casino games in Wall Street masquerading as a worthy economic system, on blind ways to preach denial while continuing to emit carbon dioxide, thus guaranteeing the warming of the planet and the disappearance of countless beautiful and amazing species, all this carries us into a place collectively from which we see no escape. That is a dark night. It is ours. We are in it together. The mystics tell us that important lessons are learned in the dark night, lessons of the purification of our longing, lessons of the real meaning of compassion and of wisdom. Are we up to such teachings? Are we warriors enough to enter the dark night and not settle for the pills and shopping and other addictions to distract us from the lessons our species needs to learn?

Still another reason for the rise of the apophatic Divinity in our time are the multiple stories emerging about dark matter and dark energy. As astrophysicist Joel Primack and Nancy Abrams put it in their book, *The New Universe and the Human Future: How a Shared Cosmology Could Launch a Global Society* (2011), we are living in a "Golden Age" of astronomy and one gift of today's science is to have discovered that we ride in a sea of darkness. Over 97% of the matter of the universe is "dark matter" or "dark energy" and we ought to synchronize our theologies and spiritualities with these facts (as Aquinas put it, "A mistake about creation results in a mistake about God"). The "Double Dark" theory of the universe was "unknown and even unimagined until the twentieth century. Between dark matter collapsing the galaxies into being and dark energy accelerating them apart from one another, our evolving universe has turned out to be far more dynamic than the old picture of endless space scattered with stars." What we call "dark energy" constitutes about 70% of the density of the universe and it is "the most powerful entity in the universe and yet until 1998 no one knew it existed . . .. Dark energy powers the expansion of the universe." The authors invite us to imagine the entire universe as an ocean of dark energy.

On that ocean there sail billions of ghostly ships made of dark matter. At the tips of the tallest masts of the largest ships there are tiny beacons of light which we call galaxies. With the Hubble Space Telescope, the beacons are all we see. We don't see the ships, we don't see the ocean—but we know they're there through theory, the Double Dark theory. Dark matter is indeed primeval and came out of the Big Bang, and it surrounds and permeates our Local Group of galaxies, but dark energy, which dominates outside our halo of dark matter, only became important later, because it has been creating more of itself all the time. The larger the universe expands, the faster more dark energy gets created.

This sounds like mother power if I have ever heard it—creativity and more creativity, expansion and more expansion of the universe going on. The Cosmic Mary, the Black Madonna, at work in the universe.

Merton promised us that from a shared communion that is wordless and speechless and concept-less we "discover a new unity" which is "an older unity." We all come from the darkness of the universe; we all share what Merton calls an "original unity." And that original unity is not morally neutral, nor is it beauty-neutral. It is about shared goodness. It is an original unity *and* an original blessing. The original unity *is* an original blessing. Goodness is our origin ("blessing" is the theological word for "goodness") and it is our destiny. Consider Rabbi Heshel: "Just to be is a blessing, just to live is holy." Consider Eckhart: "Whenever we talk about God the Creator we are talking about goodness." If it is true that the essence of authentic religion is not buildings or structures or dogmas or ordained ones but rather *the virtue of giving thanks,* as Aquinas taught, then original grace and original blessing lie at the heart of all authentic religion. What does one give thanks for if not goodness?

Here is where we share an ancient and original origin and unity: in a place of gratitude and of praise. "Praise precedes faith," warns Rabbi Heschel. All our religions need to drop lots of faith concepts and dogmas to return to a shared oneness which has everything to do with praise and gratitude: the *Via Positiva*. It is there that our communion as humans will restart what we call religion. There lies our origin because, in Julian of Norwich's words, "We have been loved from before the beginning." Before the beginning of our religions, before the beginning of our earth, before the beginning of the Milky Way galaxy, way before the beginning there was love that brought us here. We ought to return kind for kind and blessing for blessing. We can and ought to restart our religions and put Praise and the *Via Positiva* out front, and doing our work in the *via negativa* and the apophatic Divinity assists us in this task, just as fasting assists one to appreciate water and food more fully after the fast.

In this way we "become who we truly are," in Merton's words. We become human beings again, late-comers in the universe with both larynx and consciousness for praise. Or in Mary Oliver's words, "There is only one question: How to love the world?"

Three Nuggets About Tom And Me

Judith Hardcastle

Tom would have liked this view. He would have liked this place. I'm at Rivendell, a non-denominational contemplative retreat house on Bowen Island, three nautical miles from Horseshoe Bay. Although Horseshoe Bay is less than 24 kilometers from downtown Vancouver, it is literally "the end of the road" for anyone wanting to travel by car further north along the west coast of British Columbia. It is also the hub of British Columbia Ferry Corporation activity whose ships depart frequently to Vancouver Island, the Gulf Islands and the Sunshine Coast.

A translucent mist almost shrouds the mountains behind Snug Cove, which is directly in my line of vision, and the 400-year-old cedar trees that surround Rivendell stretch their old limbs skyward without a sound. I'm watching an eagle patrol the beach in the distance; its wings spread wide and its white head appears like a beacon of wordless light as it effortlessly rides the thermal air currents. Silence is spoken here. Even the deer that are dining on Rivendell's flowers come and go silently. Everything in this sacred place reminds me of Tom.

Merton burst into my life in February, 1997. I remember the year only because my mother died in 1997, and I remember the month because I took an unscheduled leave of absence from my work at SkyTrain, Vancouver's light rapid transit company, to read anything I could lay my hands on about (and by) Thomas Merton.

In January I had produced a play about Dietrich Bonhoeffer, which was based on author Herbert O'Driscoll's CBC radio drama by the same name. After its successful run, I received a note from Herb suggesting I might want to do something on Thomas Merton. I enthusiastically said "Yes!" But when I received and read his original typewritten radio script of *Hermitage of a Thousand Windows*, my heart sank. I realized it would be impossible to turn this aged script into a one-act play. It was a personal testimony of how Thomas Merton affected Herb's life as a young priest—a beautiful, heartfelt testimony, but testimony nevertheless; not drama.

However, the venue was booked. Announcements had been made. John Juliani, a well-known and talented Canadian actor, was committed to the project. I had exactly seven weeks to turn a radio-script about someone I didn't know into a one-act play.

The play happened (it was dreadful) but I was bitten by the Merton bug in the process of producing it and, as anyone will tell you, once bitten by the Merton bug, your life is never the same.

Shortly after the play was staged, I met Donald Grayston, Anglican priest, professor of Religious Studies at Simon Fraser University and long-time Merton enthusiast. He told me about a pilgrimage program he had organized through the Institute for the Humanities at Simon Fraser University called "Thomas Merton in France" and encouraged me to join the group for ten days of sun and conviviality in Prades, Merton's birthplace. This first pilgrimage became the forerunner of the Thomas Merton Society of Canada's pilgrimage programs. Merton pilgrimage programs do focus on Merton (his life, his writings, places he has lived or visited such as Prades, St. Antonin, Rome, Cuba, New York, Alaska, Gethsemani) but the real *boon* of pilgrimage is the relationships formed along the way. Some are transitory; some become permanent; all transform what starts as an ordinary journey into a sacred one.

On the last day of that first pilgrimage program in Prades, I remember making a decision to continue my Merton journey when I returned home by finding folks who would like to accompany me. And so, as they say, the rest is history. The Thomas Merton Society of Canada was birthed and has grown from a small group of Merton readers in 1997 to a vibrant national organization seventeen years later.

It is tempting to go down the meandering path I have travelled with Merton, telling you everything about Tom and me. A homiletics professor once told me a good preacher should be able to reflect on a text and distill its meaning into two or three clear, well-delivered nuggets (gold nuggets of course) that anyone hearing the sermon will remember. "There's no need" he said "to go on and on." I think the professor's approach is the best one to take, even though this is not a sermon, just a personal statement about Thomas Merton. So here they are: three nuggets about Tom and me.

He helped me to grow intellectually. I admire Merton's intellect. Reading Merton was (and still is sometimes) a circuitous affair, though I make fewer detours these days than I did seventeen years ago in order to unpack philosophical, religious and literary references he casually makes.

I am continually amazed that Merton wrote on issues which are relevant today, nearly four decades after his death. I respect his analysis and stance on justice issues—for speaking out against war, abuse of the environment and racism, to name a few. I am glad he explored and embraced spiritual practices of other religious traditions while remaining firmly rooted in his Christian faith. I am thankful he retrieved Christianity's contemplative past and showed us how to incorporate spiritual practices such as meditation, prayer and silence into our daily lives. I applaud his critique of institutional religion. I still laugh at his humor and wit, especially in his lectures to the novices at the Abbey of Gethsemani.

I doubt if I will ever get tired of reading Merton. When Epiphany comes round, I shamelessly use his well-known "shining like the sun" passage to illustrate my sermon, and on Remembrance Sunday, when I want to show how war can break your heart, I read his poem, "For My Brother Missing in Action." That's the glory of Merton: he's a man for all seasons, a man for all times; a source of ancient wisdom and bold new ideas.

He led me to ordination. When I was going through the long discernment process required by my denomination for ordination, I was repeatedly asked when I felt called by God to ordained ministry. I insisted there was no defining moment; rather, a growing certainty of God's call that was revealed to me by reading Merton. Merton's prose, poetry, journals, and letters helped me to write my own spiritual autobiography, to ask difficult questions about my faith, and to be as vulnerable and as honest as Merton was about my relationship with God and the world, and especially about my relationship with myself.

He showed me life is all about relationships. Merton was Fr. Louis to his brother monks; Tom to his family; Thomas Merton to the world. He corresponded with literary giants, political and religious leaders, theologians, peace activists, and ordinary folks like you and me. His relationships were diverse and often complicated. But the penny dropped for me about the *value* Merton placed on relationships when I listened to Trappist monk and priest Matthew Kelty talk about his relationship with Fr. Louis. "Merton asked me to be his confessor," Kelty explained, "not because he needed me but because he knew I needed him."

I am not a Merton scholar. But as you can see I have been indelibly marked and blessed by Thomas Merton. He helped me to grow intellectually. He led me to ordination. He showed me life is all about relationships.

The new moon is edging its way to the porch. It is well past midnight. Rivendell is engulfed in the sound of sheer silence. If Tom were here, I bet he would be out amongst the cedars gazing up at the night sky, composing a west coast sequel to *Fire Watch*.

Happy Birthday, dear Tom: mentor, friend and spiritual companion.

Merton's Voice

J. S. Porter

Thomas Merton's voice drew me in almost 40 years ago when I first began to read him and that's what keeps me returning to his work. In 1988, in *The Thomas Merton Poems*, I attempted to borrow his voice on the twentieth anniversary of his death. Twenty years later in *Thomas Merton: Hermit at the Heart of Things* I revisited his life and work. I've tried to say farewell on numerous occasions and somehow a voice calls me back. Perhaps I've taken a lifelong vow of conversation with an American monk.

Merton has a way of speaking where, by the intimacy of his voice, he convinces you that you're a co-writer of his words rather than a mere listener to them. In his best writings, in his most personal confessions, he establishes an extraordinary degree of intimacy between writer and reader.

He speaks to you as if you're on the same level as he is. He speaks brother to brother, brother to sister. He doesn't speak as an authority; he speaks as a beginner. He doesn't lecture from the pulpit or a similarly elevated platform. He speaks from the table at which the two of you are seated. He shows you his cuts and bruises in words as simple as bread, as full-bodied as wine.

And when he finishes talking, you ask yourself: is he talking about himself or about me? The barrier between the self and the other is dissolved. His voice is your voice. As he says in the "Preface to the Japanese Edition of *The Seven Storey Mountain*," "I seek to speak to you, in some way, as your own self" (*Introductions East & West: The Foreign Prefaces of Thomas Merton*, 47).

You don't read Thomas Merton; you hear him; he speaks directly to your ear. You don't read him; you meet him. I can't think of another writer who gets out more of who he is and what he stands for than Merton; he's able to put his body on the page; his soul on the page. He invites you into his life by a kind of tonal alchemy. I am you, he says time and again, and you are me. What moves in you moves in me.

If I had to pick one sentence from the Merton canon that instantly defines his character, it would be this one: "This is simply the voice of a self-questioning human person who, like all his brothers, struggles to cope with turbulent, mysterious, demanding, exciting, frustrating, confused existence in which almost nothing is really predictable, in which most definitions, explanations and justifications become incredible even before they are uttered, in which people suffer together and are sometimes utterly beautiful . . .." (*Contemplation in a World of Action*, 160). That's the voice. That's why I return.

> Of all the sounds
> in Japanese,

the most powerful
        is oh
for the death of a child.

I've never had an oh,
        but I've had
        an ah
for a mother,
        an eh
for a father,
        an uh
for a brother.
Just about all the sounds,
        except oh.

From my *The Thomas Merton Poems*, 24

His Words, My Life

Dianne Aprile

From the beginning, it was his way with words that drew me in and kept me reading until I wondered if I could ever stop. It was the late '90s, and though I'd grown up a Catholic-school girl, spending the first 12 years of my formal education with Ursuline nuns in Louisville, Kentucky, I had never been exposed to Thomas Merton's works. (Or if I had been, I paid no attention.) I graduated from Sacred Heart Academy in 1967, some 18 months before Father Louis died. Though he was certainly known well in my home state, as an underground war protestor and civil rights advocate, I didn't read him, didn't know his work, didn't notice his passing when it came at the end of a long year of deaths that included other extraordinary men whom I mourned and still count among my heroes.

It would take three decades, a marriage, a child, and a career in journalism for me to turn to his words, seriously, and absorb their influence—their depth and intensity. For a time, I read one book after another. Some stunned me. Some put me to sleep. Any avid Merton reader can figure out which were in the latter category. I started with an outlier, a book that is rarely cited in recommended Merton titles. But its playfulness and intimacy—its literary magnetism—made me a believer. It was the collected letters between Merton and his college pal and lifelong friend, the poet Bob Lax, titled *A Catch of Anti-Letters* that made me curious. And kept me reading. Here was a mind and literary voice that could not be contained. Later, the letters were re-issued as *When Prophecy Still Had a Voice: The Letters of Thomas Merton and Robert Lax*.

Oddly, the next Merton book I read was Monica Furlong's biography. These two books actually belonged to my husband Ken Shapero who, though Jewish, had been interested in Merton's writing long before I met him. Tommie O'Callaghan, a friend of his family and a co-worker at *Louisville Today* magazine in the 1970s, had given him the two books. They sat on our bookshelf for close to two decades before I picked them up to read. But I eyed them regularly, and somehow each time I crossed their path, I felt Merton eyeing me, too.

Immersing myself in Merton led to changes in my life, big and small, personal and public. I was 40 when I began to read his books, the classic Jungian time of big change in an individual's life. I was ready for a shift, and his words and thoughts and actions (alive more than ever in the '90s) nudged me in the direction I needed to go. My dissatisfaction with the rigidity of the Catholicism I grew up with seemed to be affirmed by his prose. (More than any writer he taught me how to be constructively critical.) His explication of the mystical, meditative, contemplative aspects of Catholicism, which I'd missed growing up in the '50s and '60s, opened doors for me, offered me a taste of the spirituality I would find nourishing and nurturing in the years to come.

I devoured his poetry, his letters, his tracts, his biographies and histories—but it was his journals, the story of his own remarkable life, that taught me who I was. Today, as a teacher of writing, I realize that the best writing—of any kind—must do just that: make the reader more aware of who she is, what she wants, how she wishes to live the short span of time known as her life.

Through Merton, I was led to the Abbey of Gethsemani, where I wrote about the place and its monks, but more importantly, I was embraced by the place and its monks. Always, whether it was walking the knobs with my friend Brother Raphael Prendergast or listening to Brother Paul Quenon recite Emily Dickinson on the porch of Father Louie's hermitage, I felt Merton's shining sun lighting up the moment, uniting me with the rolling Kentucky landscape, the monks who give their lives to the Abbey, the long history of Trappist life, and always a feeling of union with Merton, too.

My affection for and curiosity about Merton and his Abbey ultimately led me to write two books about the monastery and numerous essays about my experiences there. Through the pull of Merton's life of contemplative action, I grew as a human being, and as a writer. I was exposed to people and ideas that built bridges for me to places of the heart and mind I might never have discovered. Sitting with the Dalai Lama at Gethsemani; sharing days of conversation and meditation with activist priests, like John Dear; activist nuns like Sister Helen Prejean; activist leaders like Barbara Mikulski—all of this came about because I couldn't keep my eyes off those Merton books on my husband's bookshelf.

My ideas about God, the Church, American culture, diary-keeping, solitude, struggle, and, of course, love were never the same after reading Merton.

Today, I live in the Pacific Northwest, a place on the far side of this country from Merton's Trappist monastery, near a coast where Merton spent some of his final days. I think of him often, as I contemplate my own big move from my homeplace of Kentucky, leaving it for the first time at the age of 60. There's a sorrow in losing that stability, that deep-rootedness in landscape and collective history. I've struggled with it, God knows. But I've also found that, when roots are torn out of their native ground, they look to silence, solitude and contemplation for comfort and support. They find peace in nature, as Merton's journals so convincingly argue. It's there, in the heart of it all, (be it rolling Kentucky hills or the Olympic range at sunset) that they find union with the whole shimmering hurting world—and, yes, with themselves.

Thomas Merton: A Reflective Essay

John P. Collins

The following remarks reflect actual events in my life, albeit anecdotal in nature, described in a literal fashion, rather than a philosophic reflection. I believe the events demonstrate my search for unity within my family, friends and other acquaintances. Thomas Merton once wrote: "Whatever I may have written, I think all can be reduced in the end to this one root truth: that God calls human persons to union with Himself and with one another in Christ" ("Concerning the Collection in the Bellarmine Library," *The Thomas Merton Center,* 14).

I consider myself a prodigal in a faraway country, "the 'region of unlikeness' and ... [I] must ... travel far in that region before [I] seem to reach [my] own land" and then I will realize that I have been in my own land all the time (*New Seeds of Contemplation*, 280-281)! But I have not yet arrived and I am still a prodigal searching and, at best communicating in an incomplete way. Alas, I have not yet recovered my original unity or "older unity." I have not yet reached that level of communion with my brethren advocated by Thomas Merton in his informal remarks at the Temple of Understanding in Calcutta, India just prior to his untimely death in 1968. But I am trying. The following remarks perhaps will help the reader understand this prodigal's attempt to find his "own land."

It all began when I was serving with the 8th Army during the Korean War. I had been deployed to Korea early in 1952 after serving with the 508th Regimental Combat Team at Fort Benning, Georgia. I had suffered a broken shoulder during a Regimental parachute jump and, instead of enjoying the night life of Columbus during my off duty hours, I found myself trying to adjust to the reality of war in the little town of Sokcho-ri located on the 38th parallel of Korea. On July 27, 1953 the armistice was signed. I was getting ready to rotate back to the States in December of that year. For many months we had been living in tents but after the armistice we had the "supreme luxury" of living in Quonset huts. On a regular basis the American Red Cross would drop off boxes of books for us to read. Although some of the books were on the best seller list, most books were of a salacious nature and predictably the box would empty quickly. It was there in my Quonset hut that it happened! In my later years I learned to call the moment "epiphanic." When I arrived at my Quonset in late evening the box was empty except for two books, *Life on the Mississippi* by Mark Twain and *The Sign of Jonas* by Thomas Merton. *Jonas* was a brand new hard cover edition and evidently just came off the press as it was published in 1953. Many Thomas Merton scholars and enthusiasts explain that their first Merton book was *The Seven Storey Mountain.* In my case, *Storey* was the second Merton book which I read in the spring of 1954.

Why was finding *The Sign of Jonas* in that battered and torn carton an epiphanic moment for me? The best answer to the question can be found in Thomas Merton's emblematic prayer—"My Lord God, I have no idea where I am going. I do not see the road ahead of me." Indeed, I did not know where I was going in 1953 and in 2014 I still don't know the way but "I will not fear, for You are ever with me, and You will never leave me to face my perils alone" (*Thoughts in Solitude*, 79). During the remaining weeks in Korea in the fall of 1953, I read my new found Thomas Merton book and I intuitively knew that its "Epilogue, Fire Watch, July 4, 1952" was a masterful piece of writing. As I read it, I was struck by the paternal feeling that Merton felt for his fellow monks sleeping and some snoring in their cells. Although I did not realize it at the time, Merton was describing his search for unity with his scholastics. One of the scholastics, Father John of God, used the new kiln to make a clay crucifix. Merton writes about Father John Of God and the other sleeping scholastics:

> And I think of the clay Christ that came out of his heart. I think of the beauty and the simplicity and the pathos that were sleeping there, waiting to become an image. I think of this simple and mysterious child, and of all my other scholastics. What is waiting to be born in all their hearts? Suffering? Deception? Heroism? Defeat? Peace? Betrayal? Sanctity? Death? Glory? (*The Sign of Jonas*, 354).

When I left Korea, I was able to enter Providence College in January, 1954. I lived with my parents as their residence was only 30 minutes from the College. Before the Army I had attended the University of Notre Dame for a year and, after three years in the Army, I was ready for some good home cooking. Also I was not up for returning to college dormitory life as my Army experiences had created within me a desire for more solitude which I found in the quiet of my room at home. The Trappist life described by Thomas Merton was appealing to me and in the spring of 1954, I began reading *The Seven Storey Mountain* along with two new friends I had made at college. Both Mario and Richard were serious students and, ironically, they were also attracted to the writings of Thomas Merton. We had great discussions in the cafeteria about the book and later we made a retreat together at Saint Joseph's Abbey in Spencer, Massachusetts. Richard contributed poetry about Thomas Merton to the college literary journal *The Alembic*. Upon graduation the three of us were accepted to the Boston College graduate program for history and we lived together for a year in Newton Highlands. Our discussions about history, religion, literature, and philosophy continued far into the evening and Thomas Merton was referenced on many occasions.

After I received my M. A. in History, I married Pauline Carroll and moved to Rochester, New York where I taught at McQuaid Jesuit High School. Later I moved to Massachusetts where I continued my educational career culminating with eight years at the College of Holy Cross and a professorship for the International Education Program, Inc. Along the way I became the father of four wonderful children, Jack, Mary, Patrick, and Erin. Unfortunately in 1979, my wife Pauline died of cancer and my reading of Thomas Merton helped me cope with this painful time of my life. I remember especially turning to his autobiography and re-reading the following passage related to the loss of his brother, John Paul, in World War II: "I passed the *pieta* at the corner of the cloister, and buried my will and my natural affections and all the rest in the wounded side of the dead Christ (*The Seven Storey Mountain*, 402)." Truly, Merton had captured the moment of grief that resonated with me. Merton's own experience of losing his parents, Ruth and Owen, at an early age, gave me the courage and hope to provide some comfort to my children during this dark period of their young lives. As my children reached their adult years, my hope for them was realized through their service to others, community and country. My interest and reading of Merton had, somewhat, a contagion effect on my son, Jack, as he has read several of his books and in the sixth grade he wrote a Thomas Merton essay. For a confirmation present on May 4, 1975, I gifted Jack with *Thomas Merton/Monk, A Monastic Tribute* edited by Patrick Hart. Indulge me a moment as I quote the message of hope I had inscribed in the book: "Dear Jack, Reading Thomas Merton has always provided me with hope to cope with life's problems. May he inspire you to fulfill your spiritual life on earth. A special gift from Dad." For the past eleven years both my sons, Jack and Patrick, have edited my monthly Thomas Merton columns in *The Catholic Free Press*. Daughters Mary and Erin have read my various journal articles about Merton with interest through the years providing me with the inspiration to continue as long as I am physically able. Indeed, I believe our family unity has been enhanced by the works of Thomas Merton.

In 1991 I attended my first ITMS General Meeting at Nazareth College and was pleased to see friends Edward Farley and Tom Del Prete, who received the first Louie award for his book entitled *Thomas Merton and the Education of the Whole Person*. This meeting was an important event for me as I discussed with Ed Farley the possibility of starting an ITMS Chapter in Massachusetts. Ed graciously assumed the duties of director and for close to twenty years I was able to make contributions under his competent leadership. Later in 2002, through the encouragement of Frs. Paul O'Connell and Dennis O'Brien, I organized and led the ITMS Chapter at St. Mary's Parish in Shrewsbury, Massachusetts. The Chapter met monthly on a designated date. On the St. Mary's website there was a program description with the titles of the books to be read and discussed during the year. As the group progressed, I was able to integrate other writers whose lives intersected with Thomas Merton. Readings from Flannery O'Connor, Walker Percy and Dorothy Day enriched our discussions about Thomas Merton's influence upon all of us. I present a brief excerpt from the St. Mary's Newsletter from a member of the Chapter regarding his reflections on the group. From John:

> What does the group offer? The group offers each one an opportunity within a friendly environment including people of varying backgrounds with a common interest in learning what it means to be 'human' . . .. We talk, we listen, we agree, we disagree. Everyone has an opportunity to contribute a little or a lot as you wish.

In May of 2013, when I led my last discussion with the St. Mary's ITMS chapter, I thought my chapter days were over, so that I could spend more time with my writing projects. I had agreed to lead a Confraternity of Christian Doctrine group that included four of my grandchildren, Meghan, Haley, Paulina, and Holly. I decided that Scripture was the best way to approach the program as I was influenced by Father John Dear who used the same method with a group of his New Mexico students. I had attended one of his lectures held at St. Rose of Lima Parish in Northboro, Massachusetts, and I was impressed with the simplicity but profundity of his approach. I had previously heard one of John's Thomas Merton lectures at an ITMS General Meeting and felt a kinship with this gifted priest. I hoped to devote more personal time to further my knowledge of Holy Scripture. It was not to be, however, because in June, 2013, I received a much delayed letter dated February 12, 2013 from Sean, an inmate of the Massachusetts Correctional Institution at Shirley, Massachusetts. The following is an excerpt from the letter:

Our community is extremely interested in Thomas Merton and are hoping that you may be able to come and present a talk on his life and teachings. Our community is truly blessed and we know that you would come away from any visit very uplifted. Jesus said, 'When I was in prison you visited me' and we can think of no better visit than to have you share the blessings of Thomas Merton with us.

The letter was another epiphanic moment for me as I believe the Holy Spirit had guided the convergence of events, that is, ending my St. Mary's group and the letter from Sean. I contacted Chaplain Arthur Rogers and the one time lecture became the beginning of an ITMS Chapter at the prison. After my first visit to the prison, I learned that the inmates had learned about Thomas Merton primarily through my monthly Merton column in the *Catholic Free Press.* Perhaps through the guidance of the Holy Spirit I was, at least partially, fulfilling my vocation as a "messenger of hope." During the summer of 2013, we decided to read *The Seeds of Contemplation* as our first book. At one of the fall, 2013 meetings we viewed Paul Wilkes film: "Merton: A Film Biography" and we have read selections from *A Year with Thomas Merton* edited by Jonathan Montaldo. The group is serious and dedicated to learning how Thomas Merton can enhance their spiritual life during their years of incarceration. There is a newsletter published through the prison chapel "Our Lady of Guadalupe" and Thomas Merton reflections are beginning to appear in the publication. The following is a partial commentary from an article entitled, "Where is Christ?" by Joe:

> In his book, *New Seeds of Contemplation*, Thomas Merton opines: 'It is the gift of God Who in His mercy completes the hidden and mysterious work of creation . . . by awakening in us the awareness that we are words spoken in His One Word, and that the Creating Spirit (*Creator Spiritus*) dwells in us. That we are 'in Christ' and that Christ lives in us.' How many times have we looked up to the skies seeking God? Is heaven there above us? Is that where Christ awaits our return home . . .. Ergo, if we do not listen to the voice inside us (the voice of God) then we need to be silent and reflective in our daily meditations. Be still. Be quiet. Listen. You will hear the love of God has instilled in all of our hearts.

What can I say? Joe had captured the divine moment that resonates with my own journey as a prodigal trying to find my way home.

There is much more of course. My joy has been in the many hours devoted to researching and writing about Thomas Merton, especially as his life intersected with other religious and literary personages. The best way to end is where I started, with my first book, *The Sign of Jonas*: "You who sleep in my breast, are not met with words, but in the emergence of life within life and of wisdom within wisdom. You are found in communion" (*The Sign of Jonas*, 361-362). My journey as a prodigal is not quite over and may it be consummated with a discovery of my "older unity" that includes my "brothers and sisters" culminating in a wordless communication—a communion with "You who sleep in my breast."

The Older Brother Who Leapt

Simeon Leiva-Merikakis, OCSO

Thomas Merton burst unexpectedly into my life when I was fifteen years old, a sophomore in high school. During religion class that fateful day my ears perked up when I heard Brother Hugh relate with his usual dry humor the story of a man who had now become a famous writer and whom the Franciscans would forevermore bemoan having rejected from their novitiate, apparently on account of his shady past. It seems that, after enjoying a lion's share of the bohemian life in New York, that young man had, by a stunning reversal of lifestyle, suddenly become a monk in, of all places, the Kentucky boonies, and in the most austere of all Catholic Orders. He had traded Manhattan for Appalachia.

MONK! From history books I knew that such mysterious beings had once walked the earth. But in *my* place and time? I was then living in the South, and the year was 1961.

Right after class I shot like an arrow to the library, and I shall never forget the moment, or the shelf just above my head from which I took down a copy of *The Seven-Storey Mountain.* Even better were its companion volumes—*The Waters of Siloe, The Silent Life*—because these contained explicit photos as well as seductive text, both of ancient Cistercian abbeys in Europe and of American monasteries of more recent foundation. The photos included an anonymous shot of an American monk (whom I only later identified as Father Louis himself) as he alluringly walked away from the camera into the woods. "Why not join me?" the monk seemed to be whispering.

The experience of seeing those pictures and reading those captions, as I stood there transfixed in the library of Christopher Columbus High School in Miami that random day in 1961, was very much like the experience of falling in love. The lightning bolt had hit home irreversibly. Brother Hugh's casually entertaining story in religion class on that particular day, in fact, changed my life forever; witness the fact that I am writing these lines as a 67-year-old Cistercian monk of St. Joseph's Abbey in the boonies of Massachusetts.

For the rest of my high-school years I systematically devoured every line Merton had written that I could find. Years passed before I found anyone else who nurtured a similar "secret relationship" with the famous writer-monk. The more I read him, the more certain I was—with a kind of overwhelming self-evidence—that I, too, was destined to become a monk.

With time I noticed that I much preferred those books in which Merton described monastic life and history in detail to others in which he held forth more generically about spiritual subjects. My all-time favorites were *The Sign of Jonas* and *Conjectures of a Guilty Bystander,* because here I could re-live moment by moment the feelings and thoughts of an honest-to-goodness contemporary monk. Merton's enthusiasm for Cistercian life lent a preternatural aura even to his trials of physical endurance and the long stretches of interior desert. Merton's narrative captured the monk's odyssey so vividly that the vicarious experience made me giddy with anticipation. Within a few months I surrendered, and accomplished the unthinkable: I boldly broke through what I then considered an awesome time-barrier into the medieval world by penning and sending a letter to the vocations director at Gethsemani.

It is Merton the Monk that has always appealed to me, much more so than Merton the Guru. True, every genuine monk should in some sense blossom into spiritual fatherhood as guide and teacher; but what most powerfully affected me in this writer, I realized years later, was not so much his thoughts and "teaching" as the life of radical faith he had freely embraced, as embodied in a monastic setting with its traditional daily round of work and prayer. Through Merton's witness and instrumentality I had fallen in love with the way of life he led and that now I desired for myself as well.

But what was it specifically about the literary medium crafted by Merton that could so magnetically draw the very young person I was into a state of enthrallment with the whole monastic project? Obviously, since all I had were Merton's *words,* my growing love for the monastic life was intimately bound up with the power of his written language.

I would say, first of all, that in Merton's style it is *experience* that holds the primacy. He is fundamentally a confessional writer: at bottom, he is always communicating or processing on paper some aspect of his own life. Though analysis and speculation are by no means foreign to him, he never takes his departure from an abstract theme or principle, but always from his own lived experience. This is why I consider that his best writing is to be found in his journals and his letters, and not in the more speculative books on the spiritual life or other subjects, although these are by no means mediocre.

Even this latter speculative-meditative genre, moreover—I refer to books such as *No Man Is an Island* and *New Seeds of Contemplation*—may in an extended sense be said to be "autobiographical," since all of Merton's books were generated out of the context of daily monastic life and cannot be properly understood, I think, apart from this concrete culture-medium. Merton always speaks as a monk. His rootedness to the very end in his identity as Christian monk of Gethsemani Abbey is illustrated for me most movingly when I remember the inventory of the homey, use-worn items that were found in his possession in Bangkok at the moment of his death: his eyeglasses, his Cistercian prayer book in Latin, an icon of the Mother of God, a broken rosary.

Merton's *style of experience* is also marked by the bare-bones rhetoric of the Hemingway generation: any highfalutin flight of language, any verbal flourish that seems enamored of itself and aimed at an artificial effect, any imaginative impulse that would leave behind the nitty-gritty human coordinates of time, space, carnality, and the ambiguities of psychophysical existence: all of this is instinctively excluded by Merton as inauthentic. Merton is forever hunting for new ways to distinguish the artificial from the authentic "self," so as to move forward to a greater fullness of existence, and his skill and human warmth in verbalizing this journey continually invites new wayfarers to join him.

Merton speaks the genuine idiom of mid-20th century people, fresh from the calamity of world war and desperately searching for interior meaning against all the frantic distortions of humanness by the slogans of Hollywood, Wall Street and the Pentagon. To the contemporary malady of chronic suspicion and distrust, spawned in people's souls by disillusionment with such gospels of deceit, Merton responds with the antidote of radical honesty and self-disclosure as the necessary beginning of the path to God.

Merton didn't mind presenting himself in disarmingly naked fashion as every bit a child of his age, conspicuous for its garishness, ambition and mutual exploitation. What was it, however, that fueled Merton's life-long and extravagant generosity in self-revelation? No exhibitionistic compulsion, I presume, but, as with Augustine of Hippo, I believe the energy that drove him was the total certainty that all his doubts, vanity and wrongdoing were already cradled from the outset within an unimaginable abyss of Mercy. Merton could make himself known to us without cosmetic beautification because he had gratefully discovered himself as *already known and embraced by the love of God*. After such a discovery, why waste energy pretending?

Reading him, I too wanted to commune with the One whose healing violence and power of attraction had whisked Merton away from the neon-lit turmoil and frenzy and ruthless achieverism of the Big Apple and plunged him into a life of silence and prayer and seeming emptiness in rural Kentucky; a life of seeking, out of an avowed darkness, the radiant face of Christ. From the start Merton intuited that this vision augured an unsurpassable joy that made all renunciations infinitely worthwhile. The lure of such a transformation of soul stirred me deeply and beckoned to me far more urgently than any other endeavor I could think of. Merton had taken a leap of faith, a *salto mortale,* which to my eyes far exceeded in intensity, heroism and long-range promises any of the career possibilities or alternate ways of living proffered by contemporary American society.

When I finally met Father Louis briefly in the Gethsemani guesthouse in June, 1968—only six months before his death—I simply wanted to speak to him a heartfelt thank-you in person. He had shown me through his own struggles and choices, shared with me by those writings with their irresistible tone of intimacy, that it was not an inane romantic dream to aspire toward eternal Beauty even in the midst of a hard-nosed, pragmatic age. He had taught me by his life, more than by his words, how to distance myself from the shallowness and ruthlessness of the world in which I lived. But, above all, he had modeled for me the thrill of humbly bowing the neck of my own conceited ego to the tender persuasion of a faithful Love that does not pass away.

Grace Insists

Alexis Leiva Letayf

The meaning of life is to find your gift. The purpose of life is to give it away.

Pablo Picasso

There is no doubt that Thomas Merton both found his gift and lived his life giving it away. By fearlessly answering the call of his heart he became an inward adventurer of the Holy Spirit, paving the way for followers seeking to cultivate a radically intimate relationship with God. In *Man's Search for Ultimate Meaning*, Viktor Frankl writes "A human being is a majestic being who, when he rises to full human stature, is recognizably created in the image of God" (85). In Merton's powerful writing I recognize a majestic being who rose to this kind of full stature. Frankl also spoke of human beings as "repressed angels." Despite fear, neuroses and human limitation, Merton took action, never stopped growing and gave away his light like a bright angel.

At twenty years old, when I discovered Merton, I was in need of light. I was desperate to find both my own purpose and reasons to believe in humanity. I also needed to know that a human being was capable of the greatness and power Frankl spoke of. In my heart I knew that all was already one and that God was Being itself, and though I had at times experienced oneness and the dropping away of a separate self, my prevailing, day-to-day reality was full of alienation, hate and distrust. Why so much Divorce if we are already one? Are we really "repressed angels"? Had we all, in deed, fallen from Grace? Did God abandon us? At this crucial juncture in my search, I discovered the great Thomas Merton. What a blessing indeed!

Merton once said that we carry within ourselves the mystery of transformation. Despite the intimidating level of existential accountability this statement implied, I was enthused to take it on because it put the power in my hands and gave me something to immediately work with. He also described that, "Prayer and love are learned in the hour when prayer has become impossible and your heart has turned to stone." To hear it explained in this way and to know I was not alone infused my dark hour with a sense of glorious purpose and faith in the human journey. With Merton as my guiding light, I decided to face my own gloomy soul and find God in the dark. As Carl Jung stated, "We come to enlightenment by making the darkness conscious" ("The Philosophical Tree," Alchemical Studies, 335).

After learning more about the man and reading *New Seeds of Contemplation*, *Dialogues with Silence* and *The Intimate Merton*, I chose to both believe in and imitate Merton. I realized that if I were to find the key to redemptive transformation within, I would have to wholly serve the all-encompassing referential point we call "God" with the same unflinching tenacity and drastically disciplined Faith that Merton embodied. In the book *Acedia and Me,* Kathleen Norris writes that the monk "has bet everything that he is on his vocation. It is a question of resolve that arises in the wake of a decisive choice for which the monk has risked his life and to which he must hold to realize full potential in oneness with God" (43). Merton made these vows, and from my point of view, his life became an offering in the form of total service to his Beloved Other. Completely giving himself to monastic life and showing up day after day, with all his human limitations, willing to continually put himself at issue in the name of something bigger than himself is extra-ordinary. This is life as an act of courage: to bet one's whole life on God! And that we, his readers, get to nourish ourselves with the wisdom, insight and even humor of his epic journey inspires a magnitude of gratitude in me. What a marvelous contribution to humanity to have both captured and shared the story of his great spirit in literary form!

Beyond the priceless content that Merton brought forth in his writing, what most inspires me about the man is the seemingly bottomless, unparalleled doggedness with which he cultivated a relationship with God. Under the microscope of his heartfelt faith, he seemed always open to take on a not-often-seen level of existential answerability. By taking the whole of his humanity on, in the heart of silence and community, with what I recognized as a will for utmost sincerity and transparency before his Creator, he showed the rest of us just how deep our faith and spiritual inquiry can go.

After fourteen years of staunch self-introspection in my own, Merton-inspired, daily journaling routine, I unearthed a broad-spectrum source of the despair I mentioned earlier and learned that it grew out of unresolved childhood sadness. Finding no clarity or resolution as a child, my sadness turned into teenage anger, which after time, spread thin and turned into self-righteous resignation, overgrown resentment and full-blown mistrust. I got caught up in a mostly unconscious and delusional lifestyle of insistence on separateness. What I didn't realize was that by habitually running from my darkness I gave monstrous mass to it. In attempts to understand my melancholy, I spent much time belittling and blaming everyone for the unworkability of my life, including God, society, my family, and myself. My defensive posture of strategic and faithless love tangled me up in a dualistic double bind trap that became reconcilable only when I took on the level of introspection and existential accountability that Merton himself became the incarnation of. "It takes real courage," Merton insists, "to recognize that we ourselves are the cause of our own unhappiness" (quoted in *Acedia and Me,* 273). And, what I know for certain now is that without letting Grace have Her way with me, the possibility of redemptive transformation would be impossible. That redemption even be a possibility is a testament to the benevolent order of our merciful universe. That a wholly unified plane of inextricable Being be here for the human being to tune into and be is reason enough to run to the top of Earth's highest hill to enthusiastically shout out, "*Grace insists till kingdom come!*"

Thomas Merton clearly found his gift and spent his life giving it away. When Merton spoke of communion being the deepest level of communication possible, I again remember the words of Viktor Frankl: "Whenever you are talking to yourself in utmost sincerity and ultimate solitude, he to whom you are referring may justifiably be called" God (171). Merton was touched with a living fire that burned with radical curiosity for ever-deepening levels of being, knowing and faithfulness before his Creator. His very desire to pray and reach the deepest level of pure authenticity before God mirrors Grace's bottomless indwelling and is evidence enough to see the Holy Spirit alive, "at full stature" in his human being. The exceptional standard Merton held himself to points to a kind of bottomless well of holy fuel all us humans draw our life from. His thirst for Truth was such that he must've needed to draw more out than the average Joe for his light shone bright!

What I have learned from Thomas Merton is that we are all created in the image of God. Though some of us may be more or less "repressed" than others, we are all equally sacred and angelic. Merton's life clearly mirrored God's own unquenchable thirst to know and expand what is possible through us, His own curious creations. I wildly assert that perhaps even God doesn't know what's coming next because He so loves us that He grants His creatures the miraculous power and freedom to create fate. God's along for the ride too and oh, how He must delight in the light of His Merton!

A Spiritual Guide For Social Change

Thomas Del Prete

Thomas Merton was both a man of his time and a man who lived on the margins of his time, a man in his world, but not necessarily of it. Driven partly by the sense of rootlessness and seeming self-destructiveness of the middle twentieth century that weighed heavily on him as a young man, he began an intellectual quest that turned increasingly spiritual. Encouraged to search inwardly, he struck out on what he would come to call the real journey of life, the interior journey (*The Asian Journal of Thomas Merton*). Along the way he discovered for himself and drew our attention to our deeper selves, our selves beyond socially constructed temporal, geographical, psychological, and interpersonal boundaries, our selves in "the hidden ground of love." In the face of anomie, he offered the possibility of authenticity; confronted by various forces saying "no" to life, he said "Yes." When questioned about "what" to do, about taking action on pressing issues of war and peace, he responded, "Who are we who ask?" Searching for who he was, he found others as well; in a time of division, he apprehended our deeper unity and communion.

There can be little doubt that today, well into a new century, Merton would respond similarly to persistent signs of our inwardly and outwardly divided humanity: struggles with personal and social identity, economic disparities, political and cultural animosities, ideological polarities. For Merton, like Augustine and others before him, could not rest until he was on solid ground about who he was and who we are and living authentically. I can only imagine him pursuing his vocation as a Christian contemplative and spiritual writer, as an intercultural and interreligious interlocutor, as a voice for peace and social justice, as an active contemplative witness. As before, I think he would appropriate language in a way that would communicate across the fractured surfaces of our lives and resonate with some of our deeper intuitions and with our deepest experience of being. Presumably he would take some advantage of new technologies and tools for communication.

What I am suggesting is that Merton is at least as important to us now as he was before, that we still need to hear his message calling us to be what we are and to make the contributions that we can uniquely make in discerning and meeting the particular human needs and possibilities of our time. Merton might say, as he suggests in *No Man Is an Island*, that we all have a particular vocation in this regard, not simply our work vocation, but our vocation to be, to say and to do as the unique persons we are, loved by God. In other words, as Merton makes clear in his essay "Learning to Live" (*Love and Living*), our contributions will come from who we are, and get expressed in ways which cannot be measured in the conventional terms of success which exert such powerful influence in our social worlds.

Perhaps, like me, you feel strongly the challenge of understanding and fulfilling your vocation as a person in the context of your everyday life and work. On the one hand, there is the daily challenge of opening up an interior space in which our sense of a deeper or authentic self and, correspondingly, our deeper relatedness to others, might grow and deepen. On the other, there is the challenge of acting and responding in a complex social world in a way that flows from this deeper integrity. Of course, this is not necessarily a one-way process. As Merton reminds us in characteristically paradoxical terms, we find ourselves by losing ourselves, we discover ourselves by discovering others (*No Man Is an Island*) or in "mature collaboration with others" (*Contemplation in a World of Action*). We become who we are in relatedness, in our common identity in the hidden ground of love, or what Merton might say is our "Christ-self" (At one point in a talk on Faulkner's "The Bear" that he gave to his fellow monks, he refers to his Christ-self).

In my own case, the struggle to act authentically is located in work tied to teacher education and urban public schooling in the United States. While this work is defined at its core by a commitment to the development of each child intellectually and personally, with implicit respect for who each is and belief in the contribution each can give, it is situated in a complex environment, one rife with tension and contradiction. In the effort to close the achievement gap which separates, in large part, poor students of all backgrounds from others, policy for more than two decades has shifted to systems of test-based accountability in which teachers and students both are measured and evaluated against some set of standards. The dominant assumption is that the root cause of underperformance is lack of quality effort on the part of teachers and schools. The theory of change appears to be that you will get more if you measure more and hold accountable those who do not measure up, including penalizing them. After years of following this formula, however, it seems clear that we have exhausted whatever usefulness it has had in drawing attention to and solving a persistent problem. And it is hard to say that the impact has been salutary overall: there is certainly evidence that education and the vocation of teaching in some places have been diminished in the process, taking the life out of one in the service of a curriculum based solely on what can be tested and taking the heart out of the other.

I do not mean to question the motivation of policy in the name of education reform. Or to suggest that there is a simple solution to the truly complex problem of improving public education for all children, particularly those in under-resourced schools, challenged neighborhoods and unstable lives. What I can try to do is to put into some kind of Mertonian perspective the question of how to define and approach the problem and, perhaps, other similar large-scale efforts at social change.

In general terms, the approach in education has followed a familiar script: focus on outcomes or results and what is measurable; focus on outcomes that will increase economic competitiveness; employ technical or uniform solutions as the most efficient and effective. Merton understood our increasing cultural tendency to frame problems and their solutions in these technical and instrumentalist terms, borrowing the approach found in a certain corporate or pseudo-scientific mind-set. He emphasized the importance of balancing quantitative values with qualitative human ones such as personal integrity, authenticity and the capacity to love (*Contemplation in a World of Action*). He kept us focused on personalistic values. He saw the importance, even in the reform of religious communities in the 1960s, of shifting to more person-centered institutions (*The Springs of Contemplation*). He also saw the danger, in movements for social change, of letting the ends justify the means, of putting so much emphasis on results as to neglect the people and work in front of us. As he advised James Forest, seeking guidance as a young leader of the peace movement, learn to focus on people, not results, learn "to be used by God's love" (*The Hidden Ground of Love*).

This is the guidance I try to heed. The question framing work such as mine is how to build authentic inclusive person-centered learning communities not only within a particular set of urban schools, but in the space formed by the intersection of the schools, a distressed but very alive neighborhood, and a university. The theory of change, such as it is, has much to do with enacting human and democratic values, a shared sense of educational purpose focused on helping students discover themselves and making college possible for all, and shared responsibility for the well-being and development of the neighborhood. It is heartening to hear of others, many inspired by the Harlem Children's Zone, moving in a similar direction, working to revitalize urban neighborhoods and schools simultaneously. There is much to hope for in person-centered, community-centered and relatedness-aware efforts such as these.

Cultivating Seeds Of Hope And Love In The 21st Century: My Personal Ruminations On Thomas Merton

Cristóbal Serrán-Pagán y Fuentes

Thomas Merton is one of my spiritual heroes. My first encounter with Merton's writings was as an undergraduate student at St. Thomas University (Miami, Florida). I took an honor's class where we read Merton's autobiography, *The Seven Storey Mountain*. Later on as a graduate student I went to Boston College and Boston University where I fell madly in love with studying mystics from all cultures and religious traditions.

Every day when I wake up I begin my ritual honoring the great spirits of St. Teresa of Avila, St. John of the Cross, Mohandas K. Gandhi, Teilhard de Chardin, Martin Luther King, Jr., Thomas Merton, Howard Thurman, Dorothy Day, Abraham Joshua Heschel, Thich Nhat Hanh, and His Holiness the XIV Dalai Lama. All these spiritual leaders share in common a deep love for humanity that transcends cultural and religious boundaries.

Merton's spiritual legacy has left a profound effect on my whole being. I am fascinated by the mystical theology of hope and love in his life and writings. The Trappist monk invites each one of us to become full partakers in building the kingdom of heaven on earth. Merton's contemplative-prophetic message is even more urgent for us today because we are in the midst of great social, political, ecological, spiritual, and religious turmoil.

Genuine mystics are able to integrate a contemplative desire for the glory and love of God with an apostolic and social commitment for their neighbor as well as for all creation. The prophetic voice demands witness and response to the most pressing moral and religious issues of our time. True contemplatives stand up as prophetic witnesses to justice and peace in their unique ways, asking for forgiveness and reconciliation in times of crisis. True mystics do not turn their backs to the suffering inflicted on millions of people in different parts of the world. They do not withdraw completely from society in a search for solitude. Instead, they protest against the individual and structural evils of their respective societies. Their spirituality is based on the ideal of building a compassionate world where peace, justice and love reign, which includes even the act of loving one's enemy.

The goal of the Christian mystic is to become God by participation so that the contemplative can share the fruits of his or her mystical vision with others by becoming a messenger of God on earth. In the Christian mystical tradition, the contemplative and the prophetic are two aspects of the same reality. Mary often symbolizes the contemplative mystic, while Martha best represents the active mystic. They complement each other. Together they symbolize the mixed life by combining action and contemplation respectively. Clearly, Merton follows this mystical tradition of contemplatives in action.

In 1958, Merton reported having a mystical vision at the corner of Fourth and Walnut Street (today renamed as Muhammed Ali Boulevard) in the business and commercial district in Louisville, Kentucky. This experience narrated in *Conjectures of a Guilty Bystander* marks Merton's transition from a life solely dedicated to prayer and contemplation to a life more engaged with the world. After this, Merton began addressing social issues more directly, and started to publicly denounce the Cold War in his letters and writings.

Merton saw the divine reflected in all things and developed a sense of cosmic interconnectedness. The epiphany that took place in Louisville has its spiritual root in his personal encounter with the source of life. Out of this contemplative experience he gains a new perspective on life. Merton is able to reach out to the world compassionately and, in doing so, he no longer ignores his moral responsibility towards both the stranger and the neighbor.

In his final year, Merton describes his own mystical experiences in his journals. Perhaps the most famous account is when he writes about his visit to Polonnaruwa. He said that he could not write adequately what he felt while he was contemplating the giant statues of the Buddha at Polonnaruwa. Merton experienced peace in its fullness, resting in complete silence before the extraordinary faces of the Buddhas. There was a sense of gratitude and awe.

On December 10, 1968, Merton received an electric shock from a faulty fan after coming out from his bath. He was in Bangkok, Thailand, attending a monastic conference. Merton the peacemaker lost his life in his beloved Asia after denouncing on numerous occasions the American participation in Vietnam. Ironically, Merton's body was transported home to North America from an Air Force Base along with the dead bodies of American soldiers who were killed in Vietnam.

Merton thought that the root of war and unnecessary violence is fear of others who are not like us or who do not think like us. The antidote for this fear is to cultivate a spiritual practice of love in action, which is based on mutual trust. Again, Merton's personal conviction has its origins in his own contemplative vision of love's transformative power, which led him to keep his high hopes in humanity intact. Merton believed that it is only through compassionate love that we can treat the other as one of us, because God is love. Each one of us is a reflection of God's love, even if we are not fully aware of it. Furthermore, Merton extended his arms not only to the oppressed but also to the oppressor. And yet, Merton did not remain neutral. He took sides with those who suffer.

Merton became a witness to the truth that God is against all forms of injustice in the world; that unnecessary suffering and moral evil is a question that affects all humans because we have the capacity to choose evil, and therefore it is our responsibility to avoid evil; and finally, that God is calling humans to participate as co-creators in building the heavenly kingdom on earth by denouncing the deepest troubles of humanity and by announcing the good news of a new reality, a new order that will definitely put a stop to the affliction and unnecessary suffering of the *anawim*, or the marginalized ones.

Merton was well aware of the need for the monk to reach out to those who suffer in this world. Merton's contemplative message stresses the practice of love in our daily lives. However, Merton did not define this Christian love as being "sentimental." In fact, Merton suggested that a theology of love cannot be authentic if it serves the interests of the rich and powerful to the detriment of the *anawim*. Indeed, Merton recognized the danger of escapism, especially within monastic circles. He warned his religious brothers and sisters not to remain indifferent to the social and religious problems of their fellow human beings. Merton clearly spoke out his mind as a mystical prophet by fulfilling his contemplative vision in the world.

Children of the twentieth-first century are witnessing similar fears to those of Merton's age. On the one hand, we are facing the fears of personal insecurities such as conditions of poverty, of unemployment, of misfortune, of domestic violence, of lack of success, or of social acceptance. On the other hand, the global fears of terrorism, of unjust wars, of fundamentalisms, of illegal immigrants, of ecological tragedies, are the signs of our times.

The people of the world are desperately crying out for signs of hope. They are longing for new leaders who can address their social, economic and spiritual needs of the world in humane ways. Many of us wonder what our leaders are saying and doing in the midst of massive turmoil. I believe the contemplative message of Merton can help us identify the root of our contemporary problems by asking the right questions. This deep questioning in search for solutions will require from us a creative response that can directly and effectively address the most urgent problems of our time.

The Trappist monk has become a beacon of hope for humanity because he never gave up in his search for truth, peace, justice, and love. Merton devoted his life to the pursuit of building a more just and humane society where each sentient and non-sentient being is respected and valued. Merton understood the unique role each being plays in the unfolding drama of the universe. For him, a true mystic is one who actively engages and participates in the social and spiritual struggles of his or her time.

I am thankful to Merton for having planted the seeds of hope and love in his own days. His contemplative message is universal in scope. The Trappist monk brought us a prophetic message of real and everlasting peace, justice and love. His impact in today's world resonates even louder since most of his writings are available to us now. The major task ahead of us today is to reinterpret Merton's own words using a contemporary language that speaks to new generations. I see myself as one of those Mertonian scholars who have taken seriously the great responsibility of passing the torch to younger generations so that we can all become real agents of love in action.

Celebrating Merton's 100th Birthday

Erlinda G. Paguio

As we celebrate the 100th birthday of Thomas Merton, we look back at the informal talk that he delivered in Calcutta in October, 1968 during the First Temple of Understanding Conference (*The Asian Journal of Thomas Merton*, 305). He identified himself as a monk and a marginal person who withdrew deliberately from established society to deepen his experience of life. In his essay, "Love and Solitude," he teaches us, however, that solitude is not a withdrawal from ordinary life; solitude is the ground of ordinary life (*Love and Living*, 22). Speaking from experience, Merton also writes that the marginal man accepts the basic irrelevance of the human condition as it is manifested by the fact of death. He struggles with the fact of death in himself and attempts to find something deeper than death. The monk or the marginal person goes beyond the dichotomy of life and death to become a witness to life. In Merton's section on "Death," in his essay "Seven Words for Ned O'Gorman" (*Love and Living*, 97-105), he asks readers to see death as part of a living continuity that contributes something decisive to the meaning of life. Returning to his essay, "Love and Solitude," he writes about living like a seed planted in the ground and dying in the ground to become fruitful. He believes that our fruitfulness is at once an act of faith and an act of doubt. The act of doubting and "dying" to what we have always conceived ourselves to be, dissolving our ego-identity, becomes fruitful as it leads to faith, a being "born again" to the person we couldn't imagine ourselves to be, that is, new persons in Christ (*The New Man*, 88-91).

Merton spoke confidently of God as the only ultimate reality Who lives and dwells in all of us and Who speaks to us and calls us to find our relevance in Him. Merton admits the presence of loneliness in our life and the need for us to admit our loneliness and to live with our loneliness. He added that our capacity to love is limited and it has to be complemented with our capacity to be loved. Merton gifts us with his insight that the deepest level of communication is communion. His fidelity to his vocation as a monk and a solitary gave him a real experience of communion with persons of other religious traditions such as the Zen Buddhist, D. T. Suzuki; the Sufi, Abdul Aziz, from Pakistan; Sheikh Abdeslam from Algeria; Rabbi Abraham Heschel; the Dalai Lama; and many others.

The reality of communion being the deepest level of communication is possible also in our own ordinary life and in our relationships with persons who are given to us in this moment in our life. I am called at this time in my life to be the primary caregiver to my mother in Louisville and to some extent to an aunt in Michigan. As I became more aware of a vast segment in our society who are aging and who need much attention, I was moved to look into Merton's writings for his observations and attitude towards the elderly.

On August 16, 1960, Merton visited the Little Sisters of the Poor in Louisville. He was so impressed by the work of the Little Sisters among the elderly poor that he wrote to Mother Sylvia Marie, superior of the Little Sisters. He was saddened by the fact that old age was not well understood:

> There is a kind of foolish legend about old people, a legend in which the old are rendered acceptable because they retain some vestiges of youth, but for that reason and no other. (We use foolish platitudes which praise the old for being 'like kids' rather than for the dignity of their age.) It is certainly very fine for old people to be full of vigor and verve of youth, but they should not have to cling to that *alone* as a way of being acceptable to the rest of the world. On the contrary, love. This is what the Little Sisters of the Poor are able to recognize and live for. What they see in the old people is not some vestige of natural 'pep,' but the light and the joy and the mystery of Christ, which gives them a far greater and wonderful energy, in spite of the feebleness of their limbs (*The School of Charity*, 135-136).

Merton expressed his joy at visiting the Little Sisters of the Poor and seeing their work among the elderly. He commended the Little Sisters for seeing not just "specimens" of aging humanity but temples of God, persons of dignity who were travelling to the threshold of eternity and were waiting to be called into the joy of their Lord.

Merton was only 53 when he died in 1968. When he turned 50 in 1965, he wrote in his journal that he realized that he was just beginning to awaken and that there was still much awakening to come. He wrote: "To take my fiftieth birthday as a turning point and to live more abandoned to God's will, less concerned with projects and initiatives" (*Dancing in the Water of Life*, 195). On his 51st birthday he summed up the activities that engaged him. He was concerned about his health, with his back problems, the dermatitis in his hands and his stomach problems. He wrote that "in all these things I see one central option for me: to let go of all that seems to suggest getting somewhere, being someone, having a name and a voice . . .. What matters is to *love*, to be in one place in silence, if necessary in suffering, sickness, tribulation, and not try to be anybody outwardly" (*Learning to Love*, 13-15). On his 52nd birthday, Merton waited for a well to be dug near his hermitage. A month later, in February, 1967, he evaluated his publications and thought that some of his best work had been published since 1957. A few days after his 53rd birthday, January 31, 1968, Merton wrote in his journal: "I need quiet. I need to get down to more reading and meditation. The problem of people is of my own making—as problem and as ambiguity" (*The Other Side of the Mountain*, 50).

Some of Merton's writing reveals his relationship with old monks in his community. He wrote about Brother Gerard, an aged monk who had made baskets for a long time. Brother Gerard told him about a Brother Stephen who used to make baskets for everyone at Gethsemani. Brother Stephen died suddenly so no one made baskets for the monks anymore. Brother Gerard learned to repair the old baskets and eventually learned to make new ones. Brother Gerard told Merton that he had made many baskets and sold them at the gatehouse of the monastery. Merton valued Brother Gerard's weaving skills greatly. He wanted his novices to learn how to weave baskets from Brother Gerard before he died or before he grew too old to weave them. Merton wrote that "when a brother is very old he sits only in the infirmary chapel, close to the window, right at the side of the altar, reading from a prayer book or a book of meditations, no longer weaving baskets" (*Conjectures of A Guilty Bystander*, 26-28).

In one of his conferences in Alaska, Merton talked about another old monk, Father Stephen, who was obsessed with gardening. One abbot insisted that he should stop gardening, but the next abbot assigned him to be a gardener. Merton had a great affection for Father Stephen and thought that he was a saint. Merton recalled how Father Stephen put his whole life into gardening and how he would sometimes surprise the visiting parents of a monk with a big bouquet of flowers. He died in a little garden by the gatehouse. During his funeral, it seemed like the whole of nature was in attendance, the sun shining brightly and the birds singing.

While he was in Singapore in 1968, Merton informed Brother Patrick Hart in a letter that the mail he received included a nice newsy letter from Father Idesbald (*The School of Charity*, 415). As Timothy Kelley, the former abbot at the Abbey of Gethsemani, described him, Father Alphonse, who used to be called Father Idesbald, was a very old monk from Belgium. He had come to the United States right after World War I. He had forgotten his Flemish and did not speak English well and did not speak much French either. He apparently was considered a real "character" in the community. Although he was a good person, he was someone to whom you did not pay much attention. Father Timothy then went on to recall that on the day Merton's death was announced as the monks ate in the refectory, Father Idesbald approached Father Timothy and said: "You know, they said he died, but I just got this postcard from Father Louis." The postcard was from Bangkok, Thailand. Father Timothy recalled this moment to highlight that here was the true Thomas Merton: "Very much aware of people in the community and specially the marginal people, and very willing to acknowledge their presence in just a simple show of friendship" ("The Great Honesty: Remembering Thomas Merton," *Merton Annual 9*, 202-203).

Dementia and loneliness are present among the aged. I see it in my elderly relatives. The phone rings and it is a relative from another state reaching out to visit with me and share some stories with me. I have heard some of these stories already, but I listen as if it was the first time that I had heard it. My 91-year old mother asks me when she wakes up: "What day is it today?" "It is Monday," I reply. She asks me the same question a few more times during the day and I silently pray that I will have patience to say gently again and again: "It is Monday today." I write a short note to my 87-year old aunt in Michigan and tell her we miss her and will visit her soon. I call her up on the phone, too, but her hearing is not as sharp as it used to be. I worry about her when she gets sick and is taken to the hospital. I appreciate the care that relatives and professional caregivers give to her. Being so far away, I can only pray that she will be well.

Every summer, my aging neighbor, who lives across from the front of our house, never fails to bring me fresh vegetables that he has grown in his garden. He always helps me whenever I need some assistance in the yard or in the house. He had heart surgery a year ago and after a few days a stroke left him less able to do the gardening that he loved to do. His wife said he did not want to talk about his health and did not want any visitors. I brought baked goods for his wife and him when I could. I looked out of the window one day and saw him sitting on his porch. Hoping it was the right time to visit with him, I was moved to walk over. I greeted him and he welcomed me and we talked about our yard and about our health. He could not grow as many vegetables as he used to, but last fall he brought me a variety of hot peppers. "Give some of them to your officemates," he said.

Merton said that solitude is the very ground of our ordinary life. All of us are called to *be*—to be one with Christ and to be one with whomever He sends to us or to whomever we are sent.

A Gift For My Faith

Mario Zaninelli

Thomas Merton has been a gift for my faith. I never met him. I have read most of his books. I can say that, without presumption but in humility, he formed my spirituality, too. As many people, I can say that I would have wanted to meet and know him, but when he died, I was only 7 years old. Now, a hundred years after his birth, I have the possibility, through this volume in honor of his centenary, to express my gratitude. It is an honor for me to take part in this volume that remembers the great man and priest whom Merton has been and continues to be for all of us. I hope he can be the same for all who will read this book and who have not yet read his books.

To be a messenger of hope in our time is not easy, but Merton's approach to this vocation is illustrative and helpful. First, he helps us to look inside ourselves, contacting our own deep sense of spirituality and humanity. He also looked inside himself to make his own definition of what it would mean for him to be a monk. One of the characteristics Merton discovered in being a monk was that he was not an ordinary person and lived on the margins of society. However, this marginality is deliberately chosen, a responsible and sincere withdrawal. To be a marginal person is to exercise one's right to freedom. The monk is a very strange kind of person, a marginal person because in the modern world he is no longer an established person with an established place in society. He is essentially outside all establishments, not part of an establishment.

Is it not true that for us, too, as Christians today, we find ourselves living, acting and working at the margins of our societies? The difference, however, between a Christian and a vowed monk is that we, unlike monks, do not choose marginality as a deliberate choice with a view, as Merton wrote "to deepening fundamental human experience." We Christians in "the world" are, however, also "marginal" by desiring to find God in each person we meet in our life and doing so without any sort of judgment. We are not monks but we strive, too, in our own everyday ways to become "marginal in Christ," living our lives in Him and only for Him.

We, too, share Merton's vocation to live as messengers of hope to anyone who crosses our lives' paths, especially those who with us experience both faith and doubt. Merton understood that faith also implied doubt. Our lives of faith, our vocations to be as salt for the earth, obliges us continually to study the roots of our faith and the historical conditions in which Christian faith evolved. In this way, we can realize that God lives and dwells in us. We can become witnesses to life, understanding that our lives have only one direction towards the only ultimate reality who is God, and this because we live out our Christian faith accepting and admitting that our lives are totally irrelevant in order to find our relevance in Him. This life of being on the margins through faith is not just for monks. This marginal way of life is for everyone who seeks to be

God's companion in this magnificent adventure we call Life.

Christian life at the margins ideally represents a life that is an openness to gifts from God and others. Christians realize that they are part of a larger society and that we have to inter-act with one another so as to build a new and a better world. Our marginality does not make us solitaries but opens us to communion as we develop, as Merton taught, not only our capacities to love, but also our capacities to be loved by others, admitting to others our loneliness as everybody is lonely.

Living lives of faith is to live conscious of our communion with everyone, not only at the level of communication but also at the deepest level of our contemplative daily prayer. We must daily be converted to living a life of Christian faith and hope. We need to live the value of *conversio morum* (conversion of manners) as found in *The Rule of Saint Benedict*. During his last conference in Bangkok on 10 December, 1968 Merton spoke to his fellow monastics about this essential vow that is relevant for all Christians vowed to *conversio morum* or not:

> When you stop and think a little bit about St. Benedict's concept of *conversio morum*, that most mysterious of our vows, which is actually the most essential, I believe, it can be interpreted as a commitment to total inner transformation of one sort or another—a commitment to become a completely new man. It seems to me that that could be regarded as the end of the monastic life, and that no matter where one attempts to do this, that remains the essential thing (*The Asian Journal of Thomas Merton*, 337).

As Novice Master, Merton taught that our *conversio* is toward becoming God's own image of Himself in us:

> What God seeks of us is 'His own image in ourselves.' This image is not something that we can produce by our own efforts. Indeed we do not have to produce it. It is already there. It is the simple reality of our true being as sons of God by grace. Our job in life is not so much to produce anything, as to 'be what we are supposed to be,' to let the divine image come out and manifest itself in our life by the 'way in which we live.' The life of the vows is not ordered to producing anything special, or at least not primarily. It is supposed rather to create certain conditions under which we live in a certain way which is most adapted to make us grow in likeness to God: The life of the vows is a life of divine sonship, a life in which we deepen our realization of our kinship with God by deepening our holiness, our likeness to Him, our union with His will. The concept of man as the image of God is incomprehensible to modern thought. The very idea of God, for modern materialism, is at best a subjective need of man, a sort of illusion that is psychologically necessary for the happiness of some—and hence it can be accepted in so far as it 'works'—in so far as it 'produces a desirable effect.' No question [is raised] as to whether or not religion is 'true.' This conception has nothing to do with a truly religious outlook on life (*The Life of the Vows*, 9-10).

The only useful thing to accomplish in our lives is finding union with God. Our contemplative work is to receive the beautiful gift of the faith in the revelation that God loves us and wants our Unity. One indispensible means to our "original unity" is the silent prayer that each of us is enjoined to pray no matter what our faith tradition. In prayer we discover our communion and that "what we have to be is what we are." In prayer we receive the grace to become "messengers of hope."

God's love for humanity is our hope. In his journal for 27 November 1961 Merton wrote:

> From this kind of love necessarily springs hope, hope even for political action, for here paradoxically hope is most necessary. Hope is always most necessary precisely where everything, spiritually, seems hopeless. And this is precisely in the confusion of politics. Hope against hope that man can gradually disarm and cease preparing for destruction and learn at last the he 'must' live at peace with his brother. Never have we been less disposed to do this. It must be learned, it must be done and everything else is secondary to this supremely urgent need of man (*Turning Toward the World*, 183).

To be faithful to a life of "hoping against hope" is to accept a consciousness at the margins of the habitual ways of "the world." But we should not fear this fidelity to living at the margins. Beyond all our doubts, Merton declared and prayed, "Our hope is victorious" (*A Search for Solitude*, 71).

Somebody's Gift:
A Universal Language For The Contemplative Vision

Joseph Quinn Raab

The poet Robert Lax envisioned a day when somebody would come along and start telling us what we've really been wanting to hear and needing to know; somebody "who is capable of telling [us] of the love of God in language that will no longer sound hackneyed or crazy, but with authority and conviction: the conviction born of sanctity" (*The Seven Storey Mountain*, 259). Perhaps the prophetic Lax knew that *that somebody* would turn out to be *his buddy*—Tom Merton. Lax's vision captures, perhaps more than anything else, what Merton means to me. He is somebody whose beautiful language convicts and consoles, and in myriad guises of poetry and prose, sounds the singular truth that Love is "all in all." One hundred years since he came into the world and lived so passionately a beautiful and brief life, his language continues to speak with authority and conviction of the God who is Love.

I want to resist being too effusive—that would only disgust both Merton and me. He was just a man after all. I belong to an age suspicious of authority, guarded against those whom J. D. Salinger described as "conceited little tearer-downers, pedants, wisenheimers, and charlatans." But Merton was able to sneak past my defenses because he was not perched on a pedestal—he was messed up like me. Yet, because he was so endearingly honest about his constant struggles, he possessed an attractive humility, and from his authenticity emerged his authority. So I, like countless others, have been able to listen to him and have learned some marvelous things.

If I had to identify his most precious gift to me it would be his training me, through the power of his own language, "to see heaven in a wildflower"—as William Blake had put it. This vision is rarely granted with visceral consolation, but Merton's perpetual pointing and his opening with wonderful words the window blinds to the omnipresent God makes it much easier to see. These visions, and Merton's language expressing them, fortify my feeble faith—keep me hopeful and in love. As a parent and a teacher I long to be a messenger of this hope and love to my own children and to students. I'd like to be able to share with them this sacramental vision and to do so I continue to learn from Merton.

The clarity of Merton's sacramental vision correlates with the strength of his conviction that the Word through whom all things were made assumes in the Incarnation much more than an abstract human nature. Becoming flesh, the omnipresent God assumes all life and all matter, "fruit of the vine and work of human hands"—all of it. Through his masterful and powerful language, Merton could share his vision, leaving his readers wide-eyed and gasping in the divine, mystical body of God. This is his gift.

Even if I must endure long periods void of ecstatic or even mildly comforting spiritual experience, I can always return to his words for a shot of vicarious wonder. Many times I have returned to *The Asian Journal* and to his epiphany before the stone Buddha statues in Sri Lanka. I invite you now to return there with me.

On the first of December in 1968 and in the last days of his life on earth, Merton was visiting the caves and giant stone carvings in the park of Gal Vihara in Polonnaruwa. He arrived at the tourist destination with his escort, the Vicar General of the Kandy Diocese. Upon their arrival "a mustachioed guide" who exuded formality and nobility greeted them. He led them through the ancient caves adorned with gold Buddha statues and frescoes depicting and celebrating various scenes from the great expanse of Buddhist mythology. As the docent elaborated on the artifacts, Merton's desire intensified while the Vicar General's interest only waned. Merton later recalled that his clerical companion was unmoved by the "pagan art" and suspicious of the cunning *bhikkhus* whom he thought were out to cheat them. Soon the Vicar decided to drop back and sit down under a tree to peruse the guidebook he had brought along. This allowed Merton to approach the giant stone Buddhas at the end of the path winding down into Gal Vihara alone and undisturbed.

Attending fully to the massive and fluid figures of stone, to *Parinirvana* reclining in an oceanic swoon of peace and bliss, to the standing Buddha, whom Merton mistook to be Ananda, and to the reclining Buddha, Merton was suddenly "jerked clean out of the habitual half-tied vision of things" and with the overwhelming clarity of a sudden insight he "pierced through the surface and got beyond the shadow and the disguise" (*The Asian Journal of Thomas Merton*, 233-234).

It would take Merton a couple of days before he would attempt to unpack this experience in his journal. The epiphany, like others that had graced his life, left him struggling to shape a language that could meaningfully communicate its abundantly rich and over-determined quality. He even wondered if he had not already spoiled it by trying to speak of his realization in casual conversations with mere acquaintances. Yet the writer did submit to his impulse. A few days later, about one week before his untimely death at the monastic conference in Bangkok, Merton sat down with his journal and pen. After conceding that he "could not write hastily" of the experience and could still not write "at all adequately," he began to piece together an image of those Buddhas whose faces shone with peace, with *samadhi*, a calm tranquility of heart. Remembering how he marveled at the carved rock, he described the figures:

> The great smiles. Huge yet subtle. Filled with every possibility, questioning nothing, knowing everything, rejecting nothing, the peace not of emotional resignation, but of Madhyamika, of sunyata, that has seen through every question without trying to discredit anyone or anything—without refutation—without establishing some other argument. For the doctrinaire, the mind that needs well-established positions, such peace, such silence, can be frightening (*AJ*, 233).

Seeing these figures he became enraptured by the overwhelming insight that suddenly seized him; he wrote:

> An inner clearness, a clarity as if exploding from the rocks themselves became evident and obvious . . . All problems are resolved and everything is clear, simply because what matters is clear. The rock, all matter, all life is charged with dhar-

makaya, everything is emptiness and everything is compassion . . . I know and have seen what I was obscurely looking for (*AJ*, 233-234).

What strange providence had brought this man all the way from Prades to Polonnaruwa just so that he might have a vision, like Simeon's, permitting him "to go in peace" (Luke 2: 29-32). This integrating vision occurred on Buddhist soil, was facilitated by Buddhist art, articulated in Buddhist language, and yet was nonetheless profoundly incarnational and sacramental. The transcendence and immanence of "emptiness and compassion" converge inseparably in the *dhrmakaya*—the truth-body. Everything culminates here and we can see along with him, in this rock, in these stones, truth's mystical body. What a gift!

Merton was very good at seeing "truth in all its various manifestations" and then writing convincingly about it. Yet he never intended his own words to be the focus— they were merely functional—enabling us to move to the silent communion that precedes and transcends all the illusory divisions, all the labels. I am still a novice learning how to glimpse this unifying love. I am still like a wide-eyed child on Christmas morning, delightfully un-wrapping his gifted words to unveil the omnipresence of the one Word's mystical body. Thomas Merton is somebody like you and me. Yes he is, thankfully.

Seeing The Gates Of Heaven Everywhere

Donna Kristoff, OSU

Thomas Merton has spoken most clearly to me at times of transition in my life. My drawings interpreting Merton's writing, especially from his journals and poetry, initially served as the means for me to learn to use the computer as a new drawing medium after I left teaching. In order to think about each movement of the mouse, to struggle to get a line to go where I wanted it, I needed to have in my heart something deeply personal, something I "knew" by intuition so as to free myself to concentrate on mastering a new technique. Hours would fly by, and, except for a sore neck, I was never tired. Eventually I was able to forget about the tool and draw as freely as I did with a traditional brush and pen. Having become familiar with Gethsemani and the hermitage and sketching on my retreats there in every season, I could easily imagine Merton in his landscape and one that had also become mine. Some of my drawings/paintings try to hint at the *point vierge* (virgin point) and the *temps vierge* (virgin time), contemplative moments that Merton describes in some of his most beautiful passages. I hope my images convey a sense of solitude and silence, a stillness full of presence and prayer that I found in meditating with Merton. It was a joy for me to discover in Merton someone who felt the impact of art on one's life as I had since childhood and to share with him his love of Eastern Christian iconography. Merton's life and experience, from birth until death, demonstrate clearly that the arts are a powerful, even integral, means to union with God. I cannot think of any saints canonized by the church *because* they were artists. This seems to me to be terrible oversight. From my viewpoint, Thomas Merton's struggle for sanctity was worked out fundamentally *through the arts*. What a gift to the future of our world would a "martyr" or witness to human creativity and artistic work be in a canonized Father Louis, OCSO.

The Gate of Heaven is Everywhere, digital drawing by Donna Kristoff, OSU.

The poet enters into himself in order to create. The contemplative enters into God in order to be created, digital drawing by Donna Kristoff, OSU.

Turning To Thomas Merton
As Our Guide In Contemplative Living

James Finley

I am grateful to Thomas Merton for his wise and trustworthy guidance in the gentle art of contemplative living. In the brief space available here, I will focus on some foundational aspects of his wise and trustworthy guidance. I will begin with Merton's emphasis on the importance of grounding our search for God in our customary experience of ourselves as human beings. The ring of authenticity that resonates in Merton's writings flows, in part at least, from the honesty with which he shares with us his own struggles and breakthroughs in the day by day realities in which he searched for and found God in his life. His down to earth honesty lets us know he is like us and in doing so he lets us know we are like him. We, too, are endowed by God as human beings to seek and find God in the nitty-gritty details of our own daily struggles and aspirations. In a passage that expresses this aspect of Merton's teachings he writes:

> Often, the inertia and repugnance which characterize the so-called spiritual life of many Christians could perhaps be cured by simple respect for the concrete realities of everyday life, for nature, for the body, for one's work, one's friends, one surroundings, etc. A false supernaturalism, which imagines that the supernatural is a kind of Platonic realm of abstract essences totally apart from and opposed to the concrete world of nature, offers no real support to a genuine life of meditation and prayer (*Contemplative Prayer*, 38-39).

More overtly contemplative aspects of Merton's guidance begin to appear as he invites us to realize that the dignity of our daily life flows from God, who is the creative origin of our lives and of all things. In speaking to the novices at the monastery Merton once said that it is important to realize that creation does not simply refer to the first moment God brings all things into being. For creation is going on all the time. Creation is God's ongoing act of giving reality to all that is real. The point being that, if God were to cease loving you into the present at the count of ten, you, at the count of ten, would instantly vanish and cease to exist. Seen in this way, God's oneness with us, with others and all things, is the reality of ourselves, others and all things. Contemplative experience is this experience of God's oneness with us being the very reality of ourselves, others and all things.

In a conference Merton gave to the novices, he quoted Meister Eckhart as saying that "For God to be is to give being. For us to be is to receive being." The crux of the matter is that giving being is not an act that God performs, but is rather the act God is. And, inversely, the act of receiving being is not an act that we perform, but is rather the act that we are. Such is the moment by moment mystery of creation in which we are nothing, absolutely nothing outside of and other than God, whose infinite reality is endlessly poured out as the sheer immediacy of all manifested reality in its nothingness without God.

In the concluding paragraphs of *New Seeds of Contemplation*, Merton speaks of God's creative presence permeating all of reality in the poetic imagery of a cosmic dance. Merton writes "The world and time are the dance of the Lord in emptiness. The silence of the spheres is the music of a wedding feast." Then, in these same concluding paragraphs, Merton invites us to consider those utterly simple moments in which we are granted fleeting glimpses of the cosmic dance of God ecstatically poured out and given away as the primordial rhythms of life itself. Merton writes,

> We do not have to go very far to catch echoes of that game, and of that dancing. When we are alone on a starlit night; when by chance we see the migrating birds in autumn descending on a grove of junipers to rest and eat; when we see children in a moment when they are really children; when we know love in our hearts; or when, like the Japanese poet Bashô we hear an old frog land in a quiet pond with a solitary splash--at such time the awakening, the turning inside out of all values, the "newness," the emptiness and the purity of vision that make themselves evident, provide a glimpse of the cosmic dance (*New Seeds of Contemplation*, 296-297).

Merton encourages us pay attention to what tends to happen as these fleeting flashes of spiritual awakening dissipate. What we discover is that, as these moments of awakening pass, we tend to return to our customary, ego-based way of experiencing ourselves. We tend to move on, as if no moment of awakening had ever been granted. A foundational aspect of Merton's guidance in contemplative living is found in how he encourages us not to break faith with our awakened heart. His guidance consists in encouraging us to stand in the experiential self-knowledge in which each of us can say that in my most childlike hour, I was intimately awakened to a fullness of presence with which my life will be forever and complete.

Merton once said that there are some things that we simply have to accept as true or we go crazy inside. And these are the very things that we are unable to explain to anybody including ourselves. Dan Walsh in his philosophy classes at the monastery used to say, "I know it. I know it. The trouble is it is I who know that I know it. And, when I try to tell you what it is that I know, I don't know what to say."

Here then is another foundational aspect of the spiritual guidance Merton offers us. It consists of a willingness to have faith in the revelatory nature of our moments of spontaneous awakening that we cannot explain, and then to stand in that faith as a stance or way of being in the world. I am reminded at this point of John of Cross encouraging us to continue on with "No light to guide us except the one that burns in our heart."

It is easier to recognize when we are in the presence of this intimate awakening than it is to define or explain it. Once I was leading a silent weekend retreat on Thomas Merton in which I was sharing the kinds of things I am sharing here. After one of the conferences an elderly woman approached me. She said that, as she was listening to the conferences, she found herself recalling moments in her childhood growing up on a farm. She said that in the summertime she would go alone into the orchard. She would lie down in the tall grass and watch the clouds pass overhead. With a sense of immediacy in her eyes and sense of quiet confidence in her voice she said, "Something was given to me there." I could tell that the moment she was sharing was as fresh and new to her as when she first experienced it. And I could tell that it mattered to her that I understood what she was talking about.

I always feel grateful and blessed to be in the presence of someone who is opened up like this to the intimate immediacy of what they cannot comprehend. For they bear witness that they are finding their way along the path that Merton invites us to explore. We might say that, in encouraging us to live this way, Merton is inviting us to discover a deeper way to understand what it means to understand. Typically, we say we understand something when we conceptually comprehend it. But here is a deeper way to understand that consists of seeing and accepting how intimately we have been accessed by a presence, beyond anything that we are able to, or ever will be able to, comprehend. Here is why solitude plays such an important role in Merton's spiritual teachings. For these intimate awakenings leave us alone in being unable to explain to anybody, including ourselves, what is happening to us. And here, too, it seems to me is how Merton helps us to understand contemplative spiritual direction in which we seek to find someone who will know by experience what we are talking about when we speak of such things. Certainly for me, Merton was such a person. When I was with him in spiritual direction, there was the sense of being in the presence of someone who was well seasoned in the transformative process of learning from God how to find our way in these obscure and intimate matters of awakening.

To reflect on transformative experience provides another way to understand the guidance Thomas Merton offers us. Transformative experience occurs when the way in which, or the level at which, we are experiencing whatever it is we are experiencing yields to a qualitatively richer, more interior experience that opens out upon previously unrecognized, more interior dimensions of whatever it is we are experiencing. Moments in which we are intimately awakened to the cosmic dance are moments we are graced with spontaneous awakenings of transformative experience. When, for example, we first began to watch children at play, we might be at a surface level of awareness. As we watch them play, the level of awareness at which we began to observe them begins to yield and give way to a qualitatively deeper, more interior contemplative experience. Poised in this deepening attentiveness we begin to be aware of and one with deeper, more interior dimensions of the children at play.

As we learn to become students of such moments of awakening, we begin to realize that Merton is trying to help us understand that we are suffering from depth deprivation in our tendency to skim over the surface of the life we are living. This tendency is all the more regrettable as we come to discover that the depths of our life open out upon the bottomless abyss of God welling up and giving itself away in the concrete immediacy of the children at play, the flock of birds descending, or whatever it might be that might occasion the subtle freefall into God welling up in a moment in which the graced awakening is granted.

As we learn to live in this way, we begin to understand how powerless our finite ego is to produce these flashes of infinite union with the infinite that are so beyond anything the finite ego can achieve. What is more, we begin to feel all the more powerless as we begin to discern growing within a desire to live in more daily abiding awareness of the depths so fleetingly glimpsed. A kind of ache or homesickness for an ever more habitual awareness of God's oneness with us begins to emerge in our life. A certain somber quality begins to emerge in which we go about wondering why we spend so many of our waking hours trapped on the outer circumference of the inner richness of the life we are living. Why is it that our graced moments of awakening have to be so fleeting with such long dry spells in between?

Merton is especially helpful in the guidance and encouragement with which he helps us find our way at this particularly delicate phase of contemplative living. We are grateful for this guidance, for we realize we can use all the help we can get. Merton encourages us to accept that, by our own finite powers we are powerless to bring about graced moments of communion with God that utterly transcend our finite ego and all the ego can attain. Even less can we master the art of learning to live that habitual underlying state of contemplatively experiencing God in all that we experience. But it is precisely at this point that can discover the graced efficacy of meditation, contemplative prayer and other spiritual practices.

The transformative efficacy of spiritual practices is found in discovering that yes, it is true, that by our own finite powers we are powerless to attain the infinite union that we long for. But it is also true that we can freely choose to assume the inner stance that offers the least resistance to being overtaken by the greatest event of intimately realized oneness with God that we are powerless to attain.

Lovers cannot make their moments of oceanic oneness happen. They can, however, freely choose to assume an inner stance that offers the least resistance to being overtaken yet one more time by the graced event of oceanic oneness in the love that sustains them day by day. A poet cannot make poetry happen. But a poet can freely choose to assume the inner stance that offers the least resistance to the graced event of poetry pouring out onto the blank page. Those committed to healing cannot make healing happen. But they can freely choose to assume the inner stance that offers the least resistance in which the gift of healing occurs.

So, too, Merton would have us realize that the fullness of a presence that we are powerless to attain, attains us in our powerlessness to attain it. Hence, the sense of amazement and joy that comes in being so inexplicably overtaken and unraveled by our arrival in that sweet communion that alone puts to rest the restless longings our minds and hearts.

It is in the light of such considerations that we can begin to appreciate that reading Thomas Merton comes into its own when it becomes a spiritual practice in which we learn to be overtaken by God in our powerlessness to find God. Reading Merton becomes a spiritual practice when it becomes an act of contemplative *lectio divina*, a kind of prayer in which we learn to listen to and trust in God, reverberating in the insights and cadences of Merton's words. As we read Merton in this way, we come to discover the subject matter of any passage is never simply a topic on the printed page. Rather, the subject matter is Merton's gifted way of sharing his very subjectivity undergoing transformations into deeper more interior experiences of God's presence in the depths of himself and in the world around him. As we read Merton in this prayerful attentive manner we begin to realize that something subtle and wonderful is happening to the qualitative texture of our own mind and heart. We realize that our own mind and heart are being transformed as we read. As this occurs we realize that the subject matter is our own subjectivity, yielding and giving way to ever-deeper more interior realizations of God's mysterious oneness with us in life itself. Deeper still, Merton would have us realize that the subject matter is God's infinite subjectivity pouring itself out and giving itself away in and as the transformations of Merton's subjectivity, the transformations of your subjectivity and the subjectivities of all people all over the world who are being intimately accessed and sustained by God's all encompassing, life giving presence.

To end on a more personal note, I was fourteen years old when I first read Thomas Merton. The depth and beauty of his words had a profound effect on me that led me to enter the monastery. At eighteen years old, right out of high school, I was amazed to be sitting face to face with Thomas Merton in spiritual direction. Each time I would go in to see him I knew I would be invited to be honest and vulnerable with him in a way that helped me to be honest and vulnerable with myself. And as I opened up in this way, I shared with him how deeply I longed to experience the deep union with God I had come to the monastery hoping to find. The foundational guidelines he offered are among the ones I have been sharing with you here.

Once, when I told Merton how much I valued the guidance he was giving me, he told me that once in awhile I would find someone with whom I could speak of such things. But, he said, I would, most likely, spend most of my life without such a person. This, he said was part of the solitude that contemplative living entails.

When I left the monastery, I experienced the sense of aloneness that Merton spoke of that helped me to appreciate all the more the ongoing guidance and reassurance I found in his writings. But what I also found was what Merton also spoke of: the graced ways in which fidelity to seeking solitary communion with God creates community. For as we move in ever closer to the all encompassing center of oneness with God, we realize we are becoming one with everyone who is being drawn with us into same center, "the hidden wholeness where everything connects."

When I was in the monastery, I experienced contemplative community in the presence of the other monks, a number of whom, like me, had been drawn there by Thomas Merton's writings. After I left the monastery, I experienced contemplative community when I began to lead silent retreats on Thomas Merton. For the silent retreats drew together men and women who felt kinship with each other in their shared desire to enter into more interior, contemplative ways of experiencing and responding to God's presence in their lives. I have experienced this same sense of contemplative community in writing these reflections. For the very fact that I am writing these words and that you are reading them invites us to be grateful together for having found in Thomas Merton such a wise and masterful guide in the gentle art of contemplative living.

Almost Full Circle

Marianne Hieb

> In a world cluttered and programmed with an infinity of practical signs and consequential digits . . . one who makes such non-descript marks as these is conscious of a special vocation to be inconsequent . . .. In effect, these writings are decidedly hopeful . . ..
>
> *Raids on the Unspeakable* (181)

> Every man has a vocation to be someone: but he must understand clearly that in order to fulfill his vocation, he can only be one person: himself.
>
> *No Man Is An Island* (133)

So, on a vocational journey of evolving roles in family and friendship, of exploring art, art therapy, spiritual direction, retreat ministry, and the community of the Sisters of Mercy, Thomas Merton wants me to believe that my vocation is to be myself. Ever since I was sixteen, and received my first Merton book, I have wanted to believe that too.

It was a Sunday afternoon. Dad unpacked the suitcase from his weekend retreat and handed me a blue paperback copy of *No Man is an Island*. Although it was the early 1960s and we were Roman Catholic, attending a religious retreat was an unusual event for my father. In our family, I was the oldest and only daughter; my brother was six years younger. We had just lost the third child, a boy, stillborn. Although I didn't know it at the time, we had all been caesarian births, and the doctor had counseled my parents on the dangers of having any more children. It was in this context, I suspect, that dad made the trek to the local men's retreat, to ponder the future of our family. Somehow, the title *No Man is an Island* had spoken to him from the gift shop shelves as a source of assistance.

But now the book was mine. I read it because it was a special gift and somehow held the secrets of part of our family's life.

The passages were beyond me, but were beguiling in their poetry and in their paradox. I searched for answers. I was a young person, interested in my religious education, trying to do the right thing in life. I wanted to know how to know God.

I still remember the visceral "aha" as I moved through these phrases and reached their conclusion:

> If I find Him with great ease, perhaps He is not my God.
> If I cannot hope to find Him at all, is He my God?

If I find Him wherever I wish, have I found Him?

If He can find me whenever He wishes, and tells me who He is and who I am, and if I then know that He whom I could not find has found me: then I know He is the Lord my God: He has touched me with the finger that made me out of nothing (*No Man Is An Island*, 232).

In those measured phrases, I sensed the basic shift: If God can find me, and tells me who He is and who I am, then I know . . . .

In the final days of high school, I had a calm wondering: was I called to religious life? I was attracted to the warmth and work of the Sisters who taught me. The scriptures indicated that the Works of Mercy were the way God judged if one were worthy of heaven, and getting to heaven was an active goal in my adolescent circle of friends.

But how could I know the will of God for me? I was in the era between theologies. In the air was still the instructive warning: "If something is difficult, it is what God wants. If you desire it, you should probably give it up."

In the pages of *No Man is an Island*, Merton's words began to create the structure of discerning vocation:

If I hope in God, I must also make confident use of the natural aids which, with grace, enable me to come to Him. If I trust in God's grace, I must also show confidence in the natural powers He has given me, not because they are my powers but because they are His gift (16-17.)

There was a profound buildup of reassurance: that as I become myself, I am doing God's will. Could it be that what was "me" was God's desire, because that is who He created? This person with gifts, talents, yearnings, imperfections; this "who I am" is God's will. My adolescent mind was happy to consider this.

I suspect the passages about God's will allowed me to say yes to the life of a Sister of Mercy and perhaps even persevere in the seasons when my *gestalt* seemed not quite in sync. If I believe that God places in us certain qualities and ways of becoming, then by "showing confidence in the natural powers He has given me" we become the Self of God's will. This glimpse into discernment still serves me. In spiritual direction sessions and in my retreat ministry, I go back to that reassurance, paraphrasing and filtering Merton's words through my own experience, trusting this grace and perspective on "becoming."

And so, I continue to become an artist, an art therapist, a workshop leader and more recently, a traveler to Merton events.

The Merton traveler part began in Chicago. After proposing a workshop for "With Roots in Eternity: The Desert and the City," I attended the ITMS Conference many windy months later. There, waiting in the soft ice cream machine line in Loyola University's cafeteria, grace struck again. Chatting ensued and I admitted to the gentleman in front of me, "Yes, this was my first time at an ITMS Conference." He countered, "Perhaps you might come to our Merton Conference in Oakham next year."

The chance conversation found me perusing *Raids on the Unspeakable* in search of a workshop theme. Paging through the book revealed black on white calligraphies introducing each chapter, and the visual impact grew until I reached the final essay, "Signatures: Notes on the Author's Drawings." I learned that these four pages were Merton's artist statement, carefully prepared to accompany a mid-1960s traveling

exhibit of his Zen drawings. The calligraphies scattered through the book were repro-
ductions of some of those works.

Merton's "Signatures" led me into more focused inquiry into this visual aspect of
his prayer and his seeking. As a reader of Merton's message, I tried to learn more
about the historic and relational contexts of this work. As an artist, I tried to notice the
cadence and phrases, the hidden and the revealed, the denial and the attraction. Might
I catch a glimpse of Merton's becoming?

I suspect that Merton would not have liked this. In "Signatures" he is insistent: do
not analyze, or try to figure out these ciphers . . . they are signs of someone who is not
there. Nonetheless, and perhaps despite himself, even here he holds out hope. "These
abstractions—one might call them graffiti rather than calligraphies—are simple signs
and ciphers of energy, acts or movements intended to be propitious." Merton adds cau-
tiously that, if these images live on, they might awaken possibilities; they might effect
hope (*Raids on the Unspeakable*, 180).

It was on that note of hope that we ended the workshop I presented in Oakham,
England. Perhaps for the participants it revealed glimpses of "becoming," through a
combination of some visual marks and some verbal excerpts from Merton's work in
Raids. For me, as facilitator, the experience remained connected to that early gift and
grace: continue to become who you are and, in so doing, come to know hope, and give
that hope to others. "Upon our hope then depends the liberty of the whole universe.
Because our hope is the pledge of a new heaven and a new earth, in which all things
will be what they were meant to be" (*No Man Is An Island*, 19).

Almost full circle, like a Zen calligraphy of a circle not yet quite closed . . . a decid-
edly hopeful sign.

Thomas Merton: Hope "Pops-Up" In My Life

Donald P. St. John

I don't know what it is about Thomas Merton. He began to "pop up" in my life to offer help and hope beginning around 1960, and has continued that practice—sometimes in the form of inspiration, sometimes information and as of late, perspiration from many hours (years) of reading, reflecting and writing on his work.

The oldest son of a large Irish Catholic family, I decided to enter the U. S. Air Force a few months after graduating from Altoona Catholic High School (Pennsylvania) in 1959. For basic training and tech school I was stationed in Texas and was subjected to a lot of anti-Catholic verbal attacks—something I had never experienced. These originated from a small but scripturally zealous group of fellow Airmen. Determined to defend myself, I began to read Catholic writers and "up-popped" Thomas Merton with *The Seven Storey Mountain*. He provided me with a new confidence and sense of pride in my tradition, but Merton also forced me to raise questions about my own life that I wasn't quite ready to face. When I finally settled into a life of directing choirs, playing sports and pushing papers at an Air Force Base near Charleston, South Carolina, I began to ask deeper questions about life, including the direction being taken by the world around me. The Cuban missile crisis (1962) found many of us pencil pushers on the flight line with rifle in-hand to guard General Curtis Lemay's SAC planes which had landed at our base "just in case." Long nights walking back and forth under the wing of a B-52 allowed time for reflection on some of the personal religious questions I had avoided earlier and on new questions concerning the morality of nuclear weapons.

During this period, a Benedictine Chaplain helped my search by suggesting readings on the contemplative life, and lo! Thomas Merton "popped up" again. At some point during these years of service and searching, I went on a retreat at Mepkin Abbey near Charleston (founded by Trappists from Gethsemani in 1949). After much subsequent thought and prayer, I decided that upon my discharge I would join a religious order (but probably *not* the Trappists). Interestingly, on the day of my discharge (August 28, 1963), during the long drive back to Pennsylvania, I listened to coverage of the famous "March on Washington." I was deeply moved by the "I Have a Dream" speech of Martin Luther King, having surreptitiously engaged in protest marches in Charleston. Both King and Merton were strong admirers of Gandhi and I was to use Merton's slim volume often in later classes. King would develop a great admiration for Merton, but his hope to finally meet with the monk-hermit in the Spring of 1968 never materialized because of the Memphis tragedy.

In September, 1963 I joined the Franciscans (Merton's original choice). I was a college student—and it was the 1960s! Thomas Merton, along with other critical writers, gave me hope that we could do something about issues like civil rights, the war in Vietnam, Church reform, dialogue with other religions, poverty and social justice. News of Merton's death in December, 1968 while on his Asian journey was devastating. By that time, I had decided that my own path would lead me out the front doors of the monastery and down the beautiful hills surrounding Loretto, Pennsylvania. (My great-grandfather, who came to the United States in 1867, is buried in those hills.)

Although Merton and D. T. Suzuki had stimulated my interest in the study of Buddhism and other world religions, it was a talk given at the seminary by Dr. Bernard Phillips, founder of the new graduate program in Religion at Temple University that sealed my decision on *where* to study. "He met Thomas Merton," whispered one of my Brothers. Indeed, in October, 1966 Phillips had taken Algerian Sufi Master Sidi Abdesalam to Gethsemani for a spiritually powerful meeting with Merton (*Learning to Love*, 152-153). By serving for a while in Algeria as a spiritual director for Dr. Phillips, Sidi joined the company of a Hindu guru, a Japanese Zen Master and others who had served as mentors for the Jewish American Phillips. In his lectures, classes and private conversations his focus on the spiritual depths common to the world's contemplative traditions reflected Merton whose early essays on Zen he had read and with whom he had corresponded. Furthermore, for Temple's program, including its new program in Islamic Studies, Phillips' priority was to hire faculty who were not only top-notch scholars in a tradition but individuals who had lived in one of its respective cultures. This was an eye-opening experience for me.

TWO TOMS AND HOPE FOR THE EARTH

A few years after earning my M. A. at Temple, I headed to Fordham University to study under Thomas Berry. As I have often said, "I went to Fordham to study world religions, and ended up studying the cosmos." Fr. Thomas impressed me by his deep understanding of Buddhism, Confucianism and Taoism but especially by his empathetic grasp of Native American traditions. Berry made it clear that the future of the earth community, human and other-than-human, would require not only a New Story joining science and religion but a post-critical way of *seeing* creation that was close to the earth-spiritualities of Indigenous Peoples and also to the contemplative traditions as understood and practiced by Thomas Merton. Berry's influence on me would remain strong, but while preparing for my first sabbatical at Moravian College, Merton "popped up" again. With a host of new perceptions gained from Thomas Berry, I began to see more clearly some of the ways in which Merton's own spirituality was influenced by his experiences of the natural world, its diverse creatures and its many moods and special places.

Beginning slightly before the first ITMS conference at Bellarmine College, Merton's influence on my study, writing and teaching increased and would never cease. Fortunately, but also at what seemed a torturously slow pace, volumes of newly published letters, journals and essays were released that provided scholars with a plethora of new sources on Merton's life, thought and experience. Of special interest to me were his many new and nuanced insights into the relationship between one's inner life and one's presence to and appreciation for creation's inner life, its magnificent grandeur and its exquisite detail. He also made insightful connections between the ongoing creative work of the divine (Logos/Sophia/Spirit) in nature and in human history. My study of and reflections on the material revealed in these new publications have appeared in some articles but my ongoing project is a book length manuscript

(350+pp.) on Merton as Radical Ecologist. The process itself has been a source of spiritual nourishment, new insights and hope—especially needed in these days.

These are uncertain days for the earth and for those who care for her. Powerful economic and political interests seem bent on pushing forward a purportedly progressive and rational agenda, which as Merton reminded Rachel Carson and others, will prove itself neither progressive nor rational. Today, the overwhelming scientific consensus concerning climate change seems merely to spark more intense media propaganda and denials by the fossil fuel industries and the politically ignorant and/or well funded. For many of us, hope and hopelessness vie for dominance. But the voices of protest insist on being heard and I have my own drum beat (a Tom-Tom) urging me forward.

Merton's vision, expressed in many ways and in various places but with special power during the last twelve years of his life, gives hope to many today. Merton would suggest that those seeking a richer, more compassionate mode of contemplative life go deeper still, until they hear and touch within themselves That which groans in creation's pain and humanity's suffering, and then—act! Contemplative ecology motivates prophetic ecology. Through the inner self I discover the world "as a living and self-creating mystery of which I am myself a part, to which I am myself my own unique door" (*Contemplation in a World of Action*, 170). We can no longer afford the luxury of feeling helpless and alienated from this world.

For Merton, the Spirit of "the world" is creative, present and alive, and manifests itself richly in spiritual, aesthetic and biological diversity. It moves to deepen and connect the inner life of each person with the integrity of the whole, while strengthening the inner connections between historical-cultural and creation-ecological communities. The wisdom of sages, seers and saints that permeates many traditions is a human reflection of the shining Wisdom manifest everywhere in creation from galaxies to rainforests, from whales to insects, from burning deserts to ice-topped mountains. Both Merton and Berry strove to recapture the deep resources available in these ancient traditions and to apply their spiritual energies and wisdom to the ecological situation of the present, thereby generating new visions and hopes. But there are also among us today innumerable poets, essayists, bloggers, musicians, artists, and the hopeful, creative workers for equity and environment in so many places and groups who constitute the "movement" (see Paul Hawkins, *Blessed Unrest*, 2007). All of these creative energies from the past and present will be needed to either transform, or if necessary, eject the shriveled souls of corporate moguls and their paid politicians and introduce a new era of ecological, social and spiritual harmony.

HOPE FOR CRAZY ELDERS

Wait! Merton has not stopped "popping-up" in my life. I, as many Americans, am moving into elderhood and seeking alternatives to the terribly inadequate models of aging offered by the unimaginative minds of conventional society. Merton offers hope for elders who seek a fuller contemplative mode of being with its rich resources for a new mode of growth. Liberation from the mental and emotional saddles that conventionality has laid upon us can lead to a deeper, more personal freedom to redefine ourselves, to focus and draw upon inner resources that too often have been ignored or squandered in the workaday world. If lucky, this will, among other things, lead to the state of "useful uselessness," lauded so boldly by Merton's sage, Chuang Tzu. Rejecting society's paradoxical clichés about the "uselessness" of "old people" (except as consumers of miracle creams, retirement homes and casino or golfing vacations), let's embrace "uselessness," first, as a release from a state of being "used" by external forces, institutions or people and second, as an opportunity to embrace a way of life vitalized and directed from within by our unique powers for insight and spontaneous action as illustrated by so many of Chuang Tzu's characters. (When Merton "popped-in" with this crazy Daoist philosopher, Chuang Tzu, I did some further research into the latter and his friends and have been working on a book tentatively titled *Crazy Wisdom for Elders*.)

Contemplative practices will also allow elders to settle into a newly opened space within and, with a peaceful non-attached mind, both uncover patterns of meaning in their past and heal the sometimes hidden but painful wounds caused by events or persons or our own failings. Many elders will want to link contemplation with action, and will experience the freedom and courage to heed Merton's prophetic voice and join with activists young and old to proclaim hope to the hopeless, provide resources to the poor and power to the powerless and, especially in this age, create alternatives to the socially unjust and ecologically destructive policies that the powerful and wealthy are spawning around the globe (see also Matthew Fox, *Occupy Spirituality*, 2013). Diverse voices, diverse songs, yet at once personal and communal, resonating with a new but very old earth-harmony.

ONE BRIGHT LIGHT, MANY COLORED CRYSTALS

Wisely, Thomas Merton did not create One theological system or One spiritual discipline that purported to answer all questions or be applicable to all situations. True to our experience of life, Merton, out of his own life and rich experiences, created a collage of complementary, sometimes paradoxical insights, scores of soaring reflections, tons of tantalizing metaphors, and countless chains of captivating images in both prose and poetry which have the power to transform us and the strength and wisdom to move us into a different place. We all need him to "pop up" at different points in our lives because, in retrospect, our lives usually do not unfold according to a carefully planned-out and subsequently executed agenda, as proffered in the ads of educational institutions and the offices of career or guidance counselors. We are asked by Merton to develop a contemplative openness to life and the world, listening deeply to the messages of our inner life, of the people around us and of the voices of the earth.

Ultimately, Merton is a messenger of hope—not because he has One Message that overwhelms all kinds of despair—but because he has many messages that revolve around a hidden Mystery and at any moment can tickle us into a state of hope. The Bright Mystery can "hit" us in different ways at different times because Merton's window is full of glass crystals of many colors, themselves being crystallized manifestations of his own changing thoughts and experiences—yet all aglow because of a Central Light. We need the Light to touch and brighten the dark spots in our lives, but we also need those different colored crystals of hope because our despairs or pains themselves come at different times, in different shapes and colors, and hide in different places.

And although Merton's messages can "pop up" at different times and under different forms, the joy they impart makes us want to dance (elders and youngsters):

When we are alone on a starlit night; when by chance we see the migrating birds in autumn descending on a grove of junipers to rest and eat; when we see children in a moment when they are really children; when we know love in our own hearts; or when, like the Japanese poet Basho we hear an old frog land in a quiet pond with a solitary splash—at such times, the awakening, the turning inside out of all values, the 'newness,' the emptiness and the purity of vision that make themselves evident, provide a glimpse of the cosmic dance. No despair of ours can alter the reality of things, or stain the joy of the cosmic dance, which is always there. Indeed, we are in the midst of it, and it is in the midst of us, for it beats in our very blood, whether we want it to or not.

Yet the fact remains that we are invited to forget ourselves on purpose, cast our awful solemnity to the winds and join in the general dance (*New Seeds of Contemplation*, 296-297).

Recovering An Original Unity

Małgorzata Poks

It is so human to want to know the right answers and have the sense of control over one's life. What we have to learn, though, slowly and painfully, is how to rest in the unknown; how to obey without understanding; how to *respond* rather than reply. "In this kind of obedience there is never a full understanding of what one has to do—this does not become clear until the work has been done," writes Merton in *Dancing in the Water of Life* (342).

I used to live a relatively comfortable life in my self-styled upper-room "hermitage" of 50 square meters; now there are eight of us here: three cats, two dogs, a guinea pig, and two women, with my octogenarian parents occupying the ground floor of our country house. "What we have to be is what we are," said Merton in his last talk in the Temple of Understanding when he talked about communion being the deepest level of communication. What we are here is a little alternative community, a parable of communion, in which the dog lies with the cat—to misquote Isaiah—and I, the alpha and leader of the pack, am the servant of communion. Although I am responsible for making this community take shape, it emerged in response to situations beyond my control. My own plans turned out to be of secondary importance; my current life has chosen me, and not the other way around.

In 1962, Merton worried about the destruction of natural life by the indiscriminate use of DDT. To ward off potential criticism, he wrote in his journal: "Someone will say: 'You worry about birds. Why not worry about people?' I worry about both birds and people. We are in the world and part of it, and we are destroying everything because we are destroying ourselves spiritually, morally and in every way. It is all part of the same sickness, it all hangs together" (*Turning Toward the World*, 274). Humans deserve love and help because they have immortal souls, traditional theology tells the faithful. But do animals have souls? Half a century after Merton wrote the above-quoted words, Christians still tend to deny animals the right to the same compassion we are urged to show to our human neighbor. It might be sobering, in this context, to remember that a few centuries ago the best theologians fought one another over the question whether non-white humans had a soul. So much for theological disputes, which reflect nothing but the current state of awareness of a group of decision makers. Since when is a Christian expected to *know* first and do works of mercy later? To help the needy, whether human or animal, not because they are needy but because they have been declared to be worthy of help? Sometimes you just need to act against commonly accepted rules because your conscience tells you this is right. And not worry about the right answers. Merton extended his compassionate love towards people *and* animals. With the realization that "everything is emptiness and everything is compassion," his life reached completeness.

One December evening I was taking a walk when I heard some plaintive meowing and, to my surprise, found an adult cat among snowed-in graves in the nearby cemetery. I smuggled her into our front yard, begged my reluctant parents to look after her for a few days, and left the following morning for a Taizé-animated meeting ("Pilgrimage of Trust on Earth"). The cat, not even named, stayed with us for the rest of her short life. She loved me, there is no doubt about it. After a successful hunt, she would climb the roof and descend onto the window-sill of my second-floor flat to bring me her precious prey; her eyes smiled and you could see immortality in them.

Since then, a succession of stray cats followed. Some came to stay, many others found adoptive homes. You will hardly believe how creative a stray kitten looking for her own person can be. One even went to church on a Sunday and prayed its way into my house! Before the morning Mass started, a desperate meowing could be heard from the vicinity of the main altar; I pricked up my ears but the congregation seemed deaf and blind, only the altar boys panicked and dived after the sound. Nobody else moved, the organ sounded. The obstacle had been removed. The principle of decorum had been kept. Fearing the worst, I rushed out of the church toward the sacristy door. Just in time to see the door open and a little black kitten, scared out of her wits, her tiny tail raised, being let out—no doubt to die of starvation. I took her home as my gift from the Lord. Caressing the terrified thing, feeding it and delousing (she had more lice than fur) was my religious service that Sunday. I know God was smiling; a helpless creature of God, one of "the least of these," found love and safety.

Another one, just as black and helpless, ran up to me as I was cycling beside a churchyard. I stopped the bike and picked her up; she looked at me with gratefulness and started to purr. She never stopped purring until half an hour later, when, having knocked on a number of doors and been turned down, we reached our new home. My home. It must have been then that my house quite unexpectedly became a House of Hospitality. Sheltering the homeless, feeding the hungry, caring for the sick, comforting the afflicted. "Whatever you have done to the least of these," said the Lord, "you have done to me." We have domesticated wild animals, made them serve us and depend on us for their livelihood. "Men have forgotten this truth," said the fox to the Little Prince, "but you must not forget it. You become responsible, forever, for what you have tamed." Children still know this truth. Adults forget. So they ask with disbelief: "Lord, when did we see you hungry or thirsty or a stranger or naked or sick or in prison, and did not minister to you . . .?" Whenever we saw a helpless creature, either human or nonhuman, begging for help and passed it by or turned aside, pretending not to see; that is when.

That dogs joined the pack was equally surprising. Kika, named after a Pedro Almodovar character, a medium-sized stray mongrel, was the first. Initially, I arranged for her to be taken to a shelter because my aging parents absolutely refused to have a dog in the house. But visiting her weekly, I could see the rapid decline in her health. She lost her vigor, did not want to play with me, and hardly ate anything. Whatever will come, will come, I decided, knowing full well my parents would raise hell. I took her home. They did raise hell, and threatened to move out to "an old people's house," as they phrased it. I had all the right arguments; all they had were negative emotions and fear. I knew I was doing the right thing. With due respect for their old age and gratitude for their parental love, I could not have done otherwise. Kika barely made it: she had a bad viral infection. Daily drips, shots, strict diet—it was all necessary, but it would not have worked without the most miraculous medicine—the TLC. Now when I stroke her fur her brown eyes turn blue. This is how you know that your dog loves you to bits.

Misiek was next: a mere puppy run over on the main street by a driver who did not even stop the car. It happened in front of the local school and next to a bus stop where a few women were waiting. Nobody helped the yelping wretch. My friend who witnessed the accident called me for help. The doggy had managed to drag himself into the shrub and, to my disbelief, wagged its tail when I touched him. With a fractured hip and a broken foreleg, he still could attempt a smile as we leaned over him! How could I leave him there to die in torment? So Misiek stayed, because nobody else would have him. He underwent several operations; his foreleg is stiff and numb, and he has to wear a shoe when playing outside. But he is a happy, playful dog; whenever he is happy (almost always), he wags his tail to beat the band. And his eyes turn blue.

There have been several other stray and mistreated animals in transit here. And a needy human who has decided to stay. Animal rescue takes up a lion's share of our earnings; it is also difficult to plan a holiday. Besides, each animal has his or her specific needs. Ernie is a fine specimen of a black European cat. When we found him fifteen months ago, he was a skeleton clad in a tattered, brownish fur, barely able to walk. We just had to bring him home risking another storm. Although he will be on prescription food till the end of his life, he has made an amazing recovery and is now a healthy, six kilogram, "peace-and-love cat." (My friend claims that Ernie was starving because he had refused to take the life of other sentient beings, in other words, he refused to hunt and eat mice). Tosia, the only female cat in the group, has been with us for four months now and has only recently been taken off antibiotics. When we found her, the poor creature had severe respiratory infection, ear mite infection, swollen entrails, and a few teeth left due to malnutrition. In and out of several veterinary practices, with scores of tests and blood samples taken, on and off various drugs, she is now a plump, resolute girl who loves to play. Her third lid is still slightly swollen and, as happens with sick cats, she occasionally leaves her litter outside the box. There is no other way but wait it out. It was the same with Ernie—he dirtied the flat for a while but now is the cleanest, cutest cat that has ever lived.

Only Tom-Tom came to us as a little kitten. Dragging his feet across a busy street, he was in the last stages of exhaustion. He was also ravenously hungry. Now Tom-Tom is huge for a European Shorthair tabby; he has thick bones, lovely hazel eyes and is a royal creature in every sense of the word. A true beast of prey, Tom-Tom is proudly independent; he does not tolerate being cuddled, an occasional stroke of fur is all you will often be allowed; but when he feels like caressing, you need to drop everything and play with him—and be ready for a bite and a scratch, too. Tom-Tom's paw: cruelty sheeted in a caress. He has had a rough time recently, suffering from painful lower urinary tract disease for the last half year. Needless to say, he was a nuisance: aching and irritated, he urinated everywhere, even the bed was not safe from him and the laundry would hang out to dry on a daily basis. Another cat on a life-long prescription food.

Time, energy, expenses, worries—the consequences you must accept when you try to be faithful to a calling. The Hebrew Scripture's *hineni*, a prophet's answer to God's call, can be rendered as "see me here" (Jacques Derrida's *me voici*), the "me" appearing in the accusative case. "Here I am" is thus a response that puts us "in the accusative," under accusation, as it were, making us subjects responsible for the stranger that calls.

As soon as I say *me voici*, claimed Derrida, God is at work, God is witnessed, and I am answering in the name of God. To change the point of reference to something more familiar to a Christian ear, Peter Maurin, cofounder of the Catholic Worker, insisted that works of mercy have to be done *at a personal sacrifice.* Although he did not think Houses of Hospitality should shelter all stray creatures of God, including nonhuman animals, such a development fits our evolving post-humanist consciousness and animal rescue takes on deeply spiritual dimensions in the context of Mat. 25:40—"Whatever you did to the least of these, you did to me." The whole of creation is the work of love. Human and nonhuman animals are our brothers and sisters. Let us recover our original unity!

A Messenger With Seeds For The Desert

David Joseph Belcastro

There was no intention to ever read Merton. I heard of him in seminary from a student who had come onto a copy of *The Seven Storey Mountain*. We were partners in a first year program entitled "No Exit." In other words, here was a relationship from which there was no escape. We were told that this was similar to the relations that we would form with parishioners. He bored me to tears with his weekly reports on this guy that hid from the world in a monastery. Having selected Rochester Center for Theological Studies because of its roots in the Social Gospel Movement, I found Merton's flight and this student's enthusiasm of no interest.

Years later, having left parish ministry . . . with no faith, little hope and even less charity, I decided to read Albert Camus. There was something in his writings that now resonated with me. The prevailing silence and solitude, acknowledgement of the absurd, and the rebel as a way of being in the world provided an opportunity to explore a new direction for my life.

You might imagine my surprise when I discovered that Merton had written seven essays on Camus's literary works. After reading the essays, I became interested in Merton's reasons for taking up with Camus. That meant a trip to the Merton Center at Bellarmine College (now Bellarmine University). Robert Daggy would remove from the archive selected unpublished letters and notebooks, carefully set them before me and quietly walk away. The soft blue smoke of his cigarettes gave the momentary encounter an air of mystery and impending revelation.

Sometime later I received a phone call from Daggy asking if I would present a paper on the essays at the first conference of The International Thomas Merton Society. My response was simple and to the point, "Sure, why not." While I was willing to do that, my primary interest remained with Camus, not Merton. I planned to focus on the essays and related materials and nothing more. Those related writings, however, led to other books by Merton.

Little did I know at that time, seeds from the hand of this Johnny Appleseed of spirituality began falling into my dried-up heart. Now the parable says that the ground must be fertile for the seeds to take root, sprout and grow. This ground was not. So it is something of a miracle that anything would come from this scattering of new seeds. But it did. [Is this evidence for canonization?]

I would like to say that my faith is flourishing, hope abounds and charity is my daily work. I would like to say that but it simply is not true. There are friends and family who will testify to this if you have any doubt about my spiritual impoverishment. There is, however, faith at work within me. I can say that. Fortunately, it has a life of its own. Because of this grace, hope flowers with charity at night in the desert of my heart.

I continue to read Merton. I have to. Somehow, this monk has become for me a "No Exit" relationship. He helped me find a place in the desert. He now provides the wisdom necessary to live there. For all this, I am deeply appreciative and forever grateful.

Messenger Of Hope

Tony Russo

Thomas Merton has been with me since sometime in 1987 when for some reason I decided to read parts of Michael Mott's *The Seven Mountains of Thomas Merton.* As far as how I see myself being a "messenger of hope," I see that my reading, studying and involvement with Merton's writings has done for me what Merton hoped. All of this has helped me as I followed Merton's invitation to seek God not only in the dogmatic, approved path but on the edges of society and religion. And it has been through the communion with Merton seekers and other spiritual seekers I have met on the way that I have had the courage to grow and follow new spiritual paths.

In about 1998 I joined the International Thomas Merton Society. Since then I have attended many conferences and met many in the Merton community. At the invitation of the Board I served as chairman of the membership committee for several years. I was impressed with the work of our local chapter and the International and felt that acting in this position was my call at the time. Later I served as Coordinator of the Local Chapters which allowed me to support and coordinate Merton's ongoing influence internationally. In these positions, I was deeply moved by the interest and work of so many.

In the late 1990s, following the invitation of the Board, our local chapter began offering an annual Merton Retreat. Beginning with the second one, this was offered at the Abbey of Gethsemani. At the suggestion of Jonathan Montaldo, this morphed into what is now called "A Pilgrimage Retreat." In the months before the retreat, letters on the theme are sent to retreatants to read and pray over. Jonathan presented the first pilgrimage retreat in January, 2002. After that, he encouraged me to author the letters and facilitate the weekend at the Abbey. Some of the retreat themes which I developed were Merton and Peace; Merton and Prayer; Contemplation: Path to the True Self; Merton and Hesychasm; Merton, Prophet and Witness; and Sufism/Final Integration. The retreat letters and the weekend itself offered the retreatants the opportunity to form an electronic community travelling together to the weekend at the Abbey of Gethsemani. In November this year I will facilitate the fourteenth retreat sponsored by The Greater Cincinnati/Northern Kentucky Chapter of ITMS: "Reflecting on Merton's *Contemplative Prayer.*" In doing the reading and authoring of these retreat letters, I was led by Merton to countless other spiritual authors who are, as he is for me, "pointing me and leading me to God" and allowing me to be a messenger of hope.

I served as the chairman of the local chapter in Cincinnati for about ten years. During that time, we were fortunate enough to have Brother Paul Quenon, OCSO, Monsignor William Shannon and others present to the group. From time to time, I have given presentations to local groups and offered days of recollection and study groups on Merton. In leading the retreats and presenting to groups, I always use these words of Merton to encourage others to open to The Spirit as Merton wished everyone would do:

> Therefore, most honorable reader, it is not as an author that I would speak to you, not as a story-teller, not as a philosopher, not as a friend only: I seek to speak to you, in some way, as your own self. Who can tell what this may mean? I myself do not know. But if you listen, things will be said that are perhaps not written in this book. And this will be due not to me, but to One who lives and speaks in [us] both! (*Honorable Reader: Reflections on My Work*, 67).

Originally when I reflected on this vocation of being a "messenger of hope" I found myself thinking about what I had done and what I had read of Merton and others. Upon further reflection, I see that the vocation is not about what I have done alone, but who I have become. Reading and praying over Merton and other authors has allowed me to live more intelligently and freely in a modern America. It has led me to balance my use of technology and modern ways of living. And most importantly, it has invited me in communion with others to risk new ways of being.

Thomas Merton Saved My Life And Opened My Heart To What It Really Means To Be Truly "Catholic"

Peter Savastano

My first encounter with Thomas Merton was both accidental and providential at the same time. I was twelve years old. It was in the North End Branch of the Newark Public Library in Newark, New Jersey, the city in which I was born. The year was 1965. My mother, younger brother and I had just moved from another part of Newark to what was then referred to as the "Forest Hill" section of the city, an affluent neighborhood. Working class and considerably poor as we were, the small attic apartment my mother rented for us was located on the outskirts of the mansion-filled part of the Forest Hill Section. This was a very exciting time for me. I was enrolled in Catholic elementary school for the first time in my life. Up to 1965, I had been a student in the Newark Public School system. Because of my new Catholic school situation, I was filled with passion and fervor for all things Catholic.

My family was Catholic by heritage rather than by practice. My mother was suspicious of and ambivalent toward the institutional Catholic Church. This was especially so because my father had been married and divorced before he met and married my mother. Consequently, it was not possible for my parents to be married in the Catholic Church. My mother had little patience for Catholic authoritarianism or its orthodoxy. Ours was a Catholicism of the home and its piety was rooted in our southern Italian ancestry. We were much more concerned with the quality of our relationships with the Madonna and the saints than we were with God who seemed distant and hard to relate to. To be fair, I should also say that my religious heritage is a bit more complex than I describe here in that my paternal grandmother was a Jew who converted to Catholicism. My maternal grandfather was Greek Orthodox, though I do not have any understanding of why this is the case. As a child, my maternal grandfather would often bring me to the Greek Orthodox Church in Newark, which also had a profound effect upon me mystically and aesthetically.

My father died when I was seven years old (1958) at the age of 41 from a sudden heart attack. My mother was 34 years old and three months pregnant with my brother who was born in July of 1959. My father was a fruit and vegetable peddler who wound his way through the streets of the Italian section of Newark selling his produce from the back of a truck. After my father's death, my family life went downhill. Extreme poverty, emotional and physical abuse, and great spiritual desolation became my lot. Seven years old is way too young to enter into a dark night of the soul. In retrospect, that is how I would characterize the years of my life between the ages of 7 and 20.

My discovery of the writings of Thomas Merton in 1965 was a source of solace in the midst of all that darkness. With my newly found passion for becoming a priest, I had discovered a book in the reference section of the library, a dictionary or encyclopedia of men's Catholic religious and monastic orders which I would often take down from the shelf and spend hours paging through, fascinated to read about the history of the various orders. I loved to look at the pictures of the habits each wore. The more austere and exotic the order and the habit, the more fascinated I became. There was something about the starkness of the monk's habit that seemed to convey a quality of cool mystic light. I remember feeling a deep sense of spaciousness and freedom, outside the confines of my ordinary reality, induced by my encountering the pictures of these contemplative monks and hermits. It was a light that seemed to suggest that there were other more subtle, spiritual dimensions to life than I could perceive with my ordinary senses. Yet exactly what that subtle spiritual world was and meant to me at the time was not very clear. I am not sure it is clear to me now, some 49 years later, except that I know by intuition that there is such a world and, through regular prayer and meditation, I am somehow brought into contact with it.

Unfortunately, I cannot remember the title of that vocational handbook. And while my memory is a bit fuzzy on this, what I do recall is that the photographs I had most liked were of the Cistercians, Carthusians and Camaldolese. I seem to recall that the photographs of these monks were attributed to *The Silent Life* by Thomas Merton (1957). "Who is this Thomas Merton?" I had wondered. I remember looking for him in my public library's card catalogue. Within minutes I had in my hand a copy of *The Silent Life* along with a copy of *The Seven Storey Mountain* (1948), the autobiography which put Thomas Merton on the religious map for so many Catholics, non-Catholics and atheists alike.

As I write this, I have in front of me first editions of both of these Merton classics. Holding them in my hands and looking again at the photographs in *The Silent Life*, I can still sense the numinous quality emanating from them. Encountering these two Merton books back in 1965 was the beginning of what would turn out to be 49 years of reading Thomas Merton, each time discovering him anew as I made my way over the ensuing years through various stages of personal and spiritual growth. Encountering Merton's writings, I was all the more impassioned to become both a priest and a contemplative monk. Alas, my attempts at monastic and other forms of Catholic communal religious life did not work out. After three failed attempts in three different religious orders, two of them contemplative and one mendicant, in 1973 I gave up on my notion of a monastic religious vocation. My relationship to the Catholic Church also changed radically from that point forward.

While I consider myself Catholic culturally and by heritage, I consider myself Greek Orthodox by heritage as well, but like Merton after a certain point in his monastic career, I now live on the margins of the Church. Having read a number of books by Merton at this point in my young life, I had come to feel that Catholicism was not the only place that could provide me with spiritual support and sustenance. Reading that Merton's mother attended Quaker Meetings and that Merton himself had considered Quakerism as a possible spiritual path for him, I began attending a local Quaker Meeting. I consider all the world's religious traditions to be valuable resources upon which I can draw for inspiration and for practice as I strive to follow the leadings of my Inner Guide, a Quaker way of talking about the Divine Light or "That of God in Everyone." Along with Merton, I had come to the conclusion that: "I cannot be a Catholic unless it is made quite clear to the world that I am a Jew and a Moslem, unless I am execrated as a Buddhist . . ." (*The Courage for Truth*, 79). And I would also have to add to this list Quaker, Sufi, Tibetan Bonpo (a practitioner of the pre-Indian Buddhist indigenous shamanic tradition of Tibet), and Vodouizant (one who serves the Vodou spirits or *lwa*). My personal experience further taught me that, beneath the cultural, symbolic and historical constructions of any particular religious tradition—including Catholic Christianity—was the groundless ground of Ultimate Reality for which I thirsted and longed. I also came to understand that it was Ultimate Reality which was and is the object of desire of the many mystics I read as a young man after being introduced to them through Thomas Merton's books and journals. It was with Merton as my guide that I began in earnest what has become a lifelong journey of spiritual seeking and practice that has led me to immerse myself for many years at a time in the practices of Islamic Sufism, Tibetan Bon and Buddhism, Zen Buddhism, Christian Theosophy, Western Esotericism, the teachings of G. I. Gurdjieff, shamanic healing, and the ritual traditions of First Nation Indigenous Peoples of the Americas, and in African-Diasporic healing and ritual traditions such as Haitian Vodou and Cuban Santeria.

Merton would also be my inspiration as I became a social activist for racial justice, women's rights and LGBTQI rights and protections. As any experienced Merton reader knows, Merton wrote very little about homosexuality. There is a letter he wrote in response to a gay man who wrote to him seeking spiritual guidance. In his response, Merton does not appear to be in the least judgmental (*The Road to Joy*, 344). Some years ago I had a conversation with a monk of the Abbey of Gethsemani who was a contemporary of Merton's. This monk, who was admittedly gay himself, told me that he thought Merton was homophobic and that, had Merton lived, he would have continued to be so. I, however, do not agree. After almost a lifetime of reading Merton, as well as many books about Merton, I am convinced of his capacity for growth and personal transformation, as is well evidenced by the progression and expansion of subjects and concerns Merton wrote about from his earliest writings to those he wrote about toward the end of his life. Who would have ever thought that the author of *The Seven Storey Mountain*, who wrote so passionately and yet so smugly about his conversion to Catholicism and becoming a monk, would also come to write about Sufis and Buddhists and Cargo Cults with the same passion and conviction, minus the smugness, that he wrote about his conversion to Catholicism?

Whatever it is that Merton might have been lacking in terms of women's and LGBTQI issues particularly, I attribute to his untimely death and the fact that he was very much a product of his time. (This of course does not at all excuse the way that Merton handled his affair with "M" or the way in which he so dismissively writes about women mystics and women anthropologists.) I remain convinced that Merton's openness to other religious traditions and to the contemporary social issues of his time are strong indications that he would have continued to grow in his religious and social worldview to eventually include a concern for women's human and civil rights and for LGBTQI human and civil rights. I believe that, had Merton lived, he would have even opened himself to other religious possibilities even to the point of possibly leaving the Catholic Church and his Cistercian monastic life. I know I am in the minority of Merton scholars who share this opinion but I trust my intuition here.

Eventually, many years after these encounters with Merton in my adolescence and young adult life, Merton would once again play a significant role in my life when in

1995, at the age of 44, I would go to graduate school to earn a Ph.D. in Religion and Society with a specialization in the Anthropology of Religion, Consciousness, Sexuality, and Gender. During my time in graduate school, I took quite a number of courses on the beginnings of Christian monasticism, both East and West, and on Christian mysticism, both Roman Catholic and Eastern Orthodox. I also took a number of theology courses, most especially liberation theology and mystical theology. As a result, I found myself revisiting Merton's writings after a rather long hiatus. *The Sign of Jonas* (1953); *No Man Is An Island* (1955); *The Wisdom of the Desert* (1960); *New Seeds of Contemplation* (1961); *Mystics and Zen Masters* (1961); *Zen and the Birds of Appetite* (1968); *The Climate of Monastic Prayer* (1969); and *The Inner Experience* (2003) would become my personal spiritual reading as I made my way through the rigors of a Ph.D. program. Now much more mature in my own spiritual life and with many years of daily meditation and prayer to draw on, I had learned to trust my own inner guide in spiritual matters, making my renewed acquaintance with Merton all the more profound and meaningful.

After I completed my Ph.D., I landed a teaching job at a large Catholic university where I teach a course entitled "Thomas Merton, Religion and Culture." Rooted in the anthropological study of religion and, therefore, in the idea that no religious tradition is more or less true than another, in the syllabus for the course I depict Merton as an "ethnographer" whose field site was the world's religious traditions. Although Merton was not himself a trained anthropologist or ethnographer, he was no stranger to anthropology or the social sciences.

So far I have taught "Thomas Merton, Religion and Culture" twice. Most students who take the course have had no exposure to Thomas Merton or his writings. For the Catholic students in the course, Thomas Merton's Catholicism is foreign to them. Their knowledge of the Catholic tradition is much more informed by the conservative image the Catholic Church has created during their lifetime as well as the Church's active opposition to the so called "culture war" issues. Many of the students are shocked by the subjects and issues Merton explored and wrote about. They are even more shocked by his love affair with "M," but the majority of them find Merton to be a breath of fresh air. A few students who have taken the course have experienced radical spiritual awakenings as a result of reading Merton.

As is often the case for college professors, a professor develops a following of students who take most of the courses he or she offers. I am no exception to this unspoken rule. Students usually take "Thomas Merton, Religion and Culture" at the end or very near the end of their undergraduate studies. Many of the students in the course are students that I have already taught many times over. As such, they have come to know me as not just a professor but as a spiritual seeker. From my students, I have often learned things about myself (some of them very painful) that I would not have become aware of easily had it not been for the questions or remarks students have made about me based on their personal experiences of me as a teacher over the years. Now at the end of their undergraduate careers, many of these students are emboldened to say what is on their minds.

The last time I taught the Merton course I came to realize just how profound an impact Merton has had on my own life and spiritual journey based on comments students made about the course and about me. As the semester's end approached, I asked students to share what they thought of Merton now that they had read and talked about him for a semester. Some students felt Merton was a complainer who was obsessed with his health and the state of his body. Other students were scandalized because Merton was a monk who drank beer, had an affair with a nurse many years younger than he, and because he also explored other religious traditions. Most of the students loved Merton and vowed to keep reading him. They told me Merton showed them a way to be Catholic by which they could relate to the world in which they find themselves in the first two decades of the twenty-first century. Quite a number of students in the course also told me that they can understand why I teach a course on Thomas Merton. Like Merton, they told me, I have spent years cultivating a life of meditation and prayer and I have explored many different religious traditions. Like Merton, they also said, I have engaged and been active in social justice issues having to do with war and peace and human rights. For all my years of reading Merton, I was quite shocked to hear my students' perception of my life in relation to Merton's. Not once did it ever occur to me that I was living my own life in emulation of Merton's life pattern and what I have depicted as his ethnographic approach.

Some years ago, I commissioned an icon of Merton be drawn for me. On the scroll Merton holds in his hands is written "Our true journey in life is interior." I often stand before this icon and pray to Merton for help and guidance. In so doing, I have tried to cultivate a relationship with Merton that is more than just about reading his books. Merton believed in the mystical and he strove to cultivate a mystical relationship, not only with God but also with the Virgin Mary and with the saints and holy persons from various traditions. If Merton could reach me through his books in such a powerful way, then I am also willing to entertain this possibility that I can benefit from his wisdom through prayer before his icon. Whether I am still in touch with Merton's presence or not through my icon of him, I still feel his powerful presence in my life now some 46 years after his death and on the 100th anniversary of his birth.

Children Of The Resurrection:
Thomas Merton And The Shakers

Kathleen Deignan, CND

On December 10, 1960 Thomas Merton wrote to Shaker scholar Edward Deming Andrews expressing his interest in writing a book about the highly celebrated and enigmatic 19th century American utopian community, known as the Millennial Church and popularly called the Shakers. "... I have discussed the possibility of a book on the Shakers. My part would not be precisely a study of their religion, if by that is to be understood their doctrines, but of their spirit, and I might say their mysticism, in practice evidenced by their life and craftsmanship" craftsmanship (*A Meeting of Angels*, 12).

Sadly, Merton never realized that intention, though he did write some remarkable essays on Shakerism which no doubt would have been defining elements of such a book. But he did in fact inspire me to write a book on the Shakers. Therefore, for the sake of these remarks, I will take the playful liberty of imagining myself as Merton's research assistant, suggesting lines of inquiry he might have followed in composing his own book on the Shakers.

This most successful experiment in American communitarianism was in its terminal phase by the time Thomas Merton encountered the Shakers with all but a few members remaining in two of their societies—a vestige of the once potent religious project that had begun in England and immigrated to America around the time of the American Revolution and which grew to over 6000 members prior to the Civil War, with its decline thereafter. Formally called *The United Society of Believers in Christ's Second Appearing,* the Shakers are a unique species of Christianity, rooted in the eschatological conviction that Christ had come again, through the mediation of a woman, Ann Lee, and subsequently and progressively through the whole Shaker Society, in order to inaugurate the resurrection state here on earth. All Shaker theology, spirituality, practice, polity, art, and culture are an elaboration of the fundamental claim that the second appearing of Christ had brought the old world to an end, and a new world to beginning. The Shakers employed startling and imaginative strategies and analogies to present their gospel to the world, and their "mysticism in practice" captured the curiosity of a kindred soul, Thomas Merton.

We can trace Merton's fascination with the Shakers from his first note on the community in *The Waters of Siloe* in 1949; through his several visits to the Pleasant Hill settlement in Kentucky not far from the abbey, noted in his journals through the early1960s; and also in his photographic archive of the settlement, recently presented in Paul Pearson's *Seeking Paradise: The Spirit of the Shakers* (2003). In Merton's pictures, which would no doubt grace his Shaker book, we see something of the aesthetic geometry that captivated his spiritual and physical senses. After his first trip to Pleasant Hill in 1959 Merton said he felt *"some kind of obscure communion"* with this small nation of Christian craftspeople who, like himself, were seeking paradise: "I cannot help seeing Shakertown in a very special light, that of my own vocation. There is a lot of Shakertown in Gethsemani" (*A Search for Solitude*, 287).

Merton's book on Shakerism would somehow include his two substantial essays which display his uncanny capacity to get inside that cosmos of creativity and worship he so admired. The first, "Pleasant Hill: A Shaker Village in Kentucky," was originally published in *Jubilee*, and later reproduced in his volume *Mystics and Zen Masters*. In it he offers a wonderfully comprehensive and rather straight forward reflection on the history and values of the order. The second essay is an introduction to *Religion in Wood: A Book of Shaker Furniture*, written by Merton's mentor on Shakerism, Edward Deming Andrews. Here Merton weaves an intricate meditation on Shaker aesthetics and may be one of the most profound pieces of writing ever published on the Shaker spirit and the extraordinary culture that it crafted, particularly in the Zen-like purity of their furniture and dwellings. But Merton gives the most direct clues to the kind of inquiry he would undertake in his book on the United Society in several letters to Shaker scholar Edward Deming Andrews, his wife Faith, and Shaker conservators Mary Childs Black and Ralph McCallister. In one of these letters Merton writes:

> I believe that much is to be done in the study of Shaker spirituality in the light of Western and Near Eastern mystical traditions, and also in light of Jungian psychology. Doctrines which were heterodox from a traditional Christian viewpoint may then assume a special significance in the history of our time. I cannot help feeling that the Shaker movement is something of a mystery of the present predicament in the world.
>
> I think that this can be said for all the Utopian movements of the nineteenth century, but is especially true of the Shakers. I have as yet no way of substantiating this intuition. Perhaps some day research scholarship may help us to see more clearly into the problem (*Witness to Freedom*, 303).

In my pretend role as Merton's research assistant I would like to draw from my own work, *Christ Spirit: The Eschatology of Shaker Christianity*, to briefly point to some of the heterodox doctrines and practices that Merton might have found illuminating for us now regarding our present predicament in the world.

Four Recoveries

I think Merton would look to Shaker wisdom to aid us in at least four recoveries from impasse situations which the Shakers themselves labored with: the eclipse of the soul of America; the arrestment of human spirituality in dogma and ideology; the repression of the feminine Sophia; and the degradation of paradise into this, our wasteland world.

Recovering the Soul of America

First, under his signature rubric "recovering of the true self," Merton would point to the Shakers as exemplars of the bright spirit of America. He would call our attention to the intense spiritual practices by which Shaker Brothers and Sisters kept fresh their practicality, optimism, earnestness, and conservation. He might elaborate on how well they held the tension of particularly American mind-streams and values: the convergence of innocence and ingenuity; idealism and realism; freedom and discipline; romanticism and pragmatism; work and play; unity and diversity; perennialism and progress; tradition and invention; mysticism and prophecy; love of the land and the desire for the heavenly homeland. He might remind us that this Shaker legacy gives evidence that at root the American soul is utopian, capable of radical social, political, economic, and spiritual experimentation and renewal, invested with a self-restoring dynamic that holds the hope of our salvation.

I would direct Merton to explore the sources and logic of radical Shaker praxis found in the several major theological master works and in the various "Millennial Laws." There he would discover the rationale for their fierce social criticism, and he would see more plainly the counter-culturalism of their several shared renunciations and commitments. He would discover how intentionally the Shakers addressed the shadow side of the American psyche in those radical conversions which spoke directly to the temptations of the American nation, and he would learn how and why in the Shakers capitalism yielded to communitarianism; militarism surrendered to pacifism; and racial and gender hegemony dismantled in favor of the egalitarianism of genders and races which flourished within the order. Indeed, Merton celebrated the Shakers as a radically American variety of monasticism, who, like the Cistercians, made central the ideal of simplicity, which Merton saw in the Shakers as "a true American charism." In Merton's elegant prose he would persuade us that this life saving virtue of simplicity as lived by the Shakers could cut through the suffocating materialism for which we Americans have traded our souls and plundered our planet. Through his quasi-Shaker eyes we would see again our true face before we were born.

RECOVERING ECSTASY

The second impasse situation Merton might look to the Shakers about is the contemporary arrestment of religion, politics and even science in dogma and ideology.

The Shakers lived within a unique Christian paradigm marked by the features of millennialism, progressivism and evolutionism. They understood themselves commissioned to announce a new age of spiritual creativity and hope, and they worked tirelessly to actualize their vision by developing model societies that invited dialogue with "the world" on ways to convert the soul of the American nation.

Although Christian, the Shakers never anxiously employed a fundamentalist biblical polemic in their religious or social discourse. They generated instead a heterodox progressive gospel, committed to an evolutionary sense that, in and beyond them, the Christ Spirit was unfolding in history with greater energy and purpose, and they saw themselves as a vehicle of that development. They perceived in a vivid way that human spiritual life was suffering a surge, an intensification, an evolutionary leap, and they saw themselves as midwives birthing a new mystical consciousness, within and beyond the Millennial Church. As an essentially progressive enterprise, the Shakers were devoted to the spiritual evolution of all peoples, of all religions, of all beings.

Therefore, they did not hold tightly to their messianic mission; they did not cling to an unchanging or eternal sense of their church; they offered no militant religious ideology to buttress their gospel. Rather, they saw the very process of change itself to be the Spirit's way of working in history. Their theologians underscored how the second appearing of Christ in the body of Mother Ann gave birth and gave way to the corporate body of Christ in the Millennial Church, and ultimately that United Society of Believers itself had to make way for the pure un-embodied Spirit suffusing the world, generating the conditions for the resurrection state to be realized by any who would labor by intense spiritual practice for regeneration.

No doubt Merton's book would draw comparisons to Buddhism not just in the Zen-like sensibility of Shaker culture, but also the Zen-like quality of their consciousness, manifested in their ease with the fact of impermanence. Their serenity in seeing the ultimate "no-selfness" of the Shaker church led to a graced recognition of divine spirit in constantly changing phenomena, constantly arising and morphing into some other form or vehicle for the energy of the Christ Spirit to travel and travail in this world, with the Shakers as prime allies and midwives. It also led them to accept gracefully the closing season of the Shaker gospel.

Such openness to the progressive and processive character of spiritual life demanded tremendous creativity and spontaneity—a capacity to live NOW, in the present moment. In one of his essays Merton applauds the way Shakers made the creative imagination the central faculty of their religious life since, as he warned, if human imagination is not expressed in the kinds of aesthetic forms that serve our humanization, it becomes a dangerous destructive power fueling our dehumanization.

Shaker freedom from dogma and ideology made room for the emergence of ecstatic visionary gifts liberating them from the autism of religious sterility. The sublimation and transformation of their sexual energies in vowed celibacy funded countless forms of creativity for work and for worship. Their sacred song was powerful, their sacred dancing vigorous, as they invented novel modes of liturgy. The overflow of such ecstatic energy was meticulously employed in the design and realization of sublimely beautiful and amazingly functional environments and technologies to simplify and bring order to all the necessities of human living. Their indefatigable spiritual expressiveness manifested a spiritual affluence that funded their societies and the whole American nation for over 200 years.

RECOVERING SOPHIA

Doubtlessly Merton would find ways to bring Shaker commitment to the new revelation of Holy Mother Wisdom into dialogue with his own vision of *Hagia Sophia* as the fertile ground of the phenomenal world. I would delight in talking to him about the radical novelty of the Shaker gospel which never betrayed the centrality of a woman in its sacred schema, even when that was difficult to sell. Because Mother Ann had experienced Christ's Second Appearing not outside herself in some other, but within herself, as her very self, Shakerism was bound to integrate the *fact of woman* in a way that all other Christian formulas have denied. (Perhaps all modes of patriarchal religion, which is to say all religions, have denied the sacred fact of woman. But not the Shakers.)

To deeply comprehend the logic of this intuition, I would invite Merton to read Benjamin Seth Youngs' *Testimony of Christ's Second Appearing* (2009), in which he discloses the theological structure of Shaker thought, supported by an intricate and characteristically Shaker set of correspondences. Youngs shows the radical duality of reality from the Shaker point of view: in the human order, the bipolarity of male and female; in the messianic order, that of Christ Spirit in Jesus and Ann; and in the divine order, that of God as Father and Mother, both and at once.

And this recovery of the feminine dimension was not just a theoretical turn; the Shakers actually built not only their leadership on the fact of the equality and relation of the two—they even built their dwellings, modes of life, governance and worship, to acknowledge the sacred balance of male and female in all things—their staircases, their dormitories, their leadership councils, their constant repetitions in song and dance all rhyming out the pattern of the diad as sacred geometry underwriting all existence.

It would be interesting to know what Merton would make of this conjunction of sexuality and spirituality, and to have his take on their challenging gospel of celibacy, which intended to liberate women and men from natural generation to labor for spiritual regeneration. This was not celibacy Catholic style with the segregation of the sexes, and the marginalization and discounting of women. Rather it was a new covenant between the sexes, a daring spiritual experiment committing men and women together as totally equal partners in the generation of new families of resurrection.

Women were no longer perceived as sexual or economic objects, but as fully enfranchised subjects, dignified by an intrinsic value as the final horizon of divine incarnation and redemption. I imagine Merton would celebrate their holistic and Taoist way of seeing and being which constitutionally honored the feminine in the mother nature of God, the personhood of women, and which mandated the Shakers to protect and nurture the feminine side of all things until we recover the balance of life.

RECOVERING PARADISE

Without doubt, Merton would spend pages on the way the Shakers played out his own fascination with that "most authentic expression of the primitive American mystery or myth—the paradise myth" (*Witness to Freedom*, 31), manifesting in every facet of Believers' highly regulated life. He would, doubtless make much of the Shaker sense of place in contrast to our post-modern sense of displacement, and he would extol the brilliant ingenuity of their architecture that reverenced and worked with the sacrality of the natural world.

He might clarify that in all this is witnessed the Shaker spiritual quest, which was not for a restoration of all that was before the fall, not a *return* to paradise. Rather, they set themselves toward the paradox of the truly eschatological, the absolutely novel: a life and world born of living in the resurrection state. In this sense paradise is a task, a work in progress, and Merton would invite us to learn the particular Shaker genius for evoking its presence as a saving way out of the wasteland world we have made of our garden.

Merton's book would celebrate the Shakers as American Zen masters proficient in the art of tending to the truth of the thing before us. He would remind us too that the Benedictine commitment to *ora et labora* for the life of the world echoes in the Shaker mantra "hands to work and hearts to God." He might easily elaborate on how a style of work which was not focused on frenzied productivity for the sake of conspicuous consumption, might open a space for creativity punctuated by leisure for the sake of appreciation. He could rehearse his teaching that such a conversion might heal the human soul and save the terrestrial body.

A heady, sobering way of being, the Shaker way. A way of gifts and gifting. A world of grace. A gospel of life. Merton's book would no doubt extol these kindred souls who shared his experiential faith in a realized immediacy of life in the divine spirit—the discovery of the living presence of the Christ Spirit within us here and now. He shared their Shaker faith that "the true Christian is the . . . 'Child of the Resurrection' with his eyes open to a wholly new vision of a redeemed cosmos in which war, hatred, tyranny, greed had no place—a cosmos of creativity and worship" (from Merton's introduction to *Religion in Wood*, ix).

What We Are

Gerard Thomas Straub

"Whenever our interior life becomes caught up in its own interests and concerns, there is no longer room for the other, no place for the poor. God's voice is no longer heard; the quiet joy of his love is no longer felt, and the desire to do good fades."

Pope Francis, *Evangelii Gaudium*

"I am a sinner." That simple, honest, direct statement was uttered by Pope Francis. He took the words right out of my mouth. Mine has been a messy, imperfect life, littered with more mistakes and failures than I can count. My sinfulness was rooted in my inner poverty, my ignorance and my self-centeredness. I was empty and lost. But God's mercy proved greater than my sinfulness. I was also a committed atheist. But God's love was greater than my doubt and unbelief. I once was a Hollywood television producer. By God's grace I now make films on global poverty that feature saintly, heroic people who are living the self-emptying love of Christ by serving the poor.

During the last 15 years I've spent a great deal of time filming in some of the worst slums on earth. I even briefly lived in a dreadful slum in Haiti. My small cinder block home in the midst of the crippling poverty of Port-au-Prince was far removed from the small cinder block hermitage surrounded by a luxuriant forest where I once spent a week in solitude and prayer. The simple hermitage was located in Kentucky and it once was occupied by Thomas Merton.

Thomas Merton saw the spiritual journey as a metaphorical "going forth into strange countries." For Merton, even going nowhere required travel. Day by day, our entire lives are a journey, a journey to nowhere, a journey to God. I've been around the world, traveled to many "strange countries" in order to get nowhere, in order to arrive at an empty place within me where the fullness of life is hidden.

When the invitation came to contribute an essay for this book, I was in the middle of editing the final draft of my new book on St. Francis of Assisi which had been accepted for publication. My original manuscript had to be cut by nearly 40% to accommodate the page limit imposed by the publisher who needed to make the book affordable. In an amazing coincidence that strains credulity, at the precise moment the invitation arrived via e-mail I was actually cutting the very quotation the editors of this book used in their letter of invitation, a quote in which Merton described the character of the deepest level of communion across seemingly impenetrable boundaries: "It is wordless. It is beyond words, and it is beyond speech, and it is beyond concept. Not that we discover a new unity. We discover an older unity. My dear brothers, we are already one. But we imagine that we are not. And what we have to recover is our original unity. What we have to be is what we are." My original draft contained 73 quotations or references to Thomas Merton. Regrettably, I had to cut virtually all of them; the final draft contained only 16 references to Merton. Moreover, in my more than a dozen documentary films on global poverty, Merton is quoted in almost all of them. I mention this because it clearly illustrates the impact Merton had on my personal spiritual journey.

Thomas Merton introduced me to a spiritual reality far bigger, far deeper and far more profound than I ever imagined existed. When I first picked up a book by Merton, I was an adult dealing with a very grown-up crisis with a religious faith that had not grown beyond adolescence. My immature faith offered no guidance, no assurance, no support; what it offered was lifeless formulas, dogmatic assertions, harsh judgment, and condemnation. My childhood faith was no match for the hopeless nihilism I encountered as an adult. So I dropped the fairytale faith of my youth and opted for the only alternative that made any sense: atheism. Yet, even though I was an atheist, Merton intrigued me and prompted me to look at things differently. Merton was my only connection to the Catholic faith into which I was born. Somehow I intuitively knew there was much good in the faith I had discarded, but I had no way to connect with it, nor did I see any real evidence of it in the lives of "practicing" Catholics who seemed no different or no better than the rest of our self-centered, consumer-crazed society that ignored the poor and loved war. Jesus and the litany of saints who tried to emulate him seemed to be relics from the dustbin of history and their lives just some pious fairytales that had no relevance to my modern, secular, skeptical life. Still, there seemed to be something poetically beautiful in the way Christ and the saints confronted the reality of life and turned human expectations and experiences upside down. I hungered for a spirituality that had the transformative power to make all things new. Over the years, Merton showed me that real satisfaction comes from giving, not taking, that real love requires real sacrifice, that thinking about or striving for success is useless, that I had to look within for answers to the questions that tormented me. Merton taught me the value of stillness and silence, where I could discover and accept my false self and find real love and authentic peace.

In the limited space of a short essay, it's extremely difficult to capture the essence of the monk's life and the impact it had on me, a network television producer whose life in the glitz and glamour of Hollywood was far removed from the reality of Merton's isolated hermitage in the hilly woods of Kentucky. Thanks to the generosity and kindness of Br. Patrick Hart, OCSO, one of the great graces of my life was the opportunity I had in December of 2000 to spend a solitary week in Merton's hermitage on the snowy grounds of the Abbey of Gethsemani. That memorable week came about five years after I had a rather dramatic conversion experience in an empty Franciscan church in Rome in March of 1995.

I had not entered the church to pray. I entered the church because I was tired. I was simply looking for a cool, quiet place to sit and rest. An empty church and an empty man became a meeting place of grace. The church was silent. I was merely resting. But something happened, something highly unexpected: God broke through the silence. And everything changed . . . and all things became new. On the seat next to me was a copy of the Liturgy of the Hours. I picked it up and opened it randomly and read the words of Psalm 63:

God, you are my God, I am seeking you,
my soul is thirsting for you,
my flesh is longing for you,
a land parched, weary and waterless;
I long to gaze on you in the Sanctuary,
and to see your power and glory.

Your love is better than life itself,
my lips will recite your praise;
all my life I will bless you,
in your name lift up my hands;
my soul will feast most richly,
on my lips a song of joy, in my mouth praise.

As I read those words, my soul leapt with joy. Without warning, I felt the overwhelming presence of God. I didn't see any images or hear any words. What I felt was beyond images and words. I felt immersed in a sea of Love. I knew—not intellectually, but experientially—that God was real, that God loved me, and that the hunger and thirst I had felt for so long could only be satisfied by God. In that moment of revelation, I was transformed from an atheist into a pilgrim. I went from denying God to wanting to experience more and more of God. A few days later, after a long conversation with a Franciscan priest from Ireland, I went to confession. St. Francis of Assisi became my spiritual guide. Day after day, this medieval saint showed a modern skeptic how to enter the heart of God. The walled, hillside town of Assisi became my spiritual home and opened the mystical windows of my soul. In those early and often lonely days of reconnecting to my Catholic faith, Merton was my main companion and inspiration. For me, Francis and Merton were brothers.

Following St. Francis led me to the worst slums on earth, and I usually brought Thomas Merton with me. I carried books by or about Merton into the massive slums and refugee camps of Uganda and Kenya, into leper colonies in Brazil, into a home for 50 seriously ill and impoverished children in Peru, into the barrios of Mexico and El Salvador, into the dire squalor in the Philippines where people lived on a mountain of garbage, scavenging like vultures off the rotting waste of others. I took Merton with me to India and Jamaica, as well as to the bleakest and most violent neighborhoods of Philadelphia, Detroit and Los Angeles while making films on the homeless. After the earthquake in Haiti that killed over 300,000 people and left well over a million people homeless, I lived in a huge slum, the only white face in a sea of black faces; I had no running water or electricity, and I shared my humble, dirt-floored abode with rats and mice. I read Merton by candlelight at night and on crowded, dilapidated buses during the day. I remember someone asking me what I was reading, and after I showed them the book they asked, "Who is Thomas Merton?" I answered with the first thing that popped into my mind: "Thomas Merton is my hero." My hero introduced me to great spiritual writers, such as Alexander Schmemann, Olivier Clément, Thich Nhat Hanh, and Abraham Joshua Heschel, to name just a few. Each of those writers showed me, in their own way and in their own traditions, the unity of life.

Returning to all the Merton material in my new book *The Loneliness and Longing of Saint Francis*, at first blush it would seem that Thomas Merton and St. Francis of Assisi did not have much in common besides their passion for God, thirst for the absolute and hunger for love. Merton wrote constantly; Francis, virtually never. Merton was well-educated; St. Francis didn't place much value on education. Merton spent his religious life within the cloistered walls of a monastery; Francis considered the world to be his cloister. However, when you dig a little deeper, you see many points of connection between the verbal monk and the mendicant saint. Both placed a high value on stillness and silence; both sought out solitary hermitage settings. Both understood the importance of inter-faith dialogue; St. Francis invented it when he tried to counter the brutal violence of the Crusades by reaching out a hand of friendship to the Sultan, and Merton is well-known for his friendship with Buddhists and Sufi Muslims. Both had a deep concern for the poor, marginalized and rejected. Both understood the pain of spiritual poverty and physical poverty. Both were messengers of peace. Before becoming a Trappist monk, Merton tried to become a Franciscan friar.

In his book *Thoughts in Solitude*, Thomas Merton wrote something that clearly could have come from the mouth of St. Francis: "Poverty is the door to freedom . . . because, finding nothing in ourselves that is a source of hope, we know there is nothing in ourselves worth defending. There is nothing special in ourselves to love. We go out of ourselves therefore to rest in Him in Whom alone is our hope" (47).

Like Merton, St. Francis was unique. He was a mystic and a person of action. His actions flowed out of his contemplation, out of his longing glance at what is real. The word "contemplation" actually means to witness and respond. Thomas Merton, in *Bread in the Wilderness*, reminds us that "the secret of contemplation is the gift of ourselves to God" (47). When we give ourselves to God in prayer, we begin to experience the richness of divine love and mercy, and are better able to share that love and mercy with others. In *Conjectures of a Guilty Bystander*, Merton wrote: "Solitude has its own special work: a deepening awareness that the world needs. A struggle against alienation. True solitude is deeply aware of the world's needs. It does not hold the world at arm's length" (10).

The human heart is drawn to God. The language of the heart is love. Not soft, wimpy, fleeting, Hollywood-style love, but a bold, deep, penetrating love that requires openness and transformation, a love that perpetually gives itself away. We live in a world of hearts. Sadly, most hearts are broken, unloved and unable to love. God wants to give us new hearts, mystical hearts throbbing to love and to be loved. If you can imagine a world of divinely transformed hearts, you will see a world at peace, a world of plenty where no one goes hungry. Such a world begins within each of us, if we are able to shake off the countless distractions of modern life and pay attention to the silent voice of God.

Prayer is the only weapon we need. Prayer helps us flee from the storm of inner thoughts and the noise that engulfs modern life. Prayer slows down the frenzied pace of life. Prayer quiets negative passions. Prayer helps restore our awareness of God. Prayer is an act of humility, stemming from a mindfulness of our inadequacy. Prayer and humility go hand-in-hand: prayer deepens humility and humility deepens prayer. Prayer creates the unruffled calmness required to encounter God. To neglect prayer is to neglect God. Prayer helps you see the extraordinary hidden in the ordinary. Prayer leads us to wholeness and simplicity. Prayer prompts us to reach out in compassion to the suffering and weak, and helps us embrace all of humanity. Prayer is the breath of life, the sunrise of the soul.

Prayer needs periods of solitude where stillness and silence are more easily found. *In New Seeds of Contemplation* Merton wrote, "The truest solitude is not something outside you, not an absence of men or of sound around you; it is an abyss opening up in the center of your soul" (80-81). Merton showed me that solitude is not the same as withdrawal, which has negative connotations. Solitude has positive qualities. In solitude during a six-month-long sabbatical in 2010, I stopped running from myself and became friends with myself; solitude gave me space to enjoy my own company. In solitude I found the wisdom to forgive those who had hurt me deeply. In solitude, I learned that I am not alone; moreover, it taught me there is no such thing as aloneness. Spiritual growth, for most of us, does not come from fleeing the world, but from entering into it fully. However, for the sake of our spiritual health, we each need periods of solitude. And we also need to develop an inner solitude that can be entered no matter where we are. But Merton made it abundantly clear that entering into solitude with the idea of affirming ourselves, separating oneself from others, even interiorly, in order to be different, or by intensifying one's individual self-awareness, is not in harmony with the purity required for spiritual growth. For the Christian, pure solitude is a place of self-emptying in order to experience union with Christ; in the interior abyss we become detached from our petty false self and open ourselves up to the vastness of the Infinite Presence.

Merton showed me that who I am on the surface is not the true me. I'm not who I appear to be. My exterior is only the person I think I am, and the guy I put on display for others to see. The real me is buried deep within—unknown even to me, unknown to all but God. I must cast off this projected exterior image, my false self, and discover my true self, the person I was created to be. That process of losing and finding is the stuff of sainthood. I had lived in a dense forest of unreality for so long that finding my way out was a difficult, confusing, scary task.

The key to finding myself is finding God.

Transformation into my true self can only come through the power of the One hidden in me. There is nothing I can do on my own. Even stripping myself of all that is not God will not bring me any closer to the reality of God. The only thing I can do is to respond to God's call to enter into union with God. I created my external self, not God. Out of the clay of my own egocentric desires, my own selfish, sinful actions, I molded the person I see in the mirror, the person who loved to flee reality. The real me, my true self, sleeps silently in the depths of my being, undisturbed by all my surface activity, waiting patiently to be awakened by God. My true self was created by God, made for God. And I cannot be my true self without knowing God. I am hidden in God. And God is hidden in me.

On my own I can learn something about God through reason and reading, but, as Merton writes in *New Seeds of Contemplation*: "There is no human and rational way in which I can arrive at that contact, that possession of Him which will be the discovery of Who He really is and Who I am in Him." Merton goes on to say: "The only One Who can teach me to find God is God, Himself, alone" (36).

For most of my life, I had been moving away from God, carried along on the tide I had created. All along I was fighting a Wind which had been trying to prompt me to turn in the opposite direction. My initial movement away from God was propelled by the influence of sin, and was powered by my ego and illusions. The habits acquired while traveling in the wrong direction are hard to reverse. The superficial, fictional me I see in the mirror is far from the reality of God. The guy in the mirror is incapable of transcendent experiences. Only my openness to God's call can put me on the path to becoming more receptive to the mystical dimension hidden within me.

This stuff doesn't come quickly or easily . . . which is why we don't bother with it. I devoted a few pages of *The Sun & Moon Over Assisi* to explaining Merton's ideas on the true and false self. Mostly I quoted sources who understood. I had deceived myself into thinking I understood. In truth, my mind sort of got it—but it was just another theory neatly tucked away in a dingy corner of my brain. Slowly, I'm beginning to "see" it with different eyes.

Thomas Merton wrote so clearly about deep spiritual things that we think we get it. The fact is, his understanding was hidden in his words, which only point the way, showing us the right direction. But we must walk alone. Only God can teach us how to find God . . . which is why so many true contemplatives are so reluctant to talk about their inner life. They cannot teach us anything—aside from a few techniques to help us get started.

Find a quiet place. Sit. Be still, mentally and physically. And listen. Easy? No. It is the most difficult thing in the world. Nothing seems to be happening. Results take a lifetime. Maybe even longer. We are so far from God, it is beyond our ability to measure. Merton knew this, even after a quarter of a century as a monk. He knew he was far from his goal, and had miles to go. Perhaps he came close in Asia. Perhaps not. Only God knows.

For me, writing has become a sacramental avenue into that interior empty space where the fullness of God resides. The very act of writing demands attentiveness. Simone Weil claimed that all study and serious reading, with its required concentrated focus, was in essence an excellent preparation for prayer. The Buddhist road to enlightenment is paved with attentiveness. Thomas Merton's dance with Buddhism helped him embrace a freer, more experimental form of writing. His thoughts flowed out onto the page in clear, simple words that expressed the openness of his heart and spirit. It also helped him see the entire world in a more positive light. It seems that Buddhist meditation practices drew him into a deeper silence, which helped him to be more aware of his true self. Merton's interior journey helped him affirm and deepen his Christian understanding that (as he wrote), "Christ alone is the way." The way of Christ is all-embracing love and peace.

Despite all our longing and talk, we don't see much love and peace today. Society is becoming increasingly fragmented and polarized, which poses a great danger. We are in desperate need of a spirit of communion and compassion to wash afresh over all of us. We need to resurrect the lost art of conversation in which we truly listen to and share with each other. Through communion, compassion and conversation we can find our common ground and work together for the common good of all, while at the same time realizing that we are all fumbling around in the dark of an infinite mystery that is beyond words and understanding. While God is beyond words and shrouded in silence, God nonetheless is in a perpetual conversation with each of us, even if most of us are rarely listening; our failure to recognize and appreciate this divine conversation has caused us to turn a deaf ear to the other, to anyone who does not believe as we do, which in turn stifles communion and compassion.

Each of us is a different expression of the same divine energy and we were created to be in communication with each other and the Other. Each of us is a part of one organic whole. Each of us is only a temporary and infinitesimal fraction of a gigantic universe, and our failure to humbly grasp our individual smallness allows us to assume a far greater importance than we deserve and causes us to be human-centered rather than God-centered. We are so centered on ourselves, we have failed to grasp the organic wholeness of life and the divine beauty of the entire universe. The brokenness of any one of us is the brokenness of all of us. It is in our human brokenness that divine revelation is manifested.

If Merton were alive today, I think he would be appalled by that fact we are drowning in a flood of words and shrouded in nonstop noise. Silence was once a natural part of life. Max Picard, the famous Swiss philosopher, accurately observed: "Nothing has changed the nature of man so much as the loss of silence" (Max Picard, *The World of Silence*, 221). He wrote that long before such noise-making devices as television were invented. Today, it is normal for earphones to be almost permanently jammed into ears, earphones connected to iPods, iPads, iPhones that are channels for endless, pointless chatter. And we watch life through little screens which distract us from the real life in front of us. We now film our lives with our cell phones and then e-mail selected scenes from our self-centered lives to everybody we know. No one looks up anymore . . . we are all looking down at our iWhatevers and typing something that someone else needs to know. Writing has become "texting." We tweeter away the day and keep God at bay. Not many people these days aspire to sainthood. In *Life and Holiness*, Merton wrote: "If we are called by God to holiness of life, and if holiness is beyond our natural power to achieve (which it certainly is) then it follows that God himself must give us the light, the strength and the courage to fulfill the task he requires of us. He will certainly give us the grace we need. If we do not become saints it is because we do not avail ourselves of his gift" (17).

Whether we think of Merton's life as saintly or not, we know his life was a continuous struggle, especially his last dozen years at Gethsemani. On my last night in his hermitage, I thought about all the mental and spiritual wrestling Merton did in his humble, rustic, cinder block home in the woods, and how he poured his external and internal life out on pages covered with words carefully documenting every aspect of his life. His expansive mind and personality took everything in . . . and gobbled it up like a hungry lion. He entered fully into everything. He probed, poked, pushed, and badgered people and ideas. He was serious and funny. He was outgoing and reclusive. He was profane and personal. He loved freedom but practiced discipline. He had great intensity.

Life is a struggle, a continual search for meaning. We live in exile. Each dawn brings us the chance to wake up to the true Reality: the insubstantial, shadowy, false self must dissolve into God. St. Francis of Assisi and Thomas Merton both made the connection between poverty and prayer. In *New Seeds of Contemplation*, Thomas Merton wrote: "No man who ignores the rights and needs of others can hope to walk in the light of contemplation, because his way has turned aside from truth, from compassion, and therefore from God. The obstacle is in our 'self,' that is to say, in the tenacious need to maintain our separate, external, egocentric will" (18, 21). For me, Thomas Merton truly became a messenger of hope. In turn, I've tried to become a messenger of hope in my modest work on behalf of the poor.

Playing Chess

Laura Geary Dunson

The metal detector stood at our doorway, a bold reminder of the new world we were entering with just a single step. As we were whisked away from our comfortable suburban bubbles to a raw inescapable reality, I was struck with an overwhelming anxiety. *What did I get us into?* I asked myself. Here it was, only a couple weeks into the summer service program I was directing, and I had brought a group of naïve college students (including myself) into a men's homeless shelter. Within moments our group was assigned a personal set of security guards who already had their work cut out for them shooing away residents who were trying to get our phone numbers. *This is a horrible idea*, I thought to myself. *We don't belong here, and everyone knows it.*

I had always prided myself on having a strong service ethic, a strong desire to connect with people through anything. Maybe it came from being a part of a family of nurses and doctors, or maybe it came from hearing my parents' struggles and triumphs throughout their lives. Whatever the ethic was, it was completely undermined by my desire to lead this band of suburbanites out of the shelter and away from everything that challenged our biases, our assumptions and our prejudices we could rely on until now.

But the metal detector had been a one-way entrance and, like it or not, we were brought to this new world. We were led to the cafeteria where the residents were finishing their dinner and waiting for us to bring in the board games and cards. The walls were cold and clean, somewhere in the place where a hospital ended and a prison started—a new world within itself, speaking languages few of us could ever understand.

At the sight of games, a few men started calling out—claiming the Uno cards or challenging other residents to another round of poker. One resident, an older African American man with a thick beard and a walking cane called out to us: "Any of you play chess?"

I swallowed and smiled weakly. "I play chess."

Jacob had a thick raspy voice and a laugh that seemed to shake away dust and old memories. He watched me intently but kindly, not unlike a grandfather making sure a grandchild didn't mess up on an important project. And sure enough, he shared with me that he was a grandfather and was on his way to see his family. He had stopped at the shelter for a couple of nights because it was colder than usual and he couldn't stand sleeping in his car anymore. But soon he'd continue driving through Ohio and into Michigan to see his long-lost daughter and the grandkids he had never met. It had been three years since Jacob last worked construction, when he had been injured on the job and given the full-time companion of the ratted cane next to him. "We all go through tough times though, you know?" he added on gruffly. "It's just part of life."

We were so different. Completely different lives, completely different backgrounds, and here we sat in harmony and in community. Between us stood mountains of stigma and societal standards and it was all we could do to precariously reach out and connect.

"So kid, are you in college?"

Jacob's question drew me out of myself and into that present moment. I told him that yes, we all were and explained the program, about a group of students living in a house together and working at nonprofits over the summer. "That's good of you, kid," he responded with a gruff attempt at a smile that still managed to seem frighteningly intimidating. "You're alright."

His words surprised me, even though they were exactly the words we had all expected. Doing service so oftentimes means that you expect thank you's and you're wonderful's paired with trophies and parades. You expect the praise for being such a good person. But here, I didn't feel like a good person. I felt human. I felt small. Infinitesimally small, like I was nothing more than a cog in a greater machine than I never knew existed before that moment. Here I was, walking into the shelter ready to save and cherish each of these poor unfortunate souls—each of these people I saw as "the other"—when really Jacob was the one who validated me.

He could see how scared I was, I was sure of it. He saw how silly and naïve this white suburban girl who went to private school and private college was—how little she knew about the real world and about the struggles people had to face. How on paper her own problems could pale in comparison with the greater casualties of the world. And although he could have rightfully held any of these perceptions against me, he reached out across the divisions of age and race and background and connected with a fellow human with her unique troubles and her unique dreams, accepting her fully and completely. Recognizing a fellow human in a common struggle to find happiness and meaning in a confusing, strange, but beautiful, world.

And somehow as he reached beyond all of those divisions, it seemed as though each difference melted away. As beautifully diverse as we were—two members of an extraordinarily mixed and melded creation—we were so much the same. And how amazing it was that we two sat together breathing the same air, sitting under the same sun, loving and living in the same creation, as all the rest the world around us. That there was no other, no them, but simply a beautiful and vast and endless *us*.

Jacob's validation still rang in my ears, those few simple words bringing to life feelings I had never known before. I looked back to the chess board as Jacob again checkmated, this time in a record eight minutes. I couldn't help but laugh. "Thanks, Jacob. But I'm still pretty bad at chess."

He laughed back. "Yeah, you are." We played countless more games of chess that night, joking and laughing with one another and other residents. When it was time for our group to go, Jacob and I clasped hands. I thanked him and he smiled easily, saying, "We'll see each other again, don't you worry."

I could never have known how right Jacob was. He followed me everywhere I went from that point on—a human face where before I had only seen strangers. He laughed at me when I made mistakes and clapped me on the shoulder when I picked myself back up. Even as I hoped he had found his daughter and met his grandchildren, I saw him back in our city with me every day.

And he joined me there, standing on my own corner of "Fourth and Walnut" where I found myself realizing the same truths Merton had once learned. Seeing the world

195

with new eyes, awakened from the realm of stigmas and stereotypes to the place where our oneness in creation united us. There, in Jacob's eyes, I was able to see the dazzling reality of humanity, pulling me from my seat of comfort and safety and taking me to the very brink—where all that stood with us in creation was reckless love and sacred connections.

Another Song From Nobody

Gary Hall

How to begin? Whom to address? A simple dilemma reveals the peculiar giftedness of Thomas Merton. The strange familiarity of his abiding presence prompts a desire to address the dead monk-writer directly, as though writing him a letter, as though he were as alive as when those thousands of other letters poured into Gethsemani. He seems, still, to invite conversation, though all we have is what he once described as his paper self in what he dismissed as a strange land of unreal intimacy. A paper self, a life hammered out on that rightly Royal typewriter or scrawled in heart-leaning cursive, can over time begin to feel like a real presence in our midst. Perhaps this is a cumulative effect of the kind of attentive reading he draws readers into, leading us by the hand to a place apart, yet never really apart. In fact, the opposite. That authorial presence—not like a ghost, or some lonely child's invisible friend—remains as (here I'm groping for a metaphor) a beacon, perhaps? A homing beacon, by whose intermittent radiance readers orientate themselves towards the burning love of Christ and feel again the pulse of a more vibrant world, in all its glory and fragility. Along the way readers seem to discover one another, and we get some sense of how his writing goes on working, how it goes on communicating and stimulating the kind of communication which just might lead to a communion beyond words.

If we who never knew Merton in that flesh-and-blood way of friendship or companionship can discover one another through him, this is no more remarkable than our joining company with sundry saints and martyrs, artists and activists, oddballs and passers-by who populated his world, along with his friends and correspondents whose lives we can hardly avoid intruding upon. Merton's world and their worlds merge with our own worlds until the realization dawns on us that (as he told us) we cannot be alien to one another, that separateness is illusory. In following his paper trail we, time and again, stumble across some overgrown path leading away from manufactured worlds into ancient forests which remember an older unity; where the breeze, however ancient, is a new testament; where whispering rain becomes rivulets forming pools from which, if only now and then, our thirst is slaked.

That's one way of putting it, anyway. Other days, less poetic, are laced with foreboding. Then only seeds of destruction and engineered fruit seem to flourish in deforested wasteland, irrigated by the poisons of soulless industries which merrily go on manufacturing consent and distraction. Prometheus is fracking now and Eichmann is reinstated. Merton provides the script, while other voices keep on suggesting that the prophetic longings he conjures so eloquently are no foretaste of paradise, merely nostalgia. More Forrest Gump than John of Patmos. The bluegrass hermit with his deceptively simple ways simply had to die. Killed by electricity (of course) before Reagan and

197

Bush presided over Cold War games, before cruise missiles were replaced as weapon of choice by an armory of militarized finance. Merton left these shores before the Fat Man with his digitized matrix turned to spying on email and digi-text (forget those indiscrete phone calls from the cellarer's office) or could watch from satellite and drone, making mockery of twenty-feet-thick walls and putting an end to any prospect of wilderness. Merton didn't live to witness these developments but we can only conjecture his protests against the madness of the late twentieth and early twenty-first centuries.

But these are supposed to be variations on a theme of hope, a theme which perhaps needs to be made more explicit. Thomas Merton taught us to eschew that cheerful optimism which works so hard to suppress the tragic realities which naked minds and tendered hearts simply cannot—will not—avoid. Deep joy will always be prone to flip over into sorrow, just as love risks pain, and delight in beauty becomes grief at its destruction. Hope, like love and faith, bears all these. Merton's joyful Advent faith in the promise and the presence of Christ carried him on his own Advent journey beyond the misty realm of slogans and petty comforts, of accolades and commentaries. Only captured words remain, inviting us to our senses, restoring confidence in the life-giving activity of proper speech.

I love that he made no money from writing, nor wanted to. I love that he stayed the course, loyal unto death, despite the storms and the options. I love that, despite ambition, he cared little for office or rank, but craved only enough solitude for hospitality, silence and communication. And the occasional beer. I love that he knew his need to be noticed and didn't hide his foibles; that in the end he knew love to be more than sufficient. Sometimes overly assertive yet never too sure of himself, Merton unmasked his own contradictions and fractures, so we might dare to do the same.

It would seem strange for those of us who never knew him to say that we miss him. An occasional sense of loss nevertheless lingers. Perhaps these are innate memories of the primordial paradise Merton evokes, though the feeling is not so much about a lost world as his way of seeing it and telling it. So serious yet un-serious, a transparent blaze of paradox and integrity, disciplined and assiduous yet as playful as a child who just wants to see what happens when he points out that the emperor is naked. Gazing into the abyss or reeling in wonder at the incandescent glory of the human race, brooding beneath stormy skies or singing like birds granted permission to be, he waited and prayed, relentlessly making his art and his confession, pouring out silent words then blending the best of them on the canvas of so many hearts. So, in the end, his way of seeing and telling is far from lost, but continues to evolve amongst readers who recognize their Virgil, and wend their way back into the heart of this present moment where nothing is final. The game is never over.

Hope Is Where The Margins Are

Patrick Thomas Morgan

One day, at the Abbey of the Genesee in Piffard, New York, Henry David Thoreau introduced me to Thomas Merton. It was summer. The warm smell of Monks' Bread hung in the air inside the abbey bookstore. I could hear the buzzing hum of a Douglas C-47 Skytrain flying over Genesee Valley, playing its part in the annual historical aircraft show. In front of me on the wooden bookshelf sat a copy of *New Seeds of Contemplation* by some author named Thomas Merton. There was something about the book cover that caught my attention. Perhaps it was the way the title blended agrarian practices with mental processes, layered over a shallow-focused photograph of the imbricated grains of a wheat shoot. The first thing that struck me when I turned the book over to read its back cover was a single surname: "Thoreau." It was a sentence clause that changed my life: "... and some have compared Merton's reflections to those of Thoreau." At the time, I was in the middle of an undergraduate honors thesis about Thoreau, analyzing the intersection of aesthetics and gender within his conception of river geomorphology. *Anyone who is compared to Thoreau is good enough for me*, I thought to myself.

Some people read one Merton text, realize his genius, and then devour as many of his titles as they can find. In contrast, after reading *New Seeds* once, I read it again. I then read it a third time and a fourth, and with each new reading came new insights—a sentence that I had somehow overlooked before, a word to which I had been blind. What drew me to this text was Merton's aesthetic of instability. Suddenly, it was all right to acknowledge the fractures of doubt within one's foundation of faith. Indeed, Merton was telling me that these fractures, somehow, were the means by which God drew me closer to the source of my being. "Place no hope in the feeling of assurance, in spiritual comfort," says Merton (*New Seeds of Contemplation*, 187). Hope resides in the margins of life, between faith and doubt, emptiness and saturation, inner sense and outer sense, silence and sound. Merton gave me a new vocabulary—ordered by a different syntax—to give voice to this vibrant, protean sense of inner life.

My next several encounters with Merton were through two Trappist monks at the Genesee Abbey: Brother Anthony Weber and Dom John Eudes Bamberger. Each, in their own way, nurtured this Mertonian seed intertwining margins, instability and hope. With Brother Anthony, I participated in shared *lectio divina* alongside a group of college students, reading Merton's *The Inner Experience: Notes on Contemplation* in the abbey's Merton Hall. Merton gazed down at us, from a painting, with a serene and radiant smile, while we munched on a fresh loaf of Monks' Bread and read Merton's words with prayerful intentions. In the margins of my pages, I would summarize Brother Anthony's reflections, transforming his words into the speech acts of instruction: "Be wary of people who tell you who you are." A false stability, in other words, isn't only the hobgoblin of a shallow faith, but also the bugbear of our sense of identity, and of our vocational discernment.

Father John Eudes teetered out of the abbey's front door, meeting me near the Virgin Mary and Christ Child statue just outside the glacially deposited granite cobbled walls of the chapel. Knowing that I studied geology, he asked me how old these granite rocks were, and then told me that a Harvard geologist estimated an age between one and three billion years. In his crackly, high voice, he mentioned how he dug up several of these granite cobbles from the nearby Genesee River, back when the abbey was being built. Then he faced the statue and, gesturing toward the space surrounding the Virgin Mary and Christ child, said, "This landscaping was done in the Japanese tradition. The Japanese have a beautiful way of organizing the landscape, but it is lost on Westerners, who don't realize what's before their eyes." "If you look closely," he said, "there are two hills adjacent to the statue: a lower mound on the left, sporting several different kinds of small shrubs and other decorative features; and a higher mound on the right, composed entirely of blindingly green grass. The lower, more cluttered mound represents one world—*this* world—of chaos and change," he added, "while the higher mound represents the world to come in all its simplicity. That's something to think about," he said with a knowing look. In Father John's words I could hear the echo of Thomas Merton, expanding once again my notion of the linkage between instability and hope—a linkage that began as a commentary on faith within *New Seeds*, then sprouted into a commentary on vocation with Brother Anthony, and flowered into a commentary on the immensities of life with Dom John Eudes.

When I think of the relationship between hope and instability within Merton's work, I think of his poetry. It is within poetry—a genre that became increasingly marginalized within popular culture throughout Merton's lifetime—that Merton locates hope. In his 1964 address, "Message to Poets" (*Raids on the Unspeakable*), Merton reminds us that the poet's purview isn't the "the magic of words" (a phrase he associates with politicians and propaganda), but with life. Poets place their feet in the ever-flowing river, writes Merton, and poetry is created by the flashing up-splash of water. That is, poetry itself is born in the margin between foot and water, poet and life, imagination and experience. For Merton, the margin is where the deepest form of communication occurs: the poet's words point toward the silence of communion. It's within his image of the poet's foot contacting the protean fluidity of the river that Merton situates his message of hope to the Latin American poets gathering in Mexico City: "Let us obey life, and the Spirit of Life that calls us to be poets, and we shall harvest many new fruits for which the world hungers—fruits of hope that have never been seen before" (*Raids*, 160).

I like to think that my own vocation, as a teacher and scholar of literature, participates in this poetic harvest that Merton describes. Because the connections between margins, instability and hope are sometimes buried deep within the material reality of Merton's lyric poetry, and the art of reading and describing the lyric is a skill that we as a culture cannot risk losing. Merton, for example, deploys different techniques across the evolution of his verse to instill his language with an aesthetic of instability. In his early poetry, he often makes use of the poet's traditional tools for inscribing instability: variations of rhythm, rhyme and meter. But his later poetry, especially in the 1960s, enacts—I would argue—the knight's gambit: aesthetic techniques that played a relatively marginal role in relation to the signifying capacity of rhyme and meter are suddenly imbued—within his 1960s free verse—with a greater signifying capacity. In other words, without having recourse to meter and rhyme within his later focus upon *vers libre*, Merton is forced to make sense of specific life moments via other formal features—features that, though often present in his earlier, more formal poetry, are suddenly imbued, in the absence of meter and rhyme, with a heightened signifying capacity. By the "knight's gambit," I am referring to that side-stepping move, akin to the knight's move within chess, in which a more direct, straight-line movement is deferred for the indirection of that side-stepping minor move—a useful metaphor for the way Merton defers the more direct and traditional signifying capabilities of meter and rhyme in favor of breathing new life into relatively minor aesthetic techniques.

One example of the knight's gambit, or this significant elevation of particular lyrical techniques, includes his 1966 poem, "Elegy for a Trappist" (*In The Dark Before Dawn*, 43), a poem that relies heavily on non-metrical means of signification. Specifically, Merton inscribes an aesthetic of instability into the material reality of the poem by transforming uncertainty into an overt theme and then continuing that instability through the syntactical arrangement of words and through the way he enlists the stanza's container form to embody the poem's drama. The poem represents Merton's response to the death of an endearingly quirky, gardening-obsessed monk named Stephen Pitra—a monk who can be said to be on the margins of the monastic community insofar as the other brothers do not comprehend his utter fascination with flowers. Merton's aesthetics of uncertainty are openly declared right from the first lines: "Maybe the martyrology until today/Has found no fitting word to describe you" (ll. 1-2). The poem is beset from the start by an incapacity to define a human life and death according to formal standards. The formal standard here is the official martyrology, which is a catalogue of martyrs classified by their calendar feast day. As he writes, it isn't "until today"—or the very writing of this poem—that the unnamed Trappist's unruly identity can be emplaced within the formal structure of a martyrology, to which Merton adds the epithets: "Confessor of exotic roses/Martyr of unbelievable gardens" (ll. 3-4). This uncertainty is expressed not only in the inability to find a "fitting word" to describe the deceased monk, but also in the uncertainty of the syntax itself, since the poem's initial word to the reader, rather than declaring the bounds of a poetic vision, situates the persona himself in an indefinite space: "Maybe" (ll. 1). Through the bare content of the first stanza, Merton implicitly defines the poem as an elegy concerned with the disharmony between formalized, descriptive norms and the idiosyncratic individual, much in the same way that free verse itself represents an assertion of the idiosyncratic self.

From the first stanza's reference to authoritative martyrology and its ironically official epithets, the second stanza shifts into the register of personal memory, as Merton writes:

> Whom we will always remember
> As a tender-hearted careworn
> Generous unsteady cliff
> Lurching in the cloister
> Like a friendly freight train
> To some uncertain station (ll. 5-10)

Mixing a cliff metaphor and a freight train simile, Merton builds on the overt uncertainty of the first stanza by creating an aesthetic of insecurity via the syntactical arrangement of words. For example, notice the carefully alternating charges of the adjectival catalogue: tender-hearted, careworn, generous, and unsteady. The positive connotations of "tender-hearted" bleed into the predominantly negative charges of "careworn," which returns to the positive charge of "generous," and ends with the precarious and subtly negative connotation of "unsteady." It's as if this back-and-forth movement of positively and negatively charged words enacts the very unsteadiness of the monk, leading elegantly into one of the most unsteady—i.e. ambiguous—lines in the poem: "Lurching in the cloister" (ll. 8). Within the syntax of the second stanza, this lurching line creates a space for ambiguity because, in the organic unfolding reading process, one receives the image of a "Generous unsteady cliff/Lurching in the cloister" before one realizes that the *monk* is "Lurching in the cloister/Like a friendly freight train" (ll. 7-9). In the absence of punctuation, the lurching action at once completes the cliff image and begins the freight train image, forcing the reader into a moment of uncertainty regarding the correct location of the referent: for a moment, we are provided with the paradoxical image of a metaphoric cliff lurching in the cloister, before our poetic reality is modified by the ninth line's opening assurance that the *monk* is merely lurching "like a friendly freight train." The stanza embodies in its material reality the "uncertain station" to which it refers, insofar as the eighth line's syntactical station within the stanza is imbued with ambiguity. Thus, without recourse to rhyme and meter, this 1966 poem's syntactical arrangement is suddenly forced to pull more poetic weight.

The third stanza amplifies an aesthetic feature that remains more understated within traditional metrical poetry: instead of using the mere subtraction or addition of one or two syllables along a line as a means of signification, the stanza makes use of lines that contrast so greatly in length that the difference is visually apparent. One merely has to glance at the container form of the third stanza to get a sense of the playful use of line lengths:

> Master of the sudden enthusiastic gift
> In an avalanche
> Of flower catalogues
> And boundless love. (ll. 11-14)

Picking up on the "unsteady cliff" image from the previous stanza, Merton now casts the elderly monk as a massive, down-slope movement of material akin to an avalanche. In terms of the shape—or stanzaic morphology—of this section, it's as if Merton is winking at the reader and forming a kind of linguistic cliff with his careful apportionment of words: the extended, twelve-syllable-long first line plunges down into a mere five-syllable-long line, which varies only slightly throughout the rest of the stanza. The material shape of the poem is akin to the poetically referenced cliff, while the act of reading enacts the avalanche itself insofar as our eyes linger on the long, surficial layer (i.e. the first line) of the stanza before rapidly tumbling down the relatively short—and quickly scanned and vocalized—subsequent lines. Even though traditionally metrical poems marshal syllabic variation for aesthetic effect, the overall effect is more subtle, occasionally modifying line lengths by merely adding or subtracting a few syllables; in contrast, the free verse of "Elegy for a Trappist" brings syllabic variation to a new level, rendering the very *shape* of the stanza—and not merely the rhythm or number of syllables—aesthetically operative. Thus Merton inscribes the material reality of his poetry—from the syntactical arrangement of words to stanzaic container forms—with an aesthetic of instability that is linked to a message of hope. The hope here resides in the dead Trappist's location on the margins of the monastic community—a monk faithful to his own flower-obsessed calling, his sense of vocation, and his message from God. Brother Stephen was a monk, to use Merton's informal remarks at the Temple of Understanding in Calcutta, India, who was "not dependent on social acceptance" (*The Asian Journal of Thomas Merton*).

The intersection of marginality, instability and hope is thus a major narrative connecting my first reading of Merton with my most recent reading. Hope and instability conjoin, whether on the surface of his prose or the interstices of his lyric lines. Merton has taught me to see instability as the condition of hope in both my sense of faith, vocation and the immensities of life, allowing me to practice a degree of responsiveness that will help me as I continue to navigate a changing world. His words teach us that life is a liminal, protean state. Thank you, Father Louie, for teaching us that hope is where the margins are.

Thomas Merton As Spiritual Director

James Conner, OCSO

In May, 1951, Thomas Merton, known as Fr. Louis, was appointed as Master of Students at Gethsemani. This was a new position which had been created as a result of the fact that the community had some 35 young monks who were studying for the priesthood and were involved in studies. Prior to this, the young monks, after finishing their novitiate, would move to the professed side of the house and were simply under the Prior's supervision. As the numbers increased, it became clear that some further care was needed for this group.

Fr. Louis had been ordained less than two years himself, and during part of that time he had helped in giving monastic history classes to the novices. His own background in studies and teaching at Columbia University in New York had given him a strong inclination towards study, and he had used this well during his own years of formation. He was one of very few in the monastery who had read the sources of monastic history, usually in the Latin texts of *Migne Patrologia*, since little had been translated at that time. He had also read many of the early Fathers of the Church and the Cistercian Fathers. His reading and study had been prodigious, particularly in comparison with most of the monks at that time.

It was shortly after my novitiate that, in October of 1951, I became a scholastic under Fr. Louis and experienced him as a Father Master, Confessor and spiritual director. In his role as Father Master, he not only gave weekly conferences to the students each Sunday afternoon, but also met with each student privately at least once a month. With mutual agreement, the students were free to choose him also as their confessor and director and consequently meet with him each week privately.

When people ask me what was most memorable about Fr. Louis, I have always cited his humanity. He was warm, jovial, lighthearted, and youthful. He was about 36 at that time, but even as he grew older he retained a very youthful spirit which was almost boyish. He had a good sense of humor which he readily shared with others in a way that kept their feet on the ground.

At the same time, though, he had a serious side to himself. He applied himself to the task of Father Master with a deep sense of responsibility, serious to impart to the young monks his own love of monastic life and prayer, and most particularly his love of God. He did this both by his words and his general demeanor. He encouraged a love of God which was not limited merely to the spiritual aspects of life. In a letter to a laywoman, Etta Gullick he had written:

> As for spiritual life: what I object to about the "spiritual life" is the fact that it is a part, a section, set off as if it were a whole. It is an aberration to set off our "prayer"

etc. from the rest of existence, as if we were sometimes spiritual, sometimes not. As if we had to resign ourselves to feeling that the unspiritual moments were a dead loss. That is not right at all, and because it is an aberration, it causes an enormous amount of useless suffering. Our "life in the Spirit" is all-embracing, or should be (*The Hidden Ground of Love*, 357).

The traditional doctrine of the monastic life had held strongly to the notion of "flight from the world," seeking "God Alone." While Merton subscribed to these concepts, he both understood and lived them in a way that was quite different from the austere, almost gloomy way that some tried to live it. He viewed life in general and monastic life in particular as a gift from God which was to be valued and lived to the full.

Merton was an excellent spiritual director. He had an ability to comprehend what was being conveyed without it having to be fully expressed. He brought a clear sense of compassion and support for whatever one was experiencing, as well as a great deal of plain common sense. He maintained lofty ideals both for himself and for others, but he was fully realistic about the way and extent to which those were realized.

Merton would certainly have never considered himself "holy." He was all too conscious of his own human frailties and idiosyncrasies. And yet even these were a part of his very holiness. He was zealous in striving to live his monastic vocation and his search for God. Even in spite of his many struggles with his vocation, he remained convinced of his own call by God to seek Him in solitude and prayer. And he strove to live this as best he could. His prayer was expressed particularly in his love for the Eucharist. His own priesthood meant a great deal to him, and his daily celebration of Mass was the highlight of his day. Besides this he extended the time of his Mass by his Thanksgiving after Mass, and he encouraged the students to do the same. At other times during the day, he could be found kneeling behind one of the pillars around the sanctuary in the old Church, oblivious to all around him.

He taught us by his own way of life the meaning of prayer, reading, study, solitude, and the monastic life in general. He taught us more than that: he taught us what it meant to be human. He accepted himself as he was, and he accepted others as they were. He not only accepted them, he loved them as they were. His holiness in this way was closely based on his faith—particularly his faith in each person as being a Child of God. It has been said that his whole theology was based on his belief in Christ as the Word made flesh. But this carried over to the corresponding faith in each person and the dignity of that personhood as a share in the life of Christ. He expressed this humanly in his great openness to all people—to their ideas, their situations, their backgrounds, their beliefs. And he showed this as a spiritual director in his great openness to each one. His ability to truly listen and hear what they expressed made him the spiritual father that he was for so many, whether the students or novices or other brothers in the monastery or the many who corresponded with him through the mail.

Merton emphasized the need for learning in a spiritual director, a quality he possessed abundantly. The foundations for his learning had been solidly laid in his training in schools in France and Cambridge. It had been increased through his own studies and classes at Columbia University and at St. Bonaventure College in New York. But Merton was never one to be satisfied simply with what was required reading for a course. His intellectual curiosity was vast, and this led him to pursue many other avenues of thought besides those that were necessary. During his own studies at Gethsemani, he was not content with the theological manuals, but studied Duns Scotus and St. Thomas extensively, and drew from them much that remained with him throughout his life.

It was this same intellectual curiosity which led him into an interest in psychology. He saw this as a solid instrument to help in his own sound understanding of human nature. He did not consider himself an expert in psychology and, contrary to the comments of some writers, he did not try to use psychoanalysis on those he directed. But he did explore psychological principles as a basis for the common sense that he applied so clearly in all instances.

His common sense approach to direction was expressed in my own life just prior to my solemn profession in 1954. It seems to be quite common that people struggle with this final decision for some time before it is made. In this way I would regularly bring to him each week all the doubts I had about making solemn vows: the benefits of married life, the beauty of human love, the value of a life of ministry, the seeming purposelessness of the monastic life. Each time he listened patiently and honestly discussed the pros and cons of each point as it arose, but without any judgment or pressure. Finally a couple of months before a decision was due, I remarked to him that all these arguments still go on in my head, but that still there remained a silent conviction of the fact that when the time came, I would decide to make profession. At this he simply said: "Now you are really talking!" He listened and supported whatever was going on, but he had a profound faith in the action of God Himself in the heart.

One of the more obvious traits in Merton as a spiritual director was his humility. His humility enabled his humanity to shine forth so clearly. He did not try to be other than who he was. What you saw was what you got! Some might have preferred that at times he was a little less obvious, but that did not affect who he was nor what he said or did. This humility and love of souls also had a bearing in his involvement in social questions of war and peace, race relations, etc. that marked his later writings. He did not enter into this simply as an activist nor still less as someone who was disillusioned in the value of his own prayer and solitude. He did so precisely because of his love for people, which was the foundation of all his work as a spiritual director and an author. To this extent, I think that he must have seen his social writings as a definite part of his duty as spiritual director. It was not as if he boastfully saw himself as a director for the world at large, but simply that, in all truth, he realized that many looked to him in this light from his earlier writing, and he felt impelled to lead them to a realization that their spiritual life would be an illusion if it did not include a realism in regard to the actual situation of the world.

In *The Inner Experience* Merton wrote that prayer today cannot be simply an experience of light, and that the greatest temptation for spiritual persons today may be this seeking consolation in prayer. He wrote that we live today in an age of darkness and human atrocities. The greed, dishonesty and injustice in the world affects our prayer in ways different from the experience of prayer in the ages of Faith. Today God perhaps reveals Himself nowhere more than in the very sense of emptiness which we encounter in our own heart. When we encounter the true centers of our hearts, we also encounter the heart of all humanity with both its darkness and light.

Ultimately Merton was an excellent spiritual director because he was so emptied of himself. He admitted that even the trials and frustrations of the monastic life were valuable for this very purpose. He taught us that we do not need to wait until we have some perfect situation or perfect director before we can seek God and love others. The very difficulties we encounter may be the way that the Lord is leading us to accept our own nothingness so that His fullness can enter in. As the Lord Himself told His disciples: "For you it is impossible; for God all things are possible!"

Spiritual direction, then, is not so much a ministry that one performs in the Church as it is a simple availability to one another in a way that can be a channel of the Spirit for the other. This availability implies vulnerability and an openness to love. Jesus taught his disciples that they were to wash one another's feet in humble service.

Thomas Merton tried to do this, and—to my way of thinking—he succeeded in it to a great extent. That is why he was a great man—not because he had no faults, not because he had extraordinary spiritual experiences, not because he performed great deeds or wrote great books, but simply because "he loved much."

If we can strive to love enough to become vulnerable to one another and to the Spirit of God, then God can do great things in and through us. We will not have to wait until some great spiritual director comes along who can answer all our questions and point the way. We can strive to be like the Lord who found the Father in all things and in all people and who loved us to the bitter end—even to death on the Cross. And in this we will find life in the God who has loved us first.

Visitors

Patricia A. Burton

A chance remark by Dr. Paul Pearson from the Merton Center in Louisville set me to burrowing into the giant ramified termite mound of information and puzzles left behind by Merton. It was a casual suggestion: "Wouldn't it be great if we had a list of all of Merton's visitors in one place, to refer to whenever we needed it?" Such ideas are as catnip to me. In no time at all, I was ransacking all the information I had.

At first it seemed simple. Now that we have Merton's journals and letters as e-books, we need only search on the keyword "visits" and all will be revealed. Except that Merton didn't write that way. He used all kinds of language to indicate visits, and I had to come up with more keywords: "came down" (from Louisville), "came over" (from Lexington) "came out/came by" (from anyplace near or far away), but also the simpler ones like "was here." And sometimes no verb. Just "here." If I wanted to find the groups of Protestant visitors in which I became increasingly interested, I had to go "fishing for Baptists" as my notes report. Or Episcopalians or Methodists or Presbyterians. Gathered together, the visits look like an important element in Merton's life, and I eventually entered all that I could find into the Timeline in *Merton Vade Mecum* 3rd edition.

There is another facet to the story. In a recent article in *America*, Daniel Horan quotes a now-famous Merton letter to Pope John XXIII about an apostolate to intellectuals (*The Hidden Ground of Love*, 482). After proposing the idea, Merton goes on to suggest a way to accomplish it, through a series of "special houses" run by monasteries for the purpose. In a follow-up letter on February 11, 1960, Merton reports progress: "I have received approval for five or six retreats" for "specialized" or even "elite" groups (*HGL*, 484): "For example, there will be a meeting of several theologians and heads of *Protestant* seminaries . . . (Merton's italics)." In April of that year, Merton reports "I also thank Your Holiness for the interest you have so kindly shown in our little project of spiritual meetings . . . . A few days ago I had the pleasure of addressing more than fifty Protestant seminarians and pastors here in our monastery" (*HGL*, 485).

The idea of a separate place to house these meetings coincided with Merton's vocation and stability struggles; should he move to a Benedictine community in Cuernavaca, Mexico (as he was pondering at the time) or at least into a hermitage? Somehow, although it seemed not to be an overt and deliberate process, the idea of a separate structure for conferences on Gethsemani grounds became fused with Merton's desire for a hermitage. In any case, on December 31, 1959, Merton mentioned the possibility of meetings to Dom James Fox, who did not seem opposed. Merton says in his journal "Perhaps it is possible to do here some of the things I wanted to do in Mexico" (*A Search for Solitude*, 364). So even the idea of Mexico, it seems, had more than the element of solitude in it.

Soon enough, the meetings began to occur. Students from Asbury Theological Seminary in Wilmore, Kentucky and from the College of the Bible in Lexington arrived February 8, 1960. Others followed: students from Vanderbilt University on March 9, and 57 Presbyterians from Lexington on April 30. On May 23-24 there was a three-session meeting with College of the Bible. There were three professors from Union Theological Seminary on August 30. There was even a surprise arrival of 25 students from the University of Indiana, September 23, which Merton enjoyed. In the midst of the Protestant flood, a Catholic group from Bellarmine College arrived for the weekend of October 17 with the college's founder Monsignor Horrigan, all pledged to "broaden horizons in every direction." The meetings varied in size: 75 students from Southern Baptist Seminary came on November 7, while two students were sent over by Zalman Schachter from the Jewish Seminary in Cincinnati on November 25.

The intent to foster dialogue was obviously serious on Merton's part. In the midst of it all, plans went forward for the building, starting with meetings to plan the structure, April 29 and July 12, 1960. By October 3, 1960, they were staking out the ground, and on December 2 Merton lit the first fire in the big fireplace of the completed cinder-block structure which he had named "Saint Mary of Carmel," located fittingly on a hill called "Mount Olivet."

In 1961 the visits continued, and Merton began to pay return calls to some of the groups, as on May 15 when he visited Southern Baptist Seminary. On June 19 three professors from there visited Merton, including Glenn Hinson, and by this time Merton described these Baptist ministers as "good friends." News travels fast, however. By the end of the year, the Abbot had received a letter from the Papal Secretary of State, to urge "diminution of contacts with protestant ministers and scholars." A good thing, altogether, that Merton had acquired support from the Pope before the experiment began.

In 1961 a new note was sounded. Individuals as well as groups interested in ecumenical discussions began to show up. June 27, 1961 saw a visit of Tashi Tshering, a Tibetan. On August 3 of that year Fr Basil Kazan, an Orthodox priest from Louisville, helped everyone participate in the Byzantine Liturgy. On February 5, 1962. Douglas Steere arrived—he was later to be a Quaker Observer Delegate at Vatican II. That same month, a group from the *Catholic Worker* newspaper in New York spent a week. Later, when Merton became involved in the peace movement, he hosted a now-famous meeting of its leaders. The motto seemed to be: if I can't go out and visit the world, I will invite them to come and see me.

We know of the student visits from Merton's journals, but they do not give detailed information about what it was the groups discussed, and indeed there may have been other meetings that Merton simply neglected to mention. Generally Merton expressed satisfaction, often saying "good discussion." In a talk at the International Thomas Merton Society Conference in 1997, Glenn Hinson gave an idea of what the proceedings were like. He said that some of his young charges had never encountered a Roman Catholic in their lives. Students' questions could be startling: "What's a smart man like you doing in a place like this?" Hinson recalled that, as Merton began to explain, he was himself amazed that there could be a life dedicated simply and entirely to prayer.

In 1962 the Gethsemani Novitiate was wired for sound; Merton was able to invite well-known visitors to speak, and recordings were made (still available at The Thomas

Merton Center). To name a few: Zalman Schachter and Rabbi L. Silberman (separately and together, several times); Daniel Berrigan SJ, who spoke on poverty and other topics; R. J. Zwi Werblowsky who contributed to the talks on Judaism. Of the well-known monastics: Bede Griffiths; Aelred Graham and Brother Antoninus (William Everson) who spoke, of course, on poetry. Ivan Englesicvich had the Orthodox view, and Swami Shivaprem from Rishikesh gave the Hindu perspective. These talks we can listen to, and they indicate that when the world was invited to a dialogue, many accepted.

Of course what we have here is another famous Merton paradox: he built a place to be alone and the world arrived; once he had invited guests, they never stopped coming. When he found time to be alone, he wrote about everything that was going through his head, so that thousands of readers could finally know all about his hermit life and see connections to their own lives.

What does all this mean, especially for a solitary researcher-hermit in her high-rise cave looking south toward Lake Ontario? The significance is that the visits have never really ended. That we are already one Merton knew before the rest of us, and his hopes were in the gossamer threads that bind us together over space and time. Anyone working on Merton is connected to an expanding group of friends from all over the world. It means being only two degrees of separation from the man himself through his friends that still flourish. He built the hermitage to be alone, but ended by giving hospitality to everybody, and so it continues. The old building has become a sort of universal hub. And he's still there. In certain lights you can see him, perhaps in the slanting shadows on a wall as dusk comes down, or in the light just after dawn, when the birds have awakened for another day: there he stands, smiling, beside the open door.

O Happy Chance!

E. Glenn Hinson

Happy chance took me with my students to the Abbey of Gethsemani on 7 November 1960. Little did I know that that foolish venture would shape and mold my life from that day until this one. The reason was Thomas Merton.

I didn't take students to Gethsemani to meet Merton, about whom I knew almost nothing. I'd heard of *The Seven Storey Mountain*, but had not read it. I took them to expose them to the Middle Ages, and that happened. In 1960 Gethsemani was an austere place not unlike the Cistercian monasteries centuries before. Merton was our bonus.

Let me confess some nervousness on the way to the monastery that chilly day. None of us, almost all Baptists, had ever set foot in a Catholic facility. We didn't know what to expect, but most of us expected to find mal-adjusted men who couldn't "hack it" in the world and thus retreated or perhaps "fled" from it. They wouldn't know anything about what was going on where we lived. Merton debunked and dispelled such twisted images not merely in what he said but in the way he said it and in his presence. He was the most unselfconscious, authentic person we had ever met, someone we'd like to be like.

When he finished speaking about the contemplative life, Merton asked if we had questions. One student asked what I feared one would ask. It went something like this: "What is a smart fellow like you doing in a place like this?" I waited for Tom to open his mouth and eat that guy alive. But he didn't. He grinned and said, "I am here because I believe in prayer. That is my vocation." You could have knocked me over with a feather. I had never met anyone, even Baptist saints of fond memory, who believed in prayer enough to think of it as a vocation. All the way back to Southern Seminary that afternoon, those words kept echoing in my mind alongside the Protestant rubric, "God has no hands but our hands, no feet but our feet, no voice but our voice." The thought rushed over me: "Our world is in a desperate state if that rubric is true. We'd better hope that Merton and his brothers are right—that prayer matters enough to pursue it as a vocation!"

Two weeks after this visit, Tom sent me a card, "Glenn, I'm coming to Louisville. I'd like to stop in and see you." I wrote back immediately, "Great! How about speaking to my class?" He replied, "I can't speak to groups, but if some of my friends are around, I can talk to them." I rounded up the faculty of Southern Seminary, and we spent two engaging and fruitful hours with Thomas Merton. After his visit I heard no more warnings like I'd heard earlier about taking my classes to Gethsemani! I took them every semester until his death on 10 December 1968.

In 1964 Tom wrote, "Glenn, I'm afraid I'm not going to be able to meet with your students any more." At that time I didn't know that he had negotiated with Dom James Fox, the Abbot, an agreement not to speak to groups like ours in order to move into the hermitage built for him in 1960. Neither did I understand why he, engaging the world in such a vital way, needed to withdraw farther from it to seek deeper solitude. Thinking the abbot was punishing Merton for something, I wrote an urgent letter of protest, suggesting that he was throwing a monkey wrench into the ecumenical movement. Many students who came, I insisted, had never met a Catholic, much less a monk! How could he deny them an experience so important to their formation as ministers. Both Merton and the Abbot wrote me to explain. Dom James himself met with us that fall, but it was not the same. He didn't have Merton's charisma.

Even though he could not talk to the group, Merton found a way to speak to me privately when we visited. More important, he continued to invite me to meet with a small coterie of others in his hermitage, a practice he launched on 10 June 1961, to exchange information and ideas about critical social issues such as ecumenism, racism, the threat of nuclear weaponry, and the war in Vietnam. As his writings attest, he had an incredibly expansive outlook on life, one that shocked those of us who knew so little about monks.

I confess with some embarrassment and much regret that I didn't really delve into Merton's writings during his lifetime. His thinking seeped into mine mostly through his talks to students and then in the klatches he held in his hermitage. Of critical importance to me at the time, however, in a era when secular theology revived Nietzsche's pronouncement, "God is dead!," was the unshakable conviction of the contemplative tradition of God's "is-ness," even though beyond human cognition. Merton fed that tradition through his fertile mind and heart and "mertonized" it. I couldn't answer all of the questions my students, some returning from Vietnam, raised about God, the world, life. In Merton I found a fellow struggler who had wrestled with the deepest issues about God that we confront in life and who put me in touch with a wisdom formulated and preserved by a centuries-long fellowship of strugglers in the contemplative tradition.

A week after our first visit to Gethsemani back in 1960, Tom had sent me manuals he put together for instructing his novices. Most of them consisted of excerpts from the scriptures and the saints through the ages. At that moment I couldn't see how I could make direct use of them, but they gave me an idea for a class on "The Classics of Christian Devotion." That turned out to be the most significant course I ever offered. In that unsettling era my students and I wrestled together, as I imagine Merton did with his novices, to discover whether and how God could still fit somehow into human life in an age of irrationality and absurdity. Virtually never a week goes by that I don't receive a note of thanks from a former student for what happened in that course.

Merton's death in Bangkok 10 December 1968 supplied the stimulus for me to read all of Merton's published writings. I had read books he gave me or sent me, such as *Spiritual Direction and Meditation* and *The Prison Meditations of Father Delp*, but my education and formation up to that point hadn't taught me how to apply those to the preparation of young men and women for ministry in the church and the world. My own education left me with a great vacuum in respect to the life of God in the world of the 1960s. Shortly after he died, both Catholics and Protestants started asking me to share what I knew about Thomas Merton, and my inner prompter compelled me to read everything he wrote that was in print. Much of the Merton corpus—letters, journals, essays, recorded talks, and books—did not appear in print until 25 years or more after he died.

It won't surprise you if I admit I focused first on what I knew of Thomas Merton as a person. In my first talk I spoke about the challenges we face today in trying to interpret such a precocious, extraordinarily gifted person because of the many different ways people viewed him ("Merton's Many Faces," *Religion in Life* 42 (Summer 1973) 153-67). My students thought he would make a super candidate for Baptist ministry! By this time, however, my immersion in Merton's writings started bolstering my confidence in interpreting what he wrote to the point that I ventured to speak about his evolution as a contemplative charged with a commission to show a world torn by strife and caught up in "activity for activity's sake" its desperate need for contemplation, for seeking Wisdom for its own sake ("The Catholicizing of Contemplation: Thomas Merton's Place in the Church's Prayer Life," *Perspectives in Religious Studies* I (Spring 1974) 66-84; *Cistercian Studies* 10 (1975) 173-89). In medieval parlance I nominated him *doctor universalis contemplationis*, "universal teacher of contemplation."

As I did these studies, Merton's ideas gradually worked their way into my own thinking. You can't read much of his writing, even writing for monks, without deepening your discernment and subtly changing your way of looking at life. I liked to have graduate students read Merton simply because it improved their writing, but my real objective went well beyond that. Merton truly convinced me of the urgency of contemplation in a world so full of violence, so threatened by its own technological advances, so prone to racism, and many other crises. When invited to give the Edwin Stephens Griffiths Lectures at South Wales Baptist College in Cardiff in the spring of 1970, I did my best to transmit Merton's message to students wrestling with a secularity even more pronounced than the kind my students confronted. The lectures later appeared as *A Serious Call to a Contemplative Life-style* (Westminster Press, 1974). Given my spiritual immaturity at that point in my career and with many Merton writings yet unpublished, I had only enough equipment to share some of the most basic ideas I got from him. In the crux of my argument I relied directly on Merton. To become a contemplative does not necessitate becoming a monk, he noted. "It is sufficient to be a child of God, a human person" (*Faith and Violence*, 1968).

I saw it early on, but my continuing journey with Thomas Merton heightened my perception that, as one of his most salient long-range contributions, he would show us the way to bridge the gulf between Christians and people of other faiths. On the tenth anniversary of his death I spoke about the development of his ecumenical perceptions. Like many another convert, in *The Seven Storey Mountain* he panned, put down and made light of other Christian traditions. At that stage he exhibited what he later called a "ghetto Catholic" mentality. As his years in Gethsemani healed and assuaged some of the hurts he had experienced, he developed what I chose to call an "expansive Catholicism," ("Expansive Catholicism: Ecumenical Perceptions of Thomas Merton," *Religion in Life* 48 (Spring 1979) 63-76). which could make room for other Christians, persons of other faiths and even persons of no faith. He thought monks could play an especially vital role in dialogue with persons of other faiths.

As a Baptist, I have had a keen interest in conversion, which is also a key concern in the Rule of St. Benedict. In Merton's case what intrigued me was his dramatic shift from radical world denial (*contemptus mundi*) on entering Gethsemani to a real and deep and critical concern for the world (*amor mundi*) expressed by the monk who spoke to my students and who invited me to klatches in his hermitage. Many pointed to the "epiphany" Merton had at the corner of Fourth and Walnut (Muhammad Ali) on 8 March 1958, but close reading of *The Sign of Jonas* (1953) and the dramatically different Merton of *No Man Is an Island* (1955) caused me to look more closely at what Merton called a "submarine earthquake" he experienced between September 1949 and March 1951 ("Contemptus Mundi—Amor Mundi: Merton's Progression from World Denial to World Affirmation," *Cistercian Studies* 26 (1991) 339-49).

Whenever it happened, the "new" Merton differed dramatically from the one who wrote *The Seven Storey Mountain.* He became one of the most important prophetic figures in America. He became a contemplative at the heart of the world.

In the more than 50 years since I met Thomas Merton I've spent much time pondering what accounted for such an extraordinary person, whose life and thought have drawn so many, including me, to him. Obviously there's no simple answer to the question, but, if I may stretch your imagination, I would finger one factor on our first meeting that I sensed he and I shared—loneliness. I can see how that would figure prominently in bonding others to him in an unusual way, for assuaging loneliness is a need every human has. Reading his journals a quarter of a century after his death, I was surprised to note how persistently the word loneliness recurred throughout his writings. The reason for it is writ large in *The Seven Storey Mountain*—death of his mother when he was six, virtual abandonment by his father after her death, death of his father when he was fifteen, "grabbing life" at Cambridge when he was eighteen, and his effort to assemble an *ad hoc* family at Columbia. For a time he sought an answer to loneliness in community—Catherine de Hueck Dougherty's Friendship House in Harlem and then Gethsemani. At first the community at Gethsemani satisfied his longing. Through much travail, though, he discovered that the answer to loneliness lies ultimately in the loneliness of God. "Although loneliness can and does cause excruciating pain, it can also be a crucible of grace as it nudges and prods us to seek community with the larger family of humankind and, ultimately, in God" ("Loneliness as a Key to the Merton Story," *Cistercian Studies* 40 (2005) 410).

I finally got it: he sought more and more solitude as he exposed his heart more and more to a world desperate for contemplation!

On My Father Photographing Thomas Merton 1967-1968

Christopher Meatyard

Between January 18, 1967, and September 1, 1968, Ralph Eugene Meatyard took 116 photographs of Father Louis—Thomas Merton—mostly in the vicinity of the monastery of Gethsemani at Bardstown, Kentucky. Thomas Merton was a subject who carefully articulated his life around the terms of a singular idea. He gave up his personal possessions, his heritage and his freedom to assume the identity (the iconological mask) of the Cistercian Order of the Strict Observance, the Trappists. Merton's "mask" was not so different from anyone else's, although it was more clearly defined by the traditions and the iconography of the Catholic Church. It was from this perspective that Merton began to reach out in his last years, valuing the diversity of human relations and human freedom as a revelation of his creator's unqualified love. But he could not vividly know that freedom except by degrees of contrast to his own "masked" vigil. While most of Meatyard's work is abstract and characterized by an emotionally charged formalism, nowhere is it more justifiably narrative than in his portraits of Thomas Merton.

Meatyard, in the company of Guy Davenport and Jonathan Williams, first met Merton on January 18, 1967, at the hermitage that the monastery had built to allow him more solitude. There were no steps, so the guests hoisted themselves up one and a half

feet to the front porch. From inside the cabin, the windows, lacking vertical mullions, looked like ladders ascending to the sky. Through them one could see the rolling pastures almost all the way to New Hope. The cabin offered an abundance of chairs made with Shaker simplicity by nuns. The only structural embellishment to the concrete-block and slab-floor hermitage was a field-stone fireplace with a cross laid into it in high relief. Merton kept a wood fragment from the top of the abbot's old chair resting on the mantel like a clock, saved by its embossed cross from numerous possible stokings of the fire in the hearth below. Greek icons, gifts from friends such as Marco Pallis and Bob Rambuch, hung on the walls.

The first photographs of Merton were made around a flat pine-top worktable spread with the remains of lunch. We can see slices of bread, cheese, a tin of fruitcake, all products of the Trappists at Gethsemani. Merton leaned one elbow on his slant-top writing desk; writing was his form of monastic labor. Immediately before Merton is the two-handled mug: the monks held these with both hands to concentrate on the act of drinking and to remember their adopted childlike innocence.

Meatyard made nine images of Merton's profile as he read from the manuscript that would become *Cables to the Ace*. Each explored a different relationship between the silhouette and the outlining illumination. Meatyard modified Merton's location by degrees to draw attention to the juxtaposition of the horizontal frame of the window and the vertical support post of the porch outside. He illustrated Merton's apophatic speech by aligning one black arm of the momentary crucifix with the speaker's ebullient tongue.

After this session indoors, the four men put on jackets and coats and went for a walk. When they came to the sheep barn, Meatyard made six more photographs of

Merton; these concluded his day's work. Merton had a white notepad tucked into the waist pocket of his denim jacket, and a note on the print reminds us that this place was one of his favorite spots: "Many poems written here." In all the photographs, Meatyard sought to make visible some significant connection between Merton and his environment, and he paid special attention to even the least obvious, but nevertheless tangible, relationships of light and form. He observed details that we might discard as random coincidence, then revealed these details as pointed integrally to one subject, at one place, in one moment of time.

At Gethsemani in the early summer of 1967, Tommie O'Callaghan catered a large picnic on the edge of some woods. O'Callaghan was six or seven months pregnant. Marie Sharon, who assisted O'Callaghan with the organization of Merton's papers, was present, as were Guy Davenport and Meatyard's wife, Madelyn. Merton wore his monk's habit, and provided Meatyard with his first and best opportunity to photograph him so attired. The black and white elements of the habit represent diverse aspects of the Trappist heritage. The white robe is a reminder of the twelve apostles and of the Trappists' dedication to the Virgin, and is worn in choir. The black scapular dates back to the time of St. Benedict, the sixth century, when it functioned as an apron for those involved in manual labor. The hood of the scapular was seldom used except in processions. The contrast of black and white corresponds to Merton's own personal combination of two branches of theological discourse: the apophatic, referring to the unknowability of God, and the cataphatic, referring to the theology of "light," "good," "life." The wide leather belt "girds up the loins" and thus represents a profession of monastic vows (elsewhere Merton can be seen wearing this belt of profession even on top of another belt looped through jeans). A fishing cap bearing a pair of crossed swordfish as insignia tops off Merton's habit.

After O'Callaghan and Sharon left to complete some business at the monastery, the rest of the group went to an abandoned farm nearby so that Meatyard could take more photographs. These all incorporate as a key motif the graphic lines of cable wire

and thus relate to two subjects that had been brought up in the first meeting between Meatyard and Merton. General Electric, the original benefactor of Merton's hermitage, had wanted to build an elaborate U-shaped, glass-walled ecumenical retreat house and conference center. Merton, who usually made pretense to apologize for his humble dwelling, was clearly jubilant about his decision not to let GE build this pavilion. The company's patronage is tied into the poem Merton was writing in his modest hermitage when Meatyard first visited him. The poem, which would be titled *Cables to the Ace*, was then called *Edifying Cables*, and it refers often to the plurality of wire messages for communication but none with more resolute spring than the electrical transmission of life into afterlife.

A picnic held in the woods in midsummer brought the Meatyards together with Merton and Wendell and Tanya Berry. Merton wore a short-sleeved denim shirt. As had not happened on earlier occasions, Meatyard photographed Merton together with the others present. Interspersed among the negatives from this picnic are numerous multiple-exposure compositions that Meatyard made looking up into the tree canopy. He photographed Wendell Berry's head superimposed over Merton's and made multiple exposures of Merton alone. Meatyard spent several years working with multiple exposure, and he used it as the principle style for his nonfigurative views of landscape and architecture. With multiple exposure he could intensify the harmony and the cacophony of rhythm shifting to a fever pitch the controlled coincidence among objects.

In late December 1967, Wendell and Tanya Berry, Denise Levertov, and Madelyn and Gene Meatyard met again with Merton at the hermitage. Meatyard photographed the poets—Merton, Levertov and Berry—in two sessions, the first inside the hermitage with the three sitting around the fireplace, and the second outside, where they gathered around an old rusting wheelbarrow. Merton wore a hip-length field jacket over his denim work clothes, his jeans rolled up around his ankles. In several photographs he seems to be emphasizing his words by placing his left hand on top of his head; the movement lifts his shirt so that its white enameled snaps repeat themselves in triplicate. Levertov slices the air with open palm and fingers; Berry clasps a thin volume with both hands and appears more still.

It was at the December meeting that Levertov and Merton discussed the merits of self-immolation as a way of protesting the war in Vietnam. It is tempting to see a visual commentary on this conversation in the triple exposure with the overlapping visages of Levertov, Merton and Berry: almost every one of its overlapping forms of the cedar altar over the hearth opening recalls flames. Another image of the altar is superimposed in that of the gas heater. The horizontal exhaust of the heater intersects with the altar candle. The candle snuff reflects a flamelike light. A second image of the altar candle hovers under a thermometer, which blends together with an altar icon. Outside the hermitage Meatyard made another statement, a strangely conjunctive visual addition to the verbal conversation. Meatyard posed the poets around an old wheelbarrow

that the monks had used when building the hermitage; Merton had used the same wheelbarrow to haul young trees to replace the older ones lost during the construction. Meatyard softened the focus around the feet of the trio and placed Merton and Levertov behind the wheelbarrow, thus making them seem as if they had been dug up like trees and loaded there. The next photograph completes the episodic transplantation of young poets in front of several of Merton's transplanted trees visible in the background. The small group of photographs made around the wheelbarrow was blithely conceived. Meat-

218

yard's presence is felt here as a result of the strange hyperopic insistence of focus on the distant horizon. The logical extension of focusing on the distant horizon makes the photographer the least focused element, a formless object that is nevertheless the gathering point for the group's attention. Meatyard used focus as a means to refer to himself and humbly include himself with the group portrait. He is the gardener planting seeds for a later harvest.

Merton and Meatyard did not meet again for almost eight months. Merton, having won pronounced freedom from his monastic restrictions, had begun traveling extensively and developing new projects. Meatyard spent much of this time photographing the Red River Gorge in eastern Kentucky for the book *The Unforeseen Wilderness*, a collaboration with Wendell Berry. The last meeting between Meatyard and Merton, September 1, 1968, took place just before Merton left for the Far East. Meatyard again brought Madelyn, Melissa and Christopher. Merton was wearing his robes and was scheduled to say Mass; the meeting was thus more brief than usual. He played the bongos, accompanying a jazz record. At the right-hand edge of one of the photographs Meatyard took, a pile of Merton's calligraphic drawings sits on the pine-top worktable. Meatyard took three photographs of Merton playing the bongos; for one of these Melissa leaned into the camera dancing. As the Meatyards were leaving, Merton asked the photographer to show him how to use the camera John Howard Griffen had sent him. Merton planned to take it along on his long journey to the East; he called it his "Zen camera."

In The Company Of Thomas Merton

Lawrence S. Cunningham

I propose this question and a tentative answer: Why is it that, decades after his death, so many young people and others not so young still inquire of Thomas Merton and his writings? Why do they email me asking about strategies for reading Merton and, more precisely, *which* Merton should they read? What did they personally capture by an encounter with his writings or with his life?

My own response to that line of questioning is simple: Thomas Merton had a profound gift of writing about the reality of God, derived from his own monastic experience, without sounding "pious" or, what is even more off putting, without falling into the swamp of academic or scholarly jargon. In his writing there is something *memorable* in the deepest meaning of the word.

Anyone who has read his spiritual classics like *Thoughts in Solitude* or *New Seeds of Contemplation* cannot but be struck by the pure simplicity of his prose and the clarity of his exposition. As a long time teacher of those texts both to university students as well as to lay and religious groups, I have often challenged my audiences to write out ten or twenty "thoughts" from their reading of these classic texts to create a little anthology of meditation points.

To create such a little chapbook of Mertonian texts is to replicate what he himself (inspired by Saint John of the Cross and Blaise Pascal) did in composing his own books. It is well to remember that many of his spiritual books consisted of "thoughts" or "seeds" or "conjectures" and not treatises or *summas* or *tractates*. This does not mean, by any stretch of thought, that he was incapable of an extended essay because we have collected volumes of such extended work. What it does mean is that it is his brief observations that capture his most enduring witness. Those primordial insights stud some of his best books as he sought what was "really real" and the nature of the "true self."

Thomas Merton was badly afflicted with the *furor scribendi* and not an insignificant part of his collected writings, as he himself openly recognized, will not hold up over time. Some works, however, like those mentioned above, and parts of other works (think of "The Fire Watch" in *The Sign of Jonas*) have reached the status of the classic. A classic, as it has been observed, possesses a "surplus of meaning." The test of a classic is this: it speaks to the author's present but its enduring value is in what it projects in its after life. In the flyleaf of my much battered copy of *New Seeds of Contemplation* is a jotting indicating where and when this text was taught (over fifteen times). The fact that I can still reach for it, learn from it and gloss my learning to others is the mark of a classic.

A young monk, having decided to leave monastic life, asked Merton to write him out a "good word." In compliance, Merton wrote: "God manifests Himself in what is hidden. Therefore, if you try to find Him you don't. He shows himself where there is no 'you' to look for him. But whether He shows Himself or not does not matter because everything is a blessing for Him." Those deeply contemplative words, tense with hiddenness and revelation, were dashed off in response to a simple request. They deserve reflection and personal assimilation. Like much of what Merton wrote they ring of truth and of the Truth. That is why he is as pertinent today as he was in his twenty-seven years in the cloister.

As for us who have spent a long time reading his writings, commenting on them and grappling with how to teach others how to grow in wisdom—what have we learned? I can only speak for myself here. It was from Merton that I became schooled in the great monastic wisdom that had first schooled him. Encountering him when very young helped me to look back beyond my strict Thomist education to study the great Cistercians of the twelfth century who then pointed me back to the Patristic wisdom of both the West and the East. A short way of saying this is that I learned the path of *ressourcement*—going back to the sources, a path I follow to this day.

The great *ressourcement* thinkers of the twentieth century triggered another impetus, looking back to learn for the future. The word for that impulse was coined by Blessed Saint John XXIII: *aggiornamento*. From that dual impetus of going back to the sources and looking at the needs of today and tomorrow has led me to ask foundational questions to share with the young people at the university where I have taught: How does one live with the True Self? How does one develop that contemplative approach to life that lets us see the Ground of our being in such a way that our lives become one of gratitude? How do we become open to those "Fourth and Walnut" epiphanies by which we can reach out in love to everyone? How do we transmute our privileged lives of comfort and class and education in such a way that we see (and abhor) the ugliness of poverty and violence in the world around us?

I would love to tell you that I now have satisfactory answers to those questions but that claim would be pride-filled foolishness. When I was a young man, I had all the answers but now, many decades later, I think I am beginning to grasp what the real questions are, rather like those asked by that young monk sitting with his back to the bell tower on the 4th of July querying the immense sky over him. So, like Thomas Merton and thanks to his life and writing, I find myself sailing towards my destiny in the belly of a paradox.

The Art And Beauty Of Being Human

Ben Eisner

Like millions before me, I was introduced to Thomas Merton by way of *The Seven Storey Mountain.* I was taken immediately by Merton's honesty and vulnerability, beginning on the first page, where he acknowledges that he was born free by nature in the image of God, yet was the prisoner of his own violence and selfishness. As I plowed through one Merton title after another, I slowly but surely gained a new vocabulary not only for my own inner conversion, but also for the transformation of my entire generation—a vocabulary of hope.

Vocationally, I feel compelled to live out and share this vocabulary with those I encounter on a daily basis—my wife, my daughters, my friends, and those in my community—as well as with the broader audiences I'm able to reach through the art of filmmaking and visual storytelling. An excerpt from Merton's essay collection *Love and Living* offers a succinct definition of my marching orders as a fellow messenger of hope to those within my sphere of influence:

> Artists, poets, and others who might be expected to have some concern for the inner life of man are declaring that the reason why God has ceased to be present to man (therefore "dead") is that man has ceased to be present to himself, and that consequently the true significance of the statement "God is dead" is really that "MAN is dead." The obvious fact of man's material agitation and external frenzy serves only to emphasize his lack of spiritual life (*Love and Living*, 56).

It's the material agitation and external frenzy to which Merton refers that I seek to eradicate in my own life by daring to face myself in solitude. People who know not the art of pausing and the importance of withdrawing from the tumult of life for a time are those who have yet to learn how to truly love themselves and, thus, the world around them. Overcoming the mimetic pressure fueled by our false selves to become better versus the gentle voice of our true selves that calls us to grow deeper is an increasing challenge for a generation that is over-stimulated with technology and the "connectedness" of mobile devices and social media. This age of connectivity gives us increasingly more "important" reasons to elude inner reconciliation and refrain from allowing our true selves to shine the light of life into the world.

However, the call to true connectivity is a two-way street. Merton has inspired me not only to share life but also to receive life from everyone. Yes, I was born to draw out the best in everyone I encounter and remind them of who they truly are behind the pretense of "self improvement." But I also was born to live openly and receptively in a way that allows everyone I encounter—regardless of faith, race, nationality, or sexual orientation—to draw forth my true self and remind me of whom I truly am.

Thomas Merton's Message of Hope

One of Merton's thoughts from *Conjectures of a Guilty Bystander* captures everything in which I hope to be intimately involved as a husband, father, friend, and filmmaker.

> At the center of our being is a point of nothingness which is untouched by sin and by illusion, a point of pure truth, a point or spark which belongs entirely to God, which is never at our disposal from which God disposes of our lives, which is inaccessible to the fantasies of our own mind or the brutalities of our own will . . . .. It is like a pure diamond, blazing with the invisible light of heaven. It is in everybody, and if we could see it we would see these billions of points of light coming together in the face and blaze of a sun that would make all the darkness and cruelty of life vanish completely. . . . I have no program for this seeing. It is only given, but the gate of heaven is everywhere (*Conjectures of A Guilty Bystander*, 15).

Yes, a gentle reply turns away wrath. Yes, we are to love our enemies and pray for those who persecute us. And yet, Merton has shown me that all we hope for is impossible until we learn to live comfortably in naked solitude, until we dare to bridge the gap that separates us from our true selves.

Non Finis Quaerendi: My Journey With Thomas Merton

Donald Grayston

It's the spring of 1954. I'm in Grade 10 at Lord Byng Secondary School in Vancouver. I've heard that a new library is opening on Dunbar Street. I check it out, browse a little; and then notice a book with an unusual binding, a kind of burlap. It's *Seeds of Contemplation* (1949) by someone named Thomas Merton. I read the first two or three pages, and remember thinking, "This is deep, and I don't understand it—but someday, I will."

It's the summer of 1958. I have a job in the lab at the MacMillan Bloedel pulp mill in Port Alberni, on Vancouver Island. I am downtown in a drugstore, looking among the paperbacks for something to read, when I notice a book with a lurid cover. It depicts a number of small figures in various painful or suggestive poses; and there in the foreground, a larger figure, a man in a monastic cowl, with the hood pulled over his head. The title of the book: *The Seven Storey Mountain*, by the man who wrote that book with the curious binding, Thomas Merton. I smile now at the come-ons on the cover: "A Widely Acclaimed Bestseller"; "The Revealing Experience of a Man Who Withdrew From the World." Couldn't resist, had to buy it.

A week or two later, I was reading it on the graveyard shift. Among the students who staffed the lab, it was understood that that was a good time for reading. The work of eight hours could be done in four hours, leaving lots of time for reading; and since the supervisors never came around on the graveyard shift, why not? It turned out, however, that "never" was something of an overstatement. A supervisor came in about 3:00 A.M., frowned at me, scribbled something in the log, frowned at me again, and departed. I went over to the log and read what he had written, which was this: "If I catch you reading on the job again, your time with MacMillan Bloedel is over." OK, got it; work at half-speed, fill the eight hours. But the incident fixed in my mind the exact time that I was reading Merton's youthful autobiography. I still have that well-read edition, now held together by an elastic band.

It's the spring of 1972. I'm working in Rossland, British Columbia, just a few miles north of the US border. Our closest big city is Spokane, Washington, and I am down there for a short break. I go into a Catholic bookstore, and notice a book bearing that name again, Thomas Merton. It was by Ed Rice, and was called *The Man in the Sycamore Tree: The Good Times and Hard Life of Thomas Merton* (1972). Ah, Thomas Merton! Whatever became of him?

I read the book, and the rest is history. I had just been accepted to do graduate work in Toronto, and had a vague idea of doing it on the reconfiguration of Christian spirituality for our swiftly-changing culture. Merton (even in Ed Rice's somewhat idiosyncratic characterization) immediately commended himself to me as my guide in that endeavor. I didn't then know the term "public intellectual," but I can see now that it was that dimension of Merton's life and work that first attracted me.

Now it's the fall of the same year. I have moved to Toronto, and need to choose my courses. Would there be a course offered on Thomas Merton? Ah, very good, yes: at St. Michael's, one of the colleges in the Toronto School of Theology. The instructor was Joanne McWilliam Dewart, former wife of one of Merton's correspondents, Leslie Dewart. Two memories stand out: a dramatic reading of "The Tower of Babel" at her home, and a visit to the class by a young grad student doing his Ph.D. in the English Department at York University, a certain Michael Higgins. That was the beginning of a wonderful friendship, one of non-stop stimulation and hilarity, to which anyone who knows Michael will attest.

My first degree in Toronto was a Th.M., and a thesis was required; on Merton, naturally—but from what angle? I reacquainted myself with *Seeds of Contemplation*, and then with its successor volume, *New Seeds of Contemplation* (1962). Perhaps a comparison of the changes from the first to the second versions? Then I discovered that between these two, Merton had published a revised version of *Seeds* in December 1949 (the first version had been published in March). The structure of the thesis presented itself to me on the spot. I am happy these many years later to acknowledge here its masterly supervision (and later, of my dissertation) by Professor Herbert W. Richardson. And so, twenty years later, my intuition that day in 1954 in the Dunbar Library came full circle.

I then started on my Ph.D., and in so doing felt that the time had come for me to visit the holy city of Louisville and the Merton Center. I received a warm welcome from longtime director Bob Daggy, and, when I went to Merton's monastery of Gethsemani, from Brother Patrick Hart. My signal discovery on that visit was that there existed two typescripts related to my thesis, one a typescript of *Seeds* which pre-existed the first published version, the other a typescript containing the changes to the first two versions which appeared in *New Seeds*. These, I learned, were in the collection of Sr. Thérèse Lentfoehr of Racine, Wisconsin, who had served as extern secretary to Merton, particularly during the time when he was prohibited by his order from publishing works that in the order's view were "unmonastic" (!).

I contacted Sr. Thérèse, who invited me to visit her. We made a fine connection, and soon came to the question of the typescripts. I was prepared to photocopy them, with her permission, and take the copies back to Toronto. I suggested this, and then came a memorable moment. She held them out to me, then clutched them back to her chest, repeated these actions, and finally thrust them at me with the happy words, "Just take them." I took these precious originals with me back to Toronto, had them copied, and returned them to Sr. Thérèse, with my sincere thanks for her trust.

It's now 1977. I haven't finished my dissertation, but the time has come to move back to Vancouver and get a job. The following year would be the tenth anniversary of Merton's death; and it seemed to Michael Higgins and myself that the time was ripe for a commemoration, which in fact was the first major conference on Merton. It was held at the Vancouver School of Theology in the spring of 1978, with a number of the pioneers of Merton studies present: Bob Daggy, Naomi Burton Stone, Amiya Chakravarty, William Shannon, and others, about 120 in all. (Here I gratefully acknowledge the loan of $1,500 from my dear father, without which we would not have been able to pull this off.) The conference was immediately followed by The People's Merton Festival. The name, serious then, humorous now, suggests we were still in the penumbra of the Sixties, as indeed we were. The CBC did TV specials for both English and French networks;

and a selection of the conference papers, edited by Michael and myself, was published in 1983 by Griffin House of Toronto as *Thomas Merton: Pilgrim in Process.*

I had put my dissertation on hold for the sake of this project, and when that was completed, turned my attention to it once again. I am grateful that my parish, All Saints in Burnaby, British Columbia, gave me a three-month leave of absence in the summer of 1979 to move the dissertation towards completion. By the fall, only the final chapter remained to be written. I wrote this last chapter in an incandescent stretch of four or five hours on January 31, 1980, Merton's 65th birthday. I had the strange feeling that it was my fingers and not my brain doing the writing; and as I pulled each page out of the typewriter, I read it as if for the first time, as if it had been infused rather than composed. After pulling the last page out, I shook it in the direction of whatever realm in which Merton is located, and addressed him thus: "OK, Tom, you have eaten up the last seven years of my life, and given that you are 65 today, I am retiring you." Anyone who knows Merton, of course, will realize that he cannot be so easily dismissed. I am happy that he did not take me seriously, and continues to challenge, irritate, stretch, and inspire me. The dissertation was published in two volumes, as *Thomas Merton: The Development of a Spiritual Theologian* (1985), and as *Thomas Merton's Rewritings: The Five Versions of Seeds/New Seeds of Contemplation as a Key to the Development of His Thought* (1989).

In 1989 I went to the inaugural general meeting of the International Thomas Merton Society in Louisville. I had proposed a paper on Merton and Polonnaruwa, but a week before the conference hadn't started on the paper. I had to be in Montréal the week before, and took advantage of being there to hole up in the library at McGill. I read *The Asian Journal of Thomas Merton* (1973) three times in rapid succession all the way through; and on the third reading, it fell wide open before me, much as did the ox disassembled by the cleaver of Prince Wen Hui's cook ("Cutting up an ox," in Thomas Merton, *The Way of Chuang Tzu,* 1965). I did my presentation, telling myself that when I got home, I would write up my notes and submit the paper for publication. I finally did that, a mere 23 years later. It was published as "Merton in Asia: The Polonnaruwa Illumination," in Ross Labrie and Angus Stuart, eds., *Thomas Merton: Monk on the Edge* (2012), and presented in abbreviated form as a paper to the 2013 general meeting. I am glad, in fact, to have taken so long to commit my early intuitions about Merton's experience at Polonnaruwa to writing, because it brought me closer than I was in 1989 to the experience of which he spoke in his last talk, at Samut Prakhan. "The monk," he says (and as non-monastics, the rest of us can also desire what he describes), "is a man who has attained, or is about to attain, or seeks to attain, full realization. He dwells in the center of society as one who has attained realization . . . . Not that he has acquired unusual or esoteric information, but he has come to experience the ground of his own being in such a way that he knows the secret of liberation and can somehow communicate this to others" (*The Asian Journal of Thomas Merton,* 333).

I made my first visit to Prades, Merton's birthplace in France, in 1996. The first "pilgrimage" to Prades took place the following year; and out of this came the Thomas Merton Society of Canada (www.Merton.ca), under the energetic leadership of Judith Hardcastle. Since then the TMSC has offered perhaps a dozen pilgrimages to places associated with Merton: New York, Alaska, Rome, Cuba, and, of course, Gethsemani. It continues to flourish from its Vancouver base.

In 2000-01, I was given a sabbatical by Simon Fraser University in Vancouver, where I taught Religious Studies from 1989 to 2004, including a course on Merton. I decided to spend part of it following the path Merton took on his 1968 journey to India, Sri Lanka and Thailand. It started as a research trip and ended as a pilgrimage. For the 40th anniversary in 2008 of Merton's death, I wrote an article about it which may be accessed through the link on the Merton page of my website www.donaldgrayston.ca/projects/thomas-merton/. In that article you will find the account of my life-changing ten minutes with Chatral Rinpoche on December 13, 2000. For my introduction to him I am indebted to Dr. James George, at the time of Merton's trip to India, Canadian High Commissioner (i.e., ambassador) to India, a debt I gratefully acknowledge.

In 2007 I was elected president of the ITMS for the 2007-09 term. I appreciated the honor done me thereby, although I soon discovered that, much like Queen Elizabeth, the president of the ITMS reigns but does not rule. Paul Pearson as resident secretary of the society as well as director of the Center acts, to complete the metaphor, as the highly competent prime minister. The president does offer the presidential address at the general meeting at the end of his/her term; and as the first Canadian president, I wanted to offer some Canadian content in whatever I would say about Merton. When a couple of months before the meeting, I read in an article in *The Globe and Mail* that Leonard Cohen was "monastic in his own way," the connection was made (the address is available at www.leonardcohenfiles.com/grayston.pdf) . Manifestly Thomas and Leonard are soul-brothers: both born in francophone cultures; both poets; both tricksters; both interested in Zen; both developing into transcultural spiritual teachers; and both, for what it's worth, 5'8". I have continued to develop this connection through a non-credit course for SFU, and through presentations and workshops.

As we know, 2015 marks the centenary of Merton's birth. The occasion will generate books, papers, exhibitions, and so on; and those of us who work in the Merton industry will toil away on some aspect of the great man's significance for the edification of others. Their experience, I trust, will parallel my own, which is that in keeping company with Thomas Merton and his friends, we indeed find ourselves members of a community of hope, faith and insight.

For myself, I acknowledge that, at some point in this journey, Merton shifted from being simply the object of academic study and became my spiritual director *in absentia*. I realized that I had taken his major concerns—contemplation, war and peace, and the engagement with the world's great religious traditions—as together comprising a paradigm both for my walk as a Christian, for my pastoral and academic work and for my understanding of our world in the time of "the great turning" (Joanna Macy's term). My sense of him is that, when he died in 1968, he was operating from about 2050. We still have a long way to go to catch up with him.

I give the second last word here to Ed Rice: "Merton was part of the great Catholic tradition and yet seemed not to be confined by it. . . . Thomas Merton never left us. The journey goes on" (quoted in James Harford, *Merton and Friends: A Joint Biography of Thomas Merton, Robert Lax and Edward Rice*, 217).

And the last word to Merton himself, the phrase he put at the end of *The Seven Storey Mountain: Sit finis libri, non finis quaerendi*—The book is finished, the seeking goes on—for him and for all of us.

Caritas. Coast. California.

David M. Odorisio

Merton's geography has always been my own. Woods. Shore. Desert. These are the landscapes of my soul. I stalked his woods in central Kentucky heat, ate cobwebs and danced in the darkness along crumbling creek beds and hallowed high Kentucky hill knobs. Scraped old paint off barn sheds to see if I could not find a piece of that dead monk's spirit trapped somewhere underneath—inside it all. I ate full-summer Gethsemani-garden ripe tomatoes with chunks of dense monk cheese. Thick bread. Bourbon-jar in hand. Mosquito-bathed in monk's pond. Paced straight-line forested woods. Silenced in smoky hermitage chapel. Icons unfurled. Merton's geography has always been my own.

Merton's voice is a living voice, haunting me since age 18. I first read his translation of Chuang Tzu. Required reading. "Introduction to Buddhism." Catholic monk writes Chinese. Translates dead Daoist masters. To my parochial mind *this* was the impossible. Squared and hemmed in by the safe strict confines of my tiny Catholicism yearning to set fire—no! To be set free! Dumbfounded, I read on. *The Seven Storey Mountain. No Man is an Island.* I needed no more once I discovered The Journals. Freshly minted hardbacks from college library. I carried half of them under each arm as I waddled my way to the lower parking lot en route to devour. *Zen and the Birds.* My college thesis, "The True Self." I had had enough. I entered a monastery too.

Then I left. And time passed.

Merton's was a living voice that remained with me for many years until it didn't. At a certain point, I was on my own. My thirties found me entering unchartered waters, adrift, lost at sea. No longer held interest by voices other than my own. Living on the West Coast at that time, I made a pilgrimage to some of Merton's final American haunts: Redwoods Monastery, Lost Coast, Humboldt. At Needle Rock, I read out loud with friends Merton's late words, penned at our exact location, line by line over campfire. A fierce wind howled off the Pacific as cresting waves crashed rocky coastal shores reminding us of *all* life's vicissitudes. In the entire expanse of the universe, we were alone in that sacred moment. Three friends. Lamenting the loss of a dead monk's voice. Longing for our own.

Now. I ruminate Merton's legacy from icy laurels. It is wintertime in the Berkshires. Icy snow crunch under soft boot weight. Geography haunts me.

California. Kentucky. Places I have known. Places I have yet to know.

The in-between places.

Certainty eludes all but one small thread: *caritas*

On a Lost Coast

Thomas Merton's Message of Hope

In a cinder-block chapel
With the silence of pine-barren stillness
. . . *Ubi caritas*

For passionately embracing the soul's wild places;
For my silent response.
For the great harvest—words planted in fragile soil.
For a young man's descent to truth (*est vera*)
For you, Tom Merton, Fr. Louie,
Deus ibi est

Love's Proximities

John Giuliani

In the winter of 1952 I was living in Brooklyn studying art at Pratt Institute. *The Seven Storey Mountain* literally fell into my hands. From the start I felt a kinship with many turns in Merton's young life. These episodes prepared me for the experience of being wounded by what I can only call "an arrow of love" that quickened within me a love barely understood. Since its origin was Gethsemani, I considered a journey to the place where countless others caught in the aura of Merton's story were making spiritual pilgrimages.

For the first of the two weeks of my stay at the monastery, it was Merton's turn as hebdomadary. He chanted the Conventual Mass. The following week leading up to the feast of Corpus Christi Merton served as Deacon in the liturgy which called upon him to sing the Gospel. Retreatants were welcomed in the choir at the rear of the nave. From a distance I was able to spot Merton. Listening to his unremarkable voice chanting the Gospel did not lessen the sense of proximity to the sight and sound of him.

It was June. The summer heat peaked at over a hundred degrees. A blanket of humidity released a sweet, sweaty moisture that coated the worn kneelers whose fragrance spoke to me of love's solidarity with all who had buried their faces in the hands of their prayers and who had found consolation on those kneelers.

In his first published journal, *The Sign of Jonas*, published in 1953, the last entry is titled "June Octave of Corpus Christi." Here Merton actually records the two weeks I spent at Gethsemani. Reading that entry again and again, I see my remembered self in his journey and among the company of a hundred and more brothers swaying *con una sola voce* like some immense wave of the sea. And I am taken up into its adoration, into its thanksgiving. How then is it possible for the youthful heart to turn from this easy ecstasy? For "This is the land where you have given me roots in eternity . . . the place of peace, the place of silence, the place of wrestling with the angel."

The face of Merton has impressed itself upon my soul. In that beautiful weathered face the sense of his huge humanity and irrepressible joy gives word to every breath. The rest, as another poet has written, is silence.

Merton Centenary Icon, acrylic on gessoed board by John Giuliani, 2015.

Ishi: Messenger Of Hope

Paul R. Dekar

I was born and raised in California. As a young adult, I worked in 1965 with a Christian Ministry in the National Parks. Through that experience, I learned about Ishi, last of the Yana, the original inhabitants of the area. Ishi (c. 1860–1916) lived most of his life in the area. In 1911, he left his ancestral homeland alone and starving. He spent his remaining five years in a University of California building in San Francisco where he served as a research subject and assistant for the anthropologists Alfred and Theodora Kroeber. The latter wrote *Ishi in Two Worlds: A Biography of the Last Wild Indian in North America*. Ishi died of tuberculosis, in the words of Thomas Merton a "disease of civilization." After a long legal battle, in 2000 Ishi's remains were cremated and his ashes scattered in the area where he once had lived free.

In the Yana culture, it was rude to ask someone's name. As a result, when asked his name, Ishi said: "I have none, because there are no Yana to call to me." The Kroebers named him Ishi, meaning "man."

In 1967, Thomas Merton wrote "Ishi: A Meditation" for *The Catholic Worker*. Subsequently, the essay was one of five published in *Ishi Means Man: Essays on Native Americans* (1976). Two essays dealt with the original inhabitants of North America, two with ancestral Central Americans. William H. Shannon included Merton's essay on Ishi in *Passion for Peace* (1995). Merton's reflections on Ishi that follow are cited from Shannon's volume. I have not changed non-inclusive language although I believe that Merton would use gender-free language were he writing in the twenty-first century.

The Collected Poems of Thomas Merton (1977) reflected Merton's fascination with anthropology, Native Americans and the cargo-cult phenomenon. Merton's colleague, Matthew Kelty, a monk of Gethsemani, had served in Papau, New Guinea from 1947 to 1951 and may have fueled Merton's concern for those regarded by other humans as subhuman or worthless, having no right to exist (*Passion*, 286).

In "Ishi: A Meditation" Merton expressed his commitment—prevalent during the last decade of his life—to address what he saw as one of the grave problems of religion, namely, "the almost total lack of protest on the part of religious people and clergy in the face of enormous social evils (*Passion*, 128)." While the Catholic hierarchy reacted to Merton's addressing social issues, such issues as the Vietnam War, and ordered him not to publish on the subject, this opposition simply fueled Merton's commitment to continue to write about violence, racism and injustice. In "Ishi: A Meditation," Merton explored the dropping of bombs on defenseless Asian villages as much as the story of Ishi. Merton concluded that both atrocities rendered purported values of the United States "the most pitiful sham."

Merton acknowledged that Indians could be as cruel and inhumane as any group of people. Yet in the case of the Mill Creek people, as their numbers declined during the nineteenth century, they unsuccessfully sought someone with whom to negotiate their future. Since coexistence was impossible, they withdrew into an inaccessible area and lived as if they were not seen. Merton identified with them, in that monks too live a hidden life. He recognized a major difference, in that his choice was entirely voluntary.

While the Yana lived out their days as "peaceful, innocent and deeply wronged human beings . . . hidden . . . completely out of sight in order to escape destruction," Merton expressed horror at what he called "genocide" by "white America" of Ishi's people, as well as of "entire tribes and of ethnic groups of Indians." For Merton, the story of Ishi extended the frontier mentality, replete with enemies who were an "inferior race."

This pattern continued into Merton's time, for the Vietnam War seemed to him "part and parcel of our national identity." Merton regarded the killing of innocents as an inevitable outcome of modern warfare. He was aware that more civilians were killed in modern warfare than combatants. Merton concluded, "What a pity that so many innocent people have to pay with their lives for our obsessive fantasies."

During the 1960s, Merton also explored race, revolution and the cargo cults of Papua, New Guinea. He saw parallels in these great "crusades" of his time—the Black Power Movement, the Communist Chinese revolution, the resistance of Vietnamese to colonialism, the peace movement, and the Cargo Cult phenomenon—with the apocalyptic literature of the Middle Ages. These undertakings were not irrational outbursts, as the consensus of the dominant culture often held, but rather uprisings of subjugated peoples. For Merton, the oppressed were forging a way forward that would transform the stultifying status quo through openness to all kinds of new knowledge and goods.

In one essay on the "Cargo Cults of the South Pacific," Merton summarized why the dominant social order should pay attention to First Peoples. He observed:

> If our white Western myth-dream demands of us that we spiritually enslave others in order to "save" them, we should not be surprised when their own myth-dream demands of them that they get entirely free of us to save themselves. But both the white man's and the native's myth-dreams are only partial and inadequate expressions of the whole truth. It is not that the primitive needs to be dominated by the white man in order to become fully human. Nor is it that he needs to get rid of the white man. Each needs the other to cooperate in the common enterprise of building a world adequate to the historical maturity of man (*Love and Living*, 94).

During the 1960s, Merton asked penetrating questions about the growing gap between the rich and the poor, the environmental crisis, human rights, and the need to bring a deep spirituality to bear on all these concerns. Merton responded to such queries by beginning to shape an earth ethic.

In my writing about ecological justice, social justice and peace I have developed principles with which, I believe, Merton could share if he were alive today. First, the Earth has values for humankind that no scientist can synthesize, no economist can price and no technological distraction can replace.

A second principle is interconnection. Merton understood that all things are connected, that whatever we do to the Earth, we do to ourselves. He also believed that we should protect in perpetuity the natural world, not only for our own sake, but for the sake of the plants and animals and for the good of the sustaining earth.

Nature should exist intact solely for its own sake; no human justification, rationale or excuse is needed. We are custodians of the Earth.

Merton also was convinced that one concern led to another. He concluded that "neither the ancient wisdoms nor the modern sciences are complete in themselves. They do not stand alone. They call for one another" (*Gandhi and Non-Violence*, 1). Merton understood a task in the West as that of learning "that if we can voyage to the ends of the earth and there find ourselves in the aborigine who most differs from ourselves, we will have made a fruitful pilgrimage" (*Mystics and Zen Masters*, 112).

Truganini (1812–1876) was a Tasmanian Aboriginal woman. In 1830, George Augustus Robinson, the so-called Protector of Aborigines, moved Truganini and approximately a hundred other survivors of the conquest of Tasmania offshore to Flinders Island. At the time of her death, she was widely considered the last full-blooded Tasmanian Aboriginal person. Years later, learning of her story prompted the British writer Aldous Huxley to write *Brave New World*. First published in 1932, Huxley cautioned that, if one people could eliminate another, humans had the capacity to eliminate any people. Setting the novel in London of AD 2540, Huxley foresaw negative developments in technology, warfare and climate change.

Merton's journals reflect that he read some of Huxley's writings. Did Huxley influence Merton's subsequent interest in First Peoples or in the potentially adverse effects of technology? Merton does not so indicate. Nonetheless, the pace of technological innovation is profoundly impacting society much more significantly than either Huxley or Merton anticipated. Both writers were prophetic in calling humankind to wake up to the down side of the way we are living. By acknowledging that humans could utterly obliterate the Yana or the Tasmanian aboriginal people, Merton and Huxley warned against genocide. Merton and Huxley portrayed Ishi and Truganini as messengers of hope and warning in our dangerous times.

A Long Shelf Life: Growing Up, Growing Old(er) With Thomas Merton

Patrick F. O'Connell

For as long as I can recall, Thomas Merton has occupied at least a niche in my life—quite literally so at the outset. On the built-in bookcase that my father had made as a "secret" door from the living room to the cellar of our house, along with *Cana Is Forever* by Charles Hugo Doyle, *Life Is Worth Living* by Fulton J. Sheen and other Catholic books of the era, sat Merton's 1948 autobiography *The Seven Storey Mountain*, a year younger than myself, a year older than my brother. (They were joined somewhat later by duplicate copies of *Dear Sister* by Catherine de Hueck Doherty, which our aunt had found one year as potential Christmas presents for our teachers, but they were never given because it was unthinkable, to my father at least, that a book of letters of advice to nuns should have been written by a laywoman.) All these volumes were simply part of the decor of our living room—I don't recall any of them being taken down or read by either of my parents, though they may have done so before we were old enough to be aware of it—I never asked. (The one book my brother and I would look at repeatedly was a fat, squat anthology called *100 Great Lives*: we were fascinated and appalled by an illustration labeled "Luther Burns the Pope's Bull," an act we considered incredibly cruel—since there was no sign of the bull in the picture we decided the burning must have been going on for a while, but we could never figure out why the pope had a bull in the first place and how Luther might have captured it.)

Cana Is Forever wasn't—at least for us: it and Fulton Sheen and the Baroness and *100 Great Lives* are all long gone, but that copy of *The Seven Storey Mountain* now occupies a considerably more substantial niche. It is sitting just behind me as I type this in my "study," under the eaves of the only house we've actually owned, in a built-in bookcase, remodeled from a good-sized closet shortly after we moved here six or seven years ago—six five-foot wide shelves filled with just about every book, other than the rarer limited editions, ever written by or about Thomas Merton, along with complete runs of *The Merton Seasonal* and *Annual*, a nearly complete set of *The Merton Journal*, and almost four feet worth of *Cistercian Studies Quarterly* as well.

I didn't actually read *The Seven Storey Mountain*, however, until I was a sophomore in college, and at the time, I'm rather abashed to admit, I was somewhat underwhelmed by it. I had stayed at school for, appropriately enough, a Holy Week retreat, and picked up a paperback copy (the Signet edition if I recall correctly) at the campus bookstore for my spiritual reading. It was just a year and a half after the close of Vatican II, and in those heady days of ferment and renewal the autobiography struck me as quite pre-conciliar in its attitudes—which of course it was, inevitably. It is much else as well, much more, as I would later come to realize, but its apparent "traditionalism" was mainly what I noticed then, with at least a touch of condescension—also perhaps inevitable, or at least predictable. I left Merton alone after that until the beginning of my senior year, when I was visiting the room of one of my professors and noticed the Image Book paperback of *Conjectures of a Guilty Bystander* on his shelf. While my teacher and some of my friends conversed, I began flipping through the book, and as we were about to leave I was putting it back in its place when he told me to take it with me and to keep it.

This generous gift was a defining point for me, at the time and thereafter. That copy too, almost read to pieces, is now on the shelf behind me (finally joined just this year by the original cloth edition that had been the object of a decades-long search). *Conjectures* did what *Seven Storey Mountain* hadn't—made me a confirmed and permanent Merton "disciple." As James Laughlin puts it in *Merton: A Film Biography*, "Once you've been 'bitten' by Merton, you'll just go on reading him until you've read everything he's written." It took two 'bites' for me, but from then on I was smitten as well as bitten. At the time I was very involved in a campus retreat program but was also becoming increasingly drawn toward nonviolence and an anti-war stance, yet it seemed as though few of my fellow students committed to one of these movements had much interest in the other. The Merton of *Conjectures* showed me that this was an artificial division, that "I could unite in myself" (to borrow a phrase) prayer and action, literature (I was an English major) and spirituality, a commitment to the Church and an openness to the world—the post-conciliar perspective par excellence. Merton pointed toward a wholeness of vision and of practice that I was desperately looking for then and have tried, with mixed results, to remain faithful to ever since. His death at the end of that year—I can still vividly recall feeling shocked and disconsolate while looking at the *New York Times* obituary in the reading room of the Holy Cross library on the morning of December 11, 1968—only deepened my sense of how important his witness had been and would continue to be for me personally, and for the Church and even the country in a time of turmoil.

Merton accompanied me into the Jesuit novitiate the following fall—my parents gave me a copy of the oversized cloth edition of *Bread in the Wilderness* as a going-away gift—which I later passed on to a friend who was heading off into a sort of wilderness himself to try to figure out his future direction. (Years later I got another copy of *Bread*, identical except for a rather stained front cover, when the pastor of our parish retired, a parish where that same friend had worked as Religious Ed. Director.) During Advent some fellow novices and I put together a prayer service that was also a commemoration of the anniversary of Merton's death; it featured an excerpt from *Conjectures* I had come across in which Merton reflects on the meaning of the Incarnation while standing on a Louisville street corner—at the time I had no idea whether anyone else had ever noticed what a powerful passage this was.

Merton accompanied me out of the novitiate after a year and a half of trying out the life, when I realized that my future belonged with the student nurse I had come to know around the same time as I was reading *Conjectures* (Sue and I met on retreat, not in a hospital room, and she's actually seven months older than I am). A group of us novices had been reading *Gandhi on Non-Violence* and *Faith and Violence* in preparation for deciding to mail back our draft cards—which I did with some trepidation since at that point I had already decided that I would be leaving behind the novitiate and my "ministerial" exemption. (I later received in the mail a duplicate copy from my draft board, which I returned with even more trepidation since by this time I was about to become a father, but rather miraculously I never heard from them again, I'll never know why.)

Merton was present at our wedding—one of the readings was from *No Man Is an Island*—by then we'd been to enough weddings where Kahlil Gibran's pseudo-mystical effusions had been used that we figured Merton could safely join Saints Paul and John from the lectern. Merton accompanied me to graduate school—I spent a wonderful summer reading a chapter a day of *New Seeds of Contemplation* after lunch in the St. Thomas More Chapel at Yale where we had gotten married shortly after I entered the English doctoral program there, and I even managed to get Merton into my dissertation, on John Donne's religious poetry—a passage from *The Waters of Siloe*, oddly enough (though in fact quite apropos). While teaching at a high-school seminary (remember those?) on Long Island and finishing my dissertation, I was also taking courses for a master's degree in spirituality at Fordham, hoping to somehow work my way into a "literature of Christian spirituality" position somewhere (which never quite happened), and took an excellent summer course on Merton with Fr. George Kilcourse, a recent Fordham doctoral graduate, from whom I first heard about the Bellarmine Merton Center. I immediately wrote to be put on the mailing list for *The Merton Seasonal*, and to be sent whatever back issues were available—which turned out to be all of them, rather amazingly. I could hardly have imagined then that one day I'd be the one editing this very periodical.

Merton accompanied me to my present school and has continued to enrich my life not only with his own wisdom but by putting me in touch with an ever-expanding circle of wise and witty and wonderful people. The master's degree had actually gotten me a job (though not a tenure-track one) in the theology department of St. Anselm College in New Hampshire, where I was able to finish a Fordham theology doctorate long-distance. Merton also made a cameo appearance in that dissertation, on St. Bonaventure, on its second page and a couple times thereafter. By the time I was looking for a new position I had become particularly interested in Merton's poetry and had been trying to track down what Sr. Thérèse Lentfoehr had called the preliminary version of "Elias: Variations on a Theme," which turned out to be the same poem with an additional page that had been lost before publication. So on my way out to Erie for an interview at Villa Maria College (shortly thereafter to merge with Gannon University) I stopped at the St. Bonaventure University library to look at some of the letters between Merton and Naomi Burton—by that time I'd already come across the missing page at Columbia but was trying to figure out how that had happened, and in the process discovered at Bonaventure a couple of other poems from the same period that had never been published. So I ended up with material for two articles on Merton just as we were moving to western Pennsylvania—one on the missing materials, that I sent to the *Seasonal*, and a long one on "Elias" that was ready just as the first volume of *The Merton Annual* was being prepared.

It was at just this time, fortuitously or providentially, that the International Thomas Merton Society was about to be formed, and even though my total Merton publication record at that point was a review of Monica Furlong's biography and an article on "diaspora" Christianity that was about a third on Merton, Merton Center Director Bob Daggy, of blessed memory, invited me to the founding meeting in May 1987, shortly after I'd submitted my articles. Because of another commitment that same weekend,

I arrived only on the second day, and felt totally overwhelmed and out of my depth in the midst of the distinguished gathering of Merton scholars and friends whose articles and books I had read—people like William Shannon and Lawrence Cunningham, Mary Luke Tobin, Anthony Padovano and Victor Kramer—but in fact they were all extremely gracious and welcoming, then and thenceforth. I was able to hitch a ride down to Gethsemani with the Kramers, who were staying at the abbey, to be warmly greeted and shown around by Brother Patrick Hart, like so many others before and since, and to go back to Louisville the next day with Christine Bochen and Bill Shannon, who more than a dozen years later would invite me to coauthor *The Merton Encyclopedia* with them. Not only a perpetually fascinating subject for reflection, study and research, and a source of inspiration and insight both inside and outside the classroom, Merton became the catalyst for some of the most graced friendships of my life, with these extraordinary people and many others like them who have been part of the Merton "family" over the years. My life would have been immeasurably poorer had Merton been somehow "left on the shelf."

Of the hundreds of thousands (at least) of Merton's words that I've read over the past forty-plus years, it's difficult to say for sure which have been the most meaningful, but five key passages would certainly make the cut for any personal anthology, and taken together seem to me to provide the gist of Merton's message. The first comes from "The General Dance," the final chapter of *New Seeds of Contemplation*, and combines Merton's fundamental view of the Incarnation with one of his favorite scripture passages:

> The Lord made the world and made man in order that He Himself might descend into the world, that He Himself might become Man. When He regarded the world He was about to make, He saw His wisdom, as a man-child, "playing in the world, playing before Him at all times." And He reflected, "My Delights are to be with the children of men" (*New Seeds of Contemplation* 290).

While the language is of its day, the basic message is timeless—that is, always timely: God's will to participate fully in human life was not contingent on the fact of the fall, not simply a response to human sinfulness, but the very purpose for and culmination of creation, as Duns Scotus and others have taught; it is the epiphany of Divine Wisdom, of Hagia Sophia, so memorably expressed in the words of Proverbs 8.

This does not mean that Merton in any way underplays the need for or the centrality of Christ's redemptive work. The paschal mystery, in which Christ the Word shares fully in the human condition so that humanity united with Christ can be drawn into "the utter fullness of God" (Eph. 3), is at the heart of Merton's faith, articulated throughout his work, as in this beautiful passage from "A Christian Looks at Zen":

> It is essential to remember that for a Christian "the word of the Cross" is nothing theoretical, but a stark and existential experience of union with Christ in His death in order to share in His resurrection. To fully "hear" and "receive" the word of the Cross means much more than simple assent to the dogmatic proposition that Christ died for our sins. It means to be "nailed to the Cross with Christ," so that the ego-self is no longer the principle of our deepest actions, which now proceed from Christ living in us. "I live, now not I, but Christ lives in me" (Gal. 2:19-20; see also Romans 8:5-17). To receive the word of the Cross means the acceptance of a com-

plete self-emptying, a *Kenosis*, in union with the self-emptying of Christ "obedient unto death" (Phil. 2:5-11). It is essential to true Christianity that this experience of the Cross and of self-emptying be central in the life of the Christian so that he may fully receive the Holy Spirit and know (again by experience) all the richness of God in and through Christ (*Zen and the Birds of Appetite,* 55-56).

The consequence of this participation in Christ's death and resurrection is that Christians are empowered to see the presence of Christ and to be the presence of Christ in a world that has been redeemed, even if the signs of that redemption are often difficult to discern. Here is the gift and the challenge of Merton's realized eschatology, his call to the Church to be a sign and instrument of God's reign of truth and justice and *shalom* and compassionate love here and now, as found in "Blessed Are the Meek," perhaps the best essay on Christian nonviolence ever written, or at least the best I've ever read. Merton writes there:

The great historical event, the coming of the Kingdom, is made clear and is "realized" in proportion as Christians themselves live the life of the Kingdom in the circumstances of their own place and time. . . . Christian non-violence is nothing if not first of all a formal profession of faith in the Gospel message that the Kingdom has been established and that the Lord of truth is indeed risen and reigning over his Kingdom, defending the deepest values of those who dwell in it (*Faith and Violence,* 16, 18).

This vision of the Kingdom is the vision of unity, of Christ as all in all, transcending all distinctions between sacred and profane, between divine and human, as Merton declares toward the end of "Is the World a Problem?"

Do we really choose between the world and Christ as between two conflicting realities absolutely opposed? Or do we choose Christ by choosing the world as it really is in him, that is to say created and redeemed by him, and encountered in the ground of our own personal freedom and of our love? Do we really renounce ourselves and the world in order to find Christ, or do we renounce our alienated and false selves in order to choose our own deepest truth in choosing both the world and Christ at the same time? If the deepest ground of my being is love, then in that very love itself and nowhere else will I find myself, and the world, and my brother and Christ. It is not a question of either-or but of all-in-one (*Contemplation in a World of Action,* 155-56).

Ultimately this is a unity that transcends creation itself. To be one with Christ is to share in the Word's intimate love of the Father in and through the Spirit, to be drawn into the very love life of the Blessed Trinity, discovered and experienced in silence and stillness as a foretaste of eternity. So Merton teaches us in the concluding words of "Notes for a Philosophy of Solitude," which may serve as an apt conclusion for these notes as well:

The shallow "I" of individualism can be possessed, developed, cultivated, pandered to, satisfied: it is the center of all our strivings for gain and for satisfaction, whether material or spiritual. But the deep "I" of the spirit, of solitude and of love, cannot be "had," possessed, developed, perfected. It can only *be,* and *act* according to deep inner laws which are not of man's contriving, but which come from God.

They are the Laws of the Spirit, who, like the wind, blows where He wills. This inner "I," who is always alone, is always universal: for in this inmost "I" my own solitude meets the solitude of every other man and the solitude of God. Hence it is beyond division, beyond limitation, beyond selfish affirmation. It is only this inmost and solitary "I" that truly loves with the love and the spirit of Christ. This "I" is Christ Himself, living in us: and we, in Him, living in the Father (*Disputed Questions,* 207).

Learning From Merton:
Dates, Research, Projects, And People (1958–2014)

Victor A. Kramer

I.

In 1958, at age 17, Merton was a name, someone who, as a freshman in college, I sensed must be important. *Seeds of Contemplation, The Living Bread* were on the rack of the St. Edward's book store. 25 cent Dell editions. I bought the books. Read them in a perfunctory manner. All those words seemed a bit abstract, reflecting some ideal, which at that time seemed beyond ordinary living. Yet the seeds were planted.

Then the rush of study, activities and reading followed—undergraduate, and graduate, up to full-time teaching at Marquette University in 1966—without a lot of time for religious reading. At that time those small Merton Dell books were still on the shelf along with textbooks, including *The Pattern of Criticism* by Victor Hamm (now a colleague) and *The Imitation of Christ* (mostly skimmed).

In December of 1966, one of my teaching assistants gave me a copy of *Raids on the Unspeakable*. Surprising words and calligraphy! I read it, was awakened, changed into a real reader seeing then and there we are surrounded by the unspeakable.

In my late twenties, other Merton books found their ways onto my shelves. It was during the period 1966 to 1969 learning to teach, research, write. There was a flood of work to be done with American literature, and thinking about James Agee, but this was also a time (I realize in retrospect) of discernment. Merton was finding me.

I got the contract to do the Twayne U. S. Authors Series book on Merton. This was the first time anyone celebrated him as a literary figure. During this period, Merton remained somewhat distant, a successful monk-writer. My job was to read and comment. What, of course, was also happening was that, just as Merton says in his book about the Bible, that the Bible reads us, Merton was reading me.

His literature, I was beginning to know as a mysterious bearer of gifts. Things unspeakable were to be examined and in the process changes came to my understanding and attitude. Merton could not be only a literary figure.

II.

Merton had to be shared, not just as a good writer, but as someone who changes lives. By the late 1970s, my appreciation of Merton began to become an appreciation of his implicit spirituality—an invitation, then, to grow more in the "general dance." His monastic journey, I began to know, was recorded in so many books, saints' lives, poetry, essays, fiction. I could also see this was the outward record of an inward transformation. I began to see that the books were not a record of Merton's accomplishments. They were, above all, an invitation. His published insights were designed to draw others into mystery.

We did a conference at Georgia State on February 28, 1980. 150 people came. Elena Malits was a speaker and George Kilcourse, too. A friend at Emory, Michael Mott, came because he had been just given the contract to "finish" a biography started by John Howard Griffin. Jim Finley was also one of the main speakers.

Much followed: reading groups and meditation groups and friendships. Some of those friendships are still alive now, decades later. Fr. Tom Francis Smith, of Conyers Monastery, spoke at that 1980 conference about Merton and Contemplative Prayer. This was way before Thomas Keating and Basil Pennington did their work on what we know as Centering Prayer. Attendees stayed in contact with me, and each other.

One psychology professor years later said, "Merton pulled me through a difficult time in my life." Later I heard this was something which happened for him because of what he had learned by studying Merton who had in many ways manifested his intense respect for all of his student novices, and how Merton had learned so much over the years, not just through knowledge of psychological theory but through love and appreciation of the goodness and insights of his own students. That professor was changed; and others—a student here or there; a member of a reading group occasionally; a friend who had learned to rely upon Merton (not for scholarly study) but as the monastic who was, through his careful writing, sharing his insights so people would have the opportunity to be changed.

Teaching Merton, doing an Oral History with people who knew him, another Oral History about Conyers, sharing in programs, conferences, writing papers, and then twenty years of *The Merton Annual*—begun in 1986—those activities allowed the loving monastic insights of Merton to be shared. Programs, seminars, conferences followed; Ecumenical focus, Lay spirituality, the journals, parallels with Buddhism, and the need for silence moved me and others.

III.

These were new and different kinds of events, so different from having a few paperbacks on a college dorm shelf. This was now a Merton who was waking up people. One of my student assistants read, acted, was baptized in 1992. Another, reading carefully over years, sees Merton's work as a bridge between religion(s) and philosophies. He helped co-edit the two issues of *CrossCurrents* of 2008-2009 on Merton. Another friend, in a reading group, which has existed since 2001, a dozen years plus, sees Merton as one of his two most important guides.

My editing of volume 4 of the journals, *Turning Toward the World*, was done in the mid-1990s. This, too, has led to learning and meeting people in special circumstances because of our reading of this detailed spiritual journey. It's helped, too, with spiritual direction.

Seeing how carefully Merton's entries were made, it is now clear to me that his life, and this entire journal project was intended—right from the first page—not to be just a record of Merton's spiritual journey. It is a selective record of that journey written so others could later return to the entries, where they come to do *lectio divina*, to read and re-read.

IV.

I am convinced Merton's careful journal entries, and everything else that he wrote (from poems to class notes) were done as Labors of Love, not just to put information or poetic insights on record. Merton's vocation, especially from December 10, 1941, forward, was a call to draw others into the mystery of God's invitation to us as "life moves inexorably towards mystery and crisis," as we become more aware of how to use words.

Merton's work allows us to enter into the mystery of God's Presence, not for this or that person's redemption, but because God is and always will be present for all humankind.

The large correspondence, the hundreds of poems, the essays on Christian and non-Christian religion, the Love of persons through so many commitments, the Love of each person for other as gift: It's all there, seeds to be planted, shared for all seekers.

Merton's writings, the overflow of his love for and journey to God, are a model, a resource for all seekers.

CODA

I have lived and learned with Merton for some four decades. As I have explained some of those experiences through dates, projects and persons, I now realize that I have learned so much more than Father Louis..

Now I will turn full circle and express some of my present enthusiasm by way of still more connections which I have recently been privileged to develop. Just this year I did a retreat about the journals, and later I received a note from a retired professor who attended. He said, "I have so many of Merton's books on my shelves. I hope it is not too late to read them." Our thirteen-year old Merton Reading Group (finally) decided to read Merton's *Peace in the Post-Christian Era* as the news keeps coming about Syria and Ukraine. In September 2013, I did a course on Merton and Mary Oliver, as seekers.

Clearly Merton has flavored my life. I now know so many people, scholars and friends with whom I have worked so well and consistently to know and pray with his words. What I realize is that this group of brothers and sisters is a clear reflection of God and of this Cistercian monk-writer-saint.

Thomas Merton's Hopeful Life Of Peace

John Dear

The last hundred years has shown us the worst of systemic evil, with a hundred million dead from warfare, the use of nuclear weapons at Hiroshima and Nagasaki, extreme poverty on an unparalleled level, and the deliberate hastening of catastrophic climate change. But it has also shown us the best of humanity, with stunning peacemakers of every description from Franz Jagerstatter and Dorothy Day to Mohandas Gandhi and Martin Luther King, Jr. to John XXIII and Archbishop Oscar Romero. In this world of war and despair, these great peacemakers give me hope. They show us a way forward, along the path of nonviolence, toward a new future and the God of peace.

When I was young, I made a conscious decision to study the lives of the great peacemakers, and to meet and befriend the best living peacemakers, in the hope that I might fulfill my vocation to be a peacemaker. I realized I would not learn much about the spiritual life or following Jesus or peacemaking from our presidents, generals, TV newscasters, media pundits, mean religious officials, or others caught in the trappings of power. So I sought out the great peacemakers of our time, and sat at their feet to hear their lessons of peace—people like Daniel and Philip Berrigan, Bishop Thomas Gumbleton, Mairead Maguire, Mother Teresa, Archbishop Desmond Tutu, Dom Helder Camara, Henri Nouwen, and Thich Nhat Hanh. I also began a lifelong study of the writings of Gandhi, Dr. King and Dorothy Day.

And from day one, that list included Thomas Merton. I tried to read every book, essay and letter he wrote. I attended conferences about him, started making regular retreats at the Abbey of Gethsemani, made two retreats in his hermitage, and learned about him from his friends. For over thirty years, as I have traipsed through the war zones of the world, marched for peace, been arrested and jailed for my protests, and preached the Gospel of peace to the masses, Merton has been my teacher and guide. His writings and example have been a steady, daily source of strength, hope and light, right up to today.

It's with gratitude and consolation that I think of this peacemaking monk and writer. For while the Berrigans taught me resistance to the culture of war, Dorothy Day models hospitality to the poor and Dr. King exemplifies the methodology of active nonviolence, Thomas Merton embodies for me the creative, spiritual life of peace. By spending hours in prayer, wandering through the woods, reading about every topic under the sun, corresponding with people around the world, and sharing his spiritual discoveries with everyone, Merton lived a full life of peace and shared that peace with the world. There was no violence, no hostility, no meanness in his heart or on his journey; instead, he seemed to discover the freedom of peace within the boundaries of loving, prayerful nonviolence. Because of his soaring intellect, passionate concern for the world and ever-deepening faith, he demonstrated a life lived to the full, a life that non-cooperates with the forces of death. These days, when life is so cheap, death runs rampant and few live life to the full, I find his example to be an amazing gift, one that keeps on giving.

After three decades of journeying with Merton my teacher and guide, I look back at a few key aspects that have shaped my own journey. They may not be that unusual for other students of Merton, but I share them from the perspective of my own peculiar, public work in the struggle for justice and peace and in the hope that we can all continue to explore the spiritual life of peace.

The Prayerful, Solitary Life of Peace

Merton's solitary life as a hermit on the grounds of the monastery stands out in today's mad world of twitter, tweeting, Facebook, iphones, and GPS—not to mention the regular gun shootings, widespread hunger, drone bombings, and catastrophic climate change. While the rest of the world was charged with racism, war, nuclear weapons, and the war on communism, Merton took a solitary stand alone in the woods, like Thoreau at Walden Pond or a desert father in the northern Egypt. He refused to give in to the madness of his time, and clung with determination to daily prayer, quiet meditation and scripture reading as the basis for a more human life.

Today, everyone seems caught up in the ever-worsening rat-race of competition, consumerism and noise. The violence around us consumes us, eats away at us and destroys us without our knowing it. We grew ever more unconscious. Few people seem hopeful, happy, peaceful, or joyful.

And then there's Merton—alone in the woods with his prayer books, showing us that we need not give into violence, that we can create a life of nonviolence for ourselves, that we can reclaim our humanity, that we can be at peace with ourselves through daily prayer, quiet meditation, scripture study, and solitude. We can live at peace, he insists. We can make peace with the God of peace, with creation, with humanity. What's more, we need to do this. This is our best hope. We don't have to become monks or hermits, but each one of us has to become a person of peace and nonviolence.

This conscious, solitary life of peace and prayer has become a model for me. We can take time every day, no matter how busy we are, for peaceful solitude, for quiet meditation, for intercessory prayer. We can let the Holy Spirit of peace settle within us and move through us. In our violent world, that simple practice is too often forgotten—especially by peace and justice advocates and church people. If we want to serve the God of peace, Merton seems to say, we better get used to living at peace with ourselves and the God of peace; otherwise, how can we claim to offer the world an authentic witness for peace?

In my own life, I swing from periods of intense, active public work—traveling, addressing crowds, leading prayers, organizing demonstrations—to quiet, solitary work, writing alone in a little handmade house off the grid on a remote mesa in the high desert of New Mexico. Perhaps on that score, I've taken Merton *too* seriously. I literally sought out the same kind of solitude he searched for in New Mexico in the Spring and Summer of 1968, and I found it on a quiet mountaintop looking out over fifty pristine miles of beautiful New Mexico wilderness in the Galisteo basin. For ten years now, I've lived alone on this desert mountaintop. I've experienced the sheer joy and ecstacy which Merton extols as the fruit of holy solitude. I know what he's talking about. I've also experienced the pain and despair that can come with solitude.

The solitude of the desert slows one down, restores one's humanity and puts one in touch with the reality of creation. The silence here is unlike anything else I've experienced. Sometimes at night, a million bright stars shine overhead, and I try to reach up and touch the bright pink Milky Way. Coyotes walk regularly around my house, along with other creatures, and the Russian sage brush and green junipers give the moonscape a mysterious beauty. This peaceful solitude forces you to confront yourself, but it also opens up innumerable blessings for the present moment of peace. I never would have dared such a life without Merton's strong example.

Through the example of his own life journey, Merton invites me to pursue the life of peace, plumb the mystical depths of peace and experience the holy life of peace as ordinary. His example and zealous writings on the subject give me hope that I too can live a life of peace, that we all can. I still want to take him seriously, and urge others to pursue the life of peace as well. I hope we can catch his passion and choose the ordinary, spiritual life of peace, rooted in an authentic daily spiritual practice.

THE WRITING LIFE AS A WITNESS TO PEACE

With his magisterial autobiography, *The Seven Storey Mountain*, Merton exploded on to the world as a spiritual force to be reckoned with. In his first twenty-six years, it seems he tried everything, traveled everywhere, studied every avenue of thought, and then landed, improbably, in a Trappist monastery. From then on, it was "God Alone." He threw down a gauntlet to the world, and asked us, "Where are you going? Where are you on the road to peace? How is your journey leading you to God?"

A soaring intellectual with a one in a million gift for writing, Merton not only shared that journey to the monastery, he went on to share countless other insights. For the next twenty seven years, he churned out some of the best spiritual writing in the last century, a hundred books, journals, collections of essays, letters and poems, enough to keep us occupied for centuries. For someone who spent seven hours a day in liturgical prayer and quiet meditation, who then lived alone in the woods, who had no access to a telephone, fax, cell phone, computer, ipad, or google—this is an astonishing accomplishment.

And Merton reached an enormous audience, another unheard of accomplishment, not just for a monk or a priest, but for anyone. He reclaimed the ancient teachings on prayer and contemplation, drew us back to the interior life, invited us to live consciously, and summoned us to the search for God. He made the life of prayer interesting and exciting and real.

If he stopped there, that would have been plenty. But Merton was the real thing. He started to address war, nuclear weapons, racism, idolatry, and the war on communism. He connected the life of prayer, solitude and peace with the mad world of war and systemic injustice. This turn in his writing shocked his readers and continues to push us today. Of course, he was right on all counts. Why? Because he wrote from an authentic encounter with the God of peace. Because he followed the spiritual journey shown by Jesus all the way, a journey that leads to the cross as confrontation with the culture of war and empire, and risks the peace of resurrection.

The spiritual life, Merton teaches, leads the peacemaker to address the world with a word of peace. In particular, he demonstrates the power of writing as a way to address and change the world. He proves the adage: the pen is mightier than the sword.

The church has a long history of Christian writing—from St. Paul to Thomas Merton. Writing on God, the spiritual life and its social, economic and political implications, is a noble way to serve humanity and proclaim God's reign of peace. Reading, writing and studying can help us understand the life of peace, explore the spiritual roots of nonviolence, publicly renounce the ways of war, and promote the vision of a new nonviolent world.

As a young man, I noticed how Gandhi, King, Day, the Berrigans and Merton all wrote regularly. They taught me that, if you want to advocate for justice and peace, you have to write. With their example in mind, I started writing and never stopped. I don't claim Merton's skill or intellectual ability, but I do share his passion for writing. His writing discipline encourages me to share my own thoughts about Christian nonviolence and my own journey and vision of peace. Merton inspires amateurs like me to continue to witness for peace through writing. We need more writers like Merton who are not afraid to unpack the social, economic and political implications of the spiritual life.

THE PROPHETIC LIFE OF PEACE

Merton's life of prayer, and the daily disciplined writing practice that accompanied it, led Merton to become a prophet of peace to the world of war. He certainly aspired to be a best-selling author, but he may or may not have intended to be a prophet. His serious practice of daily meditation and prayer, his silent opening to the void before God, combined with his spectacular gifts as a writer, made him a fluid receptacle for God's wisdom. He came along just at the right moment in history after World War II, as millions of people were coming to grips with the failures of the world and the lack of hope for real nonviolent change. Just at that moment, he shared his story and spoke an authentic word about the God of peace and found a receptive audience.

A prophet is one who takes quality time to be present to God and to listen to whatever God has to say, and then shares God's word with the world. Merton listened attentively in contemplative silence for twenty seven years and he shared what he heard. The God of peace, Merton discovered, wants us to live in the truth, love, compassion, wisdom, and the Holy Spirit of peace. In our world of total violence and war, this news is surprisingly not welcome. We prefer to keep God under control, locked up and safe in church, so that we can go along with our nation, its wars, corruption and imperial ambitions. Merton remained faithful to his prayerful openness to God, and to his writing practice, and so it was inevitable that this great soul would begin to address the idolatries and blasphemies of war and nuclear weapons, and the way church people blindly support our nation's wars and weapons.

Merton announced that the spiritual life requires creative nonviolence. We can't claim to worship the God of peace authentically while we continue to support the false gods of war. This political word coming from a spiritual master was a great gift, but it cost Merton terribly. For me, it's the sign of an authentic Christian in our midst. It's also the path we all need to walk. Those of us who study and emulate Merton need to carry on that prophetic witness. If we dare maintain any spiritual integrity, we too must address the horrors of our age—such as drones, hunger, government surveillance, and catastrophic climate change. That's the next step after the encounter with the God of peace.

Merton became a prophet of peace to the culture of war, even the war-making church. As I read him over the years, I decided to take his message to heart. So many passages struck me like a thunderbolt, such as this famous text, written for *The Catholic Worker* in the early 1960s. It remains for me a kind of talisman. Is it true? Is he right? If Merton is right, then we had better heed his wisdom, and get to work opposing war and promoting nonviolence:

> The duty of the Christian in this time of crisis is to strive with all our power and intelligence, with our faith and hope in Christ, and love for God and humanity, to do the one task which God has imposed upon us in the world today. That task is to work for the total abolition of war. There can be no question that unless war is abolished, the world will remain constantly in a state of madness and desperation in which, because of the immense destructive power of modern weapons, the danger of catastrophe will be imminent and probable at every moment everywhere. The church must lead the way on the road to the nonviolent settlement of difficulties and toward the gradual abolition of war as the way of settling international or civil disputes. Christians must become active in every possible way, mobilizing all their resources for the fight against war. Peace is to be preached and nonviolence is to be explained and practiced. We may never succeed in this campaign but whether we succeed or not, the duty is evident (James Forest, *Living With Wisdom*, 152-153).

Elsewhere, Merton explained how his monastic life was a clear political stand against the culture of war and violence:

> It is my intention to make my entire life a rejection of, a protest against the crimes and injustices of war and political tyranny which threaten to destroy the whole human race and the world. By my monastic life and vows, I am saying no to all the concentration camps, the aerial bombardments, the staged political trials, the judicial murders, the racial injustices, the economic tyrannies, and the whole socio-economic apparatus which seems geared for nothing but global destruction in spite of all its fair words in favor of peace. I make monastic silence a protest against the lies of politicians, propagandists and agitators, and when I speak it is to deny that my faith and my Church can ever seriously be aligned with these forces of injustice and destruction. My life, then, must be a protest against [those who invoke their faith in support of war, racial injustice and tyranny] also, and perhaps against these most of all . . .. If I say no to all these secular forces, I also say yes to all that is good in the world and in humanity. I say yes to all that is beautiful in nature . . .. I say yes to all the men and women who are my brothers and sisters in the world (*Living With Wisdom*, 165-16).

"I am against war, against violence, against violent revolution, for peaceful settlement of differences, for nonviolent but nevertheless radical change," Merton wrote to a friend shortly before his death. This consistent prophetic stand exemplifies the ordinary public role of the Christian in a world of permanent war. Merton shows us that it is possible no matter what our state in life to speak out publicly against war and violence, and for peace and nonviolence. He urges us through his example to take our own prophetic stand.

I hear him quietly whispering to us: "Walk away from the culture of war, turn back to the God of peace, embrace everyone as sister and brother, live at one with creation, enter the communion of peace, enjoy the fullness of life in nonviolence, let love and compassion reign." That's a message of hope and healing that we need now more than ever.

"The God of peace is never glorified by human violence," Thomas Merton once wrote. The flipside, I discovered, is also true: "The God of peace is always glorified by human nonviolence."

Thank you, Thomas Merton, for your peacemaking life and loving nonviolence, for glorifying the God of peace. You continue to give me hope! May we heed your teachings and example, and do our part to practice and promote nonviolence and welcome God's peace with our very lives.

Beliefs And Politics: Thomas Merton's Political Theology

David Golemboski

In February 2014, two middle-aged men and an 84 year-old sister of the Society of the Holy Child Jesus were sentenced to three to five years in federal prison for breaking into the Y-12 National Security Complex in Oak Ridge, Tennessee. Y-12 was constructed in the 1940s as part of the Manhattan Project, and since that time has served as a manufacturing facility for nuclear weapons. In the summer of 2012, the three protesters cut fences, entered the facility, sprayed paint, hammered on the walls of one of the facility's buildings, and then lit candles and began to sing and pray for disarmament.

The three were quickly detained, and thus began a legal process leading to their eventual sentencing. In addition to trespassing and destruction of government property, the federal government charged them with a more serious crime: sabotage. At their sentencing, the nun told the judge, "Please have no leniency with me. To remain in prison for the rest of my life would be the greatest honor for me." Ultimately, they were convicted of the greater charge, under the judgment that they had "harmed U. S. war efforts."

I shared this story with my undergraduate students—many of whom aspire to careers in international politics—and asked if they thought the punishment for these protesters was appropriate. Not a single one held the view that the judge had been too harsh. A couple were broadly affirming of anti-nuclear political views, but nevertheless thought that the judge had decided rightly. While I was surprised by the uniformity of my students' views, I do not necessarily interpret it as an entirely bad thing. For one, they were not unanimously disapproving of civil disobedience. One student pointed to the arrest of Rosa Parks as evidence that punishment for civil disobedience can be a necessary impetus toward social change.

More fundamentally, though, I recognize that some of my students may be spoiled on public religion given that religious incursions into the political realm have not been entirely salutary in recent decades. After all, the defining act of religious "activism" in the lives of my students occurred on the morning of September 11, 2001. In addition to religious violence, we have seen faith-inspired politics often take the form of self-interested defensiveness, in which religious persons insist on either dictating terms to a pluralist society or on being left alone to do whatever they want, damn the impact on others. (Recent cases regarding religious business-owners who wish to discriminate against same-sex couples are a good example.)

Perhaps because of the evident self-interestedness and narrow-mindedness of some very visible religious activists, my students (and American society more broadly) have internalized the mantra of John Locke, who, in his famous "Letter Concerning Toleration," published in 1689, drew a stark demarcation between religion and politics. The former is about "concernment for the interests of men's souls," Locke held, while the latter is concerned with "outward things," such as life, health and property. While this distinction has underwritten the very necessary spread of religious toleration in the West, it has also embedded in our political culture an assumption that religion and politics do not play on the same field. The Y-12 case flies directly in the face of this assumption. The tenor of their prosecution, in turn, reveals the poverty of our language for conceptualizing the relationship of religion and politics. For all the proclaimed religiosity of the United States, when religion spills out of the church and into the munitions plant, it can only be called sabotage.

Thomas Merton, who once described himself as abiding "in the belly of a paradox" (*The Sign of Jonas*, 11), is generally a helpful guide in challenging apparently clean dichotomies. Anyone who is familiar with Merton knows that much of his charm and significance arise from the way he cut the legs from under the facile assumption that the life of the monk and the life of the world must be starkly divided. For Merton, life in the monastery was a fundamentally social act. He once wrote that "There are always a few people who are in the woods at night, in the rain (because if there were not the world would have ended), and I am one of them" (*Raids on the Unspeakable*, 307). That the world might end is perhaps hyperbole, but the sentiment is clear: Merton's monastic vocation was *for* the world, not against it.

Similarly, Merton rejected the Lockean assumption that religion and politics belong to distinct and separate realms. His concern with politics became especially evident throughout the last decade of his life, when his writings turned increasingly toward race, war and peace, and other issues of social concern. While he remained steadfastly a monastic—and even sought deeper solitude during those years in moving to his hermitage—Merton did not confine his interest in "the world" to mere prayer and writing. Throughout the 1960s, Merton counseled peace activists, lent his name in support of their work and became an ally of many who worked on the front lines of social change. He affirmed for them and for his readers more generally the necessity not only of religious belief but of religious *action*.

One of Merton's most politically pointed pieces of writing is *Peace in the Post-Christian Era*, a collection of essays that Merton's superiors did not permit him to publish during his lifetime, but which was finally published in 2004. There, Merton reflects on Christian approaches to war and peace, and on the particular urgencies of the nuclear era. He writes that "Christians have got to speak by their actions. . . . This means reducing the distance between our interior intentions and our exterior acts. Our social actions must conform to our deepest religious principles. Beliefs and politics can no longer be kept isolated from one another" (*Peace in the Post-Christian Era*, 132-33). These words were written against the backdrop of the Cold War and the nuclear arms race—an era that Merton often called "a time of crisis." In such a time, religion must not confine itself to pious devotion, but must enter into the world of political action.

Merton did not affirm ungrounded or unreflective political engagement, though. He was aware of and critical toward the pervasive distorting effects of ideology and rhetoric. He sensed beneath the surface of political activity a spiritual undercurrent, and in those waters he observed both pathology and reason for hope. On the former, Merton often diagnosed spiritual causes of political evils. In an influential essay, Merton wrote that "At the root of all war is fear: not so much the fear men have of one another as the fear they have of *everything*. . . . They cannot trust anything, because they have ceased to believe in God" ("The Root of War is Fear," *New Seeds of Contemplation*, 112). On the more hopeful side, Merton counseled faithfulness to the Gospel even in the face of immense evil and slim odds of success. In a well-known letter to Catholic peace activist Jim Forest, Merton advised the frustrated young man, "Do not depend on the hope of results." After all, "You may have to face the fact that your work will be apparently worthless and even achieve no result at all, if not perhaps results opposite to what you expect. As you get used to this idea, you start more and more to concentrate not on the results but on the value, the rightness, the truth of the work itself" (*The Hidden Ground of Love*, 294). In short, the Christian political posture cannot be simply about success, but rather about witness.

I had the privilege to work for a time as a lobbyist with an organization called NETWORK, which is a Catholic social justice lobby in Washington, DC. The organization, founded by nuns in 1971, advocates for public policy in support of the common good, including economic justice, immigration reform and international peacemaking. Working for justice by means of the legislative process is an uphill struggle, and much of NETWORK's work could be aptly described by Merton's phrase: "apparently worthless." Successes are hard to come by, and the frequent failures can be dispiriting. Merton's counsel to Jim Forest remained close in my mind when results were not forthcoming, reminding me that bringing the voice of Catholic social teaching to Washington was a valuable mission independent of tangible outcomes.

But NETWORK's story is not exclusively about futility. In 2012, the organization initiated a campaign to promote economic justice in the federal budget and in that year's presidential election season. The multi-state tour was titled, straightforwardly, "Nuns on the Bus," and it became something of a phenomenon, attracting a great deal of media attention. What made the campaign so successful, in my view, was not merely that the nuns' message of concern for the poor was substantively correct (though it was), but that it came from the mouths of Catholic sisters whose commitment to *living* their political convictions is undeniable. Nuns have educated, catechized, cared for, and otherwise blessed the lives of millions of Americans—including many politicians. The remarkable, longstanding witness of the nuns, injected into the political process that year, transformed discourse and helped influence the presidential election and the kinds of policies that worked their way into law. At the same time, the deep spiritual integrity of the nuns who founded and continue to lead NETWORK provides support against falling into mere "hope of results."

The nuns I've described here—both the nuclear activist nun and the budget-debating nuns on the bus—are, to me, examples of a religious politics that transcends the harsh division of John Locke and embodies the integration described by Thomas Merton. Merton's own life is a less obvious example of this politics, given that he remained committed to monastic life. But he wrote in an era of radical change, both religious and political, and his insights into the relationship between those two worlds is powerful. Christian discipleship, as Merton describes it, must be political. It cannot remain confined to the cloister or to the pew. At the same time, entering into the world of politics, the Christian must not lose her bearing. Political success is not the only end of life, and no real success can come from abandoning love for friend, neighbor or enemy.

Perhaps most fundamentally, if the root of war is fear, then the root of peace must be hope. Like Merton, we live in a time of crisis and, as he famously prayed, we may not see the road ahead of us. But Merton once wrote that "Christian hope begins where every other hope stands frozen stiff" (*Raids on the Unspeakable*, 5), and it is this hope that will not only influence, but ultimately transform politics as we know it.

In Search Of A Hidden Wholeness

Michael Casagram, OCSO

Merton lived with a continual paradox, his call to silence and solitude while being one of the most articulate writers of our time. His living with this tension is expressed clearly in his words that "the deepest level of communication is not communication, but communion. It is wordless." My finest experiences of Merton were glimpses into his wordlessness, the way he lived this on a daily basis.

Whether it was my noticing him pacing up and down on what was then a porch to the infirmary, his walking to and from his hermitage, his collating sheets of paper in the print shop, his insisting on my praying the *Angelus* when I was trying to get him to sign one of his books for a family member, there was always the inner stillness he kept. He even called into question the very meaning of all his writing when he perceived it in the light of what he felt his primary vocation to be.

My own vocation is to the Cistercian way of life dedicated, as was Merton's, to a life of prayer, to truly seeking God as expressed by our Rule and Constitutions. To do so is to live on the margins of society, seeking values grounded in a relationship with God so as to avoid all forms of empty pursuit or false security. To live for God is to expose one-self to the raw reality of one's humanity, to experience one's nakedness in the Divine Presence. Merton knew only too well the subtle ways we veer from seeing the true self even when we know deep down that to do so is to find that we are wonderfully graced.

> Am I sure that the meaning of my life is the meaning God intends for it? Does God impose a meaning on my life from the *outside*, through event, custom, routine, law, system, impact with others in society? Or am I called to *create from within*, with him, with his grace, a meaning which reflects his truth and makes me his 'word' spoken freely in my personal situation? My true identity lies hidden in God's call to my freedom and my response to him. This means I must use my freedom in order to *love*, with full responsibility and authenticity, not merely receiving a form imposed on me by external forces, or forming my own life according to an approved social pattern, but directing my love to the personal reality of my brother [or sister], and embracing God's will in its naked, often unpenetrable mystery (Rom. 11:33-36). I cannot discover my 'meaning' if I try to evade the dread which comes from first experiencing my meaninglessness! (*Contemplative Prayer*, 68).

My living the monastic life and experiencing the ongoing challenge it entails is finely expressed in these words of Merton. They articulate not only my journey but that of many others feeling the need for a more contemplative life. I've worked for many years with the Lay Cistercians associated with Gethsemani. Again and again I run into a long-ing for the kind of spiritual experience and freedom Merton speaks of above. Wherever we may be living, whatever the responsibilities we may have in the social structure of today, there is a way for discovering what Merton loved to call the "true self." It is a hunger to find where our full freedom lies, where we are no longer hiding behind façades. To glimpse into this freedom is to become a divine "word" for others. This has been the great incentive in my own vocation and I think the vocation of anyone willing to pursue it.

There is here a respect for the human person that not only assures integrity but leaves one drawn into a mystery far greater than oneself or this world has to offer. To enter into it means, however, having to pass through the experience of one's own meaninglessness, to experience what Christ said about losing one's life in order to find it. The experience of meaninglessness is never far from any of us. We who are destined for participation in God's own divine life are also destined to face meaninglessness in anything short of God's gift. At the very same time it is the very thing that gives us an endless and untiring hope. How we interpret what's happening to us makes all the difference. To see ourselves and every event of daily life in the light of faith brings entirely new perspective. It is one that gives us glimpses that indeed the kingdom of heaven is within us.

In so many of the comments made to me about Merton's writing I marvel at how he is able to articulate for others what they were unable to understand or put into words. Having plunged himself into his own humanity, having let himself see who he really was before God, enabled him to articulate for others what is going on or unfolding within their own journeys. There is an encouragement that happens in this encounter with Merton's words, the realization that you are on the right path despite all of one's human failing and weakness. This fills me with hope.

Merton wrote of Mary, Mother of God, as an exemplar of wisdom and a hidden hopefulness: "I can find her if I too become hidden in God where she is hidden. To share her humility and hiddenness and poverty, her concealment and solitude is the best way to know her: but to know her thus is to find wisdom" (*New Seeds of Contemplation*, 168). Merton was fascinated his whole life with a hidden holiness or, as he expressed it, a hidden wholeness. What seems ever elusive to our minds and hearts may be easily attained if one is willing to enter into the hiddenness, the humility and poverty of God. There it is that we find Wisdom.

Father Louis has highlighted for me the meaning of my own vocation, as I understand it. His approach is available to every Christian, to everyone with any real sense of the reality of God. Hidden wholeness is what we all thirst for, whether consciously or not. How restless we all are, until we rest in God. The restlessness takes a myriad forms and moves along countless paths. Merton's gift to me, to countless others, was to have shared his way to rest in God and the abundant joy that goes with it.

What we are most inclined to think as great contributions to society may not be so at all. What is most valuable and builds a better world is often accomplished in the simplest of circumstances, amid getting through a day with integrity. We strengthen our society whenever we act from our centers rather than the impositions of our ego or social structures. The option for wholeness arises with every thought, word or deed that engages us. If they come from our center, they will be moved by grace. If their origin is elsewhere, they will leave us feeling restless. How graced do we want to be? Father Louis reminds often of just how wonderful our gift of freedom truly is.

The Comeback Monk

Kathleen Tarr

> I am on the Pacific shore—perhaps fifty miles south of Cape Mendocino. Wide open, deserted hillside frequented only by sheep and swallows, sun and wind. No people for miles either way. Breakers on the black sand. Crying gulls fly down and land neatly on their own shadows.
>
> *The Intimate Merton: His Life from His Journals*

On California's rugged, northern coast, not far from where Merton first saw the Pacific in 1968, I'm walking in the headlands of Mendocino. Waves crash into rocks and boulders below me. Ocean swells—turquoise and thick with kelp—roll past the cliffs and into the small bay. Ferns and scrub brush are scorched by September's hot sun. A few patches of white sweet alyssum and low-growing yellow daisies offer spurts of color along the sandy trails.

I share Merton's special attachment to "this Asian Ocean" as he called it. For over thirty years, I have lived on its extreme northern half, on the Pacific Rim of Fire—in Alaska. Both of us dreaming and meandering to the sounds of its tumbling surf; both of us lonely and wistful for the Pacific and for the solitude it can provide; both of us filled with a sense of being unutterably happy whenever we are anywhere near its shore.

In the last years of his life, Merton wondered if the Pacific was where his true destiny lay. And I, too, in this moment, while taking a seat on a large, hand-hewn driftwood bench, am wondering if it will remain mine. Tension, contradiction and paradox are front and center in my life. Another reason for my kinship with Merton. As a monk, an ordained priest, a distinguished teacher, a famous and admired author and spiritual thinker with an Ivy-league pedigree, Merton continued to view his inner life as a work-in-progress. Nothing was settled; no real home might ever be found.

Through his intense intellectual life, he had already traveled a great spiritual distance with his investigations of heart and mind into other faiths and philosophies from the East and West. He was clearly forging his own monastic model, and by the time his much-anticipated global trek materialized in 1968, he was willing to let the winds and currents carry him where "the face of God" could be most clearly seen. In many ways, he was like a child of the Sixties—open-minded, experimental, constantly searching for ways to expand his creativity and consciousness within the confines of his religious commitment.

"I really expect little or nothing from the future," he wrote. "Certainly not great 'experiences' or a lot of interesting new things. Maybe, but so what? What really

WE ARE ALREADY ONE

intrigues me is the idea of starting out into something unknown, demanding and expecting nothing very special, hoping only to do what God asks of me, whatever it may be" (July 29, 1968).

This does not sound like a monk who was stuck in the mud. He was coming full circle, back to his "rucksack" youth in the years his artist-father took him to France, England, Bermuda, New York, and after his father's untimely death when the young Merton traveled unencumbered around Europe. Merton, the perpetual pilgrim, was dreaming about being a solitary on the move.

His basic idea was to attend various religious meetings, retreats and conferences, to visit the Flemish nuns at Our Lady of the Redwoods monastery on this same "lost coast" farther south in Whitethorn—a place I briefly visited in summer 2007. He had spent years studying Zen Buddhism and he intended to talk to as many Buddhists as possible, the culmination of which would be a special, personal meeting with the Dalai Lama. But though Merton's itineraries to New Mexico, California, Thailand, India, and his seventeen-day sojourn to Alaska, too, were well planned and organized, within his inmost self, nothing was fixed, determined and all figured out.

He believed that new choices, new possibilities should be allowed to surface in the contemplative life of a monk. The contemplative life needs space to roam, whether physically or metaphorically. Contemplation was not a safe port or a secluded cove in which to take refuge from outside storms. You could not pray yourself into penance, redemption, sanctity. Nor could you sustain a self-rewarding, blissful solitude, pretending the world with its vagaries and confusions and stupidities were far out of range from your monastic doorstep. The purpose of contemplation was not to retreat, but to engage—to gain more compassion and understanding about the crazy world we all live in. For Merton, the spiritual journey was subject to heavy wave actions and slippery foot conditions. If it's answers you want, you've come to the wrong monk.

I've been migrating around after this migrating monk for many years now—ever since, as a non-religious, I first stumbled across *The Seven Storey Mountain* in 2005. Until then, I had never heard of the jabbering Thomas Merton. His life story and the great literary works he left behind have been like a deep well I keep dipping my cup into to help quench an inner thirst I didn't realize I had.

Merton, *the solitary explorer;* it's one of the metaphors he liked best in describing himself, as Elena Malits' book of reflections and interpretations of Merton—also with the same title—pointed out. He was a man "bound to search for the existential depths of faith in its silences, its ambiguities, and in those certainties which lie deeper than the bottom of anxiety." As a renowned spiritual figure, he was trying to be more like that gull out there who is still sitting on the sun-drenched rock not doing much but shaking out his feathers and watching. As he steeped himself in the study of Zen Buddhism, he imagined a life of less striving, less busyness, less full-throttle intellectualizing.

He talked about the desire in his heart to make a journey to a primitive place among primitive people and there die. It is at the same time a going out and a return, he said. A going somewhere where I have never been or thought of going—a going in which I am led by God, a journey in which *I go out of everything I now have.* I feel that unless I do this my spiritual life is at an end" (August 18, 1959).

Merton's continuous lamentations about his lack of a real and more perfect solitude, his inner frustrations over wanting to live as a true hermit, are well known. He was the literary breadwinner for the Abbey of Gethsemani, yet secretly he yearned to be a Carthusian without a notebook. "Reincarnation or not, I am as tired of talking and writing as if I had done it for centuries. Now is the time to listen at length to this Asian ocean. Over there. Asia" (May 14, 1968).

It takes an intense personality, one not afraid of risk, to realize you might have to journey once more to a place you've never been to retain the vitality of your spiritual life. Merton was a man clearly living in the full stream of life and humanity, constantly making and re-making himself, a man who made wrong turns and U-turns, false starts, who loved and lost, who was orphaned and full of doubt, conflicted, hyper, garrulous, full of imperfections, and possessed of an intellect that resisted resolutions and couldn't sit still. It is within his example of trying to make sense of himself within the concrete realities of everyday *lived* experience and his acceptance of paradox where I find some of his greatest messages of hope.

Merton never sounded like some modern-day guru peddling a talk-show message on *The Secret of Staying Young and Becoming a Better, More Spiritual You.* He was a far cry from being any kind of spiritual purveyor. He was a poet trapped in a monk's body and he had many internal arguments to try to reconcile these two identities. "I no longer need to and will more and more refuse to write so many prefaces and articles," he said during one of his confessional, anti-writing moments.

Basil Pennington said that his friend Merton considered himself primarily a poet. "The last thing I will give up writing will be this journal and notebooks and poems. No more books of piety," Merton admitted.

He had a special, life-long affinity and solidarity for poets, and I take hope in this, too. He did his honors thesis on a complex, paradoxical, anti-conformist, and spiritual visionary—William Blake—someone who mirrored himself. Blake said man must learn to bear a certain amount of uncertainty.

Despite the spiritual discipline and stability of his monastery, he never stopped questioning, doubting, dreaming, and wanting to be part of a literary scene—if only from a distance, as a kind of *hommes d'esprit* who was up on all the latest through frequent letter-writing and through his voracious, eclectic appetite for reading any book he could get his hands on. Before he came to the Abbey, among other things, he was a failed novelist. His first published book was a collection of poems, and he went on to write several more volumes.

On the pages of his journal (November 28, 1967), he made a brief reference to the seventeenth century Japanese poet, Matsuo Basho, and how remarkable and deeply moving he found Basho's poems and brief travel reflections to be. Penguin had released an edition of Basho's translated poems in 1966 making them more widely available beyond academic audiences. It was one of the most beautiful books he had ever read in his life, Merton noted. Basho made several arduous journeys by foot and horseback through Japan's misty and mountainous landscape, relying on the good nature and generosity of his fellow poets, disciples and wanderers. And as he made his solitary pilgrimages to various Buddhist shrines and temples, passing through ancient fishing villages and voyaging to remote islands, he wrote haiku and linked verses all along the way.

Basho's *The Records of a Travel-worn Satchel* and *The Narrow Road to the Deep North and Other Travel Sketches* are treasured works of Japanese literature. Nobuyuki Yuasa translated the Penguin Classic edition of *The Narrow Road.* In the book's introduction Yuasa highlighted Basho's biography, but he could have easily been describing Merton's state of mind as he was preparing to embark on his world trek:

> Basho had been casting away his earthly attachments, one by one, in the years preceding his journey, and now he had nothing left to cast away but his own self which was in him as well as around him. He had to cast this self away, for otherwise, he was not able to restore his true identity (what he calls the 'everlasting self which is poetry' in the passage above). He saw a tenuous chance of achieving his final goal in traveling, and he left his house caring naught for his provisions in the state of sheer ecstasy.

Merton wanted to leave the spiritual fishbowl behind and become more like Basho with nothing but a change of clothes and a pile of books—a sojourner who was living squarely in the direct, unfiltered, unobstructed, un-politicized moments of life. The more mature Merton never fell into any kind of "holier-than-thou" piety nor did he collapse into self-analysis as Father James Heft of USC's Institute for Advanced Catholic Studies, remembered:

> It was in August 1968, just four months before his death. I was making a week's long silent retreat at Gethsemani. Of course, I knew about Merton. In the spring of 1962, as a novice in the Marianists, I read two of his books: *No Man is an Island* and *Mystics and Zen Masters*. In the spring of 1968, with the War of Vietnam at its worst, Martin Luther King assassinated in April, and Bobby Kennedy in June, I knew I needed to retreat into some silence . . ..
>
> On the second morning of my retreat, some of us young religious were allowed to join the monks in choir during Lauds. Merton sat nearby. I didn't dare speak to him, especially in the midst of that profound Cistercian silence. But, at the end of prayer, as we all rose, I did look him in the eye and he me. There was a slight smile on his face. I was nearly a foot taller than he. Perhaps that is what made him smile. In any event, I knew then that the books I had read with his name on them could be traced back to a real flesh and blood person who smiled. I will never forget that.

Merton was not a rank-and-file Cistercian or Catholic. On one level friendly, obedient and warm. On another, outspoken, freedom-loving, with a streak of that 1960s rebelliousness. As the more visible social critic, he spoke out on nuclear proliferation, racism, poverty, the alienation of modern man, crude materialism, the immorality of war. But as he pondered his future, he started to embrace the idea that one day even the social critic might retreat to silence. That he might put down his pen and paper altogether and disappear completely into a new, as-of-yet-undefined existence.

With all his focus on silence, the interior self and the longing to be an outright hermit, he continued to keep a close eye on the literary scene from behind the monastery's walls. My guess is, that as a writer, he was well-aware of the impact the Beat Generation of poets were having on the country's cultural landscape beginning in the mid-to-late 1950s, how they were helping to create a renaissance in poetry, making it more like natural speech in a kind of "let it out" spontaneous verse-making, less beholden to the conventions of meter and rhyme.

Though he lived without the saturation of daily media, I imagine Merton must have followed the publicity and events of the Sixth Gallery in San Francisco following Allen Ginsberg's reading of "Howl" for the first time in fall of 1955 in front of an audience that included Lawrence Ferlinghetti. Ferlinghetti went on to publish "Howl" with its sexually explicit, "revolutionary" content and much public controversy ensued. In 1968, as the monk's literary fate would have it, Ferlinghetti naturally extended an invitation to Merton to drop in to his City Lights Bookstore in downtown San Francisco. Merton slept in a small aparatment above the bookstore. (It's an interesting historical note that Merton and Ginsberg both studied literature under Mark Van Doren at Columbia University, though Merton was a student there a few years before the still-unknown Ginsberg arrived, and that Ginsberg and Merton had each experienced epiphanies while reading William Blake.)

Merton was immersed in Eastern thought about the same time as the West Coast poets, also inspired by Zen and the literary lineage of Asia (Gary Snyder, Kenneth Rexroth, Gregory Corso), were making a name for themselves.

Though Merton had written several volumes of poetry, and though he had keenly understood the close association between the rhythms of jazz and what the Beat writers represented on the poetic front, Merton never quite caught on as a well-recognized, national poet of acclaim as many of these poets eventually did. In her requisite critical appraisal of Merton in *The Solitary Explorer* which comes near the end of her book almost as an after-thought, Malits commented that Merton suffered from *hyperverbalization*, that he wrote to assure himself he was real, and that sometimes his powerful verbal gifts dominated him and that he simply said too much. Of his poetry, she said Merton was often too abstract.

In truth, he achieved a higher level of mindfulness primarily through the act of writing and reading widely and closely, not by meditating for hours under a loblolly pine or delivering brilliant lectures. His day-to-day writing, so much of it highly personal and memoiristic, was the umbilical cord to people; it's what kept him fully tuned in and mindful of the world. He used writing *not* to call attention to himself and his personal story and reflections, but to teach himself how to think. And the fact that he openly grappled with his mixed selves and identities, as both prolific writer and cloistered monk, as religious celebrity and fantasy hermit, makes him more universally endearing.

Like an actor or singer who come backs to the stage after a long absence, something neglected within the core of his being needed fuller expression by the late 1960s. Complacency and continuing to abide the status quo were not in Merton's religious rule book. Though he enjoyed a secure and stable life in a Cistercian monastery for almost three decades, the impulse to be a spiritual wanderer never left him. Merton felt empowered *to go* in 1968, and like Basho, Whitman, Kerouac—and in the milieu and spirit of the Sixties—the road beckoned.

"We need to stop thinking and start looking," he said. "Perhaps there is nothing to figure out after all: perhaps we only need to wake up."

"And yet the pilgrimage must continue," Merton wrote in *Mystics and Zen Masters*, "because it is an inescapable part of man's structure and program. The problem is for his pilgrimage to make sense—it must represent a complete integration of his *inner* and *outer* life, of his relation to himself and to other men" (*Mystics & Zen Masters* 11).

No matter how much word-less Zen spirit he hoped to someday experience, and no matter how manic and conflicted he could be about his vocation of writer, I don't think he could ever quit it altogether. Writing was his greatest gift and torment. And as he once joked in *The Sign of Jonas*, it appeared that if he were to ever to become a saint, his writing was going to be the way he could probably get there.

The Pacific is an ocean of great paradox. In Mendocino, it's known for creating foggy conditions without which the majestic redwoods would not be nourished. We often associate the Pacific with enticing images of tropical paradise—Hawaiian Islands, South Pacific atolls, crystalline Tahitian beaches. With Japan and the Phillipines, the Pacific often conjures memories of destructive typhoons. A few thousand miles north on the Gulf of Alaska coast near Cordova and Yakutat—a region where Merton also briefly visited and where I once lived—it's been called a *turbulent crescent*. There are no artsy hamlets anywhere on that part of the Pacific; it lacks any kind of vacation-center atmosphere. It's a highly seismic, more desolate and isolated place containing the world's most dramatic coastal mountains with glacial lobes and ice fields reaching down to the sea.

One immense ocean, many faces. A fathomless, boundless deep, as Blake would say. A symbol of great mystery. Frightening nautical realities. Violent natural forces. Purifying in its powers for monks and for me.

"My desolate shore is Mendocino, I must return," Merton wrote in May 1968. I don't think he'd be surprised at all to see its desolation gone today. When he was visiting tiny Bear Harbor and Needlepoint down the coast south of here, he noticed the increasing numbers of people who were starting to discover California's remaining pockets of seaside solitude. In Mendocino, Victorian-style inns and quaint B&Bs, pubs, organic restaurants serving fair-trade-certified coffee, eclectic art galleries, an independent bookstore, window displays of hand-crafted jewelry, and a grocery featuring Mendocino County wines and artisan olive oils and the freshest local produce—the bounty is all here to keep the *locavores* and the big-spending regulars from San Francisco's high-tech industry happy and comfortable.

Merton needed cold rain splashing his face. The salt air. The unnamed terns and gulls that darted in and out with the tides. The immediacy and shiver of angry seas. The sailor's chill in his chest. The vast empty of the sky, mountain and ocean where there was no longer a need to distinguish between self and mind, ideas and direct perception, external success and plain existence. Like his poetic hero, Blake, Merton lived in the certainty of the human imagination. With or without any future listeners or readers, he wanted to look at what was hidden and beyond. "I look through the eye," Blake said, "not with it."

Thomas Merton gives me hope that I am no more screwed up than anyone else, no more of a sick pilgrim than all the other wanderers I see wherever I go who are lost and then found, and who are lost again. Spiritual journeys, conversions, the need to find your center, your inner grounding—it's never over. If we're living the real truth of things, we accept that we're caught in the Pacific's green-black coat that never stops moving. The only thing I know for certain is that I keep coming back to the start of another unknown journey into the Unknown. And I take Merton with me.

Rediscovering Child Mind

Christopher Pramuk

And a little child shall lead them. Isaiah 11:6

The end of summer in our household brings both joy and dread. Joy because the kids are finally back in school, and dread because the kids are finally back in school. Packed afternoons of shuttling from school to home to practice and back to school again, slogging through math pages with grumpy-hungry kids, tending to the pot on the stove and a cantankerous four year old while slogging through math worksheets with grumpy-hungry kids—you get the picture.

September is also the time of year when Papa—that's me—begins to disappear ever more deeply into his over-stuffed head, his dreaded laptop and stacks of undergraduate papers piled in a corner of the dining room, whence they needle my conscience and cry out for attention like fingernails scraping across a chalkboard.

> Mom: "Where's Papa?"
> Kids: "He's asleep under the table with an open grade book next to his face and a string of drool hanging from his mouth to the floor."
> Mom: "Somebody kick him and tell him to put Henry to bed."

Ah, yes, it all begins in September.

And yet . . . there are hints of joy, glimmers of possibility and signs of wonder in the collective rediscovery of child mind.

My kids bustle in the excitement of new teachers, new and old friends, new uniforms one size larger, and freshly-sharpened pencils with bulging unblemished erasers. And I come alive too, in different ways, turning outward beyond the circle of family—of what is intimate and "familiar"—toward an imagined but not yet realized horizon of possibilities.

The campus stirs with new students. I lay awake at night rehearsing syllabi speeches and pondering which doors to open in the first minutes on the first day of a new class, thinking: *You only get one chance to make a first impression*, to stir the receptive (or skeptical) heart.

But that's not quite true! What my four kids and my college students keep teaching me is this: The child mind is ever open, ever resilient, ever forgiving, ever alert to *the person*—even the grownup, the teacher, the dreaded professor—who shows up ready to "come out and play." What makes a good teacher is perhaps not so different from the good parent and trusted friend: fully present, open and responsive, at once both structured and spontaneous, focused and free. I wish I could find that place of presence and balance more often.

Yes, the pot is boiling on the stove, my four-year-old is tugging at my pants with a bulging load in his, and the two girls are about to chuck their math books across the table at each other. But hints of surprise and delight break through the near chaos of it all. Even the stack of papers in the corner holds a thousand secrets, a hidden song, when I am fully present to their pages.

In one of my favorite passages in Thomas Merton's innumerable essays and books, Merton reflects on a bunch of children's drawings sent to the monastery from "somewhere in Milwaukee." The pictures, he notes sardonically, are the "only real works of art I have seen in ten years." And then, quite poignantly, he adds: "But it occurred to me that these wise children were drawing pictures of their own lives. They knew what was in their own depths. They were putting it all down on paper before they had a chance to grow up and forget"(*The Sign of Jonas* 341).

For me there is no more potent figure of hope in Merton's writings—and no more powerful image of Christ, Emmanuel, God with Us—than the image of the Child. "We do not hear the soft voice, the gentle voice, the merciful and feminine. . . . We do not see the Child who is prisoner in all the people" ("Hagia Sophia" in *Emblems of a Season of Fury*, 63). What would it take to find these hidden children and set them free? How did we let them become prisoners in the first place? Just what is it in Merton's voice that quickens the divine-human Child in me?

Merton embodies an approach to Christian formation—the way of *sapientia*, the education of the whole person—that vigorously resists and counters just about everything a corporate model of education and life in society presumes valuable. The "people with watch chains" are everywhere, saying: "Grow up! Measure it! Quantify it! Computerize it! Let's get on with business" (*Selected Essays*, 39-51)! Against their relentless static Merton's witness engenders in me a quality of fearlessness, of radical openness to the rediscovery of child mind, wherever it might lead. "The score is not what matters" (*Love and Living*, 12). We need not have it all figured out ahead of time. The way of love, on pilgrimage together in faith, implies spontaneity, vulnerability and risk.

When I am fully present to my students, when I sit and listen to my kids, really listen, what I discover being born *in myself* is hope, hidden yet beautifully manifest in the desires and dreams of a new generation. The metaphor of birth, to be clear, is no rhetorical New Age nicety. In ways altogether breathtaking, terrifying and beautiful, God calls us to be midwives of companionship and mercy for one another; midwives of resilience and radical hospitality; midwives of a primordial innocence that discerns and seizes upon the "flowering of ordinary possibilities" hidden in everyday life, in order to harvest "fruits of hope that have never been seen before" ("Message to Poets," in *Raids on the Unspeakable*, 155-64). In truth, Merton is summoning us to be born into a very daring and grownup vision of faith.

It doesn't happen every day in my classroom, but when it does, there is a kind of electricity popping and humming around the open circle as students wrestle and engage with each other, with me and with the material before them on their desk. Some days, to be sure, I walk out of the classroom disappointed and weary; other days I leave humbled, grateful and energized, thinking, my goodness, what in the heck just happened there? Each day, in every circumstance, it seems to be about opening a space for grace.

It is the Christ Child, after all, the glory of the unseen God, who hides in every person, waiting to be set free. And I have learned to wait, to listen and to follow.

Thomas Merton, The Prophet

Richard Rohr, OFM

I only saw Merton once. He walked in front of me and my family when we were visiting the Abbey in early June of 1961. I had read *The Sign of Jonas* and *The Waters of Siloe* in the high school seminary in Cincinnati, and already my youthful mind intuitively knew that this man was a prophet for my soul and for the church in the world. So on the day of my graduation and return to Kansas for the summer, I said to my parents, "Let's take the southern route home, I have a place I want you to see." Little did I imagine!

I stood back in awe as he walked two sisters and their driver right in front of us. He was returning them to their car as we approached the old guesthouse. One of the sisters was Mother Teresa of Calcutta. When I later gave the retreat there in 1985, I asked one of the brothers if I was just imagining this, and he said with a bit of disappointment (or was it resentment?) "Oh, we all heard that 'the famous sister from India' was visiting, but of course none of us got to meet her except the Abbot and probably Merton!"

Yes, I believe Thomas Merton was a true prophet, and I use that word in its classic sense as one who sees at a higher level and thus, in effect, *foresees*. A Biblical prophet is one who lives on the edge of organized religion as a truth speaker, and yet from *the loving and experienced depths of that religion.* The prophet cannot be throwing rocks from outside, but must "pay his dues" and earn the right to speak what are somehow—words from Elsewhere! The message is invariably mystical and political at the very same time; it is a *synthesis of seeing* that God grants to anyone that God chooses to speak prophetically.

I am now convinced this is what religious life is meant to structurally allow and even foster—a prophetic and listening stance as opposed to a merely priestly one. Monks, nuns, hermits, and friars are a part of para-church communities, each with different things to pay attention to, various spiritualities that encourage depth and actual God encounter, and authority structures that protect, allow and foster just such wisdom. Religious life is structurally set up to be "a room with a view," and often a view that the common parish does not have time to inspire or generate. No wonder that the young Merton raced to a place like Gethsemani with such determination, fervor and even over-excitement.

A prophet intuitively knows that he or she cannot stand alone, but needs the wisdom and protection of a living faith community, and years of the deep listening and loving that many forms of religious life can ideally provide. What the prophet has to say is going to "uproot and knock down, destroy and overthrow, build and plant" (Jeremiah 1:10), and in ways that scare into doubt the one who is saying it. No wonder that Moses stutters, Jeremiah begs out of the role and Isaiah's lips are burnt with a live coal; no wonder John the Baptist must leave his priestly family for the alternative food and clothing of the wilderness.

Thomas Merton, like almost no one else in our time, put together the mystical depths and the political implications of the Christian message. He did it in a way that confirmed for many of us a kind of "Deep Christianity." He wrote things that still now are showing themselves to be true and even central to spiritual truth. I find him read in every country and continent I have taught in, and quoted by sincere seekers of all Christian denominations and even other religions. Things he wrote in the 1950s and 60s do not always feel dated. This surely means we are dealing with big truth and high level seeing.

Although there are so many aspects of the wisdom tradition that he recovered, there is only one that I want to comment on here. I believe that Thomas Merton almost single handedly pulled back the veil and helped us see that we all had lost the older tradition of contemplation. It was no longer taught in any systematic way in the church. Clergy, religious and laity "recited prayers" and meticulously "performed" liturgies, but the older methods for quieting the mind and heart, and seeing "spiritual things spiritually (1 Corinthians 2:13)," had been lost both in theory and practice by almost all of us, even the "contemplative Orders." It was nobody's bad will, but simply what happened after we separated from the Eastern Church in 1054, and then allowed the dualistic and calculating mind to take over after the Reformation and the wrongly named Enlightenment.

In that same 1985 retreat that I mentioned, I asked my friend Brother Bruno if the monks "liked" Thomas Merton, because I had picked up what seemed like a bit of "no prophet being honored in his own country" or what could have been in-house jealousy from a few. He humbly and quietly said that it was true that many did not like him so much in the community. I said "But why?" And these were his words, which he then explained: "He told us that we were not really contemplatives! We were just introverts!"

But of course he was pointing out the elephant in the monastic living room, as prophets are inclined to do. Even contemplatives had no systematic training in what to do with their obsessive minds and errant emotions, just as Teresa of Avila had already complained in the 16th century. No one told them exactly *how* to deal with the distractions that followed them into the monastery. The daily schedule and monastic habit, and lots of chanted Psalms, did not usually eliminate their old mind, their lonely hearts and their unhealed emotions. Mere will power and good will itself were not enough to do the spiritual warfare that they had entered into. Many left all forms of religious life, feeling they had been overpromised, deceived or worse, that there was no accessible God to be found.

If we should place a monument for Thomas Merton anywhere, it would be enough if it just said "He gave us back the contemplative mind. He told us, and he showed us, that we could live with the very 'mind of Christ'" (*1 Corinthians* 2:16).

A Personal Trajectory

Michael Casey, OCSO

In the late 1950s, in the course of a pre-entry interview, I was asked by Tarrawarra's novice master whether I had read any of Thomas Merton's writings. I replied evasively that I may have heard of the author and, to my relief, the matter was pursued no further. On joining the novitiate I found that most of my fellow novices were either disciples or fans although official policy toward Merton was, at best, cool. It was not that he was considered "dangerous," like St. John of the Cross, but his was thought to be too glamorous a portrayal of the Cistercian life into which we were being inducted. What we were seeing was a reality far more "ordinary, obscure and laborious" than anything Merton described. Not surprisingly, those who were most enthusiastic about his books mostly left.

I must have read *Elected Silence* (the bowdlerized British version of *The Seven Storey Mountain*) early on, because I remember being moved by the section on his brother's death. I also gained some voyeuristic pleasure from *The Sign of Jonas*, although the everyday experience he described so appealingly was profoundly different from my own. Much later, alerted by *Time* magazine, I was entertained by *The Man in the Sycamore Tree* and was thus motivated to read the biographies by Monica Furlong and Michael Mott.

During my time of formation, I do not remember doing more than glancing at his spiritual writings except that I did try reading *Bread in the Wilderness*, but abandoned it unfinished. I was already beginning to discover the twelfth-century Cistercians for myself and these seemed a more satisfying source of nourishment. For contemporary reading I must confess that I preferred the delicious obscurities of Karl Rahner and Bernard Lonergan. In 1969, the posthumous *Climate of Monastic Prayer* (later republished with the title *Contemplative Prayer*) was the first of his spiritual books that grabbed me. It spoke to me strongly because it echoed my own experience at the time. I took copious notes to which I have referred over the years and I recently reread it. Later, when I began to be asked to conduct seminars on contemplative prayer, I read some of the books that I had earlier ignored and appreciated their content. My esteem for Merton's writing greatly increased with the publication of the articles on *Inner Experience* which, in their disarray, seemed to me like his version of the unfinished symphony.

Merton's various right-brain activities, poetry, calligraphy, photography, passed by me largely unnoticed. His interest in the religions of East Asia paralleled my own, but was far more knowledgeable. A less permeable monastic enclosure and the fact of living in a different hemisphere meant that his political concerns were no more than a curiosity. And I never had much appreciation of his enthusiasm for the eremitical life except as a fantasy escape from the trials of community living. When the volumes of letters began appearing, I was suitably astonished by the extent of his network and the breadth of his interests, but I have to admit that many of them did not interest me greatly, although I did wonder how he managed to find the time to maintain such a high-level correspondence.

For me, as I suppose for many, a new point was reached with the full publication of Merton's journals. Although a certain amount of their content had already been revealed in various biographies, the exposure of the raw entries provided much scope for analysis. In them the reader was confronted with Merton's chronic vocational difficulties and his unrealistic schemes for an ideal monastery, his unending struggles with authority, the pathos of his mid-life crisis and the restlessness of a mind constantly engaged with new avenues of reflection. All this gave context to his writings. Far less edifying was the underlying anger which seemed coiled and ready to spring out at any of the everyday idiocies encountered in community life, such as trivial Christmas celebrations and pontifical Masses. In addition, there is often an element of unreasonableness in his impatience with the practicalities of building and work organization especially since all this busyness became necessary in order to make provision for the hordes of vocations for which he was partially responsible. The author of his books and articles comes across as broad-minded, good-humored and tolerant, albeit with a sharp eye and a sharp tongue, but many entries in the journals seem to present him in a much less favorable light.

Let me suggest three ways in which, from my perspective, Merton's writings have had a positive impact at least on the monastic world and on myself.

In the first place, there is no doubt that Merton was the Cistercian Order's most successful recruiting agent since St. Bernard. And, as with Bernard, part of his impact was due to his fluid and allusive writing style. He spoke old truths in a contemporary language that made his message attractive not only within a monastic readership but far more universally. There was a breeziness about Merton's writing, even when he was considering such lofty topics as contemplation, which sowed seeds of hope in many hearts. His descriptions of Trappist life drew many to enter the monastery . . . and not all of them left. In this way he may be seen as contributing to the building of bridges between traditional Cistercian monasticism and the modern world. His post-conciliar articles on monastic renewal are incisive and challenging although it seems from the journals that he himself was unimpressed by the practical outcomes.

Secondly, I think it is undeniable that Merton's books and articles contributed to moving commonplace monastic spirituality away from Counter-Reformation devotionalism in the direction of classical Benedictine and Cistercian spirituality, with a greater appreciation of the Fathers of the Church and an incipient openness to the East. To measure the extent of this change, it is only necessary to recognize the manifold increase in library holdings in monastic history and spirituality over the last half-century.

Finally, it seems to me that Merton's most personal insight concerned what we might term a *mysticisme sans frontières*. His mystical moment in Louisville gave him an appreciation that profound spiritual experience was not confined within confessional boundaries and that there was a commonality of experience across the religions that could bring unity where dogmas divided. It was this experiential initiation into the unity of humankind that powered both his anti-war attitude and his outreach to other religious traditions. Whatever distractions he permitted himself, it was this fundamental conviction that enabled him to break out of the narrowness of pre-conciliar

Gethsemani spiritualty to forge connections with a wide variety of persons from many different backgrounds.

Meanwhile Merton's legacy continues. In part this is probably due to the pleasing complexity of his character, which enables readers to choose the elements that appeal to them and from these elements to construct a character with their own aspirations. Michael Mott began his biography by wondering how many different Mertons were being remembered at his funeral and the years that have passed since then have seen the creation of new versions. There is no reason to think that the Merton industry will terminate soon. The implicitly adversarial stance adopted in some of his writings sometimes makes them seem outdated, but there is plenty else in them that continues to be fresh and challenging. At least for the foreseeable future, it seems to me, Merton's will serve as a messenger of hope to many. In one form or another his writings will continue to be read, and that is about as much as any author could wish.

Listening To Merton

Deborah Kehoe

I'm equally honored and challenged by this opportunity to celebrate with others Thomas Merton's legacy of hope for the world into which he was born a century ago, and to reflect on how his life's work has influenced my own vocation. Discovering Merton has been a transformative journey for me. While I have bookshelves filled with the works of "spiritual writers" who bear forceful witness to the existence of a benevolent God, Thomas Merton remains my favorite for various reasons that I will lightly touch on here.

First, Merton makes me laugh. I presume I'm not the only reader drawn to his sense of humor that revels in wordplay as it apprehends the absurdity of so much human endeavor and exposes the gaps between truth and expectation or delusion, his own as well as those of others. One source of pleasure for me in reading almost anything by Merton is coming upon moments so perfectly comical that they defy analysis. "Connie had an inn called Connie's Inn" ("Queens Tunnel" 9, *Geography of Lograire*) inexplicably slays me every time I read it.

I was raised to laugh at myself, and so I have a well-honed instinct for irony and the comic relief available in almost any situation under the sun. I've found kinship in the wit of Thomas Merton, and I believe one of his gifts to all of us is humbling and uplifting laughter.

Second, in the years since I began earnestly exploring the thought of Thomas Merton, my love of nature, engendered in me as a native of the rural south, has matured into deep reverence. I've found personal inspiration in Merton's poetic articulations of the cosmic dance and his assertion that all elements of creation glorify God by merely existing, pursuing whatever purpose for which they were brought into the world by the creative energy of love. Those expressions have galvanized the core of my commitment to living a life of minimal harm to the earth and its inhabitants, advocating particularly for those not always acknowledged as members of the choir, sentient beings callously and unnaturally exploited for human vanity, appetite or profit. His prophetic environmental vision, so ably analyzed by scholars, is, to my eye, yet another aspect of Merton's legacy of peace and hope.

A third source of Merton's longevity is his gift for verbalizing what it means to embrace suffering. I suspect he has heartened many readers like me who have endured disappointments and possibly have had moments of crippling distress wherein they felt like abject failures. Merton's provocative writings about "success" have strengthened my resistance against the tendency to evaluate my or anyone's accomplishments according to a popular, yet ultimately false, set of standards. And his evocation through journals, essays and poems of the indestructible peace that comes from total surrender to the will of God, however confounding, has furthered my own progress in prayer and contemplation. I personally know of few other writers with Merton's facility for talking someone down from life's ledges.

Finally, I marvel at the perhaps obvious and hardly uncommon fact that my relationship with Merton was established and sustained by the written word. Years ago, as the timid person I've always been, I found what is commonly called "a comfort zone" on the margins of most communities in which I moved. From there, I became an acute listener, intensely sensitive to voices. Not surprisingly, I soon became a constant reader, not for escape, but for connection. Books became my primary mode of safely entering the world. Eventually, I became adept at reading behind the words, reading the silences, reading the writer. Although I could not have said it then, my ear was becoming most attentive to writing that was genuinely humane. Every reader is searching for something, and I now understand that my most intensive reading throughout my life has been one avenue by which I have searched for God.

I first encountered Merton's writing almost twenty years ago in a copy of *No Man is an Island*, which I found in a secondhand bookstore near Wrigley Field—in retrospect, a serendipitous merging of three of my life's passions: books, baseball and Thomas Merton. I was stirred by the immediacy and compassion of his voice; it penetrated my solitude as clearly as if he were standing before me. That kind of power is extraordinary in a writer, and as a teacher of academic writing for many years, I'm confident that it can't be contrived. One can learn to make writing clear, concise and overall less burdensome to an audience, but writing that makes itself at home in the soul of a reader has a more mysterious origin. Merton's compulsion to record and recreate the spiritual journey, to put its anguish and joy truthfully into words, communicates itself magnetically. When he writes, the reader can hear affirmation of God's enduring love. Surely, the pull of that voice will never lessen as long as people ache for unity, and as long as such people, out of such loneliness, continue to open books.

As A Seeker Of Truth

Roger Lipsey

Looking toward Merton, I see a seeker of truth. His dedication, depth and persever-ance as a seeker of truth created an enduring model, a way of moving toward light and engaging with darkness. He modeled root, branch and leaf: the imperative need for rootedness in the home ground of a specific world view and practice, the further need to follow the branching of other cultures and teachings that absorb just as much solar energy and send nourishment to the roots. One relates to Merton's search through one's own; his writings and example are potent enough to give birth to others' search for truth, and for those already engaged in a serious search he is a stunningly intel-ligent and good-hearted companion, often ahead on the path, looking back, waiting, cheerful because *this* is what matters, this is what he knew to be good.

But does the paradigm "seeker of truth" still matter? Is it meant, at least for some people, to be the center of their lives as it was for Merton—no matter what else we do, as we all must do many things? Models of search and accomplishment yield their lessons, their mood, their compass markings in response to sustained attention. That explains why so many have read all of Merton, or very nearly. There is a great deal to read, it is greatly rewarding, and it is rarely dull because his life remained in motion to the end. There are few *formulae* in Merton's writings; the result is nothing like a cate-chism. But there is the bright energy of search and a sure sense of direction. "Transub-stantiation is the rule," wrote one of his preferred authors, Ananda K. Coomaraswamy. It was so for Merton. He lived for inner growth, and his life moved along an often rough path of transformation. "The law of all spiritual life," he wrote in 1962, "is the law of risk and struggle, and possible failure" (*The Hidden Ground of Love*, 37).

Given his responsiveness to other traditions, Merton's rootedness in Catholic and monastic tradition needs to be remembered. To have a spiritual home, firm and tested, means that one can travel far and return with new knowledge. He was that kind of seeker of truth. He entered the monastic life, welcomed its austerities, and—no mat-ter how far he traveled in the spirit—never denied its value or ceased its fundamental practices. "In its essentials," he wrote in 1957, "—solitude, poverty, obedience, silence, humility, manual labor, prayer and contemplation—monastic spirituality does not change" (*The Monastic Journey*, 59). Within this rather unchanging context, prayer and contemplation flowered and flowered again for him; his writings over the years record a pilgrim's progress from narrow certainty to an incomparably deeper state of ques-tioning and insight in which he was wholly engaged, as if his body knew what his mind knew, feelings knew what mind knew. This is why he was not a willing or especially skilled theologian but an excellent guide on the path. He had thought about this issue: "The most important thing . . . is not to reduce the idea of God to that of an *object*," he

270

wrote in 1965. "The best approach is existentialist, and the existentialist approach, in theology, is not through abstract dogmas but through direct personal confrontation, not of a subject with an object but of a person with an inner demand" (*The Courage for Truth*, 226). The air clears with such a statement. One nearly knows what to do next, where to turn.

The authority and ease with which he often wrote came from his wholeness, but wholeness was a work in progress. "The voice of God is not clearly heard at every moment," he wrote at much the same moment in spring 1965, "and part of the 'work of the cell' is attention, so that one may not miss any sound of that voice." What this means, therefore, is not only attention to inner grace but to external reality and to one's self as a completely integrated part of that reality. Hence, this implies also a forgetfulness of oneself as totally apart from outer objects, standing back from outer objects; it demands an integration of one's own life in the stream of natural and human and cultural life of the moment. "When we understand how little we listen, how stubborn and gross our hearts are, we realize how important this inner work is. And we see how badly prepared we are to do it" (*Dancing in the Water of Life*, 254-255). Passages of this quality from his writings deserve a place on seekers' bulletin boards or in their journals. How can one keep these thoughts in mind and live by their light? One's own search, however structured and inspired, must be similarly alive—and complex enough to address the human condition as a whole. We are our own workshops. Merton knew this.

In Merton's search for truth there were hidden doors leading from his tradition to others and back again. For example, notions of radical simplicity in St. John of the Cross are akin to Zen practice. "The task for Zen in the West," he wrote in 1963, "is probably a healthy reaction on the part of people exasperated for four hundred years by the inane Cartesian spirit—the reification of concepts, the idolization of reflexive consciousness, the flight from being into verbalism, mathematics and rationalization. Descartes made a fetish of the mirror which Zen shatters" (*Turning Toward the World*, 304). A further example: the subtle oscillation in contemplative prayer or meditation between doing and non-doing is a fundamental experience in all traditions dedicated to inner exploration. Merton knew this also. "Contemplative prayer," he said in a conference at Gethsemani, "is a deep interior activity in the very roots of our being in response to God who has the initiative and yet draws us into certain very subtle forms of obedient initiative on our own side" (*Contemplation in a World of Action*, 341). Obedient initiative: a paradox encountered not on the page but in seekers' experience, which is what Merton most cared for. The page bears witness to experience and derives its validity only from there. The theme of obedient initiative recurs in his writings; in the later years it is a center around which much turns. "To be a flexible instrument in the hand of God is a great and sometimes terrible vocation. . . . We are all in some way instruments. And we all have to be virtuosos at taking a back seat when necessary. Way back. The prayer life of a flexible instrument cannot be well ordered. It has to be terribly free. And utterly responsive to a darkly, dimly understood command" (*The School of Charity*, 271).

Merton's encounter with paradox as a seeker of truth cannot be dissociated from what he writes here about the "dimly understood command." It is as if paradox and its intrinsic uncertainty lie somewhere toward the nucleus of experience, not necessarily as an obstacle: on the contrary, sincere and unsparing encounter with paradox releases religious energies otherwise bound. We know too much and too little. Merton can be quite extraordinary in his commentaries on uncertainty and the need for courage, as in autumn 1966: "Actually one decides one's life by responding to a word that is not well defined, easily explicable, safely accounted for. One decides to love in the face of an unaccountable void, and from the void comes an unaccountable truth. By this truth one's existence is sustained in peace—until the truth is too firmly grasped and too clearly accounted for. Then one is relying on words—i.e., on his own understanding and his own ingenuity in interpreting existence and its 'signs.' Then one is lost—has to be found once again in the patient Void" (*Learning to Love*, 160-161).

There is so very much to explore in Merton's writings as a seeker of truth, but this is only an homage, a suggestion of great things to be found. Faith of course had its place in Merton's spiritual economy, but not a faith that settles all questions; it plays a far more dramatic role. To his friend Dorothy Day he once wrote, "We should in a way fear for our perseverance because there is a big hole in us, an abyss, and we have to fall through it into emptiness, but the Lord will catch us. Who can fall through the center of himself into that nothingness and not be appalled? But the Lord will catch us. He will catch you without fail and take you to His Heart" (*The Hidden Ground of Love*, 138). This is faith: the Lord will catch us—but only when we risk falling through the center of ourselves. In another passage he records with no less lucidity and faith a transcription from his own experience: "He who is called to be a monk is precisely the one who, when he finally realizes that he is engaged in the pure folly of meeting an impossible demand, instead of renouncing the whole thing proceeds to devote himself even more completely to the task. Aware that, precisely because he cannot meet it, it will be met for him. And at this point he goes beyond philosophy. . . ." (*Conjectures of a Guilty Bystander*, 292).

Prayer had its great place. If so many people love and revere the "Merton Prayer"—spoken together at the beginning of many Merton gatherings and no doubt in other venues—that must be because it starts from a position of uncertainty, our position of uncertainty, and prays from *there*. Capturing in simple words the hope of an utterly uncertain human being, in later lines it discovers faith with the warm certainty of a modern psalmist. It is from his book of 1958, *Thoughts in Solitude*, but long since released from there to wander the world and find a home in many people's minds.

> My Lord God, I have no idea where I am going. I do not see the road ahead of me. I cannot know for certain where it will end. Nor do I really know myself, and the fact that I think I am following your will does not mean that I am actually doing so. But I believe that the desire to please you does in fact please you. And I hope I have that desire in all that I am doing. I hope that I will never do anything apart from that desire. And I know that if I do this you will lead me by the right road, though I may know nothing about it. Therefore I will trust you always though I may seem to be lost and in the shadow of death. I will not fear, for you are ever with me, and you will never leave me to face my perils alone (*Thoughts in Solitude*, 83).

As Merton demonstrates without meaning to do so, the mature seeker of truth can possess wonderful, life-giving confidence: he or she has a flexible mind, a heart that has learned to respond and wait and reflect, a fund of experience at many levels from openness to the *ruach Elohim*, the spirit that blows where it will, to openness to others, creatures, plants, landscapes, skies—to all that is, including oneself. What a joy to be so, to have earned that confidence. And yet the seeker is also acutely aware of his or her ignorance and fragility; that the end is not yet and the end is unknowable; that faith can tell us what is to be but faith must be handled like rare tea, not to be spilled in all directions, not to be wasted. The seeker loves the journey, no matter how hard. "Can I tell you," Merton once asked, "that I have found answers to the questions that torment the man of our time? . . . When I first became a monk, yes, I was more sure of 'answers.' But as I grow old in the monastic life and advance further into solitude, I become aware that I have only begun to seek the questions. . . . I have been summoned to explore a desert area of man's heart in which explanations no longer suffice, and in which one learns that only experience counts. . . ." (*The Monastic Journey*, 220). He need not explore alone.

There is a further aspect of search in Merton's practice which we should know. Speaking with a priest about the social problems of the American south, he said, "Don't do a damned thing. Just take the time to become what you profess to be. Then you will know what to do" (John Howard Griffin, *Follow the Ecstasy*, 201). We could end this homage with something beautiful and lofty, but the search for truth isn't only about the beautiful and lofty, far from it. It is about finding one's role in life and fulfilling it with modesty, with all the precision, dignity and creativity one can summon, under the steady gaze of whatever or whoever it is one knows to be there, looking on.

What Merton Has Meant To Me

Morgan C. Atkinson

Who is Thomas Merton?

It's 1977 and I don't know or care. My home, Louisville, Kentucky has a lot of Catholics but I am a Presbyterian. More accurately, I was raised a Presbyterian. Now I would say I have no faith.

I see a story about Merton in the local paper. I read a lot of newspapers, but not much in the way of spiritual literature. Still, I attempt to read *The Seven Storey Mountain*. I check the book out of the downtown library. I learn later that Merton spent time there. I return the book in a hurry. Too hothouse for me! But there is something about the man. He has purpose and passion and a gift with language. A few weeks later I check the book out again. I get a little further but again bog down. Focus is a definite issue. But, my pilgrim's progress, or lack of it, continues. Finally after four or five attempts I am through. What keeps drawing me back? It's hard to pinpoint but this man has gotten my attention. Here is a man who hasn't walked the straight and narrow but has found great meaning in a serious spiritual commitment. A spiritual commitment of all things! Absurd—or intriguing—or both.

I think I need to see where this man lived. It is only 50 miles away. Somebody tells me the monks of Gethsemani let people come for visits. Retreat? It seems like I need to go forward but, having little money, it's probably a moot point. I don't think I can afford staying at the monastery. The post card from the guestmaster says don't worry about it. So I go, Easter weekend 1977.

For a place where one is supposed to slow down a lot happens fast. I imagined one thing and this goes beyond, far beyond. The chant. The monks so solemn and mysterious. They must be giants! The silence. The chant. So many hours! The chant—it touches something I didn't know was in me. Come Monday and back in Louisville I need to talk to someone about this place. At Pentecost I enter the Church.

Years later there was an ad campaign for sneakers—"I want to be like Mike," referring to the great Michael Jordan. Sheepishly, I will concede that I wanted to be like Tom. Like any convert there were extremes. They seem silly now. I'd be embarrassed if not for the gratitude. I'm thankful for Abba Anthony and Dorothy Day; Hannah Arendt and Julian of Norwich; Czeslaw Milosc and Chuang Tzu; Ad Reinhardt and Br. Raphael Prendergast; Herbert Marcuse and Fr. Matthew Kelty; and so many, *many* more. There's always more! All these life-giving doors that Thomas Merton continues to open for me. Focus is still an issue but what a guide! Thomas Merton is the stone that sends ripples through my still waters. The ripples continue, for me and, as this book attests, for so many others. That gives me hope.

So, What Is Hope?

Anthony T. Padovano

Hope has a way of being elusive and imperative. Because it is elusive, we wonder at times if hope drifts into a fantasy, an evasion of reality. Hope's elusiveness makes it difficult to measure it, at times even to engage it. Because it is imperative, it summons us regularly and emerges relentlessly from all the ways we seek to banish it.

Hope may be elusive, but it is woven into the fabric of everyday life. We can't walk or speak without hope. Despair leads us to immobility and incommunicativeness. Albert Camus, an alleged non-believer, noted that even to take breakfast is an act of hope. He was not speaking theoretically when he said this. Perhaps the only way to reflect critically on hope is to consider what happens to us when it is gone.

Human truth is not fully defined by cognition and reason, by logic and clarity. The truth of something is also validated by the effect it has on our life and on the lives of others. The measure of the damage the absence of something causes is reason enough to justify its presence and validate its necessity.

THE WORLD A SACRAMENT OF HOPE

It is facile and reductive for believers to dismiss the so-called secular as unreliable relativity. There are no secular realities. Christians should have known this all along, even more clearly than others. If grace is everywhere, it has no boundaries. Like love, it finds its way to all of us.

There are many signs of grace and hope along the secular paths of history. In the last century, we have experienced the lowest level of violence since the paleolithic age. Harvard professor Steven Pinker has traced the statistics of this phenomenon in his book, *The Better Angels of Our Nature.* Those of us who see only the horror that tragically broke our hearts in the last century are those who read history less deeply. Sometimes this selective reading of history happens because people assume, cynically, that there is depth in negativity and hopelessness.

The last century expanded rights and justice for women and minorities, for homosexuals and dissenters on a scale unimaginable just a few years previous. We may get a measure of the enormous progress by imagining ourselves living in 1900, shorn of all the human development that followed. Women could not vote and homosexuals had no rights. There was no ecumenical movement, and interreligious dialogue was nonexistent. Higher education and regular health care were simply out of reach for almost everyone. Retirement was not a possibility, and travel, before airplanes, was circumscribed. The European Union did not exist, and, in the United States, segregation was enforced and the idea of an African-American president was exotic. Women priests or bishops, women Supreme Court justices, or Secretaries of State, indeed, President or Speaker of the House, were the stuff of fantasy. The list could be continued but the point is made.

The Soviet Union collapsed and the Third Reich was destroyed. Some of humanity's worst diseases were eliminated. The population of the world reached seven billion and every day the vast majority of this number are fed and sheltered. The large number still malnourished is sad beyond all description, but we must not take for granted the billions who survive or even thrive.

I hope, therefore, because I experience the world as a sacrament of hope. I do this, at times, when I find the Church is not. I become more confident when the Church joins the world and the best moments of each converge. The Church achieved this in the Second Vatican Council. The magnitude of that Council is all the more evident when one compares it to its two immediate predecessors, Vatican I and Trent. Catholics experienced the world before Vatican II as one in which attendance at Protestant services was grievously sinful and the slightest sexual deviation merited eternal damnation. The Mass was in a language almost no one understood. And laity were banished from proximity to its celebration in all but minor ways. Indeed, the laity accepted its distance from Church life and leadership as proper. The New Testament was not a book Catholic leaders urged people to read on their own or to interpret critically.

The Church, as a sacrament of hope, united to a world as a sacrament of grace, enable me to see my own life and the lives of my contemporaries as sacraments of hope. It would be dreadfully naïve and inexcusably obtuse to disregard the effects of evil and sin, to make light of the unbearable suffering we inflict on one another and the damage we do by our arrogance and predatory exploitation, our greed and narcissism. The catalog of these aberrations and deviations, the prevalence of dysfunctionality and willed diminishment of the other, the bigotry and torture, war and homicide, sexual abuse and financial corruption, this catalog is well-documented and graphically inescapable. My intent is not to add to this, since it is well-known and obvious. My intent is to draw attention to the sacramentality of human existence in all its many forms and its awesome capacity to receive and incarnationalize grace. Humanity is not primarily defined by its lapses.

I find great comfort in the spiritual lessons that so-called pagan and classical literature give us. Cicero's essays on friendship and aging, Aristotle's ethics and Plato's *Republic* show the human spirit, before Christianity, as capable of impressive spiritual depth. Homer's *Odyssey* gives us the choice by Odysseus to leave the island of a goddess even though she offers him endless sexual pleasure and everlasting life because he does not love her and wants to be with his wife Penelope and his son Telemachus. Homer reminds us that there is no greater happiness than a marriage built on love.

Virgil, in the *Aeneid*, begins with Aeneas running from the destruction and flames of his native city, Troy, with his aged father on his shoulders, his young son at his side and his household gods in his arms. The symbol is unforgettable. It tells us that when our lives are in ashes, we gain hope again if we preserve our memories (his aged father), our hopes for the future (his young son) and our values (the household gods).

Merton as Mentor

When Dante journeyed to the Inferno, he had Virgil as a guide. When he ascended to

Paradise, it was Beatrice who led him there. He did not encounter the darkness or the light without mentors.

The spiritual life is a journey that takes us through the dark corners of our life into the truth and the love which give us peace and bring us hope. We seek guides for such a journey, people who reassure us that the journey is not a phantom venture, that, indeed, there is more to life than the few decades we have from birth to death. Even more to the point is the character of the life we have while we have it. How do we find God, and how do we deal with one another? Does prayer reach God and does it benefit others? What is our responsibility toward the poverty and the pain of people? What do I do with the envy in my life, or the greed, with the arrogance and narcissism, with the fears that God may not exist or that others are not worth my effort, with the enemies I make and my ingratitude to those who love me?

Thomas Merton encapsulated this message in his life. There were paradoxes. He embodied what he wanted to say in the silence he chose. He became a prophetic witness for social justice in seclusion. He changed the lives of others by what he experienced in contemplation. He made us hopeful by the simplicity of his life, a simplicity which convinced us that we could follow such a path, not in monastic confinement only, but in the seemingly ordinary journeys of our lives. We could all readily be silent and allow time for seclusion and contemplation.

Clearly, one of Merton's great books, a spiritual classic, *Seeds of Contemplation,* made mysticism not an exotic calling, but a vocation to which we are all summoned. He showed us that the arc of our individual lives is not limited to the emergence of consciousness and intelligence, reason and conscience, morality and compassion. All of us take this journey and know that human development requires these steps. We readily conclude that those who reject this path are humanly underdeveloped.

Merton, however, insisted that we are capable of more. There are mystic moments in all our lives. Those instances when we are willing to give ourselves totally to something larger than ourselves. We do this in love when we willingly lay down our lives for others. We do this with our deepest commitments which carry fidelity with them, to a life partner or a friend, to children or country, to universal peace and non-violence, to social justice for the oppressed. At the heart of our relationship is the yearning to encounter beauty. It is mysticism which forms the soul of the artist and creates the voice of the prophet. We reach for God and experience God as the source of the mystery and mysticism in our lives.

Mysticism is the experience we undergo when we see that all the opposites are at one with their alternatives. We behold the universe as a harmony, and discern that the discordant notes blend and that we are one with the universe in its great symphony. We touch mysticism when we fall in love and when the joy and exhilaration of it makes us want this for everyone. At such moments, we have no enemies and choose to have no one excluded. Mysticism brings our lives to wholeness.

Merton crafted in his silence the words to assure us of this. He did this in the singularity of his own Cistercian life, by writing, not so much about monasticism, but about us. He stated that monasticism is validated if it brings with it not only an encounter with God, but a connection with all humanity.

Merton gave us hope and became our mentor by assuring us that our lives were exalted and that there really were no hierarchies separating the ordinary from the special, the everyday from the exceptional.

Life itself, humanity lived, is the great sacrament. Like all sacraments, it is the visible expression of a reality inexhaustibly sacred.

Hope and mysticism belong together, each of them not justified by logic, not requiring evidence, not able to be done away with, without discarding human life itself. We are mystically called to love a life of hope even though the arguments contrary to hope seem more logical and rationally compelling. There is no way to justify with logic alone the power of love or our universal vulnerability before it. Love is mysticism's finest moment and it leaves hope in its wake.

Merton led us in these directions and invited us to become pilgrims with him. He called us as a brother and made us feel that someone in our own family, someone who knew us well and cared for us, someone able to find the words we needed most to hear, was addressing us. This was Merton's great genius to reveal to us in his life and writing how to find hope in who we are and how to become mystically one with those larger realities which bring us peace and make us feel at home. Merton's own life was not easy, nor is ours. Love is not an easy commitment. It costs not less than everything. But it gives us, in return, ecstasy and happiness and freedom and peace. In a word, it gives us hope.

Thanks

James Martin, SJ

There are four persons who are the most responsible for my Jesuit vocation: the Father, the Son, the Holy Spirit, and Thomas Merton.

When I was 25, I was working at General Electric's financial services division in Stamford, Connecticut. After six year of toiling in the corporate world, I finally had to admit to myself that I was miserable. Worse, I was lost. After graduating from the Wharton School of Business, I had taken a job with GE hoping that it would be a good use of my talents. It wasn't. While many of my friends found business to be an enjoyable and satisfying vocation (and still do), I felt like the proverbial square peg in a round (though high-paying) hole. Gradually, the sadness and stress started to get to me, and I developed some stomach problems.

My life seemed to make no sense to me. What was I doing? And I doubt it made little sense to many of my friends or family, who knew that I was unhappy.

One night, after an endless day of work, I came home and plopped down on the couch in front of the television set and started channel surfing. Presently I stumbled upon a show on PBS, a kind of documentary entitled "Merton: A Film Biography," which I would later discover was produced by the author Paul Wilkes.

What I saw captivated me. This man, Thomas Merton, who I gathered was a "famous" Catholic, had left behind a rather dissolute life to enter a Trappist monastery somewhere in Kentucky. Even now, almost 30 years after I first watched it, I am unable to identify precisely what called out to me so clearly and forcefully: the expression on his face in the photographs shown on television, the story of his often sad and finally joyful life, or the idea of living in a monastery which seemed at once so romantic and so impossible. All I knew was that Thomas Merton's way of life seemed so much more beautiful than mine. And the smile on his face meant that he had seen something that I hadn't. I set out to discover what that was.

The next day I bought *The Seven Storey Mountain* and read it over the next few nights before going to bed. By the time I had finished, I knew with some certainty that this was what I wanted to do: not to enter a Trappist monastery, but seeking a life of purpose and meaning.

Without boring you with details, I can say that within two years I had read all the books of Merton's I could find, left my job at General Electric and, to the shock and surprise of everyone, myself included, entered the Jesuit novitiate. It was certainly the best decision I ever made.

Merton has continued to follow me; or, better to say, that I have continued to follow Merton. In addition to Jesus of course, whom we both follow(ed)! Merton's life continued to speak to me, and still does, though in new ways now. For example, shortly after entering the Jesuits, I realized (as did he, shortly after entering the Trappists) how utterly rosy was the picture of religious life he painted in *SSM*, as devotees call it, and how unfairly critical he was of "the world." The shorthand seemed to be: Monastery good, world bad. Funny enough, when I wrote one of my first books on vocation (*In Good Company*) I fell into that precise trap, though it took me several years to realize this. My life at GE was all bad, as I described it in the book, and the Jesuits were all good. I smiled when it dawned on me that I had repeated what I had harshly judged as Merton's naïve "mistake." I'll bet he was smiling somewhere too.

Just last month, during my annual retreat, which came in the middle of my celebrating 25 years as a Jesuit, I read *SSM* again—perhaps for the tenth time in my life. There I heard that voice that had so entranced me at age 25: honest, sorrowful, larky, questioning, enchanted, wondering, critical, judgmental at times, forgiving, and most understanding. And as is always the case with a classic, the book seemed brand new to me.

During that retreat I realized a few things with a start. First, I hadn't known that he had taken "James" as his confirmation name. How had I missed that? I took "Thomas." Second, the *SSM*'s frequent protestations of Merton's awful sinfulness make almost no sense if you don't know about his (and this is a complicated topic) belief that he had fathered a child during his time at Cambridge in England.

Most of all, I was reminded that Merton died at age 53. How had I not realized that earlier? Now, don't think me a fool: I knew that Merton was born in 1915 and died tragically in 1968, and, when I first read his book, had probably quickly calculated his age. But perhaps in earlier years, in my 20s and 30s, I thought of that as simply "old." But now I'm 52. So that, when I read his book and see photos of him now, I see a peer, someone who was in religious life around as long as I have been. A brother.

Several years ago I visited the Abbey of Gethsemani for the first time. And the first thing I did after dropping my bags in the guest room was visit Merton's grave, not far from the walls of the abbey church.

There were so many things I wanted to say as I stood under the baking Kentucky sun. That without him I wouldn't be who I was. That he continues to be a guiding light for me. That I try to emulate his writer's desire to write only for God's glory. That though I had spoken to dozens of people since who had known him, I would have given almost anything to have met him, known him and asked him a few things. That I think he's a saint, despite his many flaws.

I didn't know what to say to this man who had changed my life, so I simply knelt down on the grass and said aloud, "Thanks."

100 Years Since His Birth,
Thomas Merton Is Completely Irrelevant

Mark C. Meade

This is not an academic paper. The title is not followed by a colon and a long subtitle. My point is simple. There is one overarching lesson I have learned in over ten years as an archivist at the Thomas Merton Center. It is that Thomas Merton is not relevant to us in the 21st century. The hundreds of books, poems and essays are, to today's reader, incomprehensible. If you are possessed of tender sensibilities, you might choose to stop reading now. You may not like what I have to say.

It was never my plan to like Thomas Merton, but after taking the job in 2003, I had the misfortune of being thrust into the center (at "The Center") of all things Merton. Like most people born in the 1970s, and like those born in years after, Merton was pre-history. Just ask the students at Bellarmine University, home to the Merton Center. "We are nurses and accountants, not philosophers or theologians." Never mind that neither was Merton. You have lost them already.

Like others, alas, I was drawn in by Merton. Do you know the feeling? It is like he is telling your story. You might argue that this is his genius, that it is what keeps him as fresh today as any time. Do not be fooled. You are reading yourself into the story and making Merton into your image.

It would be one thing if Merton had succeeded as a novelist. This is at least respectable these days, even if he failed to weave zombies or vampires into the narrative. However, he has completely lost us as essayist. In a consumer society, it is not important to read to shape your opinion. You have an opinion already and are asked to express it through online social media, whether it is mustering the courage and effort to add your name to an online petition or to "like" a brand of shaving cream on Facebook.

Merton was also a poet. In the era of digital media, his words might as well be scrawled on a Grecian urn because they are certainly not easy to squeeze into a 144-character Tweet that makes any sense. Besides, old "Luddite Louie" would likely complain about the Twitter medium if he were alive today, probably communicating his complaint in a text message no less.

Worse than simply a writer of poetry, Merton often penned religious poetry, for Christ's sake. Catholic literature and all Christian literature are dead. As religion is a topic to be avoided at parties and at the water cooler, the United States is a more polite nation by sticking to the antics of the "real" housewives, the hoarders, the "bride-zillas," and the moonshiners of reality television than tread into the controversy of belief.

Most of us want uplifting messages in popular spirituality. How many of us "shining like the sun," aglow from brief snippets of cheery Merton, have delved into grouchy unabridged Merton, the prophet of doom, endlessly nagging about race wars or nuclear apocalypse. What a downer. Had he only access to some modern self-help like *The Secret* or a healthy dose of the power of positive thinking found within the prosperity gospel, he could have known to surround himself with more successful people. Better look to horse farms instead of monasteries and cow pastures in rural Kentucky, Fr. Louis. There remains hope that in the unlikely event a cause is initiated for his canonization, a more sanitized version of Merton will emerge without all the rough edges. For example, few know that Martin Luther King, Jr., like Merton, spoke out against Vietnam, when "I have a dream" are the only words repeated on King's holiday.

Merton did not learn that, in the United States, you have to take sides in the partisan divide which pervades our politics and that we apply to religion. Any traction Merton gained with conservatives by reviving and defending forgotten traditions in the contemplative and eremitical life, or by his continued use of the Latin Mass after the vernacular was approved, was completely undermined by his willingness to engage in dialogue with Jews, Atheists, Protestants, and Buddhists. I guess you have to forgive Merton on the last point and chalk it up to personal weakness. Everyone knows these days to come to a discussion armed with the right answer. An open mind is just an unguarded fortress. Here again, you will point to his ongoing lifelong conversion as a good thing. If he were a politician, we would call that a "flip-flopper." There is nothing worse than character development in politics. Why would we allow for it in our heroes?

There are only two possible solutions to the problem of Thomas Merton. Since he is difficult to put neatly into a box—something easily marketable, consumable and digestible—it is best to just ignore him and to wait until he is forgotten and his fan base fades away. As mentioned, it is only a small minority under middle-age who recognize his name. The very intelligent, enthusiastic and committed fans he has in this demographic we must view as an anomaly. The other unseemly option is to read him slowly and deliberately over many years and re-read him after many more years. In fact, it would help if you organized your whole life with much more time devoted to silence, prayer and contemplation. Joining a religious order or a simple cabin in the woods would not be a bad idea to accomplish this. Seriously, though, with the current array of dizzying distractions and entertainments available to us now, I am at a loss to think of a writer with the gifts to inspire us to do this.

Becoming What We Are

Cynthia Bourgeault

> His students said to him,
> "So tell us, then, what our end and destiny will be?"
> Yeshua answered,
> "Have you already discovered your origin so that you are now free to seek
> after your end? It is only at your source that you will find your destiny."
>
> *Gospel of Thomas, logion 18*

One Sunday many years ago when I was living along the coast of Maine, I put my teenage daughter Lucy on a ferry from our island to the mainland four miles away to meet her boyfriend, Scott. Standing on a high bluff overlooking the bay on an exceptionally clear afternoon, I could watch the whole little drama play out, each of the sequences unfolding in its turn: the ferry approaching the dock, Scott's old yellow Toyota winding down the landing road. I could feel their rising excitement about the rendezvous that was finally almost upon them. But from my vantage point, it was all present already, all contained in a huge, stately "now." The dimension that for them was still being lived in time for me had been converted to space, and the picture was complete.

In an instant it came to me that this must be what Jesus meant by "the fullness of time." There really *is* a kind of fourth dimension, a reality or realm all its own, in which our usual sense of forward motion does not apply. In my brief epiphany that afternoon I suddenly saw that time, *all* our times, are contained in something bigger whose dimension is no longer temporal. The fullness of time becomes space—a vast, gentle wideness in which all possible outcomes, all our little histories past, present and future, all our hopes and dreams, are already contained—and mysteriously *already fulfilled.*

The name traditionally given to this realm in the great inner traditions of the West is the Imaginal Realm—which despite the name does not mean "imaginary" but something closer to "hyper-real" or objectively true. It truly is a kind of fourth dimension, where "beginning" and "end" are not opposite points on a line, but adjacent points on a sphere. And it is only here, in the spaciousness of this additional dimension that the *koan* posed by Jesus—and by Thomas Merton—will finally yield its secret.

"Imaginal" may be the technical term, but the great mystics of the Christian and Sufi visionary stream have known this realm by a simpler, more affective name: "The Mercy." Again and again they give lyric voice to that core intuition that the entire rainbow of times and colors, past and future, individual paths through history, flows out of and back into the great white light of the simple loving presence of God. And in that presence—in that *Mercy*—all our possible pasts and possible futures, our loved ones lost and children never born—are contained, fulfilled, in a wholeness of love from which nothing can possibly be lost.

It is not a vision we can stay with for long. It is too vast for us, too beyond our limited power of reckoning. "To apprehend the intersection of the timeless with time is an occupation for the saint," says T. S. Eliot, and most of us are just not there—or there only briefly, in moments of very great love or freefall.

General Lowenhielm got it briefly in that sublime scene in the movie *Babette's Feast*. At last, briefly reunited at the banquet table with the woman he has always loved, though the time wrenched to a separate destiny, he rises and offers a toast:

"Mercy and truth have met together. Righteousness and bliss shall kiss one another," he begins, quoting a verse in Psalm 85. Then, in what becomes the film's eloquent climax, he continues:

> Man in his weakness and shortsightedness believes he must make choices in this life. He trembles at the risks he takes. We do know fear. But no. Our choice is of no importance. There comes a time when our eyes are opened. And we come to realize that mercy is infinite. We need only to await it with confidence and receive it with gratitude. Mercy imposes no conditions.
>
> And lo! Everything we have chosen has been granted to us. And everything we have rejected has also been granted. Yes, we get back even what we have rejected. For mercy and truth have met together. Righteousness and bliss shall kiss one another.

"What We Have to Be Is What We Already Are."

Thomas Merton, of course, was no stranger to imaginal reality—either the term or the experience itself. And it was very great love and very great freefall that no doubt precipitated his extraordinary imaginal epiphany at the corner of Fourth and Walnut in Louisville, in March 1958. Reflecting later on what had erupted in his being as a single explosion of primordial light, he concludes:

> At the center of our being is a point of nothingness which is untouched by sin and illusion, a point of pure truth, a point or spark which belongs entirely to God, which is never at our disposal, from which God disposes of our lives, which is inaccessible to the fantasies of our own mind or the brutalities of our own will. This little point of nothingness and of absolute poverty is the pure glory of God written in us. It is, so to speak, His name written in us as our poverty, as our indigence, as our sonship. It is like a pure diamond blazing with the invisible light of heaven. It is in everybody, and if we could see it, we would see these billions of points of light coming together in the face and blaze of a sun that would make all the darkness and cruelty of life vanish completely. I have no program for this seeing. It is only given. But the gate of heaven is everywhere (*Conjectures of A Guilty Bystander*, 142).

In these justly famous lines, Merton is describing something he names as "*le point vierge*"—the virgin point. Most Merton fans know that, shortly before his Louisville epiphany, Merton had been reading Louis Massignon's commentary on a treatise of the heart by Al Hallaj, a ninth century Sufi saint. The phrase "*le point vierge*" translates what Sufi mysticism refers to as the Srrr—"the Secret"—the innermost veil of the heart. It is the place where one stands at the intersection of the timeless and time, where the lived reality of our life in time coincides seamlessly with the archetype of the Self, sometimes called the angel of our being. The angel and the Self are not identical, but nor are they different. They are a *syzygy*—"not one, not two, but both one and two." In a way which our minds cannot conceive yet our hearts can intuitively live, the timeless and time are interwoven in a single tapestry; they are the warp and weft of our whole Selfhood. In the lineage of Sufism Merton was exploring, this realm of union and origin is called the Imaginal. And Merton rightly intuited, from the resonance with his own deeply lived Christian mysticism, that this living from this point of origin is the key to getting ourselves oriented rightly.

My own hermit teacher, Brother Raphael Robin, had his own way of working with this idea, his own powerful image for it. I think all mystical teachers have their own way of working with this idea, because it really is the key to everything. One brilliantly clear October evening, only a couple of months before his death, we watched the fiery red sun slowly sink beneath behind the jagged horizon line of the mountain ridge. It was a poignant foreshadowing of the parting we both intuited was in store, and tears began to fill my eyes.

"Look!" Rafe suddenly exclaimed and pointed fiercely toward the east. I turned toward the east and saw a perfect sliver of a crescent moon, brilliantly poised for its October debut, so delicate and perfectly suspended in the luminous night sky that it almost took my breath away.

"Look again," he said. I did, and then I saw what he was so fixedly pointing to. There behind that delicate sliver of a new moon was the perfect outline of the full moon, completely round and whole.

"What we have to be is what we already are."

Yes, the journey in time is real. Yes, we must grow and change, and come round and full in time, and actualize in time what would otherwise only be there as potential, the mirror-like reflection of another realm. But there, in the center of our hearts, sits that gateway to the infinite: "this little point of nothingness" that is "the glory of God written in us," the intersection of the timeless and time, the *Srrr*, the secret. And it is also, claims Merton, the point of communion, as each of those "everybodies," reunited in that inner sanctum of the heart, re-create our time-torn world breath by breath, from our common place of paradise regained.

"It is only at your source that you will find your destiny."

You sit with this *koan* for a while, and suddenly you see the secret, which like all *koans* is so obvious once you've finally grasped it. Time doesn't flow in a linear direction. Never did, never will. It spirals out, like a nautilus shell, from the worm hole of the *point vierge*, weaving the tapestry of finitude as the glory of God. We are full at point of origin, and from that fullness flow out synchronously, into time. Like the moon, growing toward what it already is. Meaningful coincidence, not ruthless linear causality, knits our hearts onto the poetry of God's body. And if we can learn to flow in this direction—like learning to row a rowboat, facing your origin, and hence effortlessly flowing toward your destination, the journey through time becomes a sacrament of God's own compassionate aliveness.

And at the end, you say—as that great saint Bede Griffiths is reputed to have said on his deathbed, "Receive the growing Christ."

The Perennial Philosophy And Thomas Merton

Arthur Versluis

Thomas Merton's work as a whole, and in particular his mysticism, reflects the perennial philosophy or *philosophia perennis*. The perennial philosophy often has been presented in confusing ways, chiefly by attempting to make it a result of combining different religious traditions, or by claiming that there is a single religion behind or inside the different world religious traditions. But the approach of the *philosophia perennis* is neither of these, and although the second (the concept of a single religion behind or inside different religions) may or may not be warranted, it is simply not intrinsic to the perennial philosophy, which is not a method for comparing religions anyway. What is it? That is what we will begin to address here.

Thomas Merton wrote in his *Asian Journal* "We are already one. But we imagine that we are not. So what we have to recover is our original unity. What we have to be is what we are." Such a perspective goes completely against the current academic fashion, in which "God is not one," as a recent book title has it. But perennial philosophy does not mean that all religions are one. Rather, it means that there is an underlying basic shared human metaphysical reality, and that is what Merton is referring to, an insight that resulted from his traveling Eastward, both literally and figuratively. Platonism and Hermetism are the model for perennial philosophy in the European tradition, and Vedanta serves an analogous role in India. Buddhism is distinctive from all of these, of course, not least because of its unique emphasis on emptiness. And perennial philosophy does not hold that all these traditions are identical, or that they all point toward exactly the same goals or kinds of realization.

Perennial philosophy points to individual spiritual experience; and Platonism, Hermetism, Vedanta, and Buddhism all are based on direct individual realizations, on the experiential transformation and illumination of the individual. That is what Aldoux Huxley's book, *The Perennial Philosophy*, centered on, and that was how he defined the perennial philosophy. The word "perennial" in this context means that human beings can go through transformative and illuminative processes that are intrinsically open to us as human beings; that people have gone through, are going through, or may go through, such a process in the past, present and future (hence it perennially recurs). The word "philosophy" does not have the meaning of "an abstract theoretical system constructed by discursive reason," but rather that of "a virtuous life leading to the realization of love (*philo*) and wisdom (*sophia*)."

Huxley's book, first published in 1944, presents a series of thematically linked quotations from a wide array of sources both Asian and European, with a focus on mystics and mystical transformation and awakening. *The Perennial Philosophy* had a long and influential subsequent history, and is visible behind much of the California counterculture of the 1960s and 1970s, as well as behind New Age and related movements of the late twentieth and early twenty-first centuries. Of course, there is another modern intellectual current known as "Traditionalism," which is also often regarded as a form of "perennialism" too. But what we are describing here is at once both ancient and new, and in some respects distinct from these other variants.

In truth, the concept of perennial philosophy absolutely needs clarification in the wake of so many developments, new interpretations and changes in cultural-social contexts. The terms "perennialism" and "perennial philosophy" have lost any crispness of meaning. This is in part because these terms are often defined by opponents, who express great alarm at any hint of what they term "essentialism"—a term that is not so effective an accusation as it is often assumed to be. Nonetheless, many academics, particularly in the humanities, rejected out of hand all "metanarratives" and normative "truth claims," asserting instead in abstruse and opaque language what amounts finally to a kind of rarified nihilism. Given the waning of these intellectual movements and developments, perennial philosophy certainly calls for new consideration.

The perennial philosophy at heart is Platonism. Platonism, in this context, is philosophy not as a product of combative discursive reasoning, but as a way of life. It is existential, in the sense that it is centered in encouraging one to live a virtuous life, but also because it proposes a metaphysics centered on the individual's potential realization of self-other transcendence. Hence what is "perennial" about perennial philosophy is its call to the individual to live a better life and, potentially at least, to "return to the One," that is, to contemplatively realize inner unity.

Platonism is sometimes imported into monotheism, so that one then finds Christian Platonism or mysticism (the ur-figure for which is of course Dionysius the Areopagite), Islamic Platonism (which in effect becomes Sufism) and Jewish Platonism (to some extent, perhaps, in Kabbalah). But for all that, Platonism is prior to and distinct from the various monotheisms, and it provides a Western tradition that is closest to Buddhist and Vedantic religious philosophies.

Hence the perennial philosophy is inherently esoteric, in that those who practice it are engaged in a contemplative ascent that cannot be fully understood only through discursive descriptions of it. Discursive descriptions as read by an outsider and non-participant are exoteric, and as such give only indirect access to the actual contemplative experiences that accompany the individual's inward realization of Platonic metaphysics. Platonism in this regard is a philosophical translation for individuals of what previously had belonged to the Greek Mysteries as group revelations of transcendence (about which participants were famously and for the most part effectively sworn to secrecy), and in both cases the center of the tradition is experiential and transmutational.

In this respect perennial philosophy is fundamentally different than contemporary academia in general and academic philosophy in particular, where discursive reason alone is hegemonic. The dominance of discursive reason as a mode of consciousness, so prevalent in contemporary intellectual life, has many consequences, not the least of which is that other modes of consciousness are studiously ignored. Contemporary academic philosophy, by so emphasizing discursive reason, reinforces prevailing social tendencies toward dualism and materialism, separates individual subjects from objects of study, and appears to remove even the possibility of philosophy as a way of life. Contemporary academia—in its zeal to insist on a posture of objectivity based on an imagined hegemony of discursive reason, and in its prevailing fear of such buga-boos as "essentialism" and "metanarratives"—in effect stands for nothing. It is for the most part as if contemporary academics are adrift in an ocean without map, compass, sextant, or any other means of navigation—and insist that no means of navigation is acceptable!

Perennial philosophy, on the other hand, presents us with a map, a compass, a sextant—it offers us ways to navigate. Since it is so central to the history of Western European culture and religion, it is incumbent on us at least to become familiar with it. But it also may provide us with more than antiquarian knowledge. For the purpose of perennial philosophy is, ultimately, teleological and soteriological: it points us toward the higher meanings and purposes of human life. It has much to offer us concerning the nature of our world and of ourselves, in particular our relationship to nature, and the nature of our own consciousness. It offers us a coherent larger metaphysical con-text and significance to our lives.

What is more, as perennial, it belongs as much to our present and future as it does to our past. The perennial philosophy now exists in an intellectual world no longer restricted to one religious or cultural ambience, but inhabited by many religions. Among these, the advent of Asian religions in the West has been especially influen-tial, and we cannot discuss perennial philosophy (which came into being in the Greco-Roman world) in a contemporary context without recognizing signal points where it intersects with Hinduism and Buddhism.

The fundamental insight of perennial philosophy is that truth is unitary and it can be perceived by human cognition. Plato describes this kind of cognition as akin to a spark, which can be transmitted from a teacher to a pupil. The spark is of the same nature as a fire, and it is also light, illumination—but as perceived by human cognition. Perennial philosophy is insight into what is perennial, what is always accessible to us because it is the very nature of cognition itself—it is self-reflective and self-transcen-dent awareness.

The perennial philosophy is esoteric in the purest sense of the word—which, after all, has its origins in the initiatory tradition of Pythagoreanism, and no doubt before that and after, in the mystery traditions whose origins are no longer visible to us. The perennial philosophy is actually secret in our present age, because nearly all the preju-dices we inherit from our time are opposed to it and to the insights it offers. And yet it is an open secret, because it is transmitted in texts, and the key texts are all available to us now. We are in a unique moment in history, perhaps the end of an age, it is true, but also at that unique point when what always has been there now is visible to us in an unexpected way.

The perennial philosophy is all too often misunderstood. Among misunderstand-ings is the notion that the perennial philosophy results from comparison, as though it derived from the superimposition of multiple religions and the acceptance of what they might have in common. But that kind of view, however prevalent, is incorrect. Rather, the perennial philosophy is fundamentally experiential in nature, and reflects the recognition that a contemplative ascent is possible for us human beings, and fur-ther, that realization of transcendence is also possible. The perennial philosophy holds that there is a central path to transcendence, and that we find this path reflected in different religious traditions without being limited to any one of them. But there is more—for this individual path also has cultural implications.

We need to recognize how the perennial philosophy provides a metaphysical context for understanding wisdom within a culture. In contemporary society, there really is no context for wisdom. We are familiar with the word, but what does it really mean? We do not know. In the context of perennial philosophy, however, wisdom is the natural result of realizing transcendence of self-other dualism. The contemplative is not an escapist, but rather the individual in society who is most intent upon awakening into and manifesting truth; wisdom is a term for a result of that awakening. In the context of perennial philosophy, the word "sage" refers to someone who has undergone this process of awakening to truth. We need more sages in this troubled world. Thomas Merton's invaluable life work points us in just this direction.

Why Does Merton Give Me Hope?

Casey Holland

I suppose I'd have to begin with "Why Merton, at all?"

I did not go looking for Merton; rather, he found me. To this day I consider our meeting as something of an act of grace. I am hard pressed to come up with an exact explanation as to how exactly I found myself in the intellectual company of Merton. I've accepted it as one of life's many wondrous and innumerable mysteries! Looking back, I suppose these seemingly "thoughtless" actions on my part, leading to such profound personal and spiritual discoveries, only further remind me of that guiding hand of providence which has always carried me to precisely where I need to be. This provides a sense of hope that is almost essential to living a life, in which there seem to be so many possibilities for things to go wrong. The fact that, whether we know it or not, things turn out just as they should, kindles and sustains the smallest spark of hope to anyone who stands at the edge of the unfathomable depths of the cosmos, crying out "Who am I? What am I doing here?" Like a star in the night sky, hope is the light that guides us through the uncertainties of questions yet to be answered, of futures yet to be revealed.

Not only does Merton give us hope, he also reminds us of what we can hope for. Any reader of Merton will tell you that, when you read him, you read about yourself. He has a way of speaking to you through the pages. Merton reminds us that there is a world worth living in, full of people worth living and laughing with, loving and caring for. Merton had such an appreciation for all aspects of life. He fell deeply in love with God and the world He created, and this enchantment is reflected in each and every thing he did. Every book, letter, painting, and prayer.

It gives me hope that a man can find God in the midst of the confusion of young adulthood. It gives me hope that one can find peace in the quiet, mist-cloaked hills of Kentucky. It gives me hope that silence and solitude can be treasured in a world of noise and commotion. Thomas Merton gives me hope, along with the trees, the stones, the stars, the sky, the bread and wine, the bells, the mysteries and the unknown, and the rabbits. All those darn rabbits.

In The Fire Of A Wild Sun

Robert Inchausti

When I graduated from the University of Chicago in 1979, I was feeling spiritually empty and in need of something greater than the life of the mind. So I picked up the first book on prayer that made any sense to me and *found* Thomas Merton and an entirely new way to think about God and Christ, meditation and revolution, history and nonviolence, and everything else in between. Here was an entirely new way to think about what it meant to be an authentic Human Being.

In 1979 Merton had been dead for a little over ten years, so his life already had a dramatic arc. He was famous for writing *The Seven Storey Mountain* (1948), beloved by the Church; then things had gotten dicey in the late fifties and early sixties when he went "electric"—writing Beat poetry and radical social criticism. He had died in Thailand in 1968, the same year Martin Luther King, Jr. and Bobby Kennedy were assassinated, a co-martyr of sorts to those dark times.

After I read that little book on prayer, I set out to read everything Merton had ever written. And since over half of his collected works had yet to be published, almost every year some new and important collection would roll out, and my conversation with him would deepen and clarify. I read Merton, not because he had answers to my questions but because, like Kierkegaard, he had better questions and finer distinctions that did away with false antitheses and over simplifications.

Moreover, his move from literary modernism to contemplative Christianity struck me as prophetic and prefigured a shift in Western civilization. Thomas Merton had loved Blake. He had loved Joyce. He had wanted to be a writer. And yet, he gave it all up for something he found more real, more challenging and more true. But perhaps, most surprising of all, despite his turn to contemplative Christianity, he was *still a writer*. Not the same *kind* of writer he had once wanted to be, not an experimental novelist, but a mystic who owned his mysticism and sought to understand its place within the totality of human experience. As a result, Merton always struck me as more sincere than the aesthetes and clever dialecticians I had been taught to admire in graduate school. His monastic commitments gave integrity to his ideas and his brave turn away from the dogmas of modernism and the sentimentalities of the American immigrant Church gave weight to his reflections.

In the years that immediately followed my graduation, I left the heady atmosphere of academia—married my undergraduate sweetheart, Linda Garcia—and took a job teaching ninth grade in an inner city Catholic School. My students were fourteen years old, little anarchists really, who challenged every classroom convention I tried to put into place. That year Merton became more than a writer to me; he carried me through the troubled waters of professional isolation and private despair.

His works taught me how to love those young souls and how to find in their scattered, disordered lives the completion of my own. To this day, when I think of Thomas Merton, I don't think of any particular ideas or even any specific works. Rather I think of him as my impish friend always there to go me one better, to jar my complacencies, to deflate my grandiosity, and force me to think and feel in new ways toward new and unexpected ends.

The heroes of the contemplative life are not always writers. But when they are, they can reveal a world beyond and within the one we currently hallucinate, and by so doing transfigure our lives. As Merton himself put it, "It is useless to look for what is everywhere. It is hopeless to hope for what cannot be gained because you already have it. The fire of a wild sun has eaten up the distance between hope and despair. Dance in this sun, you tepid idiot. Wake up and dance in the clarity of perfect contradiction" (*Raids on the Unspeakable*, 106-107). Sturdy advice for a fragile soul, and exactly what I needed to hear.

Thomas Merton's Message Of Hope:
The Robert E. Daggy Scholars Program

Virginia Kaib Ratigan

On March 14, 1967, Amiya Charkravarty, friend of Merton and visiting professor at Smith College, organized a "Merton Evening," where students presented readings from Merton's works along with discussion. In his letter of March 29, Chakravarty reported: "We had a great evening. . . . We were immersed in the silence and eloquence of your thoughts and writings. . . . The young scholars here realize that the absolute rooted-ness of your faith makes you free to understand other faiths. . . . Your books have the rock-like inner strength which sustains the Abbey of Gethsemani, which can challenge violence and untruth wherever they may appear." Earlier when Merton was presented with the idea of such an event, he had felt "honored" and thought that "the girls at Smith" were wise enough not to let the evening "take on the aspect of a personality cult." He continued: "I am happy with the idea, and it is to me a way of being in con-tact with others like myself, with kindred interests and concerns, people who look for something more. . . ." He instructed Charkravarty to "Give them, then, my love."

In reply to Charkravarty's report, Merton wrote:

> I do really have the feeling that you have all understood and shared quite per-fectly. That you have seen something that I see to be most precious—and most available too. The reality that is present to us and in us: call it Being, call it Atman, call it Pneuma . . . or Silence. And the simple fact that by being attentive, by learning to listen (or recovering the natural capacity to listen which cannot be learned any more than breathing), we can find ourself engulfed in such hap-piness that it cannot be explained: the happiness of being at one with everything in that hidden ground of Love for which there can be no explanations (*The Hidden Ground of Love*, 115).

The legacy of love and respect for young people is an unbroken chain from little "Grace" (see "Grace's House," *The Collected Poems of Thomas Merton*, 330-331), to the "girls at Smith," to Merton's beatnik generation and to our Merton Society's nurture of a diverse group of young people down to this day. In reflecting on "Thomas Merton's Message of Hope" it appears that one thread like shining gold in our midst is the Daggy Youth/Student Scholars Program. The Mission was set down by the Board, in collabo-ration with Msgr. William Shannon, a founding member and first president of the ITMS in 1996. Courses on Thomas Merton were being taught in many colleges and univer-sities by that time and even in some high schools. Young people were encountering Merton in all of the expected places: schools, local Merton Chapters, peace and justice centers, seminaries, campus ministry programs, religious communities, parishes, and Catholic Worker houses around the country. Both then and now a random visit to a book store may engage a student who just happens to pick up one of Merton's books and becomes hooked.

The mission is simply stated: "The Daggy Program has as its mission to promote a greater understanding of the life and writings of Thomas Merton, and to help Daggy scholars to gain spiritual insight into Merton's journey and their own. Daggy scholarships enable young people (ages 14-29) to participate in an International Thomas Merton Society Conference, thereby inspiring the next generation of Merton readers and scholars." These scholarships honor the late Robert E. Daggy, director of the Thomas Merton Center at Bellarmine University for twenty-one years, and founding member and second president of the ITMS. The scholarships cover the cost of a General Meeting and subscription to the *Seasonal* along with the invitation to make retreat at the Abbey of Gethsemani the following year with scholars and members of the Society .

The first Daggy scholars were introduced at the Fifth General Meeting of the ITMS in Mobile, Alabama (1997) by Dr. Monica Weis, SSJ. I have had the privilege of working with the Program since 1998. From the beginning year onward Daggy Scholars have come from far and wide—from the U. S., Canada, Great Britain, Europe, China, and we expect candidates from Australia for the upcoming General Meeting honoring Merton's one hundredth birthday. We have had well over a hundred Daggy Scholars by now with the hope of many more for the celebration year.

With echoes of the event at Smith College our membership has been amazed and delighted at how our Daggy Scholars "have shared and truly understand" Merton's work. From that first introduction of Daggy Scholars at Mobile in 1997 these students have both participated and presented in the Meetings where they often take on the role of worship leaders and session moderators. Many continue to research, write and present papers in many other venues as well. The Daggy program has become an ongoing rich resource for the ITMS yielding a continuing stream of new and youthful members who now permeate the general membership. There is a growing presence of the former Daggy Scholars on the Board of Trustees and in special committees of the Board.

One very moving part of the work of our Daggy Scholars Committee (a Committee of the ITMS Board) is to read the applications from students who wish to attend a Meeting. These candidates share very personal stories along with their hopes and dreams. One young woman wrote: "Merton opened a door for me that I never knew existed in my life before. The teaching of *Le Point Vierge* has profoundly affected the way in which I view myself and others in recognizing the sacred indwelling presence of God in every human being. My spirituality has been transformed by this concept and has allowed me to see my greater connection to all of human kind and the responsibility that I have to it." Another applicant living at the St. Jude Catholic Worker in Champaign, Illinois for four years wrote: "It was there that I began to deepen my love for Thomas Merton. My own informal study, combined with the works of mercy became for me an integrated way of life. Merton is my spiritual rock and I often turn to his books in times of stress. He was also the main influence on my joining the Catholic Church, which I did on December 10, 2005—the exact date 65 years ago that Merton joined the Trappists, and the exact date 38 years ago that he died. This conference would enable me to deepen my relationship to Merton and his thought." One of our Chinese students encouraged by Dr. Cyrus Lee wrote: "I was totally moved by what Thomas Merton did in the last decade of his life when he went directly to Asia and received the rich hidden potential of ancient Eastern traditions. . . . Merton had an abiding love with Asia and the universe. The more I got to know him the more I was taken by this man. . . . And I am so thrilled to become closer to him just like sunshine getting through fingers. Being a young Chinese girl, the ITMS conference is a golden opportunity to get closer to Merton, his inner heart, his deep mind, his wise soul, to continually learn more from him and the people who will be at the conference. My heart is ready for it, my mind is ready for it, and my soul is ready for it."

The success of our Daggy Program comes from the solid support of the Board, the work of professors such as Dr. Christine Bochen from Nazareth College and Dr. Kathleen Deignan, CND, from Iona College, who have consistently directed students to the Program. The unfailing vigilance and encouragement of Dr. Paul Pearson and the Thomas Merton Center has provided the stability needed for the Program. The hospitality and direction offered by the Trappist Community at Gethsemani, especially Br. Paul Quenon along with Fr. James Conner and Br. Patrick Hart, all of whom have directed and mentored students through the years, has provided a rich experience for students. At the General Meetings the Gethsemani monks who are present, along with Abbot John Eudes Bamberger from the Abbey of the Genesee, have been generous with their time, sharing stories and offering support to the students. Other support and direction, especially for the retreats, has come from Jonathan Montaldo, Dr. Lynn Szabo and Erlinda Paguio. Thanks are due to so many in the Society, too many to name. I have been fortunate to co-chair the Committee, earlier with Cristóbal Serrán-Pagán y Fuentes from Valdosta University (one of the first Daggy Scholars), and now with Jamie Fazio, Catholic Campus Minister from Nazareth College. Cristobal and Jamie have connected with students and brought their own love of Merton and their rich campus experience to the students and the Committee. Thanks, too, to my husband, Jim, who has been a steady companion, offering support and guidance to Daggy Scholars along the way in both Meetings and retreats. Finally, the interest, friendship and financial support of the ITMS members has brought us to the heart of our Daggy Scholars Program's success.

Our Society is truly distinguished and almost unique among such organizations by its wholehearted support and integrative approach to ensure future generations of members and scholars dedicated to Merton's life and legacy. It is not a stretch to imagine that Merton walks along the path with all of us offering hope for the future. It has been an honor to share in that work.

Thomas Merton: Wild Bird

Ron Dart

> Elias becomes his own wild bird, with God in the center,
> His own wide field which nobody owns,
> His own pattern, surrounding the Spirit
> By which he is himself surrounded:
>
> For the free man's road has neither beginning nor end.
>
> "Elias—Variations on a Theme," *The Strange Islands*
>
> *Non omnis moriar* (I shall not altogether die).
>
> Stephen Leacock, *"Three Score and Ten," My Remarkable Uncle*

I was, initially, drawn to the life and writings of Thomas Merton in the 1970s when I was given a copy of *The Seven Story Mountain*. I was less taken, at the time, by some of the reactionary content than by the energy, momentum and, obvious, honest searching spirit of the dramatic journey. I had grown weary at the time of a form of philosophy that was hyper-rationalist and left me dry as Ezekiel's parched bones. I found in Merton's search a kindred spirit, a pilgrim that reached out his hands, like Virgil, to the furthest shore. There was in Merton a questing and passionate soul who pointed to places I faintly saw yet longed to see in a fuller way.

I was so smitten by Merton that, when I did a Master's Degree in Christian Studies at Regent College (Vancouver, British Columbia), I wrote fifteen essays on Merton. It was Merton's turn to contemplative theology that held me. I had studied Biblical, historic and systematic theology, but the more meditative and contemplative approach that the Christian mystics heralded and held high was something that charmed and won me. Merton was, in many ways, my portal and guide into the fullness of the Christian contemplative tradition—I simply followed his many leads, pointers and time tried cairns.

My journey into the contemplative tradition of classical and modern Christian mystics meant a pilgrimage, also, into the deeper life of the church. The more I immersed myself in the life of *Corpus Christi*, the more I realized the challenges and struggles of being critical yet faithful to the historic, spiritual, material, and formal body of Christ. Again, it was Merton who lived such a prophetic tension: faithful yet critical, critical yet faithful—no caged bird—wild yet hovering like a windhover over the "wide field which nobody owns." Merton knew what it was like to be opposed, silenced and even branded a heretic of sorts, and yet the faithful critic remained ever faithful—surely the anvil and spiritual discipline he internalized made him the spiritual mentor he became—the task of living into Divine Love meant much burning of egoistic dross and chaff. It was by remaining critical yet loyal that Merton towers above many others— many are critical yet not loyal—others loyal yet not critical. Merton lived the tension and such was his genius—much like Erasmus many a century before him (*Erasmus and Merton: Soul Friends*, 2006).

It is virtually impossible to live in the contemporary world without seeing and living into the multiple injustices that wreak havoc in our global village. Merton dared as a monk (and many questioned him for doing so) to face and speak to most of the significant issues of his time: civil rights, 1st Nations, ecological concerns, war and peace, wealth and poverty, the madness of nuclear war, American imperialism. It was the way that Merton deftly and wisely threaded together the contemplative, ecclesial and public that held me—here was an integrated and holistic vision that was worth living into. This does not mean that Merton read all the signs of the times the best or deepest. Merton's read of the Canadian political election of 1963 was seriously flawed ("Thomas Merton, Leslie Dewart, George Grant and the 1963 Federal Election in Canada," *The Merton Seasonal*, Winter 2007), but Merton's public commitment was there and such was the drawing point. Merton did not want to be a guilty bystander, and he certainly wanted to face into Hannah Arendt's notion of the "banality of evil." Again, I saw in Merton a modern Elias, a modern Erasmus, enveloped and surrounded by the Spirit.

I had grown up on the lore and legend of the American Beats: Rexroth, Kerouac, Snyder, Ferlinghetti, Corman, Ginsberg (I have a fine letter from Ginsberg in which he discusses Merton and Snyder), Whalen, and William Everson (a good essay is yet to be written on Merton and Everson). Many of these writers/activists turned to the Orient in their contemplative journeys—others attempted to synthesize the best and wisest insights of the Western and Eastern contemplative traditions. Again, it was the wild bird, Elias in the flesh, Merton, who corresponded and interacted, in various forms and formats, with the Beats. My interest in Merton and Beats (and the fact I live in the North Cascades where many of the Beats lived in the mid-1950s) meant I could not miss the opportunity of scribbling out a missive on these contemplative poets. Ross Labrie (one of the finest Merton literary scholars) and Jim Forest (friend of Merton's and a dear friend of mine) wrote "Forewords" to my book, *Thomas Merton and the Beats of the North Cascades* (2008). I had asked Arnold Shives (one of the best mountain painters of British Columbia) if he would do a painting on Thomas Merton for the book, and he graciously replied with both a painting and many Zen-like lookout sketches. The impressionistic painting of Merton graced the Merton Room at Vancouver School of Theology for many a year and the photographed version is on the front cover of the book on Merton and the Beats.

The fact Jim Forest and I have a correspondence that goes back to the 1980s, and Jim had not lectured in Vancouver on Merton meant I suggested to the Thomas Merton Society Canada (TMSC) that we bring Jim to Vancouver in 2004 to celebrate and reflect on the infamous 1964 retreat (a 40th year celebration) that Merton had led with such worthies as A. J. Muste, J. H. Yoder, Daniel/Philip Berrigan, John Nelson, Tom Cornell, W .H. Ferry, Tony Walsh, and Jim Forest at the 1964 retreat—many wild birds at the monastery. Jim joined the TMSC in February 2014, gave two lectures ("Merton, Nouwen and Icons" and "The Spiritual Roots of Protest"). His lecture, "The Spiritual Roots of Protest" was published as the first in the Thomas Merton Society of Canada's monograph series in 2004.

My interest in Thomas Merton was substantively enhanced and enriched in the 1980s when I was on staff with Amnesty International. When Michael Mott's *The Seven Mountains of Thomas Merton* left the press in 1984, Michael and I began a correspondence (he was a volunteer with Amnesty at the time) that has continued to this day (many are the letters that accumulate over 30 plus years). Many of the letters between Michael and I ponder the ongoing relevance of Merton.

I mentioned above that I was on staff with Amnesty International in the 1980s-early 1990s. Amnesty had published a report on Nicaragua-Sandinistas-Miskito Indians in the early 1990s and I had to meet with Ernesto Cardenal (who was Minister of Culture with the Sandinistas) to discuss the report. Cardenal had been a novice with Merton at Gethsemani from 1957-1959. Merton had suggested that Cardenal leave the monastery and return to Nicaragua and work with the Sandinistas to bring about a more just and peaceful country—Cardenal did so, and carried Merton's vision of peacemaking to his people. I sat with Cardenal for about an hour going over the Amnesty report. I listened to his justification for the position of the Sandinistas. I then, meeting over, asked him about Thomas Merton. It was almost impossible to get Cardenal to stop talking about Merton—image and metaphor tumbled over one another in praise of his mentor. When we parted, he gave me a signed copy of his recent book of poetry, *The Music of the Spheres*—such a meeting, such a gift—another Elias, another wild bird that had flown from Merton's high perched nest.

I have a certain fondness for celebration/commemoration dates, so in the autumn of 2008 (40 years after Merton's final retreat at Eagle River in Alaska), Angus Stuart and I did a three day drive from Lower Mainland British Columbia to Eagle River. We were warmly greeted by the Orthodox community in Eagle River which was once, in more primitive days, the convent where Merton led his final full week retreat. Angus and I were given the Merton Room in the Cathedral and spent an evening giving talks on Merton, Vladimir Lossky and Orthodoxy—all sorts of wild birds in the place with quite a history ("In the Footsteps of Thomas Merton: Alaska," *The Merton Seasonal*, Winter 2008).

Doug Beardsley (one of our finest Canadian poets and yet another Mertonian northern light) and I, in the autumn of 2013, made a visit to Charles Brandt (the ecological hermit) on Vancouver Island. Brandt thought, in the 1950s-1960s, of becoming a monk at Gethsemani, but Merton warned him against doing so. There is lovely correspondence between Brandt and Merton, and when Doug and I visited Charles, we taped a two-hour interview with him on his journey and the impact of Merton on his life. Charles is now in his 90s, but his memory is sharp when it comes to Merton—he has even bound (being a bookbinder) many of Merton's first editions—quite a sight to see—indeed, it was like being with an aging Elias.

Non omnis moriar (I shall not altogether die). Merton was born in 1915 and died in 1968, and he has not altogether died. The life of Merton continues to live in all the Elias like wild birds that bear his plumage, wild birds in which God is their center—such wild birds soar above the wide field and they see roads that have neither a beginning nor end.

Thomas Merton, Lifelong Inspiration

Robert Waldron

For five decades of my life, Thomas Merton has been my companion. He was with me in high school and college during the 1960s, and in every subsequent decade, and he is still with me, this year of 2014, on the threshold of Merton's birthday centenary.

I read Thomas Merton's *The Seven Storey Mountain* when I was a junior in high school, our English teacher having assigned it for extra-curricular reading. I recall borrowing the book from my local library, and that night after my homework, I started reading it. I also recall that I read the book straight through, not turning in until the wee hours of the morning.

Now in my mid-sixties, I look upon my young self and wonder what it was about Merton that captivated me. I have concluded that I was drawn to Merton for two reasons. I got caught up in his search for God. Why this intrigued me is puzzling because I had then no problems with belief in God. The other attraction was Merton's finding God and deciding to offer himself to Him, more specifically "to disappear into God." The latter is what totally piqued my interest because I was a pious young man, considering a religious vocation, desiring also to disappear into God. As with so many Catholics raised in pre-Vatican II Catholic culture, I believed that a religious vocation was the apex of life, superior to any other, for it was a heroic life and most pleasing to God, and as a young man my primary goal in life was to please God.

I recently finished writing my memoir, and I was surprised that in every chapter I write about Merton and his influence on my life. To explain this abiding influence, I must take a brief jaunt down memory lane, all beginning with Merton's autobiography, the first work of his I had ever read, the first of many of his books that I would read and study and write about.

When Merton published *Seeds of Contemplation* and later *New Seeds of Contemplation,* few Catholics, and people in general, knew the meaning of contemplation. I shall never forget the impact of Merton's definition in the opening page of *New Seeds of Contemplation,*

> Contemplation is the highest expression of man's intellectual and spiritual life. It is that life itself, fully awake, fully active, fully aware that it is alive. It is spiritual wonder. It is spontaneous awe at the sacredness of life, of being (*New Seeds of Contemplation*, 1).

I know of no book on spirituality that commences with such joy, so infectious that I felt filled with it, for it promised all that I sought in life: to be awake, to be aware, to be exquisitely alive, to be filled with wonder, and always to be awed by the sacredness of life. And how does one come into the presence of such gifts? Throughout *New Seeds of Contemplation*, Merton confidently announces that such grace is bestowed by and through contemplation.

Then the question arose: How does one contemplate? Merton offers no methodology. For such you have to go to others, but I was definitely hooked. Basically Merton proposed that there was indeed a higher kind of life possible, and he was emphatic about its being within the reach of everyone, not only cloistered monks and nuns but also ordinary people.

When I was in my twenties, I had searched within my own religion for ways of contemplation but found little literature to help me. Merton had an interest in the East, so I, too, turned toward the East. And I read writers like Alan Watts, Suzuki, Krishnamurti, Christmas Humphreys. I read about seekers who experienced *satori*, enlightenment attained by contemplating and solving a *koan*. I, too, wanted enlightenment but soon realized that what I really craved was a glimpse of divinity, and Zen Buddhism has no belief in God. I also realized that Merton's reaching out to the East was an act of solidarity. Catholics and non-Catholics alike yearned for transcendence, a state of being best described as spiritual even though it does not necessarily mean that one believes in God and the immortality of the soul.

Much of my reading of Merton during my twenties fell under the rubric of "finding myself." I experimented with a variety of masks (*personae*), but I invariably felt inauthentic because I intuitively knew I was not being myself. Who was I trying to be? Many of my friends and relatives would say I was trying to be Merton. They may have been right (my writing six books on Merton enforces this opinion). But to be candid, I never felt obsessed by Merton, and it is more likely that my interest fell under the category of hero worship.

An alternative to my hero worship is offered by Merton in *No Man Is an Island* (133). He writes that "Every man has a vocation to be someone: but he must understand clearly that in order to fulfill this vocation he can only be one person: himself."

This sentence, with its Emersonian brevity and wisdom, stopped me in my tracks. I had become a psychological contortionist, trying to be what my family, friends and church wanted me to be, but in attempting to fulfill their desires, I was untrue to myself. Thus, the too many masks I wore. And after years of studying Merton, I later realized that my hero and I shared this trait in common: Merton hid behind aliases and masks (Michael Mott counts over sixty aliases). Merton understood this dynamic, although he may not have acted on it:

> Your idea of me is fabricated with materials you have borrowed from other people and from yourself. What you think of me depends on what you think of yourself. Perhaps you create your idea of me out of material that you would like to eliminate from your own idea of yourself. Perhaps your idea of me is a reflection of what other people think of you. Or perhaps what you think of me is simply what you think I think of you (*No Man Is An Island*, 194).

I had not known when I wrote my Jungian study of Merton how much Jung Merton had read, but when the unexpurgated journals were published, I saw that he was indeed well versed in Jungian theory. The above passage illustrates Jung's concept of psychological projection. Thus, a person creates another in his own image, or he sees another as a reflection of one's ideal. After much pondering, I concluded that I was clearly involved in such a projection, not only with Merton but with others.

Thomas Merton's Message of Hope

In 1986, I suffered a personal crisis, one I could not handle alone. I was fortunate to find a Paulist priest who had just opened his Jungian practice. While with him, I experienced the most luminous dream of my life.

> Thomas Merton was seated upon a cliff overlooking the sea. I saw him clearly and decided to go to him, which meant climbing the treacherous cliff side. When I arrived, I sat on the ground looking at him as he gazed at the sea. Around him was a radiant white light. We silently sat for sometime until he finally averted his gaze to me and smiled. He said nothing, just smiled (from my diary).

My therapist and I spent an hour analyzing my dream. We decided that it was a positive one, although it seemingly had nothing to do with my brother's death but certainly with my spiritual seeking. In the dream, I looked up to Merton, as shown by my climbing to him far above me. Getting to him demanded extreme physical exertion, but after my climb, I was rewarded with Merton's presence, but I wanted more than presence. My therapist suggested that I wanted verbal affirmation. I suggested that a smile from Merton was perhaps better than words: He was pleased with me. When I asked my therapist *how* I could have pleased him, he said, "You climbed dangerous rocks to be in his presence, which is non-verbal affirmation of Merton, and Merton's smile was non-verbal affirmation of you." It was a simple explanation, and I accepted it (from my diary).

In the nineties, I still read Merton. I also attended retreats at the Trappists' St. Joseph's Abbey in Massachusetts. I love the abbey, for it is beautifully located, and the abbey itself is an architectural gem. And I had the good fortune to meet and become friendly with several of the monks. I was somewhat surprised that they did not wish to discuss Merton or his writing. I had the sense that they had not read much of his work. Except one. He and I got along famously. His favorite Merton book was *The Asian Journal*. I too love it, for Merton records in masterful prose his experience before the Polonnaruwa Buddhas. To my mind there is little in modern religious literature to match Merton's account.

> Looking at these figures I was suddenly, almost forcibly, jerked clean of the habitual, half-tied vision of things, and an inner clearness, clarity, as if exploding from the rocks themselves, became evident and obvious . . .. All problems are resolved and everything is clear, simply because what matters is clear . . . everything is emptiness and compassion (*The Asian Journal of Thomas Merton*, 233-235).

It has been many years since my therapist and I analyzed my Merton dream, but having recently reread Merton's *Asian Journal*, I now see its other significance. I had during my therapy known about Merton's experience before the Polonnaruwa Buddhas, one of them called the Seated Buddha, another the Standing Buddha of Ananda, with folded arms and smiling his sad smile. It occurred to me with blinding clarity that I had in my dream replaced the Buddhas with Merton himself; thus, the dream meant something quite different from what my therapist and I had thought: Merton had achieved Buddhahood. He had won enlightenment, and like the Buddha, there was no need to speak, a smile alone was eloquent homily. If he was a Buddha, I still remained a novice, still seeking, still hoping to find myself, still climbing rocks—even now.

We are now in the 21st century. Merton is still my companion. He has directed me to other writers. His comments on the fourteenth century mystic Julian of Norwich have now become for me sparkling stones, "The theology of Julian of Norwich is a theology of mercy, of joy, and of praise. Nowhere in all Christian literature are the dimensions of her Christian optimism excelled" (*Mystics and Zen Masters*, 142).

Lady Julian appeared in my life when I needed her, a mystic whose emphasis was not on sin but on forgiveness, not on fear and trembling but on love and joy. She is a realist, cognizant of the evil of the world, but she sees beyond it: into the very heart of God's agapetic love. I made it my business to learn more about her, for I felt that God himself had sent her to me through Thomas Merton. I also promised myself that one day I would visit her anchorage in Norwich, England.

I was again delighted to find more praise of Lady Julian from Merton.

Julian is without doubt one of the most wonderful of all Christian voices. She gets greater and greater in my eyes as I grow older and whereas in the old days I used to be crazy about St. John of the Cross,

I would not exchange him now for Julian if you gave me the world and the Indies and all of the Spanish mystics rolled into one bundle (*Seeds of Destruction*, 274-75).

And when I finally visited Norwich and sat in Julian's anchorage, I experienced the greatest peace I had ever known. I prayed by mention of their names all those I had loved and had gone on, I prayed for my living loves, and I prayed for the world and for every troubled place on our planet. And after my prayers, I realized that it was Thomas Merton who had brought me here. If Lady Julian had not received his seal of approval, I would not have read her *Revelations of Divine Love*. I would not have read everything I could find about her and her time. And I held onto her words, tightly as I would hold onto a sacred relic, "All shall be well/All manner of things shall be well."

Inspired by two writers of the spiritual life, a woman of the fourteenth century, a man of the twentieth century, I remain forever in their debt.

Thomas Merton, cast bronze by David Kocka.
In the collections of the Thomas Merton Center, Bellarmine University,
and the Pitts Theology Library, Emory University.

From Canigou To The Seven Storey Mountain To Kanchenjunga To The Other Side Of The Mountain: Tilting The Mirror—A Reflection On Thomas Merton And His Mother

Sheila M. Milton

> Oh! since I was a baby in the Pyrenees, when old St. Martin marked me for the cloister from high Canigou.
>
> Thomas Merton, *"On the anniversary of My Baptism"*

> It seems to me there is no more fascinating subject in the world than the influence of surroundings on human character.
>
> Ruth Merton, 1911

It is generally acknowledged that during his last decade of life Merton wrote his finest works as a monk, living a rigorously disciplined life of prayer and contemplation, and as a scholar of Eastern religions. The prose poem, "Hagia Sophia" (1960) and *Raids on the Unspeakable* (1966) spring from the maturity and erudition he achieved during this period, and from the faith and peace he experienced in the hidden love of God.

Much earlier, he had described poetry as the flowering of ordinary possibilities. It seems to me that experiencing the ordinary possibilities of life as a monk and writer allowed him to blossom himself, to resolve his earlier struggles with his identity, and to achieve a sense of fulfillment in his journey to Asia (for instance, his claim that he had found what he was looking for in his experience in Polunnaruwa, Ceylon). My focus in this reflection concerns another aspect of the mature Merton, namely a profound change in his perception of his mother, Ruth Calvert Jenkins Merton that occurred in 1961.

Owen Heathcote Merton and Ruth, his wife of less than a year, became parents when Merton was born in Prades, France, which is situated at the foothills of the Pyrenees Mountains, Mount Canigou. Ruth insisted that her son be named Tom, when his birth was registered, and I think she would have been amused at the many names baby Tom would later assume. Michael Mott, writing in his official biography of Merton (*The Seven Mountains of Thomas Merton*, 7) records Ruth's declaration that "Tom is one thing, Thomas quite another." A long time later, Merton would agree with his Mother.

Mott's first sentence in the opening lines in Part One of the biography indicates how important Aunt Kit's visit was for Merton. Mott writes, "In November 1961, Thomas Merton had an unexpected visit from one of his few surviving relatives. He and Aunt Kit (his great-aunt Agnes Merton) drank strong tea together in the gate house at the monastery and discussed the family history, and their last meeting . . . when Tom had been four." Aunt Kit's visit is a pivotal one because Aunt Kit talks about Ruth, while discussing the family history with Merton, and in doing so she illustrates some discrepancies between Merton's long recollected childhood memories and the actual events. Merton's remarkable journal entries for November 4 and 5, read "Whatever asceticism I have in me seems to have to do with her [Ruth] and my problems about asceticism are inseparable from my problems about her" (*Turning Toward the World*, 176-178). This illuminating journal entry reveals a new awareness of his mother as he gives her credit for the source of his vocation. Merton also writes about his mother's strong pacifism and her deep understanding of poverty. In the same journal entry he confirms a memory, "I remember Mother as strict, stoical and determined," but follows it with his new understanding of his mother, "Mother's integrity, directness, sincerity."

It is fortunate for us that Merton reveals his innermost thoughts regarding his mother in his private journal Ruth had also kept journals from an early age so it was not surprising that her son would also keep journals, or that she would keep one for each of her sons, for Tom and later for John Paul. These journals are in the possession of the indirect line of the Jenkins family; I held them in my hands and read from both of these journals when I visited Pat Priest in 1994, the daughter of Elsie Hauk Holohan, nurse to Bonnemaman, Merton's maternal grandmother, Martha (Mattie) Caroline Baldwin Jenkins. Ruth's brother, Harold Jenkins, married Elsie after Bonnemaman died. And thus Pat Priest inherited Ruth's paintings, papers, manuscripts, and many of Merton's earliest writings. A list of the contents of this uniquely valuable collection can be found in my "Some of the Treasures of a Sunday Afternoon" (*The Merton Seasonal*, Winter, 1994). That piece also explains how a series of errors made by Michael Mott in his biography (*The Seven Mountains of Thomas Merton*, 1984), alienated the Priest family and contributed to their collection's being inaccessible to Merton scholars to the present time.

Ironically, Merton is partly responsible for the rift that has now become a chasm between him and the Jenkins heirs. I was astonished by the hurt feelings that bordered on antagonism toward anything to do with Merton when I talked with Pat Priest and her son Paul on a visit to them in 1994.. I was the first person and now to my dismay the last person to speak to them following Michael Mott's interview with them for his biography. They were so angry with Mott for the mistakes he made regarding the family in the biography of Merton. Those mistakes only added to their earlier grievances regarding the poor representation of the Jenkins family by Merton in *The Seven Storey Mountain*. Pat Priest told me that Merton had explained to Elsie and Nanny Hauck, when they came for his ordination, that the reason he had portrayed the Jenkins family in such a poor light was in order to sell more books, because the Abbey of Gethsemani was hard up for money. Mott, however, claims otherwise, writing, "As far as Merton was concerned, certain people in Douglaston, Queens, were ripe for [his] revenge" (Mott, 252).

While Merton himself was responsible for some of the negative evaluations, Bob Giroux, the editor of the autobiography, also contributed with his editorial cuts.

Michael Mott writes that "...editorial cuts make Ruth more of an enigma, remote, and cold than she is in the original copy of *The Seven Storey Mountain*" (Mott, 9). Here are some lines that lie sleeping in the library of Boston College that would have provided a more balanced view of Ruth:

> But she [Ruth] had taste. She painted landscapes too. She designed houses. She designed all sorts of houses we might one day have lived in, in Prades, if there had not been so much of a war. She decorated the apartment where I was born, or maybe it was a house. Later, she wrote articles for those magazines about how to be a scientific housewife, and how to bring up children according to all the latest methods in 1915. Also, she danced. I don't mean, by that, that she would go to a dance and dance the waltz, the way they used to in those days: she danced those dances people do on the stage, with pirouettes and so on.

Ruth was an articulate, musically inclined, happy young woman when she attended Bradford College in Haverhill, Massachusetts. Ruth kept a journal, wrote articles and a poem, "The Bradford Alphabet," published in the *Bradford Annals* that provides a characterization of her: "J stands for Jenkins, the graceful sprite,/who dances in the parlor every night." Ruth graduated with distinction from Bradford College in 1909.

Ruth wrote a journal for Tom and she took extracts from it when she created "Tom's Book" (it was a gift for her mother-in-law Gertrude Grierson) which covers the period from the time of his birth, January 31, 1915 until he is two years old and the family is living in America. The photos of the family during that period also refute the negatives about Ruth as a mother during Tom's first two years of life and show, too, that Ruth and Owen were happily married at that time and as a couple they were full of the hope and the promise for their dreams to come true.

Tom's low birth weight, his having been born at home with no special assistance that we know of, points to his survival as a result of Ruth's diligent care. He would have needed to be nursed more frequently and kept warm, having been born in a snowstorm in winter. Throughout "Tom's Book" there is plenty of evidence that Tom not only thrived and was a happy child, but that he showed an early intelligence that seems to prove that Ruth was a responsible and conscientious mother. Ruth and Owen proudly reveled in Tom their first child and in being a family of three. Later would come a different story that would end in sadness and loss that caused Merton pain and many problems.

Tom was a small child when his mother died and he was unable to fathom the reason for her leaving him. The sense of stability that Ruth provided for Tom was lost and I think that by his mother dying Tom believed that she had abandoned him. However, young Tom seems to exhibit an extraordinary resiliency of spirit despite the problems that occurred during the following years. Owen insisted that Tom accompany him on his restless peregrinations in search for a home and a place to paint. I believe that the reason Owen took Tom with him may have been to reassure and comfort his own self as he grieved for Ruth. John Paul, Merton's younger brother, continued to live with their grandparents in Douglaston and did so until he left for college.

Tom never mentions the problems he encounters on Bermuda when he writes his autobiography. We have the Scott family to thank for providing a record of his visit with them. Owen took Tom to Bermuda, not long after Ruth had died (1922), and Tom stayed in a boarding house the other side of the island away from the Scott family.

Eventually, Owen brought him to stay with the Scotts, that is, with Owen's friend Cyril Kay Scott, his wife Evelyn (also Owen's lover), and their son Creighton. It was an odd *ménage à trois* and Evelyn was the likely reason for Owen's visit to Bermuda. Owen gives over his responsibility of disciplining Tom entirely to Evelyn as he had done so with Ruth. Tom took an instant dislike to Evelyn. He probably saw her as a successor for his recently deceased mother, while Owen, at that time, seems unaware of how much Tom hated Evelyn. Tom had good reasons to hate Evelyn as she dealt him harsh punishments that most likely occurred when Owen left him in her care to visit New York to set up a show of his paintings. In a review of Arthur Callard's *The Enigmas of Evelyn Scott* for *The Merton Seasonal* (Summer 1986, 13), Mary Jo Weaver writes, "It strains the imagination what the effects of her [Evelyn] punishments on the young Tom were. The boy was still mourning his recently deceased mother, and Evelyn punished Tom for crying for her."

Merton in his biography and in his private journals, where he confides so much, never, ever mentions Evelyn Scott. However, we now understand why Merton would write of the "poisons" of Bermuda in the original copy of his autobiography, ". . . that beautiful island fed me with more poisons than I have mind to stop and count" (*SSMB*, 36). The omission of any mention of Evelyn speaks volumes. Bermuda was obviously a place he never forgot because he includes it in his list of important places where he had lived in the conclusion of his autobiography: ". . . My mercy which has created you for this end and brought you from Prades to Bermuda to St. Antonin . . ." (422-23). Merton places Bermuda directly after his place of birth to indicate how important it was.

Many years later an indication of Merton's maturity is shown in the journal entry, "The need for ripeness—for the slow finishing of the work of God in me" (*A Search for Solitude*, 203). That ripeness, the slow finishing work of God in his life, was realized in his last years at Gethsemani that included the healing, pivotal visit of his Aunt Kit.

Merton's private journals and his books map his journey to maturity, to wholeness and holiness as a monk and as a writer. At the official opening of the Merton Collection at Bellarmine College's Library (November 10, 1963), Merton had written words for the occasion: "Whatever I may have written . . . I think it can all be reduced in the end to this one root truth: that God calls human persons to union with Himself and with one another in Christ, in the church which is His Mystical body" (Mott, 291). This root truth underlies Merton's devotion to his vocation, his vocation fully accomplished during his longed for trip to Asia, his final journey. Merton had traveled from Canigou to the Knobs of Kentucky to Kanchenjunga and to the other side of the mountain, "the only side worth seeing." In Calcutta, India, days before he dies Merton proclaims in his prayer: "Love has overcome. Love is victorious. Amen." (*The Asian Journal of Thomas Merton*, 319).

A Marvelous Subject For A Biography

Michael Mott

Ten years after his death, the publishers Houghton Mifflin and the Merton Legacy Trust approached me, asking if I would write Merton's biography. Houghton Mifflin had published a novel of mine. One of the editors, Robie Macauley, knew me, knew my work, and remembered that my background and early years were not unlike Merton's. Merton's mother was an American painter, mine an American sculptor. I had known English and American schools; Merton, French, English and American schools. He had flunked out of Cambridge University. I had flunked out of Oxford. And so on.

It was agreed that I should begin from the beginning, not finish what someone else, John Howard Griffin, had started. And the Merton Trustees agreed to give me a letter, saying that, when I presented the final draft of my biography, I could be questioned on matters of fact, but not on my interpretation of those facts. I didn't want the book to be a committee book. I was to take two years, so my contract said. It took well over five years. For four I was also teaching full time. One year I was on a Guggenheim Fellowship. There is no question that I had a few misgivings in 1978, misgivings about myself (biography was new to me) and misgivings about my subject.

When I met the chief trustee of the Merton Legacy Trust, Naomi Burton Stone, we talked and looked at the sea from her garden near York Harbor, Maine. As we turned back to the house, Naomi said in her very definite manner, "Well, Thank God, you're not a worshiper!" Thirty-seven years after that day, I can answer, "No, I'm not a worshiper." Merton can still amaze me. And I have a very strong, hard-earned affection for a man I never met.

The first thing I did on the day that I received the initial letter of inquiry from the publishers and before I went up to Maine to meet Naomi was to look up Thomas Merton in the *Encyclopaedia Britannica*. I have a use-and-abuse relationship with the *Encyclopaedia Britannica*, but it answers one question clearly and at once: what importance do the *Encyclopaedia's* middle-brow editors allow a subject, how many lines do they give it? Volume 12 of the *Macropaedia* gave two references to Merton's name and stated incorrectly, "Of significance is the fact that Thomas Merton was killed in an accident while in Bangkok to visit the Dalai Lama (leader of the Tibetan Buddhists)." And then, in the virtually full column given to a Bibliography on Monasticism, not one of Merton's books is listed (this was the 1975 edition of the *Encyclopaedia*). In the spring of 1978 I wondered why the publishers wanted the full life of a man who rated less than two lines, plus a reference, in the *Encyclopaidia Britannica*. Fortunately, I had better news of Thomas Merton.

Two friends, one an orthodox Jew, the second seemingly without a strong religious faith, told me how much reading Merton had meant to them. The second had had a mental breakdown and he had been institutionalized. He said that reading Merton saved his mind. When my editor claimed, then and later, that my biography would probably be bought and read only by Catholics, I knew he was wrong.

I agreed to write the book. I started by writing down questions as they came into my head, my own approach to a man I had never met—was now prevented from meeting. The questions (with spaces for answers) took up the whole of one legal pad, then another. Here are a few of the questions, with a brief version of the answers I discovered:

Did he smoke? Yes, before he entered Gethsemani.

Did he drive a car? No, and attempts to teach him were near disasters.

Was he a womanizer? Three of those who knew Merton at Columbia University said "No." A fourth, Ed Rice, said "Yes." The journals of the period are curiously lacking in specifics for a young man about town with independent means. It can safely be said he was no young James Boswell at any rate.

How did he speak? Did he have an English accent? Merton was at pains to shed his English accent on reaching Columbia. But it depended to whom he was speaking, then and later. On the tapes made of Father Louis teaching his classes at the monastery there is hardly a trace of an English accent. But English visitors to the monastery tell a different story.

Was he a dancer? Yes. His partner on many occasions during the New York years, Jinny Burton, told me that he was almost as good as professional dancers (and he and Jinny were exchanging partners with professional dancers at the New York World's Fair). Only a certain self-consciousness got in his way.

Did he make hand gestures? Grimace? Use joke facial expressions? All of the above. I have photographs of Merton in the club car on the way to parties in Virginia in the summer of 1940. He is making funny faces at the photographer, Jinny Burton.

Did he drink? Hmmm. I found a line in Merton's journal for 1939 in which he talks about how impressed his friends from Columbia were by the amount of drink flowing at the parties in Virginia. Merton's greatest friend at Columbia, Bob Lax, told me they were all impressed. When I asked Jinny Burton about this, she commented that she really didn't know. But however late the party ran, "We always had a full glass of bourbon waiting by the bedside when someone woke up."

What was his walk like? Purposeful. Bob Lax gave me a perfect description. And I must say here that my own friendship with Merton's lifelong friend, Bob Lax, brought me as close to knowing Merton himself as I was very likely to get.

Did he like to travel? Passionately.

And so on, page after page. Anything worth doing begins, and frequently ends, in a question.

In the spring of 1978 I read a book I had put off reading for thirty years. Even at school in England I had heard about *Elected Silence*, the version of *The Seven Storey Mountain* Evelyn Waugh had edited for English readers. Friends had recommended it, but having just read a conversion story called *I Believed*, I was not going to risk another one. Later in America, when I was in a bookshop, I shied away from the quite horrendous cover of the paperback edition of *The Seven Storey Mountain*.

In the summer of 1967 I went to stay with painter friends in San Patricio, New Mexico. A friend of theirs offered his whole house for me to write in during the day. I was in the middle of a book about the Albigensian and Children's Crusades. I had taken the latest edition of *The Hudson Review* (20, no. 2, (Summer, 1967): 211-218) to New Mexico because there was an article on the Manichees or the Cathars. I took breaks from my writing and weeded my host's garden as a gesture of gratitude. Sometimes I would sit on a low wall in the shade of the cottonwood trees, listen to the sound of the wind pump and read. I can remember nothing about the article I already mentioned. I can quote passages from the next article, "Day of a Stranger" by Thomas Merton. From this enthusiasm, I went on to read many of the articles and books Merton published in the 1960s. It was hard to keep up with him. I still avoided the autobiography.

When I did get to *The Seven Storey Mountain*, I had already said yes, I would write the biography. Apart from those idyllic pages, father and son in the Midi in France, it is still not a book I enjoy. I read it perhaps four or five times then. It is one of five or six Merton books I feel I never have to read again. At the time I felt compensated when I thought to myself, "Well, Merton's taken care of the first half of his life. I only have to write the second half." (The publishers were already breathing on me!)

I had yet to learn that biography and autobiography are two very different genres. I was discovering things the autobiographer never knew. For just one example, there was the fact that doctors suspected tuberculosis during Merton's childhood. This caused Owen Merton to change his plans, and must have colored the time father and son spent together.

There is something else. And here I had very good luck just when I needed it. I was writer-in-residence at the College of William and Mary, floundering in my first year as a biographer. A graduate student said she was going through letters written in the 1920s for her own biography of Lola Ridge, a figure in the New York Bohemia of the time. There were letters from Owen Merton and letters mentioning him. I thought this marginal, but I read the letters. There were references to Tom that made Tom, at eight, sound older than Owen, and certainly a threat to the letter-writer. I had blundered into a drama in which this particular small boy played a considerable part!

Look for this in *The Seven Storey Mountain*. In the short "Bermuda" section, there is nothing. Tom plays hooky from school, wanders the rocky coast alone (he was not alone) and risks, at worst, overhearing the bad language of the older guests at the boarding house. There is nothing about the *ménage à trois* Tom's beloved father had entered into after his own wife's death, nor of the woman who had nominal care of Tom, saw him as a threat to her own happiness, and had her dislike of him returned, undoubtedly playing a far greater part in forming Thomas Merton's lifetime dread of "bossy women" than poor Ruth Merton.

Is this another case of censorship in Merton's career? Absolutely. And I am absolutely sure it was Merton who did the cutting out, leaving a few hints in one of the drafts. Otherwise, nothing.

So now I realized that I should certainly have to begin at the beginning. And I had better keep my eye out for the self-censor, as well as the censor!

There was one problem I never did resolve. How do you write the biography of a contemplative? A very active contemplative, I grant you, but a contemplative? Do you put blank pages in the book? Lawrence Sterne might have gotten away with this. I doubt if I could have persuaded Houghton Mifflin, though I was grateful to the friend that suggested it.

Thus it is the activist I concentrated upon—not the man in the six hours of darkness before dawn on a cold March morning in the hermitage, Mount Carmel, praying, stirring a tin mug of coffee on the fire, reciting the Psalms, meditating over his reading, the sounds of the woods about him.

Let it be stated and understood: for every hour, every waking hour, of Merton's life that we know so much about through the journals, intimate journals, letters, books, there is another hour, a submerged hour, at least as important to Merton in those hours you and I know about.

I said I had misgivings in 1978 about myself and my subject. My misgivings about myself did not all miraculously disappear. My misgivings about my subject did. In 1984, with three typewritten drafts plus the final draft written on a word processor, each of the four well over a thousand pages, I should have said that Thomas Merton was a marvelous subject for a biography. I thank him for that, among other things. I have never been seriously tempted to write the life of anyone else. He spoiled me.

Owen and Ruth Merton. Copyright the Merton Legacy Trust and the Thomas Merton Center at Bellarmine University. Used with permission.

A Ground Of Love And Truth

Suzanne Zuercher, OSB

I met Thomas Merton when I was sixteen years old. Not in person; such was never my privilege. However, from that time on he became my deeply personal companion, and he continues to be until now, long after his death. Merton has been more than a mentor. A large, framed poster of him looks down as I write this. He has been part of many articles and books I've written over the sixty plus years of what I can only call our friendship.

He has spoken to me, unknown to him I would think, at every significant moment in my spiritual journey. I confess it does feel as though he actually hears questions that have arisen in my life, because in a way that seems almost like a conversation, he responds with answers to them, one after the other, in his published books.

It all began when I read *The Seven Storey Mountain* as a high school student in Chicago. The book was then a best seller, and I devoured every word, finally deciding I must do what Merton had done, as he had put it, ". . . give God everything." He was a Trappist; I must be a Trappistine. Little did I know how unsuited I was for such a vocation. In my ignorance, I began to make plans for entering that religious community after graduation. On Ascension Thursday, 1949, I was reading in preparation for a school seminar on prayer when suddenly I felt as though I had been struck on the head. I was definitely in a state of shock similar to what such a blow would have actually caused. I clearly knew in that moment that the Trappistines were not for me. Looking up at the clock, I noted it was 10:00 A.M. I remained with that shocked feeling for several days until, when my best friend asked me what I planned to do when I graduated, everything fell immediately, clearly and permanently into place. I turned to her and said, "I'm joining the Benedictines at St. Scholastica." Some years later I read in one of Merton's journals that he had been ordained that Ascension Day, and that 10:00 was the time the monks lined up for the procession into chapel. Somehow, I felt sure, he had reached out and saved me from what would have been a vocational mistake. Instead, I found my true path at this significant moment in his own journey.

I am not a suggestible person; in fact, I am something of a cynic when it comes to spiritual "experiences." Call it telepathy, or what you will, but this coincidence began a lifetime of Merton's companionship on my Way. Besides his presence at some of the usual issues around renewal and maturing spirituality, one special situation stands out. I became formation director for my community shortly after Vatican II, and in that capacity had to create contemporary guidelines for new members. I turned to *Contemplation in a World of Action* where I had remembered Merton's thoughts on applicants in today's society and the response they needed. One morning, in a matter of two hours, I wrote an entire program founded on his suggestions and based on quotations from the

Rule of St. Benedict, a program that in its essentials our community still follows.

As the co-director of The Institute for Spiritual Leadership, a training program for spiritual companions offered by Loyola University, Chicago, I continued to follow Merton's openness to growth and change and incorporated many of his developing ideas in my courses there. My interest in the Enneagram led me to write several books on the depth of that tool for self-awareness and the variety of spiritual pathways it describes for differing kinds of people. I decided to write about his spiritual outlook and issues, which happen to be my own, in the book *Merton, An Enneagram Profile* (1996). It was in doing this that I realized why Merton had "spoken" so clearly to me for so long. It also explained why three persons who had been close to Merton asked me how I knew what went on in his mind and heart, even though he had spoken about those things only to people close to him.

Ever since the journal *Learning to Love* was published, I have given talks on the significance of Merton's relationship with the young nurse Margie. His deep humanization, his sense of his being loveable and loved, his clarification of a call to monasticism and beyond community to a hermit life, seemed to me the final rounding out of his story. Sometimes we know who we are by realizing who we are not. I believe that is what Margie taught him. That is why I have written my most recent book, *The Ground of Love and Truth: Reflections on the Relationship of Thomas Merton with the Woman Known as "M,"* after many years of trying to find a way to express who I believed her to be in his life. I have finally done so by writing poems in his voice. They simply poured out of me as though he was doing the writing, so familiar did I feel with his content and style.

I am very aware that this contribution to a volume about Merton's influence is very personal. I have only spoken about how he has touched my own life and the lives of my students, readers and Sisters in community. He has done much more in the lives of many others, it goes without saying. And perhaps it is fine that it does go without saying, considering the people who will choose to read this book. The gifts Merton has given our world this past century are being discussed by so many people is an amazing summary of his lasting significance. All I can say is that I am but one example of an individual whose whole existence in this world has borne the stamp of his presence. I am but one example of the ripple effect his life on this earth has caused. There are countless others; no one will ever know how wide is the reach of his inspiration. Merton was a human being, first of all; and so many take heart, largely I believe from reading his journals and letters, as they walk their human pathway. I know I have. He was loved and hated, approved of and disapproved of, and through it all, ever true to himself. I can't think of a better way to describe sanctity.

On The Origins And Work
Of The Thomas Merton Legacy Trust

Anne Hutchens McCormick, Peggy Fox and Mary R. Somerville

In 1964, concerned about his literary legacy, Thomas Merton first spoke to his two most trusted literary advisors, Naomi Burton Stone, his former literary agent, and James Laughlin of New Directions Publishing, publisher of his poetry and a number of other works, about being his co-literary executors. Nothing was formalized until several years later when Merton decided that both a will and a legal instrument dealing with his literary legacy were now necessary. Local Louisville lawyer, John Ford, drew up these documents and on November 14, 1967, a Merton Legacy Trust agreement initiated by Thomas Merton was signed into agreement. It named Naomi Burton Stone, James Laughlin and Thomasine O'Callaghan, a close personal friend, the first three Trustees of his literary estate. The Trustees were given responsibility for the existing body of work and any future publication of his works, with the understanding that all income from these publications would belong to the Abbey of Gethsemani. Thirteen months later the work of the Trustees began in earnest following Merton's tragic, unexpected death on December 10, 1968.

When Naomi Burton Stone retired, she was succeeded by Robert Giroux; at James Laughlin's death, Anne McCormick, who had been acting as the Trust's Administrative Assistant, stepped into his position; and when Tommie O'Callaghan retired, she was succeeded by Mary Somerville. Peggy Fox had already replaced Robert Giroux shortly before his death.

The Trustees are responsible for approving contracts for new publications, including foreign editions, for overseeing many routine permissions for quotations, for keeping track of incoming funds from advance guarantees and royalties paid on published books, permissions fees and various other sources.

The Trustees also work to develop new places for distribution of Merton's work—trying to keep up with current times through the development of new media.

In the last past two years the Trust has:

- •worked with a new company, Now You Know Media, Inc., to disseminate the Merton recordings to a wider audience.
- •collaborated with publishers on audio book versions of Merton titles in anticipation of the Centenary.
- •enabled the rights for e-books on early Merton titles where old contracts did not provide them.
- •accepted musical settings of selections from Merton's poetry and other writings.

•authorized translations of Merton's works into Bulgarian, Chinese, Czech, German, Italian, Japanese, Korean, Lithuanian, and Russian.

•alerted publishers to renew and uphold copyrights of Merton materials.

•issued permission to quote from unpublished Merton material in books and scholarly articles, and helped a number of authors through the book publication process, including how to obtain rights to previously published Merton material.

•asked individual publishers, including their allies abroad, to help celebrate the Centenary with new editions, special publicity and enhanced visibility on their websites.

Bellarmine College (now University) in Louisville, Kentucky was named the official depository for Merton's manuscripts, tapes, drawings, photographs, letters, journals, holographic notebooks, and various personal artifacts in what is now the enormous, beautiful Merton Center.

Anne Hutchens McCormick

Naomi Burton Stone was the woman who pulled me into the Merton world when she invited me in 1975 to handle routine correspondence and permissions for the Merton Legacy Trust in the capacity of an Administrative Assistant. I was able to draw on my nearly 20 years in hardcover book publishing at Doubleday and later Alfred A. Knopf in New York and spent the next 22 years in that part-time capacity. Following James Laughlin's death in 1997, I was asked to be one of the three Trustees and joined Robert Giroux and Thomasine O'Callaghan in that role.

In 2015 I will have worked with the Merton Legacy Trust for 40 years, come to know and love Our Tom, through his works, as well as all the people connected to the Merton world, primarily through the International Thomas Merton Society and the Chapter group in New York. It is easy—but true—to say that Naomi's offer to be part of the Merton world changed my life in ways I could not have imagined and for which I am ever grateful.

Peggy Fox

I came to Thomas Merton through my work at New Directions Publishing, which began in 1975. One early task was organizing the filing for James Laughlin's work with the Merton Legacy Trust and through that I learned how seriously JL took his mandate to look after the literary legacy of his friend Tom. At that time New Directions was compiling Merton's *Collected Poems* and *Literary Essays* and continues to publish both new editions of earlier works (such as *New Seeds of Contemplation*) and new volumes such as *In the Dark before Dawn: The New Selected Poems of Thomas Merton* and even gift editions such as *On Christian Contemplation* and *On Eastern Meditation*. In addition to arranging for foreign editions of those works it published, New Directions also has acted as agent for the Trust in handling foreign editions of other Merton works.

Because of her intimate knowledge of the workings of the Trust and her tireless work for the Trust, Anne McCormick was appointed to immediately fill James Laughlin's seat upon his death in 1997; but before his death, James Laughlin expressed the hope that I would one day be appointed to the Trust which happened after the retirement of Robert Giroux. In my years at New Directions, as an editor, as vice-president and then president, I absorbed both the devotion of James Laughlin to Merton, the man and personal friend, and Laughlin's love of Merton's work, particularly his poetry, which is what drew Laughlin to Merton in the 1940s. I bring to the Trust over 35 years of publishing knowledge and the hands-on experience of editing Merton and keeping his work in print.

Mary R. Somerville

By lucky coincidence I met Tommie O'Callaghan shortly after moving to Louisville, Kentucky in 1998. Mrs. O'Callaghan generously shared her Merton books and files. When she decided to step down as Trustee, my name surfaced as a potential replacement. In September 2009, I was approved by Tommie, Anne McCormick, Peggy Fox, then-Trust attorney John Ford, and the Abbot of Gethsemani, Elias Dietz. I am grateful for Tommie's help and that of the entire Trust team, especially Anne McCormick, Peggy Fox and Paul Pearson. What a joy it is to connect daily with the international community of Merton writers, artists and scholars.

My past service as President of the American Library Association, the world's oldest and largest library association, as Director of the Miami-Dade (FL) Public Library System serving the nation's tenth largest public library population, and my 30 years' experience as a librarian and library administrator have given me a strong grounding in the world of books and media. My leadership in the global library arena, which has encompassed Russia, China, South Africa, and Brazil, has helped prepare me for the international aspects of Trust work. I love it all.

316

A Regular Guy Who Was Like An Older Brother

Tommie O'Callaghan

Dan Walsh introduced me to Thomas Merton. Dan had taught me at Manhattanville College in New York City. He had also taught Tom at Columbia and afterwards had become one of his good friends and mentors. So when Dan came to Louisville to teach part-time at Bellarmine College, at Gethsemani and Loretto, he thought his two former students should know one another. My husband Frank and my seven children would eventually host Tom at our Louisville home, usually for lunch, mostly whenever he came to town on a doctor's visit. We became "his Louisville family" and he insisted that my children should call him "Uncle Tom." I saw that he loved their attention and he loved being with them. He was always playful with them but he would also relate to them seriously, treating them almost like adults. They enjoyed his company. My oldest daughter, Kathie, was 11 years old and taking guitar lessons. One day, Tom asked her to show him what she had learned. Together, they retreated to the library where they composed the following song for the guitar:

> Old uncle Tom
> He lives in the woods
> Pining away
> Without adequate foods
>
> He is all alone
> And unconfirmed
> Thin as a bone
> And living on bacon.
>
> Old uncle Tom
> Thinking and thinking
> Lives in the woods
> Occasionally drinking
>
> But when I recall the truth to mind
> I figure he's drinking
> All the time.
>
> Poor old uncle Tom.

I was a good cook, so whenever he wanted to entertain special guests dropping in on him at Gethsemani, Tom would ask me to prepare and bring out a picnic lunch to the Abbey. Looking back today, I guess that I was in training to entertain and host Tom's many friends and students of his work in the decades that were to follow in my role as

WE ARE ALREADY ONE

a trustee of the Thomas Merton Legacy Trust, founded in 1967, a year before his accidental death in Bangkok.

When Tom asked me to be one of the three original trustees, the other two being his publisher James Laughlin and his literary agent, Naomi Burton Stone, I agreed to help him out, but had no idea of what would be required of me during my tenure that lasted from his death in 1968 until my retirement from the Trust in 2009. My first major act as a trustee was to drive our family station wagon out to Gethsemani, upon learning from Brother Patrick Hart that Merton had died. Brother Patrick had insisted that I come out immediately. Together we loaded Merton's file cabinets in his hermitage into my station wagon. I carried these documents, that included all of his personal journals, to my home and kept them there, although I put his private journals in a safety deposit box. In 1991, I transferred his files in my possession over to the Thomas Merton Studies Center at Bellarmine.

Through the years I've been asked to speak about my relationship with Tom at many events. I always offer the same observations. I found him to be a "regular guy." He was always unpretentious in my presence and never acted like a famous author with me, my friends or my family. He never tried to make an impression. He always spoke to people as equals. He was multi-faceted. He could speak with intellectuals in my presence at his picnics but was equally at home with plain folks and even children. He never gave me a reason to be in awe of him and I thought of him most of all as a friend, and even as if he were an older brother.

I retired from the Merton Legacy Trust after thirty years. I still marvel at how richer life had been for Frank and me ever since I agreed to Tom's request that I help watch over his publications, should something have happened. I'm grateful to Tom for giving me the opportunity to meet all the people I've come to know through him—many of them I count as good friends. I wish he were still alive at 100 and I could sneak up to Gethsemani's infirmary and share a word or two. Wherever he is now, I wish him happiness and peace.

Searching At The Margins

Maurizio Renzini

Thomas Merton realized the world was undergoing a profound transformation that raised new issues for human relationships. The rise in influence of Asian cultures was challenging the multi-century dominance of Western cultures in presenting ancient but heretofore unknown perspectives on human behavior and the possibilities for its evolution. The rise of new media and computer technologies was disturbing complicated geo-political relationships in the swift currents that propelled the processes of globalization. While on one side the world was entering an age of extraordinary possibilities for achieving and sharing knowledge, the diverse perspectives on human goals and achievement of desires increased conflicts based on real differences on both the macro level and the micro level of individual cultures. Merton witnessed with interest this evolution into more complicated and closer relationships between world cultures. This evolution required a delicate nuance of interpretation by those opinion makers who were analyzing the effects of a more complicated unity among diverse societies. For all the positive developments that accompany new media and technologies, this sudden paradigm shift away from "settled" and isolated perspectives of individual cultures instigated a spiritual crisis that challenged traditional societies. The digital age fostered new life-styles for all cultures that could easily devolve into a dangerous moral and anthropological drift.

Merton understood Christian faith as universal and capable of being operative through all the changes in humankind's technologies and societies. In 1967 he wrote to an Italian student who requested his advice: "[Faith] is not inexorably bound to any particular civilization or culture, and the creative power of the Spirit is without limits: hence [you should] be open to all that helps man to be more true to himself and to his vocation as a child of God in freedom" (*The Road of Joy*, 350). Merton did not believe that his Christian faith would be basically contradicted through dialogue with different religious traditions. He was a confirmed ecumenist who sought a unifying spiritual basis of communion among religious traditions since he believed that each religion contained seeds of truth and dimensions of God's complete revelation of reality to humankind.

Merton's sensitive approach to the study of other faith traditions and his correspondence with individuals who embodied these traditions was not simply diplomatic: he did not seek resolutions of diversity and differences that ignored actual conflicts in perspective. His interreligious dialogues aimed at both sides more understanding the hidden actions of the Divine Will and agreeing together where the new secular spirit of the world threatened the authentic freedoms of citizens of any culture. Merton hoped that inter-communication would reveal a common search among religionists and their parallel paths to understanding the reality of God. What was required was a communication in depth "beyond speech and beyond concepts" that always mark inter-cultural debates and confrontations (*The Asian Journal of Thomas Merton*, 308).

Inter-religious dialogue requires a common retrieval of the most essential messages of a faith understood in the cultural and societal context of each living tradition (*Contemplative Prayer*, 140). Monks in his view are privileged interpreters in this work of reunification because, living at the margins of their respective societies, they are more animated by a compassion that unites them with all people in the world.

We should ask ourselves today how Merton's "communion beyond words" can be a force in liberating persons from the "false selves" created by their common indoctrination into the narrow perspectives of individual societies which insure conflict with other societies who indoctrinate their citizens differently. It is clear that no one escapes an education in narrowness fostered by self-enclosed, ethnocentric cultures. And yet Merton's teaching is to transcend the boundaries between cultures by noticing that cultures always ignore "the basic irrelevance of the human condition" (*The Asian Journal*, 306). These acts of transcending boundaries require humility, a willingness to listen to others who appear alien to our experience and then to learn from the witness of their individual struggles to become more expansive human beings. In this way diversity becomes a resource to a more complicated, but much more authentic and actual, unity among all human beings. Our differences ultimately become irrelevant before the relevance of finding ourselves united as one people of God (*The Asian Journal*, 307).

Merton believed that, when we realize how marginalized we easily become, once we begin to question the verities of our particular society, this de-centering can open us to new understandings of what being human truly is. Marginalization is not abstract but incarnated in everyday life in times of illness, of painful estrangement from others through self-centeredness, and of the ultimate estrangement that is death. During these moments of marginalization it becomes possible to receive an epiphany from God which prompts us to communicate with one another on deeper levels. The poor, the refugees, political prisoners are among the world's victims of marginalization. Knowing they have been made irrelevant, their very existence communicates the continuing need for humankind to transcend itself in love and understanding over the brutalization of our communion with one another by ego-centric and culture-centric behavior. The realization that all our divisions are ultimately irrelevant prompts us to perceive our basic, original unity beyond all cultural boundaries.

Thomas Merton believed the monk as a marginal person had an educational role to play in translating the process of humankind's evolution from "*cupiditas* into *caritas*" (Saint Augustine quoted in *The Asian Journal*, 334). Inter-religious dialogue assists in our perceiving that "older unity" among all of us and can affect transcending our ethnicities in witnessing that everyone's experience and values point beyond themselves to extending the world's social conscience to a higher dimension. Mutual respect and hospitality toward "the Others" are the means to realizing a better society founded on a *caritas* in which all are valued and brought back from the margins to enjoy life at the center of God's grand experiment with humankind.

Walking With Thomas Merton

Mike Brennan

The biggest problem with writing a personal reflection to honor the centenary of Thomas Merton's birth is that there is so much to say. The second biggest problem is that there is nothing to say, nothing that can fully express my appreciation for having encountered him. I must write out of pure gratitude, if nothing else, to honor the remarkable way Thomas Merton continues to nurture us. I must write to express the wonder and joy of having discovered him and to celebrate the many ways he continues to help us discover ourselves. He inspired us, and he helps us to find, within ourselves, ways to inspire others.

I was 11 when Thomas Merton died. I knew nothing about him, but my folks had *The Sign of Jonas* and *The Living Bread* among their very modest collection of books. At 19, I attended a prayer service in which someone used the famous "Merton Prayer" from *Thoughts in Solitude*. I was captivated by both the humility and simplicity of that prayer, quite different from the prayers memorized in Catholic grammar school. It seemed both whimsical and earnest. It expressed conviction and determination and surrender and hope.

In 1987, when I was 30, I was invited to give a talk at the Vatican. It was a highly improbable turn of events. The conference, a gathering of Catholic airport chaplains from around the world, was sponsored by the Pontifical Council for the Pastoral Care of Migrants and Itinerant People. I was among a handful of laypeople who served as volunteers at airport chapels. I worked, then as now, as a baggage handler for an airline. I had never been to Rome, or even outside the United States.

The talk I gave began with these words from *The Sign of Jonas*: "There is no wilderness so terrible, so beautiful, so arid and so fruitful as the wilderness of compassion. It is the only desert that shall truly flourish like the lily. It shall become a pool, it shall bud forth and blossom and rejoice with joy. It is in the desert of compassion that the thirsty land turns into springs of water, that the poor possess all things" (334). I wanted to express the sense that airport chapels were like an oasis, a place of peace and quiet amid the busy and noisy airport. Perhaps it was a little flowery, but it caught everyone's attention. It's most likely that I had turned to my parents' copy of the book for inspiration.

I went on to deliver a personal testimony about my journey: a struggle with addiction and a life without meaning. I explained that, in recovery, I began to attend Mass at the airport, and the chaplain invited me to serve as a lector. When he discovered that I had been the editor of my high school newspaper, he asked me to write the weekly chapel bulletin. I noted that several other chapel volunteers were recovering alcoholics and addicts, and I stressed how deeply appreciative we were to be valued and invited to participate. I urged the assembled chaplains, in my own words, to be "messengers of hope," and to recognize that some of the most broken and alienated people working at the airport might prove to be very willing to participate in ministry if given the chance, if they were invited.

The people around the long table, many of them wearing headphones that provided simultaneous translation, appeared somewhat astonished by the intimacy of the talk, but offered warm applause and smiles. Only later did I realize that most of these testimonies were not very personal, but essentially formulaic reports about the services offered at airport chapels and problems that chaplains encountered.

So began my walk with Thomas Merton. I had not been reading him for very long, and I don't recall what led me to use that particular passage, but I was drawn to his sensitivity and openness. In high school I had a religion teacher who said that, if we remembered nothing else, remember to cultivate these attributes: to be aware, available, approachable, courageous, and to have good manners. Merton, as a writer and as a person, embodied and encouraged these characteristics. I found him fascinating. I read *Thomas Merton, A Pictorial Biography* by Jim Forest. Years later I would meet Jim when he was the keynote speaker at the International Thomas Merton Society in Memphis in 2007. A few years after that, he spoke to our Chicago Chapter of the ITMS, and stayed at my house. I came to know other people who had known Merton, like Brother Paul Quenon, Father Matthew Kelty, Father Jim Conner, and Tommie O'Callaghan. Through the people who knew him and loved him personally, I began to feel like I knew him, too. I already knew that I loved him and that he was a kindred spirit.

In 1994 I attended a retreat at Gethsemani Abbey sponsored by the Chicago Chapter of the ITMS, which was my introduction to the Merton Society. In 2001, I attended my first ITMS conference at Bellarmine. By 2005, I had become the coordinator of the Chicago Chapter, which led to meeting many Merton scholars and attending conferences in Memphis (2007) and Rochester (2009). Our chapter was proud to host the 2011 conference at Loyola University in Chicago. I gave a talk recently at a local church entitled "Thomas Merton: A Trustworthy Guide for Laypeople." I think that Merton devotees know that he speaks to monks, mystics, contemplatives, intellectuals, and ecumenists; he speaks to a wide range of scholars and religious people. But he also speaks to ordinary folks, and very compellingly. There is a great hunger for spiritual guidance and wisdom, and Merton's writings continue to nurture us.

The disciples on the road to Emmaus asked, "Did not our hearts burn within us as he talked to us on the road and explained the scriptures to us?" To me, one of the truest signs of Merton's holiness is his capacity to convey this same sense of the presence of Jesus in so much of what he wrote. Few writers have left me as energized and inspired, with my heart burning, as Thomas Merton.

I read that, when Merton died, one of the most poignant messages of condolences to his brother monks at Gethsemani came from one of Merton's oldest and dearest friends, Bob Lax. The telegram read, simply, "Sorrow." Just the thought of it makes me choke up, because nothing more was required, nothing more was possible to say.

So let me close by expressing how grateful I am for the life of Thomas Merton. I remember wondering, early in my recovery, if I would ever know joy again. I am looking at the beaming face of Merton on the tattered cover of Jim Forest's pictorial biography, and I can feel his confidence and affection, though we never met. And I know what he would say: "Yes."

The Pure Glory Of God In Us

Kallistos Ware

Among the many books of Thomas Merton, the one that has inspired me the most is *Conjectures of a Guilty Bystander*. I have read it so many times that my copy is now falling to pieces. Here, from my favorite book by Merton, is my favorite passage:

> At the center of our being is a point of nothingness which is untouched by sin and by illusion, a point of pure truth, a point or spark which belongs entirely to God, which is never at our disposal, from which God disposes of our lives, which is inaccessible to the fantasies of our own mind or the brutalities of our own will. This little point of nothingness and of *absolute poverty* is the pure glory of God in us. It is so to speak His name written in us, as our poverty, as our indigence, as our dependence, as our sonship. It is like a pure diamond, blazing with the invisible light of heaven. It is in everybody, and, if we could see it, we would see these billions of points of light coming together in the face and blaze of a sun that would make all the darkness and cruelty of life vanish completely . . .. I have no program for this seeing. It is only given. But the gate of heaven is everywhere (*Conjectures of a Guilty Bystander*, 158).

Merton's words call to mind a parallel passage from a writer of the Christian East, St. Isaac the Syrian (7th century):

> Be at peace with your own soul; then heaven and earth will be at peace with you. Enter eagerly into the treasure house that is within you, and so you will see the treasure house of heaven; for there is but one single entry to them both. The ladder that leads to the Kingdom is hidden within your soul. Flee from sin, dive into yourself, and in your soul you will discover the stairs by which to ascend (*The Ascetical Homilies of Saint Isaac the Syrian*, 11).

Jesus Christ said the same thing in a single short phrase: *The Kingdom of God is within you* (Luke 17:21).

A Meeting In Tehran That Was Not To Be

Seyyed Hossein Nasr

For several years Marco Pallis, mutual friend of both Thomas Merton and myself, was the link between us and he conveyed to me the ever greater interest of Merton in Sufism and my own exposition of it after he had read my *Three Muslin Sages* and *Ideals and Realities of Islam*. Arrangements were in fact made to have Merton spend a month in Persia, where I then lived in 1968, to be with me and to observe the various manifestations of Sufism in and near Tehran. I had made all the necessary preparations and it was only a few weeks before his planned entry into Tehran that he died in Southeast Asia. The opportunity never therefore arose for us to discuss Sufism together in person, but through an exchange of letters with Pallis as well as my own reading of Merton's books, I gained some ideas as to what within the Sufi tradition, with its multifarious manifestations containing nearly all spiritual possibilities, had attracted this Catholic contemplative to the extent that he had said that he wanted to devote much of his time to the study of Sufism and to write extensively about it.

Let it be said that Merton's knowledge of Sufism was authentic and genuine and not derived from either sentimental pseudo-Sufi writings nor from dry scholarly analyses of Sufism by a certain class of scholars who are interested in Sufism only if the spirit of Sufism is taken out of it, scholars who are much more at home dissecting cadavers than studying living beings. Merton had read many of the traditional books dealing with Islam and Sufism, including those of Frithjof Schuon, Titus Burckhardt and Martin Lings, and thanks to his own perspicacity was able to discover their authentic character. He had also read some of the best of Sufi poetry that was available to him in English translation and moreover had personal contacts with certain representatives of Sufism. Altogether he was fairly well acquainted with Sufi doctrine, practice and art.

As Merton deepened his studies of the contemplative life and his own practice of that life, he became ever more aware of the fact that in Christian mysticism, as it had been practiced in Western Christianity during the past few centuries, most of the spiritual techniques that still survive in Yoga, Zen and Sufism had been lost. He saw in the climate of Islamic esoterism the continuation of contemplative orders which had preserved their spiritual method and the presence of spiritual masters who made the practice of such methods possible. This reality attracted him highly as he tried to go beyond the realm of passive and individualistic mysticism.

Since the Renaissance, much of what survived of Christian mysticism in the West became in fact mostly individualistic, sentimental and passive. While Merton understood the value of this type of mysticism on its own level, his gaze was set upon the great medieval Christian contemplatives whose vision was not limited in any way by the individualism that was one of the characteristics of the Renaissance. The Sufi path, in which the adept plays the active role as wayfarer upon the way that finally leads to the Beloved, like the hero in quest of the Holy Grail, while remaining passive before the grace of Heaven, attracted Merton who was himself moving in this direction. He also thirsted for the kind of structured mystical life which the Sufi path offered in which the active and passive modes of the mystical life could be balanced on the basis of a reality that transcended the accidentally of individual existence.

Merton turned more and more to an appreciation of the spiritual significance of Nature of which Taoism, Zen and Sufism speak so often. The Sufi perspective which views nature as the self-revelation, unveiling and theophany of God and which sees all phenomena as Divine Signs (*vestigia Dei*), as a number of earlier Christian mystics had also asserted, was deeply attractive to Merton who found in this view of Sufism—which saw the supernaturally natural *barakah* (grace) flowing through the arteries of the cosmos and refused to separate the natural completely from the grace of the super-natural—a profound confirmation of his own most intimate vision of creation as God's handiwork and the theater for the manifestation of His Qualities.

By turning seriously to the study of the spirituality of other religions, including Buddhism which is non-theistic, Merton was acknowledging the truth of the "tran-scendent unity of religions" to use the term made famous by Frithjof Schuon. Merton saw in the classical Sufi tradition in the writing of such figures as Ibn 'Arabi and Rûmî a clear assertion of this truth, which goes back to the explicit teachings of the Qur'an itself. The universalism of Sufism, reflected in so much Sufi poetry, was of deep interest to Merton who saw in it the confirmation of a truth that he had come to discover after a long period of study and contemplation.

What would have happened if Merton had been able to come to Persia and to con-tinue his study of Sufism, only Heaven knows. In any case that was not to be. Perhaps he would have written major works of Sufism in its relation to Christian spirituality. But even what he did write and the thoughts that he did express to friends reveal the inner *sympatheia* he had towards the Islamic spiritual universe. Like a number of Catholic contemplatives and mystics before him, such as Père Charles de Foucault and Louis Massignon, Merton took important steps in laying the foundation upon which an authentic understanding can be achieved between the followers of Christ and followers of the Prophet and the Quranic revelation, which created a world in whose Islamic fir-mament the light of Christ as Sayyidunā 'Īsā (Jesus)—upon whom be peace—continues nevertheless to shine.

Fantasies Of A Pilgrimage Together

Huston Smith

I have been invited to so many conferences and have had to submit my regrets so often that it was a pleasure to receive a follow-up invitation, in 1968, to an ecumenical conference in Calcutta, India, that listed Thomas Merton as one of the scheduled speakers.

Seeing his name on the list compelled me to change my mind, for he had worked his way to the top of the list of persons I most wanted to meet.

The conference was slated to open with a 5:00 P.M. reception on the lawn behind the hotel that housed us. I was prompt, but Merton was already present, sitting at a table and sipping a soft drink. I joined him and wasted no time engaging him in conversation. He was the true celebrity at the conference, and I wasn't certain whether I would catch him alone again.

I began very honestly, confessing to him, "I could never have been a monk. My attraction to women is too strong in me. But I do have a contemplative streak in me. So I've often wondered what a monk's life is like. So, Thomas, what *is* a monk's life like?"

Of all the answers in the world, his was the last one I expected.

"Well, it's very nice," he said, simply.

"Your answer surprises me," I told him. "I would find the three vows difficult."

"Oh, those!" he said, laughing. "Poverty is a snap. Chastity is more difficult, but manageable. But obedience—is a bugger!"

As it turned out, I was able to have quite a bit of time with Merton, and we become fast friends.

Merton was scheduled to be the last speaker. There were many television crews converging on the conference, and he was asked to wear his clerical collar. He began his address by saying that he felt as if he was appearing in disguise, in costume. In his usual clothes of dungarees and work shirt, he usually felt more like a hermit.

But he became more serious when he talked about representing the people who didn't count so much in the eyes of the general public: monks, the poor and poets. Then he added:

> So I stand among you as one who offers a small message of hope, that first, there are always people who dare to seek on the margin of society, who are not dependent on social acceptance, not dependent on social routine, and prefer a kind of free-floating existence under a state of risk. And among these people, if they are faithful to their own calling, to their own vocation, and to their own message from God, communication on the deepest level is possible. And the deepest level of communication is not communication, but communion. It is wordless. It is beyond words, and it is beyond speech, and it is beyond concept. Not that we discover a

new unity. We discover an older unity . . . we are already one. But we imagine that we are not. And what we have to recover is our original unity. What we have to be is what we are.

Following the conference, Merton and I were scheduled to fly to New Delhi to catch connecting flights and we agreed to sit together on the plane. During the flight I mentioned that I had always wanted to take the pilgrimage from Kathmandu to Pokhara, a major monastery in one of the world's most majestic settings.

"The plane trip took only fifteen minutes," I told him, "and the journey on foot, which undulates up and down the mountainsides, takes seventeen days. But it's a real pilgrimage."

Tom picked up on my remark, and we became slaphappy.

"Let's do it," he said. "I will wire my superior back in Kentucky and tell him he can defrock me if he has to. You wire Kendra and tell her she can divorce you if she must. But we are pilgrimaging from Kathmandu to Pokhara!"

The pilot's announcement that our plane was landing jolted us out of our pilgrimage fantasies, and once in the airport we parted ways, I to head to the north to visit the Tibetans, and Tom to fly south to Bangkok and to his death. Tragically, he died later that evening in his hotel room due to a live electrical wire in a fan.

He was only fifty-three.

Huston Smith at Thomas Merton's Grave

Clear Light And God

Robert Thurman

His Holiness the Dalai Lama and Father Thomas Merton met in 1968, when the Dalai Lama was only 33 years of age. Merton was impressed by the Dalai Lama's kind and intelligent personality, though he was more impressed by his subsequent meetings with senior, more experienced and more contemplative Tibetan lamas. Sadly Merton died soon thereafter, and his sparkling interest in the Buddhist-Christian dialogue did not lead to the breakthrough insights he would have given us if he had time to digest his encounters and articulate their impact in his ever brilliant and heartfelt manner.

In the Buddhist Sutras, both Pali and Sanskrit versions, Shākyamuni Buddha is recorded as often speaking with former friends and disciples after they had died, encountering them in their between state forms or in subsequent both heavenly and less than heavenly embodiments. Here I imagine a short conversation between the H. H. Dalai Lama (DL) and Father Merton, now called Merton Angel Philosopher (MAP). They meet one morning around 4 A.M. in the predawn twilight, when MAP is descending to visit clairvoyant friends and DL is performing his morning contemplations. Here and there I have quoted actual statements of each, downloaded from the internet. Where they speak below without quote marks, I am imagining what they might have said to each other. If I have said anything either one would feel unhappy about, I am deeply sorry—but I think I have remained true to their usual messages. Anyway, it is to honor them both, to amuse them if they ever see this dream of mine, whether on earth or in some heaven or other.

MAP: Your Holiness, hope you don't mind taking a break from your *samadhi* to chat a bit with this curious angel. There are some things I've been wanting to tell you for some time. I had no chance to get back to you after we met, since the Good Lord called me away so suddenly! Don't worry though, I like this angelic life! Lucky for me!

DL: No problem! A great pleasure to see that you're still on the path, developing from full to full, life after life, as we say. Hope to see you around again in human form, one of these lives! Now, how wonderful it is to meet you in your shining angel self!

MAP: First of all, I congratulate you for your constant message that we of the world's religions should cease trying to convert each other from denomination to denomination—I agree with you the real thing is for each to convert oneself from the daily round of selfish preoccupations to the loving life that fulfills all the founders' real intentions. We can share the tools we have each developed and use them within the cultural and theological contexts we are born to. This also prevents conflict between the institutions.

DL: Yes, I do persist in that view. Meeting you helped me adopt it, to give credit where it is due. Did you hear me say that mixing them all into one big religion would be like forcing all restaurants throughout the world to carry one and the same menu? I enjoy delivering that one, as everyone looks uneasy at the thought.

MAP: Yes, it's a good one, though less important to me, as I don't need coarse food any more, in this present life [laughs].

DL: [chuckling] Lucky you!

MAP: Now down to business, dear Kundun—I have learned that Tibetans call you that, do you mind? I saw on the net recently—yes we angels can go on the blessed net—that you gave a wonderful discussion of "God" and the "clear light of emptiness," or the "Dharmakāya Truth Body of Buddha," and you made them almost the same! I was really thrilled. But I got stuck on one point, which I came to ask you about. After some explanation of the Samantabhadra Buddha, All-good Buddha, the natural clear light space of emptiness wherein all phenomena dissolve, and so on, you say "We can say, therefore, that this ultimate source, clear light, is close to the notion of a Creator, since all phenomena, whether they belong to samsara or nirvana, [seem to] originate therein." This was nice to hear. But then you go on to say, and herein lies my question:

> "I do not mean that there exists somewhere, there, a sort of collective clear light, analogous to the non-Buddhist concept of Brahmā as a substratum. We must not be inclined to deify this luminous space. We must understand that when we speak of ultimate or inherent clear light, we are speaking on an individual level."

Now, I can well understand you here, if you are saying that at the level of the ultimate clear light of emptiness, there is no person who is intentionally "creating" anything, and that is the difference between the Reality Body Buddha and the Creator God. You want to be clear that you are not saddling the Buddha's Dharmakāya with the role of Creatorship. I agree with you on that. But I don't see how that relates to your expressing this through the concepts of "collective clear light" and "individual clear light."

Perhaps I didn't make clear to you when we met in my just previous human life, that in our Christian mystic contemplations, we reach a stage of apprehension of what we call the "Godhead," where we no longer insist on the narrative of anthropomorphic Creator, creating the world out of nothing. Our "Creator" concept, in a sense, is put forth on a more conventional level, in order to re-assure people that the ultimate is not just utterly transcendent, but more like a loving father, who "created" them, has ultimate control of their fate, and stands ready to save them when they have become ready.

DL: You mean you don't take the Genesis story literally? Really? Actually I was surprised in my conversations with some Rabbis that some of them don't either. Yet they feel the majority of people do need a literal feeling of the presence of God being close and caring for them. And I have come to see how powerful that is! In fact, you in your past visit really helped me to see how the Christian path can lead someone who really takes it seriously to attain a full enlightenment, through its own form of transcendent wisdom and universal compassion. In our case, the Bodhisattva Avalokiteshvara is supposed to represent the universal compassion of all buddhas, in that sense being more buddha than any single buddha. He then represents that caring and loving side of divinity, but stops short of claiming any sort of omnipotence. Maybe we can say that only clear light of emptiness is omnipotent, but then we never say that it "does" or "creates" anything. Shakyamuni only said, when first enlightened; "Profound, peaceful, clear light, nonproliferating, uncreated—this Reality I have found is like an immortal elixir! Whomever I teach it to will not get it—better I stay alone in the forest without speaking!"

MAP: How marvelous! I don't think you mentioned that to me before! . . . But then he did a lot of speaking, after all [both laugh]! One Chinese Chan master said, "Such a garrulous 'non-speaking,' it filled the Dragon King's cave with scriptures [both laugh]!" But I understand that he meant that the Ultimate Reality is beyond verbal expression, and the "speaking" only concerns the path through the relative world that leads to transcendent experience!

DL: Exactly! Awareness of the inexpressibility of the ultimate is a principle of interpretation we uphold, to guard against absolutist literalism, to prevent us from falling into a kind of verbal form of what I think you call "idolatry"—here instead of a fanaticism about a physical object, an extremism of dogmatic belief. Of course many of us still do become too attached to our convictions—it is the root of our sectarianisms.

MAP: It's a big problem in all religions, and makes trouble between them also. I have discovered that "I will be a better Catholic, not if I can refute every shade of Protestantism, but if I can affirm the truth in it and still go further. So, too, with the Muslims, the Hindus, the Buddhists, etc. This does not mean syncretism, indifferentism, the vapid and careless friendliness that accepts everything by thinking of nothing. There is much that one cannot 'affirm' and 'accept,' but first one must say 'yes' where one really can. If I affirm myself as a Catholic merely by denying all that is Muslim, Jewish, Protestant, Hindu, Buddhist, etc., in the end I will find that there is not much left for me to affirm as a Catholic: and certainly no breath of the Spirit with which to affirm it" (*Conjectures of a Guilty Bystander*, 133). But this thought of mine sometimes frightens some of my colleagues, bless their hearts, and makes them think I might have left the fold!

But enough about that. Please tell me more about the clear light.

DL: When, in the Tantric context, we say that all worlds appear out of clear light, we do not visualize this source as a unique entity, but as the ultimate clear light of each being. We can also, on the basis of its pure essence, understand this clear light to be the primordial buddha. All the stages which make up the life of each living being—death, the intermediate state and rebirth—represent nothing more than the various manifestations of the potential of clear light. It is both the most subtle consciousness and the most subtle energy. The more clear light loses its subtlety, the more your experiences take shape.

MAP: How wonderfully you describe it. But the clear light itself doesn't do the appearing and disappearing. It is just primordially there, infinitely energetic yet quiet and calm. So is that why you say it is not some "collective" entity, a formless form of a being that wants to do something, but rather something to be individually experienced when an individual becomes a buddha?

DL: I think that's it. Though we can't really settle down too hard on one side or another of the individual/universal duality. We do have to remember a verse from the future Buddha Maitreya, in the *Ornament of Mahāyāna Sutras*, transcribed by the great *pandit* and saint, Asanga:

We can not say there are many buddhas,
Since all buddhas are nondifferent in their Dharmakāya;
And we can not say there is only one buddha,
Since each individual gets to experience the oneness with all!

MAP: O, I like that, leaving it open-ended. Thanks very much, Your Holiness! I've got to go now, to report back to my angelic discussion group! We meet now and then to share our new discoveries! By the way, though, we are very happy nowadays with His Holiness the new Pope Francis! Don't you love him too?

DL: I most certainly do! I really appreciate how he is addressing the worldwide rich and poor division I am so worried about. I wish him all the best! Farewell, Father Angel Tom, until we meet again!

Thomas Merton, The "Jesus Lama" In Asia

Harold Talbott

When people ask why I became a Catholic, I often answer, I'm ashamed to say, that it wasn't *The Confessions of St. Augustine*, it was *The Seven Storey Mountain*. In 1957, I was working on a newspaper in Memphis, Tennessee during my summer vacation from Harvard and reading *The Sign of Jonas*, the journal Merton kept on his way to becoming a priest. And I went to Gethsemani to meet him but the world was beating a path to his door, and the abbot wouldn't let me in. The next Thanksgiving I returned after being baptized. I had decided to take my first communion not with the Jesuits but with the Cistercians at Gethsemani. And this time the abbot said yes. Merton took me into a room and said, "I'm always very glad to meet someone who has just come into the church because they are full of grace and the grace overflows from the person who has just been received. And I have only one thing to say to you: the Church is a very big place. Always remember to go your own way in it." Ten years later in India I reminded Merton about that remark and he said, "Did I say that? That's pretty good. And look at where we both are." It was the first time I had met a great man which always clarifies your path. They raise you to their level. Shantideva (a celebrated eighth-century *Mahayana* master of India) says that if an ordinary tree grows up in a sandalwood forest, the nearness to the sandalwood makes it smell like a sandalwood tree. And if you encounter a true spiritual master and you recognize it, the recognition disposes your mind to a state which hints every now and then at what good practice will do for you.

Eventually I went to Asia as secretary to Dom Aelred Graham who had just retired after sixteen years as Prior in Portsmouth Priory in Rhode Island. He had already written *Zen Catholicism* and had gotten permission from the Benedictine Order to spend a year in Asia and the Middle East. So when Merton wrote to Aelred that he was planning a trip to Asia, and asked how he could meet the lamas in India, Aelred explained that I was there studying with the Dalai Lama and that I could introduce him to the lamas. When Merton finally arrived in Dharamsala, I remember saying to him, "An audience is scheduled for you with His Holiness the Dalai Lama," and he said "I'm not going." And I said, "Why not?" He said, "I've seen enough pontiffs." And I said, "Well I think, Tom—as you want me to call you—if you come to India to study with lamas, I think you'd be making a mistake not to meet the Dalai Lama. And furthermore, Tom, the Dalai Lama has heard all about you from the Canadian High Commissioner, James George, and he's taken the trouble of having a film shown to him of Cistercian monks and abbeys in France. He's done his homework and I think you should go up there and meet him." So he said "Okay, we'll see." My sense was that Merton didn't trust organized religion and he didn't trust the big banana. He did not come to India to hang around the power-elite of an exiled central Asian Vatican. But despite his misgivings, he went.

I was living in a bungalow and I gave my room and study to Merton and I bedded down on sort of a wooden sofa. There was no furniture at all, and we were freezing and Merton had the most colossal cold and was sick. He was sick a lot during his later life. He had been maintaining a crushing schedule as a contemplative Trappist working monk, and had also written shelves of books. He burned the candle at both ends to a frightening degree. I would see him at two o'clock in the morning because I was so cold I couldn't sleep and so fascinated that behind that wall was Merton. The light would go on at two o'clock and he would do his prayers and then I would see the light go on in the study at four in the morning.

One day Merton went out to take photographs and met Sonam Kazi. I knew this from his eyes before he told me. And that was the birth of the blues, the beginning of the *dzogchen* teachings for Thomas Merton. Sonam Kazi was the official interpreter assigned to the Dalai Lama by the government of India, the interpreter, for example, in the talks between Nehru, Chou En Lai and the Dalai Lama. Sonam ran into Merton on the road, invited him to a tea house and zapped him. Sonam Kazi had zapped me a year before and I had gone out carefully holding on to the furniture. I hate to use these words but I'm too lazy not to: Sonam can put a person in an "altered state of consciousness" and believe me, I was not used to altered states of consciousness. But Merton was a ripened and ready object of a visit from Sonam Kazi and he got it. He said to me occasionally after that, "I came to Asia to study Zen in Japan and now I have changed my itinerary and I'm going to study *dzogchen* in India with the Tibetans."

Sonam Kazi took Merton to visit with Chogling Rinpoche—a way-out yogi, a very wild man who was an incredible kick-over-the-traces, irresponsible-type person, a tremendous troublemaker, and extremely rollicking in an unpredictable way, a top-flight, wonderful *Nyingmapa* yogi. He said to Merton, "When Sonam Kazi brings someone, I know I'll be able to talk to them and that it'll be okay." He asked Merton "Do you believe in karma and rebirth?" Merton said, "Well, I think it's a very, very fascinating, persuasive proposition, but I wouldn't say I believe it, no." So Chogling said, "Okay, well then I can't teach you because the whole thing is predicated on your having faith in karma and rebirth. So let's *say* that you have faith in karma and rebirth, and this is what I have to tell you. A human being has a *srog*—a life force. He has a consciousness and when he dies, in order to ensure the proper destination of the consciousness, it's very useful to be able to practice *phowa*." There's a fontanel on the top of your head. At birth, it's a soft, big space between the head bones, and as babies grow, it closes. Through yogic training you can reopen it and then when you die, you can shoot the consciousness out the fontanel and then it goes straight to the paradise of Amitabha Buddha.

The reason Chogling Rinpoche taught Merton *phowa* practice—say I—is that he saw that Merton was going to be dead in a couple of weeks. He needed the teachings on death. He did not need teachings of karma and suffering, calming the mind, insight meditation. He needed to be taught how to dispose of his consciousness at the time of death because this was the time of death for him. And Merton scribbled in his journal: "I'm not sure about all this consciousness and shooting it out the top of the head. I'm not sure this is going to be very useful for us."

The days were going by with Sonam Kazi taking us to see *Nyingmapa* lamas, drinking scotch in taverns, and talking, talking. Merton is now saying, "*Dzogchen* is where it's at and that's what I'm going to do." I became very officious. We were about to go up the hill to meet the Dalai Lama. It seemed to me that it would be impolitic for Merton to refer to the dzogchen school because it's a different school from that of His Holiness. In the Jeep, as we are going up the hill to McLeod Ganj—the Dalai Lama's residence—I explained all this to Merton. He was wearing his white robe with black scapular to meet His Holiness. We arrived and after a flurry of exchanged courtesies, the Dalai Lama looked at Merton and said, "What do you want?" And Merton said, "I want to study *dzogchen*." And the Dalai Lama said, "It's true that *dzogchen* is the highest *yana* (vehicle for Buddhist study), but if you want to study *dzogchen*, I propose a series of meetings in which I will teach you the preliminary practices at the end of which I should hope that you will be ready to go on to *dzogchen*. "

The Dalai Lama didn't get into technical, methodological questions. He showed us posture and how to dispose the mind and how to get yourself into basic meditation practice by calming the mind and there was nothing technical. Of course, it was masterfully taught and there is an inexpressible gravity about the person of the Dalai Lama. He was—and still is—the supreme man holding the tradition together, the man who has been giving the Tibetan nation an identity and engaging in endless maneuvers for his people amidst the destruction and the torment. And here he was showing us posture and breathing!

The Dalai Lama's robe and Thomas Merton's white Cistercian habit with the black scapular looked Giottoesque. It was an image of two figures encountering each other who deserved to wear those robes, who were part and parcel of the world represented by those very robes. One really had a surfeit of visual inspiration. Both men were very solid. Unornamental, compact, strong, hard beings. Now the Dalai Lama has an external joviality and graciousness which is appropriate to a sovereign. To put you at your ease, to make it possible for beings to be in relation to him, he plays down the radiance, the dignity, the charisma, the persona that the West has developed a romantic myth about, but who in himself has his own distinct presence and radiance. There is no presumption about him. He's a person who draws a heart-breaking reverence from the people who are devoted to him, and to see him in this room with a man to whom we don't need to apply adjectives, but if we were, it would be things like *mensch,* authentic. Yes, Merton was a *mensch*—manly authentic. No gestures. No artifice. No manner. No program, no come-on—just, "Here I am folks"—and folks happened to be the Dalai Lama. And they encountered each other and, appropriately enough, there was utter silence. I was very glad to be aboard. It was the generosity of Merton that made it possible for me to attend those meetings. He said, "You're here studying with the Dalai Lama. I want you present." It's my good karma that I was there. There was so much good humor and so much laughter and so much camaraderie and so much confidence of understanding and so much no need for explanation and build-up and equipping themselves on their parts, you see. They had done their homework.

The Dalai Lama asked Merton what one did to make it possible in this modern world to live the life of a monk in the West. How do you stave off spiritual annihilation? These conversations were very much Merton equipping himself with the transmission of Buddhism from the Dalai Lama and very much the Dalai Lama equipping himself with the low-down from a reliable guide. This was not a papal legate. This was not someone setting up a conference for the Pope. This was not a front man. This was an embodiment of something which another embodiment—a *tulku*—who needs to function in the world, was drawing upon as a resource.

The Dahli Lama said to Merton, "I want with my own eyes and ears and speech to assure myself that you have the faith firmly grounded" and—let's be daring—let's think that there are certain beings who do not have to come every day and attend Zen or *vipassana* retreat. This could be a romantic projection but I have to say what I think: Merton had thirty years behind him and when he walked into a room or the cell of a meditator, monk or lama, he was greeted with a recognition. I've never seen a Western person received by a lama the way that he was received.

I wanted to make sure that Merton met all the outstanding lamas that I could dig up. In Dharamsala he met Avelokiteshvara—the Bodhisattva of Compassion—in the person of the Dalai Lama. And I think okay, I'm doing my job, I'm getting him the whole spectrum of the force field. But of course he must meet Chatral Rinpoche, too, and of course that will be an opportunity for me to hide behind Merton's skirts and also meet Chatral Rinpoche whom I'm terrified of. I wouldn't dream of studying with him, or anybody remotely like him, because he is totally and completely unpredictable. He is savage about the ego and he will put you on the spot, and I am not prepared to up the ante to that degree. He could throw stones at you—as he does do—and so I will use Merton as the front. We caught up with Chatral Rinpoche down the road from Ghoom in Darjeeling. He was painting the nuns' house and he put some planks on some bricks and we sat and talked with the help of an interpreter. Chatral Rinpoche started by saying, "Ah, a Jesus lama; you know I have never been able for the life of me to get a handle on Christianity so I'm real glad you came this morning."

Chatral explained his perplexity about Christianity. He said, "The center of your religion is a man who comes back to life after death and in Tibetan Buddhism when you have one of these people, a *rolog*, or a walking corpse, we call our lama to put him down. So I want to know what kind of a religion is Christianity which has at its center a dead man coming back to life." So Merton explained the Resurrection in tantric terms about the overcoming of fear and the utter and complete power of liberation which is the center of Christianity. And this satisfied Chatral Rinpoche. "At last I understand Christianity. Thank you very much." And then Merton says "I would like to study with you." And Chatral says "Right, we can work together. And so you've got to do your *ngon dno* (the preliminary practice of *dzogchen*, which usually takes a Tibetan about a year). We'll get you a hermitage in Bhutan and that is where you should do your retreat. And I challenge you: see, I'm not enlightened yet, so let's work together and see which one of us can get enlightened first." And so Merton said, "it's a deal." And so then we split and Merton says "That's the greatest man I ever met. That's my teacher." But they weren't his exact words.

I can only guess what Merton would have done after Bangkok. He might have studied with Chatral Rinpoche but he would never have left the Church. Having encountered Chatral Rinpoche he might have curtailed his trip to Japan but he was certainly going to go there and talk to Zen roshis. My distinct impression was that this was a man who had found what he wanted in India and was going to round out his experience in Asia as he planned, but he was going to modify it in order to go back and study with Chatral Rinpoche. How were Nicaragua, Alaska, and Canada, California, and New Mexico going to fit into that, and how could he be an active member of the Civil Rights movement, of the Peace movement, a poet and a writer and all the rest of it? I don't know. To my distinct certainty he was going to study *dzogchen* and do his preliminary practice with Chatral Rinpoche. I'm convinced of it, but he would never have left the Church.

335

He had reached a point—unrecognizable to me—where the Judeo-Christian theistic tradition of the Mother Church of Christendom and *dzogchen* of Nyingmapa Tibetan Buddhism were not in contradiction. Furthermore he had grown up in a Catholic village in France that had so deeply affected him that it had planted a seed which had caused him to enter the Church. He was a man who had spent twenty-seven years in a Cistercian abbey. His training came from the Church. He was a generous man and he was a just man and he acknowledged what he owed to the Church. It was his formation. It was not his Cocoon. It was not his prison. It was himself and it was a very good self and he needed to uphold it.

Merton stood for the contemplative life the way—to make a vulgar and irrelevant analogy—Picasso stands for art. For contemplatives there are illuminated beings, there are hidden yogis, but as far as how ordinary people come into touch with the great spiritual heritage of the West—including the apophatic tradition, the Via Negativa—it's through the mystical teachings from St. Paul and St. John, St. John's gospel, Dionysius the Areopagite, the great medieval mystics Thomas Aquinas and St. John of the Cross, and St. Teresa of Avila—and that's just about it, folks, that's it for the big league contributions to spirituality at the contemplative level in the West. And every now and then you get somebody who says "Wait a minute, I know the chips are down and the circumstances are against us, but let's get in there once more and try to stay alive spiritually." And that's Merton for twentieth-century Westerners. Despite all of his manliness, Merton was a man of the old moment before the Second World War, a man of enormous personal and cultural refinement. He belonged in a French salon as well as in a forest in Kentucky. There is no question about it. He had the qualities we're losing. Gaining other wonderful ones but losing. Merton had this consummate worldly culture as well as this jewel of spirituality. He was a gift to humanity, with the naivete and the nerve to take the writings of mystics seriously.

Merton definitely affected my life. He seduced me into leaving the Gelugpa schools of Tibetan Buddhism and spending the rest of my life studying with *dzogchen* yogis. Also, I told him I was in a lot of confusion at that moment in my life. Merton helped me by telling me that when he was at an English university he had an affair with the girl who made the beds in his dormitory, and she had a baby, and he said to me, "You know my son would be such and such an age right now and I don't know whether he survived the blitz or not." And he carried that with him. That was on his mind. And he let me know that this was the key to his life. He said, "My son." The impact was like that of St. Augustine who had been a sinner before his conversion. Merton saw himself as a man who had to purify himself of something that was a very heavy load to carry. But by the time he came to India, whether or not finding dzogchen was central—that's my organization of significance in his life—it turns out that he had lived his life and this was the Mozart finale and he was in a state of utmost exuberance, engaged, and absorbing, and eating with delectation every moment of every experience and every person that passed. He tipped Sikh taxi drivers like a Proustian millionaire. He was on a roll, on a toot, on a holiday from school. He was a grand seigneur, a great lord of the spiritual life. He radiated a sense of "This is an adventure, here I am folks," and he woke people up and illuminated them and enchanted them and gave them a tremendous happiness and a good laugh. But also there was always a communication from him that he was a representative of the religious life whether he was wearing a windbreaker or a habit. The Indian people greeted him as a pilgrim, a seeker, and that was the basis on which he was met by everybody and congratulated valiantly whether they recognized his public identity or not. People knew his spiritual quality. People in planes knew it. There was no question about it. Merton was not an object of scrutiny. He was an event.

Song To Merton: Light Of Compassion: Diptych

Russel Hulsey

Song to Merton: Light of Compassion, diptych in ink on paper by Russel Hulsey, 2012. In the collection of Christina Lee Brown.

I scrawled the following poem in a dog-eared notebook somewhere between here and there:

Everyday Is India

Pieces of a fever dream

Speaking in Hindi
A carousel with elephants

Why have I come to this place?
The other side of the world—

Where the Buddhas walked

Stop making sense said my talking head!!

In glass temple

On a calculated journey to India, I rather unexpectedly, inexplicably, found myself wrapped up in something of a vision quest; and found myself drawing nearer there within, stumbling upon—at least for myself—the inner sanctum of Thomas Merton. I had just visited the site where Gandhi was imprisoned for the last time by the British colonial court, and made pilgrimage to the grounds there where some of his ashes are kept in memorial along side his dutiful partner and loving wife. I had been reading *Gandhi on Non-Violence* by Thomas Merton, and my head seemed to be filled with noise. The sort of confusion and genuine heartbreak that one feels when contemplating the lives and subsequent tragic ends of such illuminated figures as the Mahatma, or Dr. Martin Luther King Jr., even Jesus of Nazareth. Why this, why that? I thought. Then, while standing barefoot quietly in a Jain temple, I stopped asking why . . .. I just stopped.

Life never has been, nor will it ever be about "figuring it all out." It is, more concisely, about being in motion, wielding the weight of Love—*the light of compassion*—and moving forward evermore deeply into the mystery of what is ineffable and all encompassing. As the *Bhagavad Gita* shows us, we must make a choice in this life, to follow our paths with strength and determination. What brought Thomas Merton to India in 1968 was indeed *his* calling, *his* path. He had long studied the Vedas, Buddhism and Eastern Mysticism. He had indeed long waited to meet his brothers and sisters of the East, and to engage in philosophical and monastic discourse. It was in India that he was introduced to His Holiness the 14th Dalai Lama; this meeting was one of massive socio-cultural and spiritual importance in his time, and remains ever more so today. The Dalai Lama later recalled, "*As for myself, I always consider myself as one of his Buddhist brothers. So, as a close friend—or as his brother—I always remember him, and I always admire his activities and his life-style. Since my meeting with him, and so often when I examine myself, I really follow some of his examples [. . .] the impact of meeting him will remain until my last breath.*"

I personally committed my life to the path of Art and Poetics in 1997 when I was honorably discharged from the United States Marine Corps, an active-duty combat veteran having served in the Persian Gulf and Bosnia with Fighter Attack Squadron 312. For me, the Arts are sacred; this is my vocation, and my new path of non-violence—a warrior of another kind and of a higher mind. The Arts are a platform for a higher discourse. The American Conceptual Artist Bruce Nauman said, "The true artist helps the world by revealing mystic truths." This is a sentiment that I have long taken into accord. Having worked in varying media to include Video, Sound, Installation Art, Writing, and Performance, I committed myself to a drawing and painting series beginning in 2006 entitled *Verses: Portraits of American Poets* with the specific aim of promoting poetry of an American voice that I consider to be particularly contemplative, and of a healing nature. The first part of the series focused heavily upon 19th Century Transcendentalists; the second was a meditation on the Beat Generation. I am now continuing work on *Verses III: Songs of the Commonwealth* (Kentucky Poets) to which Thomas Merton belongs.

Initially, I thought that "Song to Merton" would be only a rendering of Merton himself (as all other "Verses" works are individual entities). However, upon making a crucial journey, sometime after my voyage to India, to the Abbey of Gethsemani in rural Kentucky on a hot summer's day in 2012, things changed. I spent a day wrapped in silent contemplation at the austere abbey in both mental and spiritual preparation for this work. I sat outwardly still at the simple whitewashed cross of one of my great heroes, Father Louis (Thomas Merton). I asked for his approval and guidance in this process. After this, I sprinkled a small handful of Sacred Sand (a prayer to the Medicine Buddha), given to me by the Drepung Gomang Buddhist Monks, upon the warm grass surrounding Father Louis' humble marker and epitaph.

Shortly thereafter, I ventured to the monastery bookstore and rather auspiciously discovered: *Merton & Buddhism* (Fons Vitae, 2007). I was dumbfounded. I felt strongly in that very unmistakable instant that there remains a dire need of the highest significance for the open, mindful sharing of wisdom traditions as pioneered by such brave folks as our beloved Merton. I then turned the page, and discovered a photograph. This was an image of His Holiness the Dalai Lama (HHDL) in seated meditation at the grave of Merton, in the exact location where I had been positioned for over an hour not five minutes before this moment. I then fully realized that I must create a work of the Dalai Lama, equal in scale to that of the Merton artwork. They will be installed facing one another, I thought, as if the Dalai Lama and Merton, representing East and West respectively, were staring into one another's eyes. The works should be hung in close, intimate proximity to one another. In the middle of the two paintings (where visitors shall stand and experience the two works as one cohesive whole) there will be a soft golden spotlight shining. This light is meant to indicate what Thomas Merton wrote concerning his mystical experience, or epiphany, in downtown Louisville, 1958: "And if only everybody could realize this! But it cannot be explained. There is no way of telling people that they are all walking around shining like the sun."

After having completed the Merton painting, Gray Henry (Director of Fons Vitae Publishing) came to my studio to discuss Merton and his journey East. During her visit, I told her that I would soon be working on the second panel of the diptych, which was of HHDL. I explained that it was my intention to create a work that would specifically pay homage to Merton's final quest in his lifetime, his trek East; and that it was my intention to do so by encapsulating that life and that journey by creating an installation whereby the two would forever gaze into the deep holy void of one another's eyes. Gray then informed me that she had in her possession a bronze sculpture, an actual—to scale—life mask of the Dalai Lama at her home. She generously invited me to view it in preparation of the artwork, as I did, and this proved to be an invaluable experience. I later told Gray that I knew there would exist some transference between us that would ultimately aid in the making of this work. This did in fact occur, and I wish to express my sincere gratitude to her for sharing this treasure.

I am honored and humbly grateful to the Louisville-resident Tibetan Buddhist Monks who bestowed upon me a pouch of sacred sand from the *Festival of Faiths* Mandala Dissolution Ceremony. This sand was mixed into the paint used for this diptych with specific permission granted by the monks. These works are therefore blessed by them, and carry forth the healing properties of the Medicine Buddha.

It is perhaps ironic that Merton would be dead that December 1968, twenty-seven years to the exact date of his entry into Gethsemani Abbey, dying by accidental electrocution in Thailand, just a brief couple weeks after having met his brother in non-violent arms, HHDL. Often violent and untimely deaths occur, and especially when this happens to such saintly and profound figures we tend to ask: why? Giving and taking, and the perception of coming and going, are fundamental aspects of human life. Words are imbued with power, and healthy discourse is forever needed, but action is both king and queen. Action, itself, lies at the very heart of *ahimsa* or non-violence. Thomas Merton scaled *that* Seven Storey Mountain and ended up on the other side of the Himalayas. One never really knows exactly where one is going, but to have dared to endeavor is God Within.

May we find respite here, *shining as the sun*, and in this moment let us not forget that separateness is a grand illusion. We are eternally bound, each of us, as One body in the eternal winds of change. Where these winds do blow, is largely up to what we contribute. Between there and there, here and here, you and you, and I and I, we have but one struggle amidst one gathering reality; it is the extinction of distinction—which is to say, WE ARE *ALREADY* ONE.

Thomas Merton In My Life

Paul Wilkes

In the mid-1950s, I attended Cathedral Latin School, a Marianist high school for boys in Cleveland, Ohio. America was talking picket fences and middle class dreams, and here I was, a Catholic boy, alienated, angry, unsettled. I wanted something else, but what was it? What was my life to be? Who was I? What really mattered? Yes, it was perhaps typical teenage angst, but I acted out plenty in the process, for reasons that now escape me. Raining down chalk dust on an unsuspecting novice Marianist substitute teacher, gouging the gym floor with the heel taps of my shoes, stuffing an oozing, rotten tomato into the principal's mail slot. It was a rare week that went by I didn't have to stay for detention hall.

It was after one of these after-school incarcerations late in my junior year that I was swaggering down the hallway toward *Opere et Veritate*—Cathedral Latin's credo emblazoned on our walls, words which I so firmly believed as a freshman, but now were meaningless and empty—that I saw Brother Adolph Kalt coming out of the library. He was an old man, fifty years a Marianist, hunched over, with a terrifyingly bad breath, a virtual blizzard of dandruff on the shoulders of his black suit jacket, but with that kind of supernal smile both the holy and the mad possess. He was motioning to me, but I swaggered on, so perversely proud that I had just spent the last hour of my life writing some inane sentence of self-indictment over and over again. He stood his ground and I couldn't avoid him. He gestured for me to come into the library and, after peering up and down the corridor as if he wanted no one to know we would be there alone, he came inside, shut and locked the door. "You're in a lot of trouble around here," were his words, which I expected to be followed by a few more lashes for good measure. "So was he." His smile was at once generous and questioning, an offering and a request he was not sure I could understand. He reached out to the bookshelf, withdrew a book in a dark blue binding, and pressed it into my reluctant hands.

"Merton was kind of wild guy too, when he was young," he chuckled, perhaps remembering a moment in the book, "but he turned out all right after all. Maybe there's some hope for you. Now, off with you."

My face to the world did not dramatically change in the weeks and months ahead, but for some reason I stopped getting in so much trouble. Was it that I didn't want to be held after school when all I wanted to do was get home and up to my attic room on Forest Avenue to read a few more pages of that book, *The Seven Story Mountain*? And then move on to the next, *The Sign of Jonas* and after that, *The Waters of Siloe* and *Seeds of Contemplation* and *No Man Is an Island*. There was something in the writings of Thomas Merton I had never encountered before in the lives of the saints I had so ardently read.

There was no sanctimonious paeans to God, no once-and-for-all conversion experiences after which he was unalterably changed. No miracles. This man sounded like an actual human being. Merton continually confessed his sinfulness, his conflicts, his desire to be and do good and his ultimate failure in both. His parallel lives. (I wasn't alone!) And what was even more appealing was the way he spoke about his relationship with God. It was an uneven and unpredictable love affair, but both sides committed to its ups and downs. Merton's thirst for God rose up from those pages, fueled by passion not piety, the unflagging desire to understand his place before God. And here he was, a man of my own time, a *bon vivant* who lived a dissolute life in England, even made a girl pregnant, came to Columbia University and then turned his back on a budding literary life to join the Trappists, the most austere order of the Catholic church.

He wanted to know God, experience God. Thomas, oh Thomas, so did I. I began to have this fantasy that I would, on the spur of the moment, go to see him. He was at a monastery in Kentucky, just one state away. I would ask him how he prayed, how he could forgive himself when he sinned or failed. I would ask him how he knew what do with his life, what it felt like—in those fleeting moments of total abandonment and awareness—to be close to God.

It was about year later that I could wait no longer. I had read every Merton book in the school library; it was time to place my life before him. A friend had an older sister with a radiant coral pink '55 Ford Convertible and into its back seat we loaded great quantities of beer and headed south. We didn't exactly know where the Abbey of Gethsemani was, but we knew it was beyond Cincinnati on our side of the Ohio River, and the sin town of Covington on the Kentucky side. Top down, we drove. We drank. We played the radio at full blast. It was the middle of the night when we turned onto a drive, brilliantly lit by the moonlight (a sign of enlightenment to come, we were sure).

Over Cathedral Latin's door, it was *Opere et Veritate*. Here the challenge was more absolute: "For God Alone" read the sign over the archway leading to the main entrance. My hand reached for the knocker on the heavy wooden door. Once, twice, three times. A bolt was loosened. The door began to open. Just then, a bell high in the abbey church tower sounded, its muffled echo rolling over the knobby hills that surrounded the place. My friend and I looked at each other, a combination of fright and expectancy. We expected Thomas Merton to appear right then, see our fervor, invite us in for a simple breakfast, tell us how to find God, and we could be on our way home in a couple hours. Instead it was the brother gatekeeper, just aroused from his truncated night's sleep, and his heart was not so strangely warmed by these two reeking, besotted pilgrims.

I slept most of the day and, as best you can in a place where silence reigned, tried to find Merton. I looked into the faces of the monks, only occasionally upturned, who wordlessly cleaned the guest quarters and served our meals, but I realized I did not know what Merton looked like. Somehow, I surmised, the man who had written the words that had so inflamed my soul would somehow stand out, be different from all the rest of two hundred monks. From the visitors' loft in the rear of the high ceilinged, unadorned and impossibly elongated abbey church—I knew nothing of the elegant intent of Cistercian architecture to brook no distraction and focus everything on the simple stone altar—I peered down on the long rows of tonsured heads standing before their choir stalls. But none had "Thomas Merton" inscribed on the ample expanse of skin. They all seemed lost in another world, a world at once so appealing in its simplicity and obvious sanctity, but so alien from my own tiny universe.

It was here that Merton, who had first arrived as a jaded, lonesome, directionless pilgrim, just like I was, had famously written a line I could quote word for word: "As soon as I got inside, I knew I was home where I never had been or would be a stranger." I burned for such a home, such certitude and peace, to be a part of this life. But I knew that jumping into the Ford convertible for a visit was a very far cry from making this kind of statement with my young life. Finally I got up the courage to ask the priest who was in charge of the weekend retreatants—a group we were swept into—and he smiled. "Father Louis? Oh, yes, he's here someplace." He kindly added my request, one of perhaps hundreds he had received, to meet the great man.

Perhaps I actually saw him during that visit in 1956; I do not know. But Merton would walk with me through life, and we would meet again and again on the pages of his books in the years to come and in a very special way many years later.

I am able to approach the Buddhas barefoot and undisturbed, my feet in wet grass, wet sand.

Thomas Merton's now familiar, expectant words—some of his last—described his experience in the presence of the giant statues at one of Buddhism's most sacred sites, Gal Vihara, within the ancient city of Polunnaruwa in central Sri Lanka. They were written some twenty-seven years after he had entered the Trappists to seek his God and only four days before—his feet again wet, this time from a bath—his accidental contact with an ungrounded electric fan in a Red Cross Center outside Bangkok would end his life.

I had first been to Polunnaruwa in 1982, while filming the documentary, *Merton: A Film Biography*, which has been aired on PBS and NBC in the United States, and by networks abroad. I knew the outlines of his life and the crucial place Polunnaruwa occupied. But on that visit, over twenty years ago, I was more concerned with photographing Gal Vihara than experiencing it.

And so I returned, this time with my wife, Tracy. More a sentimental journey than anything else. I wanted to take in the statues at Gal Vihara and attempt to better understand Merton's cryptic journal notes, which, had he lived, would certainly have been expanded upon.

Polunnaruwa as an ancient city is a gem in itself, which I had either overlooked on my first visit or simply forgotten. The capital of Singhalese kings from the eleventh to the twelfth century, Polunnaruwa witnessed the rise of an advanced Buddhist culture, with exquisite palaces, temples and reliquaries, a massive reservoir system, as well as a sprawling monastic complex and libraries. The newly excavated and rebuilt remnants are breathtaking in their sheer scope, artistic beauty and diversity.

The statues at Gal Vihara, set within a hollow surrounded by trees, bear poignant testimony to the desire of the people of Polunnaruwa to dramatically present their beloved Buddha so that both current residents and future generations could stand in the presence of these immense figures and know that the journey toward enlightenment was worth the struggle. And that—as expressions on the statues' faces so eloquently bespoke—there was fulfillment awaiting them. Gal Vihara was obviously a site for continuing worship, as evidenced by the indentations in the rocks where wooden enclosures once framed each statue, presenting each in a more intimate grotto-like tableau.

> *. . . the silence of the extraordinary faces. The great smiles. Huge and yet subtle. Filled with every possibility, questioning nothing, knowing everything, rejecting nothing . . . .*

Carved into a massive outcropping of granite that sharply rises out of the otherwise gently rolling terrain are three exterior renditions of the Buddha and a smaller, seated Buddha within a cave. On the far left, Buddha sits in the classic lotus position, one hand upon the other in his lap. Then, after the cave opening, a huge, standing Buddha rises up, 23 feet tall, only to in turn be dwarfed by the reclining Buddha, stretching 45 feet at the far right of the site.

When I visited Gal Vihara years before, the statues were open to the air, but today, a metal roof has been constructed to protect them from the effects of sun and rain. But such a recent and modern addition quickly drops out of focus as one approaches the statues, barefoot as did Merton, in the quiet of a sultry, tropical Sri Lankan afternoon.

As Merton's eyes passed over the statues, he was at first struck with the look on the face of the standing figure. He initially described a ". . . smile, the sad smile . . ." but then went on to say it has more "imperative" than even the Mona Lisa, because of its simplicity and straightforwardness.

Indeed, there is somewhat of a quixotic expression on the face of the standing Buddha, dramatically accented by the lines of black segment ingrained in the rock that streak across the nose and cheeks, almost like etched lines in skin, expressing emotion perhaps wrought either from a moment's recognition, or alternately, from years of experience. The sixth century B. C. Siddhartha Gautama had, like Thomas Merton of the 20th Century, struggled for so many years to find the path beyond human suffering and cupidity to reach beyond. For the young nobleman it had been a wandering, itinerant life. For Merton, the orphaned, cosmopolitan writer, the choice was to remain in place, within the Trappist cloister at the Abbey of Our Lady of Gethsemani, in the American heartland.

> *Looking at these figures I was suddenly, almost forcibly, jerked clean out of the habitual, half-tied vision of things, and an inner clearness, clarity, as if exploding from the rocks themselves, became evident and obvious.*

If we might extrapolate those words just a bit, it appears Merton, who had a rich sense of irony and humor as well as a deep understanding of both Eastern and Western mysticism, intuited a profound insight in those at once sad, sly and knowing smiles. The hand-wringing days were over, the myriad questions rendered irrelevant, the once precisely delineated steps to enlightenment—or union with The Almighty—now but a feeble ladder that would be soon kicked away.

It was not intellect that finally decoded this Higher Power, but rather that his heart and soul had simply been so completely enveloped that there was no longer any need to do anything but, quite simply, rest in the simplicity of it all. Everything and nothing were but different words for the same reality. The venerable contemplative stages, never understood in the present, had once again worked their mysterious power in Merton. The purgative—through decades of an ascetic life—yielded to the illuminative—which was revealed in so many of his books and journal notes—and now, the final stage—the unitive—was at hand.

As I approached closer to the reclining Buddha, I was taken with two small details of this sublime figure, its head resting gently on an outstretched hand, in turn resting on a pillow—though made of stone—that looked soft and comfortable, beckoning to the pilgrim to find rest. The first detail was barely visible and I had surely not noticed it before. The Buddha's left leg was ever so slightly bent, the knee giving a gentle, almost imperceptible rise to the sculpted stone robe that covered the figure from neck to ankle. And, because of this, the massive toes on the left foot were similarly askew, just inches (on the scale of the statue, just a hair's breadth) behind the right.

My visit to the cave temples of Dambulla, where Merton also stopped enroute to Polunnaruwa, had acquainted me with the belief, certainly well known to Buddhists, that such a position represented the pregnant moment just before the Buddha received enlightenment. It is pure speculation, but I wonder now if Merton, with his exquisite sensitivity and deep knowledge of this venerable tradition, might not have paused at those misaligned toes, that extended knee, before his eyes rose up to take in the serene face of the standing Buddha, towering above this reclining image.

As I wrote in the script for *Merton: A Film Biography*, "He had struggled long and hard to find his God." These inadequate words attempted to synthesize his years in the cloister, millions of words written, intimations of transcendence experienced (as his soaring portrayals of the night fire watch and the street corner epiphany in Louisville demonstrate) and the countervailing moments of crushing darkness, doubt and conflict of his journals and his Confessions, the roiling sea that marks any true spiritual quest.

Then something happened to Merton at Gal Vihara. Although he was given to overstatement and sometimes-ephemeral enthusiasms (he once vowed to live in Russia, so if a nuclear bomb were dropped, he would be among the victims) that quickly faded, he had never before claimed what he would write in his journal that day.

> *. . . an inner clearness, clarity, as if exploding from the rocks themselves became evident and obvious . . . . I don't know when in my life I have ever had such a sense of beauty and spiritual validity running together in one aesthetic illumination.* And then the simple line that speaks volumes: *I know and have seen what I was obscurely looking for.*

Here was a thoroughly Catholic Trappist monk, who had, thousands upon thousands of times prayed the Divine Office, said Mass, immersed himself in the richness of Scripture in *Lectio Divina*, only to have that astonishing moment before what—at the time, and perhaps by some still today—were considered little more than idols. In fact, Merton notes in his journal that his host, the local vicar from Kandy was "shying away from 'paganism,' hanging back and sits under a tree reading a guidebook."

But, to Merton, such conventional wisdom of the day was totally irrelevant. He had burst through traditional boundaries of belief. The God he sought in the cloister, in prayer, in ascetic practices, the God he tried somehow to address, describe and quantify in his writing, was a God of a subtle and knowing smile, a God everywhere, in everything.

That Merton would die so soon after this apocalyptic moment at Gal Vihara was certainly tragic. But, in the cosmic economy of life and death, of which we know little or nothing, in a way he had reached his goal: he had glimpsed, if only for that instant, the face of the Divine. Who knows what more years of his life would have been like? He surely would have gone on to write more books. Perhaps he would have remained a monk of Gethsemani—there is nothing to indicate he wanted anything else. For certain, his capacious mind would have caused him to address both the issues of the day as well as the issues of the soul.

But as my own eyes took in those massive stone toes then rose to look into the face of the Buddha, I could begin to understand what he must have felt, standing exactly where I stood. It is something we all seek, that moment, the culmination of years of searching, his searching and our own, a journey on which his words have accompanied us.

> *I don't know what else remains, but I have now seen and have pierced through the surface and have got beyond the shadow and the disguise.*

The Last Audiotapes

Paul Quenon, OCSO

In the monastery, at the time when Fr. Louis died, I was in charge of the tape recordings. I had copied many of his conferences, and kept them in the basement studio, built as a separate climate controlled room installed inside a huge unused cheese chiller. Besides my sorrow at Merton's death there was an added disappointment that I would never hear his stories and reflections about his travels and days in Asia. So when an audio tape arrived from Bangkok, a reel to reel tape, it was with great anticipation that I put it onto the tape deck, eager to be one of the first ones to hear it at the monastery.

I listened to it all through to the end. What I heard at the end was utterly astonishing. At the point he finished the talk he then announced that there would be a be a break—and what I heard was: "Meanwhile, I will just disappear"—SNAP . . . tick . . . tick . . . tick . . . tick . . . and on it went for several minutes, with nothing further until silence. I knew how clumsy tape operators can be, and could well imagine someone leaving his wrist watch by the mike. But the coincidence was nothing short of *ominous.*

The clumsiness of the tape ending seemed at one with the clumsiness of the whole death incident and was frustrating. With him something had been broken off that seemed like it should go on indefinitely. There was so much more to come from where so much had come already.

I had all the 280-something talks on the shelf, the recordings originally begun by Br. Killian Sullivan, somewhat to the chagrin of Fr. Louis. He, then Novice Master, was willing to let us save the tapes and lock them up in a box (or so the silent hand signs he made to me seemed to suggest on that day in the Grand Parlor when I indicated I would do the recordings. One could never be completely sure about sign language, but the way he shut that imaginary box lid made it seem emphatic.)

This Bangkok tape, I believed, would be the last tape in the collection. It was not one of his best, but certainly one of his most significant. Others however would come, such as the panel discussion at the Center for Democratic Studies in Berkeley, where Bishop Pike would say that religion to the youth of today is "a crashing bore," where Fr. Louis would say: "I may return from Asia and do nothing more than engage in vocal prayer in choir"; and where Fr. Louis said the monk is like the rebellious young people because the monk is a man of the margins. The latter thought about marginality had been gestating in his mind and was expressed in conferences long before he departed on his journey.

But the audio tape that arrived last, from the Temple of Understanding, was the one that rounded out the whole picture for me and brought all the sad circumstances together in a whole and meaningful conclusion. It was his voice, so familiar and so in accord with the way he swiftly and effectively spoke what he might have to say: they were these words that are celebrated in this volume and stand to this day as timeless.

I left the recording studio that afternoon with the feeling that the man had come to completeness. He had moved into the universal where he was already headed, and had been able to give words to this spiritual maturity in a place where it could be heard. I was satisfied and much in admiration. It all seemed right. The words had set a goal and an enduring vision for the rest of us.

Thomas Merton: Memories Of A Brother Monk

John Eudes Bamberger, OCSO

Human memory mysteriously takes on a wide variety of forms in every person's life. The nature and workings of memory in each of us are rightly qualified as mysterious for many reasons. For one, accessible memory is notoriously selective. The nature of its selectivity is not arbitrary but is governed by laws operating for the most part unconsciously. What events and features we consciously remember often suggest a strongly subjective influence dependent on our values, moral commitments and goals. These and a broad variety of emotions color our memories to a considerable extent. The memories a person has of the past exert a large influence on the individual's sense of identity and worth, with the result that each of us has firm commitments to the meaningful past as actually remembered. Added to these features of my own memory's functioning is the fact that, as a priest and a physician, I have an obligation to exclude some matters from my account of the remembered past. These comments are certainly applicable to my recollections of Father Louis, the name we knew Merton by in the community; they find wide application in regard to Fr. Louis' memories as well.

Before I entered the monastery at Gethsemani and came to know Fr. Louis in person, I formed a lively image of Merton that is rooted in an encounter with his autobiography shortly after its publication in 1948. I was in the last intensive years of medical school at the time and so had little opportunity for reading anything but medical literature. While waiting for a friend to present herself for an evening together, I picked up a book lying on the table next to me so as to pass the time usefully. It was *The Seven Storey Mountain*. The opening pages struck me with such forceful impact that I experienced the actuality of God's reality with a fresh awareness of His transcendent existence. Resulting from that rather haunting impression was the persuasion that it is possible so to live as to enter into a fuller relation to Him. That, after all, is the major theme of Merton's book, giving purpose to the story described in its pages. Associated with this insight was the desire to know the man who could so convincingly convey the existence of a world whose center and horizon is the living God.

Once I entered the Community of Gethsemani as a novice, I was curious to know the monk who had authored the book which had spoken so eloquently of God's presence in the world. Since we observed a strict silence and as novices were encouraged to attend strictly to our own affairs, it was only some months after my entering the monastery that my curiosity was satisfied. When Fr. Louis began to give us novices a series of conferences on monastic life, I finally identified Merton. He was a very different type of person than I had imagined the author I had read to be. He was very lively, direct and simple in manner; not in the least solemn or seemingly introverted. He did not hesitate to give way to his friendliness and possessed a ready sense of humor, judiciously employed so as to lighten up the atmosphere. At the same time, he spoke of weighty topics such as the discipline needed for the spiritual life and prayer, displaying a facility of communication and a personal conviction that rendered the classes at once interesting and informative. He obviously enjoyed meeting with us and speaking of spiritual matters. His classes were anything but boring. As a result of the stimulation we received from him, a number of us novices developed a serious interest in monastic studies as a way of prayerfully seeking union with God. His classes were appealing as well as a help to entering into the life of prayer. Monastic observance and discipline were presented in the service of the personal growth in the interior knowledge and love of the living God.

My more personal relations with Fr. Louis, however, began only after I had made simple vows two years after having entered the monastery. He had been appointed Master of Juniors only about a year before. As he was the first one to fulfill this role, he was quite free to create its style, adapting the formation to the needs and possibilities of the newly professed monks. This office had been established in our Order rather recently, not being mentioned in the Rule of St. Benedict in which there is no provision for formation of those in temporary vows. Merton's lectures introduced us to such fields of knowledge as the Bible, Liturgy and Monastic History among others. Merton demonstrated not only lively interest in these fields of knowledge but a real enthusiasm. He was invariably well prepared for his classes and had an informal manner of delivery that resulted in a friendly spirit that we carried with us into the various activities of the rest of our day that included attendance at choir offices and manual labor in the fields and vegetable gardens.

Merton not only met us in the classroom and for private discussion, he also worked with us in the fields and forests. In those days he had not as yet developed the bone problem that later resulted in surgery on his spine. I recall how energetically he wielded a hoe working in company with a group of us juniors. During that same period of time (1952-1955), he would take a group of us simple professed out to the woods outside the cloister enclosure where a former tool shed had been adapted to serve as a hermitage (he called it St. Anne's) where he had permission to stay and do reading and some of his writing. As we set out on one such occasion, I remember his quoting a passage from the Scriptures that took up the theme of escaping into solitude. I am not sure of the precise passage, but recall distinctly the flavor of his exhortation. A text from the prophet Jeremiah captures it: "Flee and save your soul, be like the wild ass in the wilderness (31:6)." At this proclamation we scattered into the adjacent fields and woods to spend time in silent reflection and prayer.

On a later occasion, having now had considerably more contact with Fr. Louis so that we knew one another better, he invited me to join him at his newly constructed hermitage so as to participate in a meeting he had arranged with a Hindu monk, a member of a monastery in India who was visiting him. The three of us had a protracted exchange concerning various religious matters. Naturally one topic we covered in some detail was Hindu belief and monastic practice in contrast to our own. The discussion proceeded in a friendly climate that Merton was adept at creating. However, his contribution at times, to my mind, was too sympathetic and yielding, giving the impression he had no objections to certain Hindu beliefs that are clearly unacceptable to Catholic teaching. After the Hindu monk left us to return to the abbey, I pointed out to Fr. Louis that his comments and manner went too far at some points, giving a false impression as to Catholic teaching. He readily replied: "Sometimes you have to go along with those guys," making it evident by further comments and his whole manner that he did not at all agree with the Hindu position on the matters that are objectionable for a Christian; rather, he was making himself agreeable by dissembling any disagreements. This kind of accommodation did not seem honest to me or even productive in the end. Merton, at an earlier time at Cambridge University, had intended to qualify for the British diplomatic service. Had he pursued that course with application, he surely could have competed with the best! Americans have not always agreed with this feature of the English style. Michael Mott in his biography, *The Seven Mountains of Thomas Merton*, commented on his persistent tendency to adapt himself to others in ways that could be misleading.

This tendency to accommodate himself, without a serious commitment to the impression he made, was operative in more subtle ways and in a variety of situations as his diaries and some letters clearly establish. However, this incident was the only one of its kind involving a point of faith that I, at any rate, had witnessed. There was no such equivocating when I was with him at an encounter with Sidi Abdesalam, the Sufi master from Algeria. Fr. Louis invited me with two or three other monks to join in a meeting to discuss prayer and spiritual experience. The conversation was cordial, open in spirit and without any equivocal statements by any of us. Merton was a capable, reliable and facilitating presence. My impressions were that the tendency to make himself agreeable to others had strong roots in Merton's character, a tendency that contributed to his friendly manner as well as to his strong sense of sympathy for human suffering. This trait, in my opinion, played a prominent role in Merton's increasing contributions to causes of peace and justice.

It happened some few years later, about 1962 as I recall, on an occasion when I was free to spend the day alone, I took the customary path to Merton's more distant hermitage. As I proceeded on my way, I traversed a wooded area and observed Fr. Louis walking alone. I remained partially hidden by the trees not far away from him. Due to the disposition of the trees, he did not see me until I was rather nearby so that I could clearly perceive, by noting his features and his preoccupied way of walking, that he was burdened, preoccupied with some quite distressing matters in his thought. As I drew nearer, he suddenly noticed my presence and abruptly altered his whole manner and features. He greeted me with a warm expression and a smile that characterized his customary behavior in the presence of others, displaying only briefly the embarrassment he felt at having allowed something of his divided and weaker area of his interior self to be observed. This dividedness between the gifted, competent, lovable person, and the unlovable, isolated, lonely self, was so well concealed in daily life as to remain unrecognized by even close associates in and outside the monastery. Nor do biographers give prominence to the considerable suffering that the inner inconsistencies and contradictions within his character created for him, nor do they recognize the role it played in what was to be a real crisis in his life some time later

As I recall that scene in the woods, I associate it with a statement Merton made some years later, at the end of 1966, in a letter he wrote to me concerning a discussion we had shared the day before. After learning that Merton had been having an intense relationship with a young nurse whom he had met during back surgery, the abbot had asked me to intervene and engage Merton about his situation which was obviously provoking an acute inner crisis for him. The day after our initial discussion about this relationship, he wrote me a letter to give his reflections on our talk. He began his observations in the following terms: "Our talk yesterday has been fruitful in this: it has suggested some helpful perspectives anyway." But he soon qualified this statement in a way that gives the unfounded impression that I had implied he was previously without inner conflicts: "Anyone who thinks that I was whole and consistent before [my relationship with this young woman] simply does not know me. My fall into inconsistency was nothing but the revelation of what I am" And in subsequently referring to his letter to me about our meeting in his journals (*Learning to Love*, 106-107), he made a further comment: "However, there is no harm in taking seriously his [(Fr. Eudes'] advice. I'll accept the fact that it is perhaps a much bigger problem than I realized. And try to work it out."

I state for the record that, in my meeting with Father Louis, he was open about the vulnerabilities in his character that had led to his pursuing relations with a young woman twenty-seven years his junior. During our meeting, and in that subsequent letter to me, he discussed a basic conflict of his inner life, almost having the nature of a "wound" which made him feel that he was basically an unloving and unlovable person.

I am reminded of a talk I had with a good friend, an experienced government official, who for some years served as a driver at the abbey. On one occasion when driving Merton to town, he told me how Merton had shared with him the fact that for him the monastery had become the first real home he ever had. His mother's death, when he was five, his father's artistic interests and his various and prolonged travels in the service of his career as a painter, and then his father's death when Merton was in his mid-teens, resulted in his feeling abandoned and left largely on his own. He entered the adult world feeling he was isolated in his most personal center. In his autobiography he touched only lightly on this matter, but he continued to suffer from it affectively. A young child commonly perceives such absence, whether by death or prolonged distancing from the parent, to mean he is not lovable, and feels guilty. He interprets it to mean he must be at fault, not good enough, lacking in some essential quality or he would not be left to himself and abandoned. This deep self-doubt is at the source of an inner dividedness that Merton spoke of in his note to me. It accounts for more of his behavior throughout his life than anyone has as yet explored in adequate detail. The lack of intimate support he received as a child, coupled with his need for, but also resistance to, guidance on matters of his inner sense of himself, would be a source of turmoil that would haunt the adult Merton, although unconsciously acting on him most of the time. His need for intimacy, and yet self-defensively avoiding it, he mostly kept hidden from himself and others.

Dom James recognized and intimately knew the role that a lack of real intimacy with others played in Merton's life. Fox knew Merton the man and the monk in certain respects more fully than anyone else. He appreciated his natural gifts, his depth of commitment and the sincerity of his spiritual life. He chose Merton as master of the junior monks, then appointed him novice master—the two positions most influential for training the younger generations of Gethsemani's community. Both roles entailed close collaboration between the two men and required that each provide advice to one another and that each accept it. The Abbot took Fr. Louis as his own confessor. So while respecting his many gifts, Dom James knew Merton's earlier family history and realized keenly that, along with the strengths he possessed in abundance, he suffered keenly throughout his life from the painful loss of each parent. Dom James is said to have told someone that, even late in his life, Merton could never speak about his

mother without tears. And, in fact, Merton mentions his mother so seldom in his journals that his silence might well indicate that his feelings about her were too deep and
sensitive to be analyzed out-loud even to himself in his personal and private writing.

As Fr. Louis prepared to go on the trip to the Bangkok, he traveled briefly to Washington, D. C. to meet with the Ambassador of Indonesia, Dr. Soedjatmoko. In what
proved to be my last personal meeting with Merton, he came to the infirmary to meet
with me. After he told me of his travel plans, he asked for some medicines he would
need when in Asia. I wished him a safe and fruitful trip and provided him with appropriate medications. For his trip to Washington, D.C., I had arranged for him to stay with
a psychiatrist friend of mine whom I knew from my days on the staff at Georgetown
University Hospital. Dr. Camera-Peon lived in Georgetown and kindly agreed to meet
him at the airport. The visiting monk stayed in Nico's apartment and spent the evening
in conversation with his host. Merton met the ambassador the next day with his wife
and children at his family home. As another example of Merton's friendly charm, the
busy ambassador prolonged their meeting. By the time they parted after a five hour
visit, they were on first name terms, Tom and Koko. The Dalai Lama was to have a similar experience after his meeting with the Trappist. He who was wary of speaking with
visitors, after a first talk with the American monk, arranged for two further exchanges.
Merton described the discussions as "very warm and cordial," adding that, by the end,
they had become "very good friends." The Dalai Lama was so impressed by him that he
spoke of him as a Catholic Geshe, that is, an expert in spiritual matters. As Fr. Louis put
it, "the equivalent of an honorary doctorate."

While on his extensive travels, Merton maintained an ongoing correspondence
with his community. Perhaps the most revealing exchange took place with Dom James.
The retired abbot, now living in his own hermitage, had written him a friendly, even
warmly-worded letter, expressing to Fr. Louis his support, good wishes and prayers
for the success of his travels. From Calcutta on October 20th, 1968, some few weeks
before his death, Merton replied in what was to be his final exchange with the man
who had been his abbot during nearly twenty years. His opening words reflect the
warm and friendly tone that had marked the abbot's message. He thanked the abbot
for his message which he found "warm and gracious." He goes on to comment on their
past relations when both were in office collaborating in the formation of young monks.
After referring briefly to the differences they had struggled with in their collaboration, Merton added that he never felt resentment for the decisions Dom James made
and the policies he had pursued, for he understood that the abbot was "following his
conscience." After discussing his current activities and plans, as well as the difficulties
he had been having with his travels in Asia, Fr. Louis concluded the letter on a very
personal note: "Be sure that I have never changed in my respect for you as Abbot, and
affection as Father. Our different views certainly did not affect our deep agreement on
the real point of life and our vocation. I hope you are enjoying a beautiful quiet autumn
out in the wild knobs."

Merton continued his travels, visiting Ceylon and Singapore, and made a solitary
retreat in the Himalayas, then proceeded to Bangkok. On December 8th, two days
before the fatal accident, he wrote what was to be his last letter to Gethsemani. The
more he had traveled and the longer his absence from his monastery, the more kindly
were his comments and the deeper his feelings for the community there found expression. He concluded, after saying the brothers were in his thoughts, "I feel homesick for

Gethsemani." Although he could not realize it, these words were to be his farewell to the brothers.

When the message arrived at Gethsemani that brought the news of his accidental death, I was in our monastery in Georgia, preaching the community retreat. Abbot Flavian called to give me the news and told me to return promptly so as to be on hand when the plane from California that conveyed Merton's body arrived in Louisville. I was given the charge to view and identify the body. Driving through the snow-covered roads of the mountain country, I arrived in time to meet the plane. Upon viewing the corpse, I was able to identify Merton's body in spite of the disfigurement caused by the extensive burn from the 240 volts of electricity that operated the defective fan. Abbot Flavian also viewed the corpse but was unable to identify Fr. Louis due to the marks from the injury as well as the fact that the body had not been embalmed. I considered it prudent to write a brief note to record that I, an M.D., had examined and identified the body, for I suspected someone would eventually deny that it was Merton who was buried at the Gethsemani monastery. I eventually deposited that certification at the Thomas Merton Center at Bellarmine University. My actions were justified as, shortly after the funeral, I read a newspaper article on Merton's death in Thailand that denied that the body in the closed casket was that of Merton. It asserted that the body had disappeared when an alligator had come up from a canal of the extensive Khlong in Bangkok, and, as the American monk stood on the bank, had devoured him: thus the holy monk disappeared and entered Nirvana.

I still pray daily for my fellow monks, Dom James and Father Louis, to each of whom I owe so much by their teaching and example. As I write this memoir I see in imagination the two crosses that mark their graves, side by side under the tall pine in the Gethsemani cemetery, in the shadow of the abbey church.

A Last Visit With "Uncle Louie"

Patrick Hart, OCSO

Before dawn on a cool September morning in 1968, three of us trod our way through the wet grass up past the old sheep barn, stopping long enough to catch our breath at the top of the hill leading into the thick woods. As we crossed the fence gate we caught sight of the hermitage nestled against a curtain of dark green pine trees, and Father Louis was sitting on the lighted porch praying his morning office. Brother Maurice Flood, who would look after the hermitage in Father's absence, Philip Stark, a Jesuit scholastic from Woodstock College who had spent the summer in the Guest House at Gethsemani and who had helped with the typing and layout of *Monks Pond* (a journal of avant-garde poetry edited by Father Louis), and I, his secretary, were invited by Father to join him in his last Mass at the hermitage chapel before he left on his Asian journey.

As we approached the cabin, "Uncle Louie" (his monastic nickname and one which amused him) closed his breviary and greeted us warmly. He asked us if we had any special preference for what Mass he would offer. We decided unanimously that it would be the Votive Mass of Saint Peter Claver, which was a great favorite of his. Coincidentally, it turned out to be Phil's birthday, so it was appropriate to have the Mass in honor of a Jesuit saint.

After filling the cruets with water and wine, Father began to vest for Mass, as we lighted the candles. The chapel, which was a more recent addition to the hermitage, was just large enough to accommodate a congregation of three. On the wall above the cedar altar hung a group of five or six icons of varying sizes (one originally came from Mount Athos), and on the floor in front of the altar was a hand-woven Navajo rug, a gift from the Benedictine monks of Christ in the Desert monastery in New Mexico.

We all joined in the Prayers of the Faithful. Phil read the Epistle, and Father Louis read the beautiful Gospel narrative of the Good Samaritan, after which he surprised us with a brief but deeply moving homily. He compared himself to "the traveler" who had been attacked by robbers and was then left half dead along the road, and described how we each in our way had been Good Samaritans to him, helping him "to get out of the ditch." He embarrassed us by expressing his appreciation for all we had done for him (precious little it was!) and he said he was offering the Holy Sacrifice of the Mass for our intentions.

Before Communion he embraced each of us in the Kiss of Peace. We received under both Species of bread and wine, and I remember that he addressed us personally, using our first names: "The Body of Christ, Phil, etc." As beautiful and as meaningful a Mass as I have ever experienced.

After a short, silent Thanksgiving we heard "Uncle Louie" in the kitchen preparing coffee for our breakfast, so we came in from the porch and got in his way in an effort to help. Places were set on the wooden table in front of the fireplace, before the large window overlooking the quiet valley. By now the sun was beginning to rise behind the knobs in the east, and there in the joy of the morning we broke bread with our hermit for the last time.

During our breakfast we gave Father free advice about his forthcoming trip, over which he was as enthusiastic as a child in expectation of some wonderful new adventure. Phil and I, who had spent several years in Rome, cautioned him about exotic Oriental foods and how careful he should be. We also warned him about drinking the local tap water, and advised him to be content with wine or beer with his meals. To this suggestion he agreed wholeheartedly.

He spoke of the various places and people he hoped to visit on his Asian journey—especially the Dalai Lama and the Tibetan Buddhist monks now exiled in northern India, for whom he had the greatest respect and a lively interest. He was going with an open attitude of listening to them and learning what he could from the ancient monastic traditions of the East, as he wrote later: "I hope I can bring back to my monastery something of the Asian wisdom with which I am fortunate to be in contact" (*The Asian Journal of Thomas Merton*, 320).

We cleared off the table and went out on the porch, where the sun was not very bright. Father Louis remembered that he had some unused film in his camera, and he began at once taking pictures of the three of us. We took turns with the camera so that we had photographs with him in front of the hermitage and in the surrounding woods. When the last frame of the roll of film was shot, we returned to the hermitage and began clearing things up in preparation for his departure. Father gave us of us books and photographs, saying: "Here, Phil, a book for you, one of Victor Hammer's excellent hand-printed books (*Hagia Sophia*) and to me a copy of *The John Howard Griffin Reader*, which I was eager to read. He pinned a "hermit button" on Brother Maurice.

After some last minute instructions about taking care of his correspondence during his absence, he handed me his set of keys to the hermitage and to his post office box, where an enormous stack of mail was delivered daily. We said goodbye, never realizing that this would be our last Mass with Father Louis. With loaded arms, we headed down to the monastery.

This was my last sight of the man of God who was to me a Father, a Brother and a Faithful Friend. May the Lord be rich in rewarding him "good measure, pressed down, shaken together and running over . . . ."

His Holiness the Dalai Lama with Abbot Timothy Kelly and Brother Patrick Hart at Thomas Merton's Grave, photograph by David Stephenson, 1994.

His death was a great loss. If Father Thomas Merton were still alive, I am sure we would have been comrades working closely together to further the dialogue between religious traditions and to help bring real peace to our world.

Tenzin Gyatso, His Holiness the Dalai Lama

List Of Contributors

Dianne Aprile teaches nonfiction on the faculty of Spalding University's Master of Fine Arts in Writing program in Louisville, Kentucky. A journalist for more than 25 years, she is the author of four books of nonfiction and has had poems and essays published in journals, newspapers and anthologies. Most recently she edited and contributed to *The Book,* a fine-art collection of photographs of books (by Julius Friedman) accompanied by poetry and prose by 20 writers across the country, including Pulitzer Prize and National Book Award winners, and Poets Laureate. She has written two books about the Trappists: a history, *The Abbey of Gethsemani/Place of Peace and Paradox* and *Making A Heart for God, A Week in the Life of a Catholic Monastery.* She is a 2012 Washington state Artist Trust Fellow in literature, and is the recipient of a 2011 Hedgebrook Residency on Whidbey Island, Washington. She leads workshops and gives lectures on writing and subjects related to Thomas Merton. She lives with her husband, Ken Shapero, in Kirkland, Washington.

Morgan C. Atkinson is a documentary producer based in Louisville, Kentucky. He produces programming that focuses on people or groups seeking meaning through a spiritual search. A recent work, "Soul Searching: The Journey of Thomas Merton" was broadcast nationally on PBS. He edited a book (with Jonathan Montaldo) of the same name. He is working on a new Merton documentary entitled "The Many Lives and Last Days of Thomas Merton" (2015): http://tommerton.com.

John Eudes Bamberger, OCSO is a Cistercian monk who entered the Abbey of Gethsemani in 1950. Merton was his Master of Juniors for three years. Having entered the monastic life after receiving his M.D., his abbot sent him to pursue a residency in Psychiatry at Georgetown University Hospital. He served as Abbot of Genesee Abbey (1971-2001) in Piffard, New York. Upon his retirement he became a hermit on his monastery's grounds and resides there in solitude today. The author of many articles, his books include *Evagrius Ponticus: The Praktikos* (1972) and *Thomas Merton: Prophet of Renewal* (2005).

David Joseph Belcastro is a Professor in the Department of Religion and Philosophy at Capital University in Bexley, Ohio. He is serving as President of the International Thomas Merton Society [hereinafter referred to as the ITMS] (2013-2015) and is the editor (with Joseph Q. Raab) of *The Merton Annual.*

Harriet Hope Berman practices Japanese Handpapermaking as a meditation art. Growing up in the Jewish tradition and having travelled in India and Nepal, with a Doctorate in Humanistic Psychology, she has studied and practiced many faith traditions. She was baptized a Catholic at Santa Sabina Center where she was Program Director for the Center's retreats for 25 years. She continues her Handpapermaking practice at Santa Sabina and in Mill Valley where she resides.

Christine M. Bochen is professor of Religious Studies at Nazareth College, Rochester, New York where she holds the William H. Shannon Chair in Catholic Studies. She has edited a volume of Thomas Merton's letters to writers, *Courage for Truth*, and a volume of Merton's journals, *Learning to Love*, as well as *Thomas Merton: Essential Writings* in the Orbis Books series of writings by spiritual masters. She co-authored *The Thomas Merton Encyclopedia* with William H. Shannon and Patrick O'Connell. With William Shannon, she co-edited Thomas Merton's *Cold War Letters* and, most recently, *Thomas Merton: A Life in Letters.* She is a founding member and past President of the ITMS and is chairing the ITMS Centenary Committee in preparation for the celebration of Merton's 100th birthday in 2015.

Cynthia Bourgeault is an Episcopal priest, writer and internationally known retreat leader. She divides her time between solitude at her seaside hermitage in Maine and a demanding schedule traveling globally to teach and spread the recovery of the Christian contemplative and Wisdom path. She is a founding Director, Advisor and Principal Teacher for The Contemplative Society, and leads a network of Wisdom Schools in various locations world-wide. She has authored eight books including *The Holy Trinity and the Law of Three; The Meaning of Mary Magdalene; The Wisdom Jesus;* and *The Wisdom Way of Knowing.*

Mike Brennan lives with his wife Margaret and daughter Mary in Chicago, and works at O'Hare Airport as a baggage handler. He continues to edit the O'Hare Chapel Bulletin. He leads the Chicago Chapter of the ITMS.

Patricia A. Burton has been working on bibliography and indexes of Merton's work since 1997. *More Than Silence: A Bibliography of Thomas Merton* was published in 2008 in the American Theological Society Bibliography Series, number 55. *Merton Vade Mecum* (a Timeline with notes) and *About Merton: Secondary Sources* (with Marquita E. Breit and Paul M. Pearson) are now available through the Thomas Merton Center, and an updated edition of *Index to the Published Letters of Thomas Merton* is forthcoming. In 2005 she was awared the "Louie" for her service to Merton studies and the ITMS. She lives in Toronto, Canada.

Jeannette Cantrell has been an art dealer/archivist for her husband Jim Cantrell's work since their move from Nebraska to Kentucky in 1970. She founded the Bardstown Art Gallery and in 1980 added Thomas Merton Books to the business. Her Necessity Press was a venture into the fine press world—hand-setting the type, printing and binding Brother Patrick Hart's *First and Last Memories* in a limited edition of 250 copies. www.ThomasMertonBooks.com.

Jim Cantrell is a renowned painter with a BFA in Art Education from the University of Nebraska-Lincoln and an MA in Ceramics and Painting from the University of Northern Colorado in Greeley. He taught art for 14 years and has now been an independent studio artist for 44 years garnering numerous awards and recognition in the U. S. and abroad. He was commissioned by the St. Joseph Cathedral to paint the 12 Apostles, and Holy Family. The Abbey of Gethsemani also commissioned him to design and construct a ceramic wall piece for the entrance to the Retreat House and paint the large triptych depicting the history of the Cistercian Order for the lobby. His work is in the permanent collections of eight art museums around the country as well as in the collection of the Thomas Merton Center at Bellarmine University in Louisville, Kentucky. www. BardstownArtGallery.com.

Michael Casagram, OCSO entered the Cistercian Order in 1961 at Holy Cross Monastery in Virginia. He transferred to Gethsemani in 1964. He is a beekeeper involved in the formation of novices at Gethsemani for many years. He currently serves as Gethsemani's Prior.

Michael Casey, OCSO is a monk of Tarrawarra Abbey in Victoria, Australia. The author of numerous books and articles on Cistercian and Benedictine monasticism and spirituality, he has written extensively on Merton: "Merton within a Tradition of Prayer," *Cistercian Studies* 13 (1978) and 14 (1979); "Merton's Notes on 'Inner Experience': Twenty Five Years Afterwards," *Tjurunga* 44 (1993); "Merton's Teaching on the 'Common Will,'" *The Merton Annual* 12 (1999); "Afterword" in *Survival or Prophecy? The Correspondence of Jean Leclercq and Thomas Merton* (2008); and the forthcoming "Thomas Merton: Nomad of the Spirit: An Introduction to an Exhibition of Merton's Photographs."

Joan Chittister, OSB is a Benedictine Sister of Erie, Pennsylvania, and an international lecturer and award-winning author of over fifty books, for which she has won thirteen Catholic Press Association awards. For over thirty years she has dedicated herself to advocating for universal recognition of the critical questions impacting the global community—peace, justice and equality—and has received numerous awards and recognition for her work. She served as President of the Conference of American Benedictine Prioresses and was prioress of the Benedictine Sisters of Erie for 12 years. She is the founder and executive director of Benetvision, a resource and research center for contemporary spirituality located in Erie, Pennsylvania.

John P. Collins received his Ph.D. from Boston College and served on the faculties of the College of the Holy Cross, Worcester State University and the International Education Program, Inc. He has contributed articles to: *Cistercian Studies Quarterly*, *The Merton Annual*, *The Merton Seasonal*, *The Merton Journal* and *Religion and the Arts*, as well as a chapter in the book *Destined for Evil*. For the past twelve years, he has written a monthly Thomas Merton column for the *Catholic Free Press*, the Worcester, Massachusetts diocesan newspaper. He has served for over a decade as director and facilitator of the ITMS Chapter at St. Mary's Parish, Shrewsbury, Massachusetts. He is the facilitator for the ITMS Chapter at the Massachusetts Correctional Institution, Shirley, Massachusetts.

James Conner, OCSO entered the Abbey of Gethsemani in 1949. He was a student under Merton from 1951-55. After ordination he served as Undermaster of Novices under Merton from 1958-61. He pursued studies in Rome at the Gregorianum University from 1962-64. He lived at the Monastery of Christ in the Desert and was Superior there from 1973-77. He was Chaplain at Osage Monastery in Oklahoma from 1978-90, when he returned to Gethsemani. In 1994 he was appointed as Superior and later elected Abbot of Assumption Abbey in Ava, Missouri, and served there until 1999. He is currently Chaplain for the Abbey of Gethsemani's Retreat House.

Lawrence S. Cunningham is John A. O'Brien Professor of Theology (Emeritus) at the University of Notre Dame. The author or editor of over twenty-six books, including *Thomas Merton: Spiritual Master* and *The Monastic Vision*, he has lectured on Thomas Merton in this country and abroad.

Ron Dart has taught in the Department of Political Science/Philosophy/Religious Studies at University of the Fraser Valley (British Columbia, Canada) since 1990. He was on staff with Amnesty International in the 1980s. He has published twenty-five books in the areas of spirituality, church, politics, mountaineering, and Thomas Merton. He is one of the "Northern Lights" on the National Executive Council of the Thomas Merton Society of Canada and contributed to the recent book by Canadians on Merton, *Thomas Merton: Monk on the Edge.*

John Dear is an internationally recognized voice for peace and nonviolence. A priest, pastor, peacemaker, retreat leader, and author, he served for years as the director of the Fellowship of Reconciliation, the largest interfaith peace organization in the U. S. After September 11, 2001, he was a Red Cross coordinator of chaplains at the Family Assistance Center in New York, and counseled thousands of relatives and rescue workers. John has traveled the war zones of the world, been arrested some 75 times for peace, led Nobel Peace prize winners to Iraq, given thousands of lectures on peace across the U. S., and served as a pastor of several churches in New Mexico. He writes a weekly column for "The National Catholic Reporter" at www.ncronline.org. Archbishop Desmond Tutu recently nominated him for the Nobel Peace Prize. John's many books include: *The Nonviolent Life; The God of Peace; Transfiguration; You Will Be My Witnesses; Living Peace; The Questions of Jesus; Put Down Your Sword; Jesus the Rebel; Peace Behind Bars; Lazarus Come Forth; Disarming the Heart;* and his autobiography, *A Persistent Peace: One Man's Struggle for A Non-violent World.*

Kathleen Deignan, CND is a sister of the Congregation of Notre Dame and Professor of Religious Studies at Iona College in New Rochelle, New York, where she founded and directs the Iona Spirituality Institute, the Merton Contemplative Initiative, and is a founding Convener of the Thomas Berry Forum for Ecological Dialogue. Dr. Deignan holds a Masters Degree in the History of Christian Spirituality and a Doctorate in Historical Theology from Fordham University. She completed post-graduate studies as a GreenFaith Fellow, a training program for religious environmental leaders, and is a recipient of Fordham University's *Doctrina et Sapientia* Award for her work in Church renewal and ministry of spiritual animation and teaching. Her articles on topics in classical and contemporary spirituality have appeared in *Franciscan Studies, The Way, Review for Religious, Sisters Today, Sacred Journey, Monastic Interreligious Dialogue Bulletin, Journal of the Canadian Conference of Religious, The Journal of the American Benedictine Academy, Diakonia, Sacred Journey, Cross Currents, The Merton Annual,* and *The Merton Seasonal.* She is the author of *ChristSpirit: The Eschatology of Shaker Christianity; When the Trees Say Nothing: Thomas Merton's Writings on Nature;* and *Thomas Merton: A Book of Hours.* A board member and past President of the ITMS, she is psalmist and composer in residence for Schola Ministries which has published a dozen collections of sacred songs (www.ScholaMinistries.org).

Paul Dekar, a member of the ITMS, is active with the new monastic movement and is the author of *Thomas Merton, Twentieth Century Wisdom for Twenty-First Century Living* (2011). A Quaker, he lives in Dundas, Ontario where he is active with local peace and justice groups.

Thomas Del Prete is director of the Adam Institute for Urban Teaching and School Practice at Clark University in Worcester, Massachusetts. He works with developing and practicing teachers and schools and community partners in an urban neighbor-hood. A former President of the ITMS, he is author of *Thomas Merton and the Education of the Whole Person*; *Improving the Odds: Developing Powerful Teaching Practice and a Culture of Learning in Urban High Schools*; and *Teacher Rounds: A Guide to Collaborative Learning in and From Practice*.

Laura Geary Dunson is a recent graduate of Baldwin Wallace University where she studied psychology and religion. She was awarded a Robert E. Daggy Scholarship from the ITMS. She currently works in North Carolina as a member of an AmeriCorps homelessness prevention program, and has plans to study Mental Health Counseling.

Ben Eisner owns Knitted Heart, LLC, a production company based in Milwaukee, Chicago and Nashville. He has directed numerous music videos, television pilots and documentary projects for marquee music companies like Capitol Records, Warner Brothers, Sony BMG and EMI Music Group. In 2011 Ben served as Cinematographer/Director of Photography on the feature-length documentary, *Hellbound?*, which ran in theaters across North America during the fall of 2012. Ben has also directed and served as director of photography on commercials and marketing campaigns for such global brands as Harley Davidson, GE, Verizon Wireless, Case IH, Wilson Sporting Goods, Oscar Meyer, Marquette University, and Master Lock. Ben is the principle writer and director of *The Divine Comedy of Thomas Merton*, a forthcoming feature-length film produced to honor Merton and his legacy.

James Finley was a monk at the Abbey of Gethsemani where Thomas Merton was his spiritual director. He is the author of *Merton's Palace of Nowhere: The Contemplative Heart* and *Christian Meditation: Experiencing the Presence of God*. He is a clinical psychologist in private practice with his wife in Santa Monica, California. He leads retreats and workshops throughout the United States and Canada.

James Forest is the author of biographies of Dorothy Day (*All Is Grace*) and Thomas Merton (*Living with Wisdom*) as well as books on pilgrimage, the Beatitudes, icons, confession, and overcoming enmity (*Loving Our Enemies*, Orbis, 2014). A co-worker with Dorothy Day, he was a managing editor of *The Catholic Worker*. Earlier in his life, before joining the Catholic Worker staff in New York, he worked as a meteorologist with a Navy unit at the U. S. Weather Bureau; he was given an early discharge from the military as a conscientious objector. In 1969-70, he spent a year in prison after participating in the destruction of draft files in Wisconsin. In 1977 he was appointed General Secretary of the International Fellowship of Reconciliation, work that brought him to Holland, which has since become his home. In 1988, he became a communicant in the Orthodox Church. He currently serves as the international secretary of the Orthodox Peace Fellowship.

Matthew Fox is a spiritual theologian and author of thirty-one books on spirituality and culture including *Original Blessing*; *The Coming of the Cosmic Christ*; and *A Spirituality Named Compassion*. His most recent books are *Christian Mystics: 365 Readings and Meditations*; *The Pope's War: How Ratzinger's Secret Crusade Imperiled the Church and What Can Be Saved*; and *Hildegard of Bingen, A Saint for Our Times: Unleashing Her Power for the Twenty-first Century* (2012).

Peggy Fox took a summer job at New Directions Publishing in 1975, and was eventually offered a full-time position. She managed contracts, copyrights and foreign rights, but soon added editorial responsibilities, becoming Senior Editor, Vice-President in 1993, and then President and Publisher in 2004. She retired from New Directions in 2011 but remains a Trustee of the New Directions Ownership Trust, as well as a Trustee of the E. E. Cummings Trust. She became a Trustee of the Merton Legacy Trust in 2008 when Robert Giroux stepped aside due to ill health, fulfilling the wish of James Laughlin, founder of New Directions and an original Merton Trustee, that she would eventually follow him to the Trust. In 2012 she was honored by her undergraduate college, Wittenberg University in Springfield, Ohio, with a Doctorate in Humane Letters for her service to literature.

Fiona Gardner is a psychoanalytic psychotherapist, spiritual director and co-editor of *The Merton Journal*. She is the United Kingdom's International Advisor for the ITMS and has presented at both TMSGBI and ITMS conferences. Her latest book is *Precious Thoughts, Daily Readings from the Correspondence of Thomas Merton* (2011). She is currently working on a book about Thomas Merton and the child-mind.

John Giuliani, born of Italian immigrants, was ordained a Catholic priest in 1960. He has earned M.A. degrees in Theology, Classical literature, and American Studies. In the late 1970s he founded a small monastic community in Redding, Connecticut, where he continues supervision of a variety of missionary activities. After years of teaching he returned to painting, drawing upon the Byzantine iconic tradition for depicting Native Americans as Christian saints. His many works are found throughout Indian reservations as well as in museums, churches and private collections throughout North America. He is currently preparing for an exhibit of his work in the Gallery of Contemporary Sacred Art in the church of Santa Maria del Popolo in Rome.

David Golemboski is a doctoral student in the department of Government at Georgetown University, where he studies political theory, focusing on the liberal tradition, religion in public life and Catholic social thought. He graduated from the University of Louisville and Harvard Divinity School. His writing has appeared in *America*, *Commonweal*, *The Merton Annual*, *The Merton Seasonal*, and other publications. He has served on the ITMS Board of Directors and is currently co-chair of the ITMS Retreats Committee. David is also chair of the Board of Directors for Witness for Peace, a grassroots organization working for peace, justice and sustainable economies in Latin America and the Caribbean.

Donald Grayston, an Anglican priest, taught Religious Studies at Simon Fraser University in Vancouver for fifteen years before his retirement in 2004. He was director of SFU's Institute for the Humanities (2001-04), President of the ITMS (2007-09), and director of the Pacific Jubilee Program in Spiritual Direction (1988-2012). Currently he is involved in responding to the Israeli-Palestinian conflict through Building Bridges Vancouver, and is working on a book on Merton's mid-life attempt to move to Camaldoli, in Italy.

Robert Grip is a former President of the ITMS. He has written for *The Merton Seasonal*, *The Merton Annual* and *Cistercian Studies Quarterly*. In addition to his work as a news anchor for WALA-TV in Mobile, Alabama, he teaches communications at Spring Hill College in Mobile and currently serves on the Board of Directors of the Byzantine

Catholic Seminary in Pittsburgh, Pennsylvania.

Gary Hall is a Methodist Minister who teaches practical theology at the Queen's Foundation, Birmingham, United Kingdom. A former editor of *The Merton Journal*, he has published regularly in several journals and contributed to Merton conferences in the United Kingdom and United States in the past twenty years. He recently presented a keynote address at the Oakham Conference of the Thomas Merton Society of Great Britain and Ireland, and is currently writing a book on the practical theology of Thomas Merton.

Judith Hardcastle is program director and founding member of the Thomas Merton Society of Canada. Ordained in The United Church of Canada in 2008, she works in ministry full-time at St. Andrew's United Church in North Vancouver, British Columbia.

Patrick Hart, OCSO, a monk of Gethsemani Abbey and Merton's last secretary, has edited numerous volumes of Merton's work including *Thomas Merton, Monk*; *The Monastic Journey*; *The School of Charity*; *Survival or Prophecy?*; and *The Intimate Merton* (with Jonathan Montaldo). He served as the General Editor of Merton's complete extant

journals published in seven volumes by HarperSanFranciso, and edited volume 1, *Run to the Mountain*, and volume 7, *The Other Side of the Mountain*. He served as editor of *The Merton Annual*, the editor of *Cistercian Studies Quarterly* and of *The Monastic Wisdom Series* for Liturgical Press. His reflection in this volume is an excerpt from his own edition of *Thomas Merton, Monk*. (Editor's note: Patrick Hart has been significantly responsible for the progress and evolution of

Brother Patrick Hart and Jonathan Montaldo, 1999

Merton studies since the monk's death in 1968. He embodies monastic hospitality at its best and has few equals in being a supportive friend and mentoring scholar of anyone interested in the legacy of Thomas Merton.)

Marianne Hieb, RSM holds a D.Min. She develops and presents Wellness Creativity/Spirituality programs and writings through Lourdes Wellness Services in Collingswood, New Jersey. She authored *Inner Journeying through Art-Journaling*, and facilitates Art-Journaling as a way of prayer and as a wellness tool in spiritual direction and retreat ministry. She is a Sister of Mercy.

Michael W. Higgins is the author and co-author, editor and co-editor, of over a dozen books including award-winners *Heretic Blood: the Spiritual Geography of Thomas Merton*; *Suffer the Children unto Me: a Critical Inquiry into the Clerical Sex Abuse Crisis*; and *Genius Born of Anguish: the Life and Legacy of Henri Nouwen*. He most recently published *Thomas Merton, Faithful Visionary* (Liturgical Press, 2014).

E. Glenn Hinson is Emeritus Professor of Spirituality and Church History, Baptist Theological Seminary at Richmond, Virginia, where he taught from 1992 to 1999. Previously he was the David T. Porter Professor of Church History at The Southern Baptist

Theological Seminary, Louisville (1962-92). He served on the Faith and Order Commissions of the World (1977-92) and National Councils of Churches (1981-87). He taught at St. John's University in Collegeville, MN (1984), Catholic University of America (1987), and Notre Dame University (1989) as well as at Wake Forest University (1982-84) and Emory University (2000-2001). He has published thirty books and more than 1200 articles and book reviews. His latest book is his autobiography, *A Miracle of Grace*, which highlights his friendship with Thomas Merton.

Casey Holland is a senior undergraduate Philosophy major at Nazareth College, with a minor in Religious Studies. His research interests in addition to Merton include philosophy of language and meaning, sacred texts and interpretations, medieval philosophy and literature. He plans to continue his education toward a Ph.D. He attended the 13th General Meeting of the ITMS at Sacred Heart University in 2013 as a Daggy Youth Scholar and plans to attend again in 2015. When not in school he can be found with several books close at hand, and a cup of tea in the other, around family, close friends and good food, or outside in the company of trees.

Daniel P. Horan, OFM is a Franciscan friar of Holy Name Province of the Order of Friars Minor, a staff columnist at *America* magazine, and serves on the Board of Directors of the ITMS. He is the author of several books including *The Franciscan Heart of Thomas Merton* (2014); *The Last Words of Jesus: A Meditation on Love and Suffering* (2013); *Dating God: Live and Love in the Way of St. Francis* (2012); and *Francis of Assisi and the Future of Faith: Exploring Franciscan Spirituality and Theology in the Modern World* (2012). He previously taught in the department of religious studies at Siena College and was a visiting professor at St. Bonaventure University. He lectures in the United States and Europe on topics that include the Franciscan intellectual tradition and spirituality, Thomas Merton, and themes in contemporary systematic theology. He is working on a Ph.D. in Systematic Theology at Boston College. His blog is http://*DatingGod.org*.

Russel Hulsey, a Marine Corps combat veteran, served in the Persian Gulf, and in Bosnia with NATO supporting the United Nations. He is a recipient of the NATO Medal presented by the Secretary General of NATO, and an Expeditionary Medal, issued by the United Nations. His unit, Fighter Attack Squadron 312, while deployed aboard the USS Theodore Roosevelt was awarded the Navy Unit Commendation for outstanding and heroic actions in combat. He states, *"I am spiritually indebted to my time spent in the Corps and in combat service, transcending rigors and immense struggle, 'suffering' in this way has been an immeasurable teacher."* Today, Hulsey works as an Artist, Poet, Performer, Educator, and Lecturer. Recent publications include *Songs to Poets*, VISION Magazine (Beijing, China), and the book/collection *How Does It Feel: Reflections of Bob Dylan*. Exhibitions include a Solo Show at 21c Museum, The Contemporary Arts Forum, Santa Barbara, Delaware Center for Contemporary Art, and the Itami Museum of Arts & Crafts, Japan. Hulsey is an Al Smith Fellow; and a graduate of the University of Louisville in Philosophy and Comparative Religions. He is a committed Buddhist Meditation practitioner, continues to be an avid reader/student of Thomas Merton, and is husband to fellow Artist and collaborator, Shelley Vaughn Hulsey

Robert Inchausti is a Professor of English at California State Polytechnic University in San Luis Obispo, California. He is the author of five books including *Thomas Merton's American Prophecy*; *Thinking Through Thomas Merton*; *Subversive Orthodoxy*; and *The*

Ignorant Perfection of Ordinary People. He has also edited two anthologies of Merton's writing, *Seeds* and *Echoing Silence.*

Edward K. Kaplan is Kaiserman Professor in the Humanities at Brandeis University, where he has taught courses on French and comparative literature and religious studies since 1978. He organized the conference on Merton and Judaism, derived from the Fons Vitae volume edited by Beatrice Bruteau. His publications on Heschel include *Holiness in Words: Abraham Joshua Heschel's Poetics of Piety* (1996). His two-volume biography of Heschel won a National Jewish Book Award: *Abraham Joshua Heschel: Prophetic Witness* (2007) and *Spiritual Radical: Abraham Joshua Heschel in America, 1940-1972* (2009).

Deborah Kehoe lives in Oxford, Mississippi, where she teaches writing at the University of Mississippi and at nearby Northeast Mississippi Community College. A member of the ITMS since 2001, she has regularly attended General Meetings, presented papers and published a number of essays, predominantly book reviews, in the *Merton Annual* and the *Merton Seasonal.* She sees her commitment to ethical veganism as part of her vocation to be, in the tradition of Thomas Merton, a messenger of hope for the world.

David Kocka is a bishop of the Ecumenical Catholic Church, USA, a poet and artist. His sculptures have been collected internationally. He designed the "Louie," a bronze that serves as an award of excellence in several categories granted bi-annually by the ITMS. His life-sized sculpture of Thomas Merton is part of the collection of sculptures exhibited on the grounds of Bellarmine University, Louisville, Kentucky.

Victor A. Kramer is Professor Emeritus of English, Georgia State University, and the former Director of the Aquinas Center at Emory University. He began teaching at Marquette University in 1966, and he is still at it. He has written many articles, reviews and books. He is most fond of the fourth on James Agee, the third on Walker Percy, the first on Frederick Law Olmsted, and many pieces about Merton, including *Thomas Merton: Monk and Artist* and his edition of the fourth volume of Merton's journals, *Turning Toward the World.* He has been a Senior Fulbright Lecturer twice in Germany and is a Certified Spiritual Director. He founded and edited *The Merton Annual* for twenty years. He teaches for Spring Hill College, Atlanta, and presents retreats for Cistercian and Benedictine Monasteries. He resides in Atlanta with his wife and collaborator, the scholar and author Dewey Weiss Kramer.

Donna Kristoff, OSU, an Ursuline sister of Cleveland, Ohio is a teacher, artist and graphic designer. She has served the ITMS as Secretary and board member, and chairs the ITMS Cleveland Chapter. She has written on Merton and icons and has contributed logos for the ITMS General Meetings. In 2013, she was awarded a "Louie" for her service to the ITMS.

Ross Labrie, Professor Emeritus of the University of British Columbia, is the author of a number of books and articles on American literature. These include two books on Thomas Merton, *The Art of Thomas Merton* (1979) and *Thomas Merton and the Inclusive Imagination* (2001). He is also the editor (with Angus Stuart) of *Thomas Merton: Monk on the Edge* (2012), published by the Thomas Merton Society of Canada, of which organization he is the President. In the past he served as an international advisor to the ITMS. He has been the recipient of a "Louie" award for his writing on Merton.

Alexis Leiva Letayf, born in San Francisco in 1980, is a writer, musician, professional interpreter, and a big fan of family life. His poetic book, *A Fuller Pulse*, is a collection of confessional-form journal entries. All he creates stands as a declaration of interdependence and contributes to the view that a Universal and Benevolent Being inextricably links us all. More at www.fllow.net

Simeon Leiva-Merikakis, OCSO is a Cistercian monk and priest of St. Joseph's Abbey, Spencer, Massachusetts. For many years previous to entering the monastery he enjoyed engaging undergraduates in theological and literary discussions as a professor in the Saint Ignatius Institute at the University of San Francisco. He is the author of *The Blossoming Thorn: Georg Trakl's Poetry of Atonement; Love's Sacred Order: The Four Loves Revisited; The Way of the Disciple;* and *Fire of Mercy, Heart of the Word,* a three-volume commentary on the Gospel of Matthew. He is also the beamish father of three and grandfather of six.

Roger Lipsey is the author of the forthcoming *Make Peace before the Sun Goes Down: Thomas Merton's Long Encounter with his Abbot Dom James* (Boston and London: Shambhala Publications, 2015). He received a "Louie" from the ITMS for his book *Angelic Mistakes: The Art of Thomas Merton* (Boston and London: Shambhala Publications, 2006).

Susannah K. Malarkey, a Dominican Sister of San Rafael for sixty-five years, taught high school Latin and Religion before serving for 11 years in the Central Administration of her congregation. She was the Director of the Santa Sabina Retreat Center in San Rafael, California for twenty-seven years, 1982-2010. She is currently living in San Rafael.

James Martin, SJ is a Jesuit priest, editor at large at *America* magazine and author of several books including *Jesus: A Pilgrimage; My Life with the Saints; The Jesuit Guide to (Almost) Everything;* and *Becoming Who You Are: Insights on the True Self from Thomas Merton and Other Saints.*

Gray Matthews is an Assistant Professor of Communication at The University of Memphis. He has served the ITMS as a member of the Board and on various committees, as co-editor of *The Merton Annual,* coordinator of the 2007 general meeting in Memphis; regular presenter at ITMS conferences and has published work in the *Merton Annual* and *Merton Seasonal.* He has served as the coordinator of the Memphis Chapter of the ITMS since 2001 and is a member of the Lay Cistercians of Gethsemani. He strives to live a contemplative life with his wife and daughters in Memphis, Tennessee, where he also teaches courses on Merton, Eckhart, John of the Cross, and other mystics and contemplative themes for the Catholic diocesan Institute for Liturgy and Spirituality. matthews@memphis.edu

Susan McCaslin, Ph.D. is a Canadian poet whose critical work on Merton has appeared in *The Merton Annual, The Merton Seasonal* and Fons Vitae's *Merton & Hesychasm.* Her most recent volume of poetry, *Demeter Goes Skydiving* (University of Alberta Press, 2011), was nominated for the British Columbia Book Prize and was the winner of the Alberta Book Publishing Award for 2012. She also published a volume of essays called *Arousing the Spirit* (Wood Lake Books, 2011). She is Faculty Emeritus of Douglas College in New Westminster, British Columbia where she taught English and Creative Writing for twenty-three years. Her forthcoming books include *The Disarmed Heart*, a volume of peace poems (The Saint Thomas Poetry Series, 2014), and *Into the Mystic*, a spiritual autobiography about her years spent learning from an elderly Christian mystic from Port Moody, British Columbia (Inanna Press, 2014). Inspired by Merton's tree-planting activities in the '60s, She recently spearheaded the Han Shan Poetry Initiative to save an endangered, ecologically sensitive rainforest in Langley, British Columbia. (See http://www.theglobeandmail.com/news/british-columbia/writers-hang-poems-in-trees-in-bid-to-save-langley-land-parcel/article5983994/).

Anne Hutchens McCormick is a native New Yorker, born and raised in Manhattan and in Rye, New York. She earned her B.A. in English from Wheaton College in Norton, Massachusetts. She retired from her career in trade publishing, first at Doubleday, and then at Alfred A. Knopf, in 2003. Naomi Burton Stone, Merton's literary agent and a trustee of the Merton Legacy Trust introduced her to the work of the Trust in 1975 when she became the Trust's Administrative Assistant. In 1997 she became a Trustee of the Merton Legacy, a position she still holds today. In 2013 she was awarded a "Louie" by the ITMS at their bi-annual meeting at Sacred Heart University in Connecticut.

Mark C. Meade is the Assistant Director of the Thomas Merton Center at Bellarmine University, serving on the faculty since 2003. In 2011, he was the featured lecturer for the book launch at the American Embassy in Buenos Aires of *Fragmentos de un Regalo*, the correspondence of Thomas Merton and Argentine writer and intellectual Victoria Ocampo. He is a member of the National Council of the Fellowship of Reconciliation and a board member of the Kentucky Coalition to Abolish the Death Penalty. His reviews and essays have appeared in *U. S. Catholic, The Merton Annual, The Merton Seasonal, Cistercium,* and *Cistercian Studies Quarterly.*

Christopher Meatyard is the son of the late photographer, Ralph Eugene Meatyard. He studied photography with his father and Robert C. May; he studied literature and philosophy at the University of Kentucky. He worked as preparator at University of Kentucky Art Museum and studied for seven years with Caroline Hammer at the King Library Press. He taught filmmaking at the University of Kentucky. He serves as liaison for the Estate of Ralph Eugene Meatyard.

Sheila M. Milton (formerly Hempstead) lives in the woods of Rhode Island. She is a member of the ITMS and has presented papers at conferences in England and the U. S. She has published articles in *The Merton Annual, The Merton Seasonal,* and *The Merton Journal.* She edited *Tom's Book: To Granny With Love from Tom* (2005).

Rusty C. Moe is the author of three books of poetry: *Our Presence Together In Chaos, Where God Lives* (Black Moss Press), *Way-Marks: New Poems* (Fourth Lloyd Productions). His memoir is entitled *Bright Wild Stone: A Contemplative Journal of Roots That Shape A Life* (Fourth Lloyd Productions). A native of Midland, Michigan, He is a psychotherapist in private practice in Indianapolis, Indiana. He is a supervisor in the marriage and family therapy program at Christian Theological Seminary, an instructor with the Indianapolis Gestalt Institute and an occasional retreat animator at Bethany Spring Retreat Center in New Haven, Kentucky.

Jonathan Montaldo is the General Editor (with Gray Henry) of the Fons Vitae Thomas Merton Series. He is a former director of the Thomas Merton Center at Bellarmine University and served as associate director of the Merton Institute for Contemplative Living. He has edited numerous volumes of Merton's writing including *Entering the Silence: Becoming a Monk and Writer*; *The Intimate Merton* (with Patrick Hart); *Dialogues with Silence: Prayers & Drawings; A Year with Thomas Merton*; and *Choosing to Love the World*. He created the ten-booklet series for small group dialogue *Bridges to Contemplative Living with Thomas Merton*. He has recorded five Thomas Merton audio books for Franciscan Media: *The Intimate Merton*, *No Man Is An Island*, *Contemplative Prayer*, and most recently *New Seeds of Contemplation* and *Thoughts in Solitude*. He is a former President of the ITMS.

Thomas Moore is the author of the bestselling book *Care of the Soul* and nineteen other books on psychology and spirituality. For thirteen years in his youth he was a brother and seminarian in the Servite Order and since then has been a professor of religion, a psychotherapist and a lecturer. He has a Ph.D. from Syracuse University and has won several awards for his writing. His most recent book is *A Religion of One's Own* (2014).

Patrick Thomas Morgan is currently working toward his Ph.D. in English at Duke University, where he is a scholar of nineteenth-century American literature. Science and aesthetics have been a key part of his research ever since Laura Dassow Walls published his essay, "Aesthetic Inflections: Thoreau, Gender, and Geology" in the 2010 *Concord Saunterer: A Journal of Thoreau Studies*. More recently, he co-wrote (with Priscilla Wald) the March 2013 preface to *American Literature's Thoreau Symposium*. His book chapter, "Let's Get Heretical," unveils a lesson for introducing students to the analytic shapes and logics of lyric poetry through a systematic close reading and writing exercise, and is forthcoming in *The Pocket Instructor: Literature* (Princeton University Press, 2015).

Michael Mott, a former professor of English at Bowling Green University in Bowling Green, Ohio, is the author of eleven poetry collections, four novels and the best-selling biography of Thomas Merton, *The Seven Mountains of Thomas Merton* (1984). The biography remained on the *The New York Times* non-fiction best-seller list for nine weeks and was a runner-up for the Pulitzer Prize in biography for 1985. He currently lives and writes in Williamsburg, Virginia.

Seyyed Hossein Nasr is the author of over fifty books and hundreds of articles on aspects of Islamic studies and Sufism, comparative philosophy and religion, philosophy of art, and the philosophical and religious dimensions of the environmental crisis. His publications include *Three Muslim Sages; Science and Civilization in Islam; Knowledge and the Sacred; The Garden of Truth;* and *Religion and the Order of Nature*. He is Professor of Islamic University studies at The George Washington University in Washington, District of Columbia.

Tommie O'Callaghan, having been chosen by Thomas Merton as one of three original trustees of the Thomas Merton Legacy Trust in 1967, served in that capacity for forty-two years until her retirement from the Trust in September, 2009, a longer period than any trustee has served to date. Along with Abbot Timothy Kelly of Gethsemani and President James McGowan of Bellarmine University, she founded the Thomas Merton Center Foundation and later served on the Board of the Merton Institute for Contemplative Living. She approved her reflection for this volume based on an interview with the editor and on her remarks in the film "Women Who Knew Merton" (1998).

Patrick F. O'Connell, who received his Ph.D.s in English Literature (Yale) and in Theology (Fordham), is professor of English and Theology at Gannon University, Erie, Pennsylvania. He is a founding member and former President of the ITMS, and has served as editor of *The Merton Seasonal* since 1998. He authored (with Christine M. Bochen and William H. Shannon) *The Thomas Merton Encyclopedia* (2002) and edited Merton's *Selected Essays* (2013). He has edited to date seven volumes of Merton's monastic conferences, most recently *Charter, Customs and Constitutions of the Cistercians* (2014). His edition of Merton's *Early Essays* will be published in 2015.

David M. Odorisio is a doctoral candidate in the East-West Psychology department at the California Institute of Integral Studies, San Francisco, California. While enthusiastically claiming a lifetime of Merton's influence, his current work focuses on the integration of Jungian and depth psychologies within the field of Religious Studies. His articles have appeared in *The Merton Seasonal*, *Hugoye: Journal of Syriac Studies*, and *Philosophy East and West*. He lives in Berkshire County, Massachusetts.

Anthony T. Padovano is a Distinguished Professor of Literature and Philosophy and a founder of Ramapo College of New Jersey. The College campus has two buildings named after him, the Padovano Peace Pavilion in the Spiritual Center, and the Padovano College Commons. He is the author of twenty-nine books and hundreds of articles. His work has been translated into nine languages; his personal and professional papers are housed in the Archives of the University of Notre Dame. He has doctorates in theology and in literature, and has been a professor in both disciplines. He lectures across the country and the world, and has been interviewed in major media outlets on both sides of the Atlantic (http://apadovano.com).

Erlinda G. Paguio is a former President of the ITMS. She served as Program Chair for the ITMS Tenth General Meeting in Memphis, Tennessee. She is a co-founder of the Thomas Merton Louisville Chapter of the ITMS. She has presented papers at Merton conferences in the U. S., Great Britain and Spain. She recently retired as Director of Development Research at the University of Louisville.

Parker J. Palmer is a writer, speaker and activist who focuses on issues in education, community, leadership, spirituality, and social change. Palmer is the founder and Senior Partner of the Center for Courage & Renewal. He holds a Ph.D. in sociology from the University of California at Berkeley, as well as eleven honorary doctorates, two Distinguished Achievement Awards from the National Educational Press Association, and an Award of Excellence from the Associated Church Press. He is the author of nine books, including several best-selling and award-winning titles: *Healing the Heart of Democracy, The Heart of Higher Education* (with Arthur Zajonc); *The Courage to Teach; A Hidden Wholeness; Let Your Life Speak; The Active Life; To Know As We Are Known; The Company of Strangers;* and *The Promise of Paradox*. In 1998, the Leadership Project, a national survey of 10,000 educators, named Dr. Palmer one of the thirty "most influential senior leaders" in higher education and one of the ten key "agenda-setters" of the past decade. Since 2002, the Accrediting Commission for Graduate Medical Education has given annual Parker J. Palmer "Courage to Teach" and "Courage to Lead" Awards to directors of exemplary medical residency programs. In 2005, *Living the Questions: Essays Inspired by the Work and Life of Parker J. Palmer*, was published. In 2010, he was given the William Rainey Harper Award whose previous recipients include Margaret Mead, Elie Wiesel, Marshall McLuhan, and Paolo Freire. In 2011, the *Utne Reader* named him one of 25 Visionaries on its annual list of "People Who are Changing the World." A member of the Religious Society of Friends (Quakers), Dr. Palmer and his wife, Sharon, live in Madison, Wisconsin.

Rob Peach is currently pursuing a Ph.D. in Interdisciplinary Studies at the Graduate Theological Union in Berkeley, California. A long-time Merton lover and former Robert E. Daggy Scholar (2005), he has written, published and presented various papers pertaining to the monk's role as activist, mystic, poet, and messenger of hope for our time. Merton's injunction to take up the hard work of racial reconciliation informs Rob's present research interests in the poetics and politics of rap music, about which he blogs at www.hiphopmatrix.wordpress.com.

Paul M. Pearson is Director of the Thomas Merton Center in Louisville, Kentucky, and Chief of Research for the Merton Legacy Trust. He is Resident Secretary of the ITMS, and served as the 10th President of the Society. He edited *Thomas Merton on Christian Contemplation* (New Directions, 2012); *Seeking Paradise: Merton and the Shakers* (Orbis, 2011); and *A Meeting of Angels* (Broadstone, 2008).

Małgorzata Poks, Ph.D., is an International advisor of the ITMS for Poland. She teaches courses in American Literature and Culture. Her main interests concern spirituality and modern literature. In 2009 her monograph *Thomas Merton and Latin America: A Consonance of Voices* received the "Louie" award. She is interested in Merton's late poetics.

J. S. Porter, Canadian poet and essayist, is the author of *The Thomas Merton Poems*; *Spirit Book Word: An Inquiry into Literature and Spirituality; Thomas Merton: Hermit at the Heart of Things*; and most recently, *Lightness and Soul: Musings on Eight Jewish Writers.*

Christopher Pramuk lives with his wife Lauri, a pediatrician, and their four children in Cincinnati, where he teaches theology and spirituality at Xavier University. His award-winning essays have appeared in *America* magazine, *Theological Studies, Cross Currents*, and the daily prayer journal *Give Us This Day*. He is the author of five books, including *At Play in Creation: Merton's Awakening to the Feminine Divine* (2015); *Hope Sings, So Beautiful: Graced Encounters Across the Color Line* (2013); and *Sophia: The Hidden Christ of Thomas Merton* (2009), which was awarded the ITMS's 2011 Thomas Merton Award, a. k. a. the "Louie." His current work focuses on racial justice and interracial solidarity in society and church.

Paul Quenon, OCSO entered the Abbey of Gethsemani at an early age and was a novice under Thomas Merton. He is a photographer and author of many books, including *The Art of Pausing*. His poetry has been published in the volumes *Terrors of Paradise* (1996); *Laughter: My Purgatory* (2002); *Monkswear* (2008); *Afternoons with Emily* (2011); and the forthcoming *Unquiet Vigil*. A volume of his selected poems is forthcoming from Paraclete Press.

Joseph Q. Raab is Professor of Religious Studies at Siena Heights University in Adrian, Michigan. In 2000 he received his Ph.D. in systematic theology from the Toronto School of Theology at the University of Toronto. He has published numerous articles on Thomas Merton and he edits (with David Joseph Belcastro) *The Merton Annual: Studies in Culture, Spirituality, and Social Concerns.*

Virginia (Jenny) Kaib Ratigan is professor emerita in Religious Studies at Rosemont College, Rosemont, Pennsylvania. She currently serves on the Boards of the *Won (Buddhist) Institute of Graduate Studies* in Glenside, Pennsylvania and *The Women's Sacred Music Project* in Philadelphia, Pennsylvania. She has served on the Board of the ITMS and co-chairs the Robert E. Daggy Youth/Student Scholars Committee.

Maurizio Renzini is co-founder and the current President of the *Associazione Thomas Merton Italia.* He is a biologist with specializations in clinical analysis and nutrition. He served as director of the Industrial Institute for vocational training in Foligno, Italia, where he currently resides. Fascinated by the books of Thomas Merton at a young age, his interest in the monk's writing was re-kindled in 2000. He is deeply engaged with the dissemination of Merton's work in Italy.

Richard Rohr, OFM is a Franciscan priest, a member of the New Mexico Province. He directs the Center for Action and Contemplation in Albuquerque, New Mexico which he founded in 1987 (www.cac.org). CAC conducts "The Living School" for students of the perennial mystical tradition and the Franciscan "alternative orthodoxy" which emphasizes practice over theory, especially for people involved in various efforts at social change and church reform. He is the author of many books including his primary teachings on the contemplative path: *Everything Belongs*; *The Naked Now*; *Immortal Diamond*; *Dancing Standing Still*; and *Silent Compassion.*

Tony Russo is a retired teacher, chemical dependency counselor and director of counseling in an inpatient chemical dependency unit. He has been a member of the ITMS and The Greater Cincinnati/Northern Kentucky Chapter since 1998. In those years he has served at different times as Chairman of the Membership Committee, Chapters Coordinator for the Board of the ITMS and coordinator of the Cincinnati Chapter. Since 2003, he has led a Merton-themed retreat annually at The Abbey of Gethsemani. He resides with his wife in Cleves, Ohio, where he continues as a member of the Cincinnati Chapter of ITMS. In his spare time he continues to study Merton and other spiritual writers.

Peter Savastano is Associate Professor of the Anthropology of Religion, Consciousness, Sexuality and Gender at Seton Hall University in South Orange, New Jersey. He has been reading Thomas Merton for over forty-five years and teaches a course at Seton Hall entitled "Thomas Merton, Religion and Culture." He will edit *Thomas Merton and Indigenous World Wisdom* forthcoming from Fons Vitae Press. peter.savastano@shu.edu.

Cristóbal Serrán-Pagán y Fuentes is an Assistant Professor of Philosophy and Religious Studies at Valdosta State University in Georgia. He received his Ph.D. in Religious Studies from Boston University. The title of his dissertation was, "Mystical Vision and Prophetic Voice in Saint John of the Cross: Towards a Mystical Theology of Final Integration." He has a Masters degree in Sacred Theology from Boston University, a Masters degree in Philosophy from Boston College, a Bachelor of Liberal Arts and a Bachelor in Business Administration from St. Thomas University. He is a member of the ITMS and an advisor to the Robert E. Daggy Scholarship Program. He is a regular contributor to Merton conferences in Europe and the United States. His publications include articles on

Merton and the Spanish mystics in Thomas Merton. He also teaches world religions and Spanish mysticism courses in his native Spain as part of a study abroad summer program in Madrid. He recently edited *Merton and the Tao: Dialogues with John Wu and the Ancient Masters* for Fons Vitae Press (2014).

Judith Simmer-Brown has been Professor of Religious Studies at Naropa University in Boulder, Colorado since 1978. She has practiced Tibetan Buddhism for 40 years and is an Acharya (senior dharma teacher) of the Shambhala Buddhist lineage of Sakyong Mipham, Rinpoche and Chogyam Trungpa, Rinpoche, Naropa's founder. She serves on the steering committee of the American Academy of Religion's Contemplative Studies Group. She lectures and writes on Tibetan Buddhism, American Buddhism, women and Buddhism, interreligious dialogue, and contemplative education. Her books are *Dakini's Warm Breath: The Feminine Principle in Tibetan Buddhism* (Shambhala) and, with Fran Grace, an edited collection of articles called *Meditation and the Classroom: Contemplative Pedagogy for Religious Studies* (Religious Studies Series, State University of New York Press, 2010). She is married to Richard Brown, a Naropa University professor, and has two young adult children and three grandchildren.

Penny Sisto was born and raised on the northernmost of the Orkney Islands off the northern coast of Scotland. The remote beauty of her island, North Ronaldsay, was an inspiration for a lifetime of art which she began creating spontaneously at age 7. She has broken boundaries by using fabric, embroidery, applique and hand dying, combined with masterful drawing and painting technique. The result is a multi-dimensional tapestry. The varied themes of her work are a reflection of her life of service as midwife and healer of body and soul. She spent three years living with the Masai tribe in Kenya and over a decade running a free clinic in northern California and has delivered over 2500 newborns.

She has shown in prominent galleries and museums in Beijing China, London England, New York, San Francisco, Santa Fe, New Mexico, Los Angeles and the Smithsonian in Washington, D.C. Her work is in the private and public collections of a wide variety of people including Ethyl Kennedy and Senator John McCain. Her Church works include a collection used for feast days at the Abbey of Gethsemani, as well as other pieces in many churches of all denominations throughout the U. S. www.pennysisto.com.

Richard Sisto was born and raised in Chicago and spent his youth listening to many of the great jazz musicians who performed in the numerous and prominent clubs of that time. He studied the vibraphone at an early age with Jose Bethancourt, mallet artist with the Chicago Symphony, and attended Quigley Preparatory Seminary, but transferred to another high school that had a jazz band. He was named 'best soloist' in the statewide competition and spent one year at North Texas State University, studying music before returning to Chicago where he co-led a quartet with drummer Maurice White, who later created Earth, Wind and Fire. Since that time Sisto has performed throughout the U. S. and Britain and has collaborated with the poets Gary Snyder and Lawrence Ferlinghetti. He recorded seven jazz CD albums as a leader with Fred Hersch, Kenny Werner, Bobby Broom, Barry Ries, and others. He authored a popular instruction publication by Hal Leonard, entitled *The Jazz Vibraphone Book*. He has given master classes at numerous colleges and universities throughout the U. S. and is currently teaching Vibraphone improvisation and

African Drumming at the University of Louisville. He composed the music for the DVD documentary *Soul Searching, The Journey of Thomas Merton.* He hosts two weekly jazz shows at WFPK public radio in Louisville and concentrates on his current work of performing concerts in Churches and Cathedrals featuring the music from the Merton Film and the spiritual music of John Coltrane, Duke Ellington and Billy Strayhorn. He met his wife Penny Sisto in 1969 at Ananda Meditation Retreat in the Sierra Nevada Mountains of northern California. www.dicksisto.com.

Huston Smith is Thomas J. Watson Professor of Religion and Distinguished Adjunct Professor of Philosophy, Emeritus, Syracuse University. For fifteen years he was Professor of Philosophy at M.I.T. and for a decade before that he taught at Washington University in St. Louis. Most recently he has served as Visiting Professor of Religious Studies, University of California, Berkeley. Holder of twelve honorary degrees, Smith's fourteen books include *The World's Religions* which has sold over 2½ million copies, and *Why Religion Matters* which won the Wilbur Award for the best book on religion published in 2001. In 1996 Bill Moyers devoted a 5-part PBS Special, "The Wisdom of Faith with Houston Smith," to his life and work. His film documentaries on Hinduism, Tibetan Buddhism and Sufism have all won international awards, and *The Journal of Ethnomusicology* lauded his discovery of Tibetan multiphonic chanting, *Music of Tibet*, as "an important landmark in the study of music."

Mary Robinson Somerville has directed one of America's largest and most diverse public library systems in Miami-Dade County, Florida. As President of the American Library Association she established an Emerging Leaders' Institute, appeared in national print and broadcast media, and represented ALA in China at the International Federation of Library Associations. Earlier in her career she visited Russia and the Ukraine as part of a five-person library delegation. Following her ALA presidency, she taught fundraising and library advocacy in seven areas of South Africa and also spoke in Brazil. She's been included in *Who's Who in America* and *Who's Who in American Women.* Tommie O'Callaghan, one of the three Merton Legacy Trustees originally appointed by Thomas Merton, introduced Somerville to Merton work. In 2009 when Mrs. O'Callaghan decided to step down, becoming Trustee Emeritus, Mary Somerville was named her successor.

Donald P. St. John is Emeritus Professor of Religion at Moravian College, Bethlehem, Pennsylvania. He holds a B.A. in Philosophy from St. Francis College (Pennsylvania), a M.A. in Religion from Temple University and a Ph.D. in from Fordham University. He has written articles and book reviews on Thomas Merton for a number of journals and collections, including *The Merton Annual, The Merton Seasonal* and *Merton & Taoism.* He was winner of a 2004 Catholic Press Association Award for *Teilhard in the Twenty-First Century: Spirit of the Earth,* co-edited with Arthur Fabel. He has served on the Board of Directors of several organizations including the American Teilhard Association where he was also editor of *Teilhard Studies* from 1994-2007. His teaching and research interests include Asian and Native American religions, religion and ecology, environmental philosophy, Thomas Merton, and Teilhard de Chardin. He is completing a major work on Thomas Merton as a radical ecologist and a book tentatively titled *Crazy Wisdom for Elders,* which draws heavily on Taoist/Daoist philosophy including selections from Merton's "rendering" of Chuang Tzu/zhuangzi.

Gerard Thomas Straub is an award-winning author and filmmaker. His book *The Sun & Moon Over Assisi*, was named the Best Spirituality Hardcover Book of the Year by the Catholic Press Association in 2001. His latest book, *The Loneliness and Longing of Saint Francis*, was published in the summer of 2014 by Twenty-Third Publications. He is a former network television producer at all three major TV networks, working in Hollywood and New York. He has written and directed twenty two documentary films, most of which explored global and domestic poverty; three of the films were broadcast on most PBS stations. He is the founder and President of Pax et Bonum Communications, a non-profit Franciscan ministry that strives to serve the poor through the power of film. In the last dozen years he has given over 220 presentations titled "Poverty and Prayer" at churches, high schools and colleges across the United States, as well as in Canada, France, Italy, and Hungary. He taught a course on film writing at the Pontifical Gregorian University in Rome. He has been awarded honorary doctorates from three Catholic universities. His ministry has been written about in *The New York Times*, the *Los Angeles Times*, as well as numerous Christian publications including the *National Catholic Reporter* and *Sojourners* magazine. He lives in Burbank, California with his wife, Ecarlatte, an artist from Haiti.

Angus Stuart is an Anglican priest in Vancouver, British Columbia, and has been a board member of the Thomas Merton Society of Canada since 2005. He was Chair of the Thomas Merton Society of Great Britain & Ireland 2000-2004. With Ross Labrie he co-edited *Thomas Merton: Monk on the Edge* (2012) to which he also contributed a chapter on Merton and the Beats. He also edited two volumes of papers from conferences of the Thomas Merton Society of Great Britain & Ireland held in 2000 and 2002: *With the World in My Bloodstream* (2002) and *Across the Rim of Chaos: Thomas Merton's Prophetic Vision* (2005). He presented papers at ITMS conferences in Vancouver (2003), San Diego (2005) and Chicago (2011) exploring the inner and outer vision of Thomas Merton; Merton and the counterculture of the sixties; and the parallels and convergences in the lives and writings of Thomas Merton and Henry Miller. He has given numerous talks on Thomas Merton in Canada, the United Kingdom and the United States. For the past three years he has been performing "Testament of a Naked Man, a one-man story-telling dramatization of the Gospel of Mark (NRSV), and is currently memorizing the Gospel of John (www.testamentofanakedman.com).

Lynn Szabo, professor of English at Trinity Western University, Vancouver, Canada, is a long-time scholar of Thomas Merton's poetry. She has authored numerous articles on his poetics and is the editor of *In the Dark Before Dawn: New Selected Poems of Thomas Merton* (2005). She has also recently co-edited *Through a Glass Darkly: Suffering, The Sacred and The Sublime in Literature and Theory*. Her current research is focused on narrative theory as well as the mystery of *logos poiesis*. She has served as Vice-President of the ITMS and as a board member of the Thomas Merton Society of Canada.

Harold Talbott works with Tulku Thondup Rinpoche, under the aegis of the Buddhayana Foundation, on translations of Nyingpapa scriptures which include *Buddha-Mind* (Snow Lion, 1989) and *Enlightened Living* (Shambhala Publications, 1991). His reflection in this volume is an approved by him edited (by Jonathan Montaldo) excerpt of an interview with him for *Tricycle* (Summer, 1992) conducted by editor Helen Tworkov.

List of Contributors

Kathleen Tarr was born in Pittsburgh, Pennsylvania. Her work has appeared in the *Sewanee Review*, *Creative Nonfiction*, *Cirque*, *TriQuarterly*, and in several other magazines and anthologies. In 2013, she was named a Mullin Scholar through USC's Center for Advanced Catholic Studies, one of six writers from across the country who were chosen for the new program. She has completed a memoir, *We Are All Poets Here*, about a modern-day spiritual quest involving Alaska, Russia and Thomas Merton. She is a long-time Alaskan who lives in Anchorage. She has recently spent six months living and writing in Krakow, Poland.

Robert Thurman is the Jey Tsong Khapa Professor of Indo-Tibetan Buddhist Studies at Columbia University. At H. H. Dalai Lama's request, he co-founded the American Institute of Buddhist Studies, in order to translate the Tibetan Tengyur collection, currently being translated and published volume by volume with Columbia University Press, as *Treasury of the Buddhist Sciences*. He is the translator of *The Tibetan Book of the Dead*, and author of many other books, including *Inner Revolution*; *The Central Philosophy of Tibet*; *Brilliant Illumination of the Lamp*; *Wisdom and Compassion: The Sacred Art of Tibet*; *Infinite Life*; *Jewel Tree of Tibet;* and *Why the Dalai Lama Matters*. With Richard Gere and Philip Glass, among others, he co-founded Tibet House dedicated to the preservation and renaissance of Tibetan civilization. He recently founded the Menla Mountain Retreat Center in the Catskill Mountains to advance the healing arts and life sciences of the Indo-Tibetan Buddhist medicine tradition.

Bonnie Thurston, after years in academe, in 2002 resigned the William F. Orr Professorship and Chair in New Testament at Pittsburgh Theological Seminary to live quietly in her home state of West Virginia. She wrote her doctoral dissertation at the University of Virginia on Merton's poetry and inter-religious thought and has authored or edited 18 theological books and 5 collections of poetry. A founding member of the ITMS, she has held all its offices, served several times on its Board and received a "Louie" Award for service to the Society. She has written over 30 articles and given retreats and lectured widely on Merton in the United States, Canada, the United Kingdom, and Europe. She edited *Thomas Merton and Buddhism* (Fons Vitae, 2007); *Hidden in the Same Mystery: Thomas Merton and Loretto* (Fons Vitae, 2010); and *Thomas Merton on Eastern Meditation* (New Directions, 2012). In 2004 the Thomas Merton Center of Pittsburgh granted her a New Person Award for "connecting spirituality and social change," and in 2005 she received the Mary Virginia De Roo Ecumenical Service Award from the West Virginia Council of Churches.

Arthur Versluis is Chair of the Department of Religious Studies and Professor in the College of Arts & Letters at Michigan State University, holds a doctorate from the University of Michigan, Ann Arbor, and has published numerous books and articles. His books include *Magic and Mysticism: An Introduction to Western Esotericism* (2007); *Restoring Paradise: Esoteric Transmission through Literature and Art* (2004); *The Esoteric Origins of the American Renaissance* (2001); *Wisdom's Book: The Sophia Anthology,* (2000); *Wisdom's Children: A Christian Esoteric Tradition* (1999); and *American Transcendentalism and Asian Religions* (1993). He is editor of *JSR: Journal for the Study of Radicalism*, and the founding President of the Association for the Study of Esotericism. His forthcoming book is on perennial philosophy.

Robert Waldron is the author of eighteen books, six of them devoted to the life and work of Thomas Merton, including *The Wounded Heart of Thomas Merton*; *Thomas Merton, The Exquisite Risk of Love, A Chronicle of Monastic Romance*; and *Thomas Merton, Master of Attention*. He lives in Boston, Massachusetts.

Kallistos Ware, born Timothy Ware on 11 September 1934, is Metropolitan of Diokleia within the Eastern Orthodox Church under the Ecumenical Patriarchate of Constantinople. He is one of the best-known contemporary Eastern Orthodox theologians. He has authored and translated many books including *Praying with Orthodox Tradition* (1990); *The Orthodox Church*, 2nd edition (1993); *The Inner Kingdom: Collected Works*, Volume 1 (2000); and *In the Image of the Trinity: Collected works, Volume 2* (2006).

Monica Weis, SSJ, recently retired Professor of English at Nazareth College, is well-known in Merton circles for her presentations on the influence of nature on Merton's spirituality. She is the author (with Harry Hinkle) of *Thomas Merton's Gethsemani: Landscapes of Paradise* (2005) and *The Environmental Vision of Thomas Merton* (2011), and is currently writing a book on Merton and Celtic spirituality.

Paul Wilkes is the co-producer, director and writer of the documentary *Merton: A Film Biography*, the author of *Merton: By Those Who Knew Him Best* and other books. Some sections of this essay appeared in his autobiography, *In Due Season: A Catholic Life*.

Mario Zaninelli is a priest of the diocese of Milan, Italy since 1992. He is one of the five founders of the *Associazione Thomas Merton Italia* and organized its first annual meeting at the Abbey of Fiastra in 2008. He translated into Italian Michael O'Laughlin's *Henri Nouwen: His Life and Vision*, Lindau. With Montanari and Renzini, members of the *Associazione Thomas Merton Italia*, he is working at the first Italian biography of Thomas Merton written by Italians and it will be published by Edizioni Paoline. Additionally, Gabrielli has commissioned his new Italian translation of *The Asian Journal of Thomas Merton*. He is working on his Ph.D. in Spirituality at the Theological University in Milan where his dissertation will present his Italian translation with commentary of Thomas Merton's *Cold War Letters*.

Suzanne Zuercher, OSB was a Benedictine Sister of Chicago, a clinical psychologist and spiritual director. She authored several books on the Enneagram, a book of poetry and two books about Thomas Merton, *Merton: An Enneagram Profile* (2001). She died on June 14, 2014 shortly after the publication of her book, *The Ground of Love and Truth: Reflections on the Relationship of Thomas Merton with the Woman Known as "M."*

A Bibliography Of Thomas Merton Sources Cited In The Reflections

A Meeting of Angels: The Correspondence of Thomas Merton with Edward Deming and Faith Andrews. Broadstone Books, 2008

A Search for Solitude: Pursuing the Monk's True Life. HarperSanFrancisco, 1996

The Asian Journal of Thomas Merton. New Directions, 1973

At Home in the World: The Letters of Thomas Merton and Rosemary Radford Ruether. Orbis Books, 1995

Bread in the Wilderness. New Directions, 1953

Cables to the Ace, or Familiar Liturgies of Misunderstanding. New Directions, 1968

The Climate of Monastic Prayer. Cistercian Publications, 1969

Cold War Letters. Orbis Books, 2007

The Collected Poems of Thomas Merton. New Directions, 1977

Conjectures of A Guilty Bystander. Doubleday, 1966

Contemplation in a World of Action. Doubleday, 1971

Contemplative Prayer. Herder and Herder, 1969

The Courage for Truth: The Letters of Thomas Merton to Writers, 1993

Dancing in the Water of Life: Seeking Peace in the Hermitage. HarperSanFrancisco, 1997

Dialogues with Silence: Prayers and Drawings. HarperSanFrancisco, 2001

Disputed Questions. Farrar, Straus and Giroux, 1960.

Elected Silence. Hollis and Carter, 1949

Entering the Silence: Becoming a Monk and a Writer. HarperSanFrancisco, 1996

Faith and Violence: Christian Teaching and Christian Practice. University of Notre Dame Press, 1968

Gandhi and Non-Violence. New Directions, 1965

"The Great Honesty: Remembering Thomas Merton. An Interview with Abbot Timothy Kelly," *The Merton Annual,* Volume 9. The Liturgical Press, 1996

The Hidden Ground of Love: The Letters of Thomas Merton on Religious Experience and Social Concerns. Farrar, Straus and Giroux, 1985

Honorable Reader: Reflections on My Work. Crossroad Books, 1989

In The Dark Before Dawn: New Selected Poems of Thomas Merton. New Directions, 2005

The Inner Experience. HarperSanFrancisco, 2003

The Intimate Merton: His Life from His Journals. HarperSanFrancisco, 1999

Introductions East and West: The Foreign Prefaces of Thomas Merton. Unicorn Press, 1981

Ishi Means Man: Essays on Native Americans. Unicorn Press, 1976

Learning to Love: Exploring Solitude and Freedom. HarperSanFrancisco, 1997

Life and Holiness. Herder and Herder, 1963

The Life of the Vows. Liturgical Press, 2012

The Literary Essays of Thomas Merton. New Directions, 1981

Love and Living. Farrar, Straus and Giroux, 1979

The Monastic Journey. Sheldon Press, 1977

Monks Pond. The University of Kentucky Press, 1968

Mystics and Zen Masters. Farrar, Straus and Giroux, 1967

The New Man. Farrar, Straus and Cudahy, 1955

New Seeds of Contemplation. New Directions 1962

No Man Is An Island. Harcourt, Brace and Company, 1959

The Other Side of the Mountain: The End of the Journey. HarperSanFrancisco, 1998

Passion for Peace: The Social Essays, Crossroad, 1995

Peace in the Post-Christian Era. Orbis Books, 2004

Raids on the Unspeakable. New Directions, 1966

The Road to Joy: The Letters of Thomas Merton to New and Old Friends. Farrar, Straus and Giroux, 1989

The School of Charity: The Letters of Thomas Merton on Religious Renewal and Spiritual Direction. Farrar, Straus and Giroux, 1990

Run to the Mountain: The Story of a Vocation. HarperSanFrancisco, 1995

Seeds of Contemplation. New Directions, 1949

Seeds of Destruction. Farrar, Straus and Cudahy, 1964

The Selected Poems of Thomas Merton. New Directions, 1959

The Seven Storey Mountain. Harcourt, Brace and Company, 1948

The Sign of Jonas. Harcourt, Brace and Company, 1953

The Silent Life. Farrar, Straus and Cudahy, 1957

Spiritual Direction and Meditation. Liturgical Press, 1960

The Springs of Contemplation: A Retreat at the Abbey of Gethsemani. Farrar, Straus and Giroux, 1992

Thirty Poems. New Directions, 1944

A Bibliography Of Thomas Merton Sources Cited In The Reflections

The Thomas Merton Studies Center. Unicorn Press, 1971.

Thomas Merton: Essential Writings. Orbis Books, 2000

Thomas Merton: Selected Essays. Orbis Books, 2013

A Thomas Merton Reader. Harcourt, Brace and World, 1962

Thoughts in Solitude. Farrar, Straus and Cudahy, 1958

Turning Toward the World: The Pivotal Years. HarperSanFrancisco, 1996

The Waters of Siloe. Harcourt, Brace and Company, 1949

The Way of Chuang Tzu. New Directions, 1965

The Wisdom of the Desert. New Directions, 1960

Witness to Freedom: The Letters of Thomas Merton in Times of Crisis. Farrar, Straus & Giroux, 1995

Zen and the Birds of Appetite. New Directions, 1968

Acknowledgments

The Editors gratefully acknowledge and praise:

The Contributors for the generous donations of their time and talent in producing this volume's reflections.

Terrell Dickey's portrait in oil of Thomas Merton, photographed for the cover of this centenary volume, appears through the courtesy of his children who have authorized its use in loving memory of their father.

Annie Langan for her photograph of the Terrell Dickey Portrait of Thomas Merton used on the front cover.

Neville Blakemore, Jr. who with his usual contemplative patience designed and typeset the text.

Steven Stivers who beautifully produces all the covers for Fons Vitae's publications.

Anne Ogden for her invaluable collaboration as primary proof-reader of the text.

Nicole Kowalczyk for research assistance and Christian Tate for his contributions to proof-reading the text.

The Thomas Merton Legacy Trustees, with Paul M. Pearson and Mark C. Meade at the Thomas Merton Center, for their support of and assistance with this volume's publication.

Permissions for the extended quotations in the Editor's Introduction:

Excerpts from "Letter at St. Bonaventure, New York, December 6, 1941" from *The Road to Joy: Letters to New and Old Friends* by Thomas Merton, selected and edited by Robert E. Daggy. Copyright ©1989 by the Merton Legacy Trust. Reprinted by permission of Farrar, Straus & Giroux, LLC.

Excerpts from *Run to the Mountain: The Story of a Vocation* by Thomas Merton, edited by Patrick Hart. Copyright ©1995 by the Thomas Merton Legacy Trust. Reprinted by permission of HarperCollins Publishers.

Excerpts from books and articles cited are acknowledged parenthetically within the text of each reflection. Publication credits for the works of Thomas Merton cited in the reflections appear in the formal Bibliography.

Index of Contributors